CHELMSFORD AT WAR

a chronicle of the county town of Essex during the Second World War

Andrew J Begent

Ian Henry Publications

© Andrew J Begent, 1999

ISBN 0 86025 497 6

First printing September, 1999
Second printing December, 1999

Published by
Ian Henry Publications, Ltd.
20 Park Drive, Romford, Essex RM1 4LH
and printed by
Whitstable Litho Printers, Ltd.
Millstrood Road, Whitstable, Kent CT5 3PP

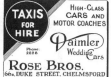

CHELMSFORD AT WAR

1939 TO 1945

A CHRONICLE OF THE COUNTY TOWN AT WAR

No 120665 BY ANDREW J BEGENT CHELMSFORD, 1991 - 1999 PRICELESS

WAR DECLARED

THE COUNTY TOWN REACTS

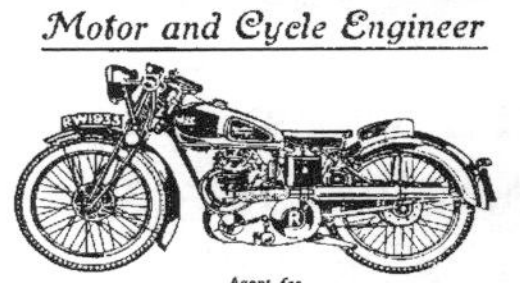

AT 9.00 A.M. a final British ultimatum was presented to Germany, giving Hitler until 11 a.m. to give an undertaking to withdraw his forces which had invaded Poland two days earlier.

At 11.15 a.m. the British Prime Minister, Neville Chamberlain, in a broadcast to the nation stated that "no such undertaking had been received and that consequently this country is at war with Germany." Within half an hour after the declaration of war, air raid sirens sounded in Chelmsford and throughout the south of England as an unidentified aircraft was detected approaching the south coast. In the event it turned out to be a false alarm, but also a portent of things to come.

In Chelmsford, several thousand evacuees, including children, mothers and pregnant women had been arriving since the previous Friday from London's northern and north-eastern suburbs. Up to the previous Wednesday only about five hundred had been expected, but during the day some eighty double-decker buses arrived at Chelmsford bus station, with about four thousand evacuees on board, of whom a quarter were set to travel on to other towns in Essex. Contingency plans for the evacuation appeared to work well. In the Chelmsford Rural District they had been the responsibility of Cecil Plumtree, the Chief Reception Officer and in the Borough, Mr. S. H. MacArthur, the Chief Education and Chief Billeting Officer. It was later revealed that under the Government Evacuation Scheme 2,543 evacuees, of whom 1,437 were school children, had been billeted in the Borough. Many of the children were said to be in a 'verminous condition'.

Some twenty pregnant women who arrived as evacuees from the capital were given accommodation by Mrs. J. T. Wigan at her home at Danbury Park. Following this gesture, the Ministry of Health were to quickly recognise Danbury Park as an emergency maternity hospital and within the month a nursing staff was to be established there, with twenty beds for expectant mothers. Ironically, before the war Mrs. Wigan had offered the premises to the Red Cross, but this had been declined on the grounds that they were too vulnerable to enemy attack.

With the outbreak of hostilities the re-opening of schools after the summer holidays was postponed for an indefinite period.

Sunday 3rd September 1939

EYEWITNESS ACCOUNTS: OUTBREAK OF THE WAR

"A quotation made at the start of the First World War went through my head, something about the lights are going out over Europe. I thought that they were going out yet again."

As told to our our Special Correspondent

"It was a Sunday morning and as usual I was in the choir at the Holy Trinity Church in Trinity Road. One of the churchwardens had a portable wireless, or one connected in the vestry, and he stayed behind when the vicar, Charles Hodgins, rose to commence the service. Within minutes the churchwarden came through and told the vicar that war had just been declared so the vicar announced the news to the congregation.

In those days the church was usually full and the congregation took the announcement stoically, though there was a distinct hush. Sitting in the choir I could view the congregation and I sensed a difference in reaction between the older and the younger people there. The younger ones, who didn't know too much, couldn't really comprehend what might happen, whilst the elders appeared to be very grave and serious.

People were disappointed rather than surprised at the news. They knew that an ultimatum had been given and in their heart of hearts most had thought war inevitable. Even as a young boy I was attuned to the fact that in all probability there would be a war. There wasn't a word said by anyone I'd ever met to the effect that the decision was wrong or that we could have done something else.

Matins proceeded and I think I'd left the church and was on my way home when the siren sounded. I was worried stiff because I felt it was so soon. When I got home my parents didn't say much to me. They weren't given to long family discussions but I could feel that they were questioning one another as to what was going to happen. Beyond that I think there was a feeling of 'Oh well, we've got it now, we've got to put up with it. Even in those days I felt that we would come through."

Ray Knappett

"It's rather like President Kennedy's death in that I can remember exactly what happened. I was ten years old and on that Sunday morning I sat in the back room of our house in Braemar Avenue, listening to the wireless with members of my family. Soon after 11 a.m. the Prime Minister announced the fact that we were at war with Germany.

It was obviously very worrying news, but it was possibly made more worrying by the attitude of the adults around me. War had not been unexpected. The day before we had come back early from holiday at Holland-on-Sea because my father was billeting officer for Chelmsford Rural District Council and he had realised he would be needed at work. The most immediate effect for me was that I didn't have to go back to school at K.E.G.S. until after Christmas because they were busy building air raid shelters there."

John Plumtree.

"I remember the day vividly - I was just coming up to 12 years old and I was living with my family at Newland Hall in Roxwell. My father, John, farmed Newland Hall and the adjoining farm, Mountney's. He was also a county councillor, Chairman of the Chelmsford R.D.C., a J.P. and Chairman of the Parish Council.

That particular sunny Sunday morning my father, mother and my 9 year-old brother were all at home. Soon after 11 am. the air raid warning went off. We had a large snooker table in our dining room, which doubled up as a dining room table, and we all dived under there for shelter. As my father was over 20 stone there wasn't too much room for the rest of us. Fortunately it was a false alarm and no enemy planes came.

The summer that year was the first that I'd done a full harvest and I was very much an integral part of the farm. We'd all been acutely aware that war was brewing up and it had worried us all. I think that you needed to have been very young or terribly unaware not to have realised that things had been very serious, None of us thought that the war would last that long - we didn't realise what a force Germany was."

Leonard Menhinick

"It was just an ordinary day. We heard the news on the radio, but it was not a surprise - war had been on the books and it was a wonder that it hadn't come before. My father said 'We're in for it now, the Germans are only across that little bit of water'. We didn't know what to expect so we weren't frightened, though we never thought it would last so long and that we would have to through all that we did."

Winifred Wales

"I married on 23rd August 1939 and for our honeymoon my wife and I went to stay in Cromer. We had been there for just a over a week but it was reckoned that there was going to be a war so we decided that the best thing to do was to come home. We returned to Chelmsford by train and it was just like the Great War all over again with soldiers embarking and wives and children crying on the platform. I could remember those scenes clearly from the 1914 war when I had been just a young boy. People were apprehensive, but there was an excitement too.

Back in Chelmsford our first job was to buy blackout curtains and things like that to board up the windows as much as we could. We put up strips of plaster over the panes to help prevent the glass from smashing.

The morning war was declared we listened to Chamberlain's speech on our next door neighbour's wireless. It was a beautiful day - in fact the whole of that summer had been too. After the speech had finished there was a false air raid alert. I think that we were all expecting German planes to come over straight away and bomb us, but of course there was nothing at all and they didn't come for months.

War hadn't come as a great surprise to me. During the 1930's I used to go on holiday in Germany quite frequently with my brother and we had seen a lot of this Nazi business then. It had seemed obvious to us then that war would come sooner or later. Apart from the Nazis, I had got to know many Germans who were jolly nice people and I was very sorry when we were at war with each other. Like most people, although I thought that the war would last a long time, I didn't think that Germany would beat us. There was never any question that we were morally right, but in the end I think that it was our spirit that really saved us."

Gilbert Torry

"When the first siren went I was at home with my family at number 19 Victoria Crescent. We all ran downstairs and I can remember plain as anything, we stood around the table putting our gas masks on - except for my dad who didn't think he needed to. The rest of us thought that we were all going to be gassed and were worried to death about it."

Betty Pryke

"I was a driver in the Territorial Army - 536 Company, Royal Army Service Corps - stationed at Chelmsford. My regimental number was T/79697. On Friday 1st September 1939, in response to a mobilisation call over the radio, I reported for duty at the Drill Hall in Market Road soon after 4 p.m. that day. I was immediately given a job in the Quartermaster's Stores issuing equipment.

Although my home in Navigation Road was relatively close to the Drill Hall I, along with many of my Company personnel, were billeted with private residents in Rectory Lane, close to the junction with Henry Road. Our duties then consisted mainly of fire watching.

On the declaration of war two days later I well remember being on guard duty outside the Corn Exchange in Tindal Square. In the ensuing days we all received inoculations in the Corn Exchange itself. This event became rather serious as I, along with many of my comrades, was taken ill shortly afterwards. In fact our Sergeant Major was even admitted to hospital because of these inoculations. However, we all subsequently recovered satisfactorily.

536 Company was then dispatched, together with our heavy vehicles, to Ingatestone, where again we were put into civvy billets. Shortly after this, and in very bad conditions we embarked for service overseas with the British Expeditionary Force in Europe."

Vic Wilks

"During the morning they talked about the war being declared on the radio, but it didn't actually happen til 11 a.m. by that time my husband, Harold, and I had gone out from our home in Ash Tree Crescent with our three week-old baby.

It was a nice day. As we were going through the Recreation Ground, just by about by the railway viaduct the air raid siren went off. We weren't prepared for that and we were a bit scared as neither of knew what we had to do. We had no where to go so we just kept walking."

Winifred Orrin

"I remember sitting on the back door step in the morning sunshine when Chamberlain came on the wireless to announce that we were at war. One of my first thoughts was for my parents because they'd been through the First World War and they'd dreaded another one.

I was their only son and I knew my mother was worried that if war did break out I would probably be called up. As I sat there a quotation made at the start of the First World War went through my head, something about the lights are going out over Europe. I thought that they were going out yet again. I then went off to work.

When the first siren went off it was very frightening and many people panicked. Before the war we'd all been told to expect that the German planes would come over and bomb us straight away and we'd given all sorts of air raid advice in the newspapers.

With this in mind my wife, who was at home on her own, went and sheltered under the stairs as that was supposed to be the safest place, put cotton wool in her ears and a cork in her mouth so that if she was knocked unconscious she'd be able to breathe. The whole thing was a bit of a farce really because it was a false alarm the war proper didn't start until 1940."

George Brown

OVER 1,400 EVACUEES NOW IN COUNTY TOWN

They've come mainly from the Capital

CHELMSFORD'S elementary schools re-opened for the autumn term after a summer holiday prolonged by the outbreak of the war. The number of pupils had been swollen by some 1,400 evacuees who were accommodated in the following way:

(1) Evacuees from the Cann Hall Junior Boys School in Leyton were accommodated at the Trinity Road Boys School, (2) Cann Hall and Mayville Junior Girls Schools, Leyton at the Trinity Road Girls School, (3) Cann Hall Senior Boys School, Leyton at Moulsham Senior Boys School, (4) Cann Hall Senior Girls School, Leyton at Moulsham Senior Girls School, (5) Aldersbrook Senior Mixed, Wanstead at Moulsham Senior Boys & Girls Schools, (6) Devonshire Hill Junior & Infants School, Tottenham at Springfield Mixed & Infants School, (7) Cann Hall & Mayfield Infants School, Leyton at Trinity Road Infants School (double shift), and (8) Deanery Senior Boy's School, West Ham to King's Road Boys School (senior classes only & double shift).

A considerable number of privately evacuated children had also been admitted to local schools.

Monday 18th September 1939

ALIEN FINED

At the Chelmsford Petty Sessions the new wartime defence regulations saw a 32 year-old unmarried woman from Dorset Avenue, Great Baddow fined £6 for failing to register as an alien and to having a camera without the permission of a registration officer. Her 33 year-old common-law husband was also fined £2 for failing to report her presence at his home. The court was told that despite being German-born, the woman had strong anti-nazi feelings and had lived in England for more than six years.

Friday 27th October 1939

THE CONDUIT IS DEMOLISHED

The Weekly news reported that throughout the week the contractors Messers A.J. Arnold had been busy at work dismantling the Conduit from the High Street and Springfield Road corner. The structure had been deemed a danger and an obstacle to traffic at this busy junction and its removal would allow the installation of traffic lights there. It was removed by the 11th April 1940 and re-erected in Tower Gardens by the 5th May 1940. Traffic lights at the junction were to come into operation for the first time on 16th April 1940.

Friday 5th April 1940

EYEWITNESS ACCOUNTS: EVACUEES

"The evacuees looked bewildered, somewhat disoriented and seemed totally uncertain as to what was going to happen."

As told to our our Special Correspondent

"I can remember standing outside our house in Springfield Park Avenue on the day that the evacuees began arriving from London, mostly from Tottenham. I watched as groups of them came up our road and adjoining roads from the station in little crocodiles, led by adults.

The evacuees were mostly between six or seven to about twelve years old and each carried little battered suitcases and brown paper parcels wrapped with string. They looked bewildered, somewhat disoriented and seemed totally uncertain as to what was going to happen. As they came down the street the adults knocked on each door on spec to ask people if they could house any of the evacuees.

One or two were taken in by each household and as they carried on up the road their numbers diminished. I could see that they were concerned that they might have to lodge with someone who would be unkind, and towards the end of the few that were left were worried that they wouldn't be found anywhere to stay at all.

My mother was unable to take anyone because she had us three children living at home, plus the fact that she'd undertaken to have our cousin from Tottenham in a private evacuation. He was to eventually stay for two or three years before going back.

We lived in a cul-de-sac in Springfield and as a result there was very little traffic so we could play in the road most of the time. After the evacuees had got themselves established they came outside into the road to look around and there was a sort of 'them and us' situation, with the evacuees and us locals.

We tried to make friends with them and eventually we managed to get to know one or two who we invited to join in with what we were doing. Even so, from most there was a reticence to get together with us, though there was never any outward sign of violence or disagreement between us.

At the grammar school our classes were doubled up with pupils from Tottenham Grammar School. It was difficult for the staff who had tremendous problems coping, and eventually that arrangement ceased. It was not long before the evacuees, in ones and twos, drifted back to Tottenham. After a while they all seemed to have returned, which was a pity in a way because I suspect that some went back to worse times."

Ray Knappett

"When the war first stated hundreds of soldiers congregated at Pollard's Garage, which was on the southern corner of Cedar Avenue and Broomfield Road. The officers came round to all the houses nearby, including ours in Victoria Crescent, and told us that we had to put some of the soldiers up - you had to have them whether you liked it or not.

Our house had three bedrooms so I moved in with my mum and dad so that two soldiers could share my bedroom. My brothers remained in their room. The soldiers used to have breakfast with us and then go over to Pollard's for parade and so on. They stayed with us for a few weeks before leaving, I suppose for France. We got quite friendly with one of them and mum invited his wife to come and stay with us before they left.

Soon after they were gone we had a boy evacuee billeted on us. He came from the East End of London and went to the Grammar School while he stayed with us. I can see his face now, he was a right little monkey, always getting into trouble! His parents never visited him. I don't think the headmaster could stand him as he did so many naughty things so it wasn't very long before he was sent back to London. We weren't given evacuees after that!

A few months later my dad went drinking in The Steamer where he met this big family who had been bombed out from Canning Town. They had nowhere to live. There was a mother, a father, a teenage girl and three other children. They'd had an horrendous time up there and had lost everything. My father was a very generous man so he brought them home and kindly invited them stay with us. My mother was furious with him, she did her nut!

They were given the bottom part of the house and we lived in the top part. The trouble was that we couldn't get rid of them. They stayed on and on - they were there for months!

They weren't particularly clean and used to accidentally break bits and pieces! In the end my mum had enough and went to the council to get them a house of their own as they wouldn't go themselves. Whenever the sirens went and our family went into our shelter outside they'd stay indoors."

Betty Pryke

SANDBAGS AT POLICE STATION BREAK THE LAW

TOWN COUNCIL IN GOOD HUMOUR

At the monthly Council meeting, in a light-hearted exchange, concerning the recent sandbagging of the Police Station in New Street, Ald. Frank Fox asked whether it was against the law to put sandbags half way across the footpath.

"Yes" was the Mayor's reply to which Cllr. Albert Hodge enquired "Can we move that the council be asked to prosecute the police for breaking the law?". Amongst other matters, members were informed that the Recreation Ground, Admiral's and Oaklands Parks were being used by the military for training purposes, even though the Council's permission had not been sought.

Wednesday 29th November 1939

NO CAMOUFLAGING OF COUNTY HALL

War emergency hospitals set up

A MEETING at County Hall of the County Council decided not to camouflage the building, having surprisingly concluded that 'from the air it does not stand out from other buildings'!

The decision came days after Chelmsford Town Council had requested that the work be approved. Another decision was to indefinitely postpone construction of the £862,692 Margaretting Mental Hospital, due to have been built on land south-west of Margaretting Hall. However, members decided that Broomfield Court Sanatorium (today's Broomfield Hospital), due to be completed as a tuberculosis hospital in January 1940, should be finished as soon as possible and be utilised to treat civilians under the Ministry of Health's emergency hospital scheme. Amongst other matters, it was revealed that two of the six emergency maternity hospitals, established by the County Council since the outbreak of the war, were at Moulsham Grange, Moulsham Street (25 beds) and at Danbury Park (20 beds). The former was to be vacated as soon as possible once the 30 bed Writtle Park Hospital was available in the near future.

Tuesday 3rd October 1939

CHELMSFORD M.P.'S NEW YEAR THOUGHTS

THE ESSEX CHRONICLE published a new year's message from Chelmsford's M.P. Lt. Col. John Macnamara, which was to turn out to be strangely prophetic.

He wrote "Be prepared for a strange war, a long war, a war which like a bog fire, will spread underground through the turf and flare up in unexpected places, a war during which previously held convictions may be upset, when even sides may be changed, a war of many surprises which makes it even more necessary for us to combine level-headed judgment with our daring. But it is also a great chance for our generation to build something new".

Friday 5th January 1940

CHELMER FREEZES AS BITTER WINTER CONTINUES

The winter is turning out to be one of the most severe for many years, though news of this was censored in most of the local press. Even so, according to the Essex Chronicle, during the day a party was able to skate along the frozen River Chelmer from Little Baddow to Brown's Yard, Chelmsford and repeat a similar exercise the following day from Beeleigh Lock near Maldon to Paper Mills Lock, Little Baddow, save for one or two sections near certain lock gates where water covered the ice. It was said to be the first time the distance had been skated in forty years.

Monday 22nd January 1940

EYEWITNESS ACCOUNT: RESERVE POLICE

"He was a bit overzealous and seemed to be out for promotion."

As told to our our Special Correspondent

"I was a carpenter by trade, but at the beginning of the war there was no building work around so, along with several other chaps from the trade, I joined the police as a war reservist. I wasn't particularly interested in police work but at the time there was little other work and at least it was a job.

We went along to the Police Station in New Street where we were sworn in and given our uniforms and equipment. Instead of a normal copper's helmet we wore peaked caps, and we were all issued with steel helmets.

After a short period of training, which mainly consisted of lectures, I was based at the section office at Greenways under Sergeant Bridges. He was a good old fashioned copper, the sort that would give you a clip round the ear if you misbehaved.

As well as the sergeant there were a couple of probationary policemen and several other war reservists. I wasn't so keen on one of the probationers. He was a bit overzealous and seemed to be out for promotion. He was always be arresting people and it wasn't long before he became a sergeant himself.

Normally I would be on duty with one other war reserve. There were three shifts, 6 a.m. to 2 p.m., 2 p.m. to 10 p.m. and 10 p.m. to 6 a.m., and I earned about £3 a week, plus a bob or two boot money. The worst shift was the night one. I never liked that because I could never keep awake. As well as staying at the section office to man the phones we used to go out on patrol to places along the whole length of Broomfield Road. One of our regular beats went up through Broomfield into the countryside beyond.

Before the war I'd done some carpentry work at Woodhouse, near Broomfield Hospital, where the Ridley's and their servants lived. If I was passing by on the beat I used to drop in and have a cup of tea and chat with them. On another beat we'd time our break so that we could pop into the Maltings in Townfield Street and have a cuppa there where it was always nice and warm.

I never arrested anyone or saw anything interesting, though as I was coming off duty one night I stopped a fella on a bike without a light. I took his name and address but when my colleagues went to see him they turned out to be false. To be honest I didn't really enjoy police work. I hated interfering with other people's business, so after a few months, when things had picked up in the building trade, I went back to that."

Norman Hume

FORMATION OF LOCAL DEFENCE VOLUNTEERS ANNOUNCED

OVERWHELMING RESPONSE IN CHELMSFORD

WITH THE situation on the continent becoming grave Anthony Eden, the War Minister, announced the formation of the Local Defence Volunteers (L.D.V.s).

He called for 'men not presently engaged in military service, between the ages of 17 and 65, to come forward to offer their services. The intention was that the volunteers would help to defend key installations and points in their localities from parachute troop attack. Experience in Belgium and Holland showed that this would be Germany's leading tactic in the now expected invasion of Britain. It was anticipated that the L.D.V.s, later renamed the Home Guard, would initially be set up in rural areas with volunteers expected to remain in their own parishes.

The appeal was met with an overwhelming response. The following day large queues of men, many veterans of the First World War, were to form at police stations ready to enlist. In Chelmsford over a hundred would do so in the first morning and by the weekend that would rise to over a thousand. One of the first to enlist was to be the Bishop of Chelmsford who had suggested the similar idea of a 'town guard' three months earlier.

Colonel Sir Edward Ruggles-Brise was selected as the Essex Zone Commander of the new force. He was to quickly set up his headquarters at the Territorial Offices in Market Road and begin the huge and urgent task of organisation and training the new force.

Tuesday 14th May 1940

EMERGENCY MORTUARY AT GALLEYWOOD RACECOURSE

Chelmsford Council met the Rural District Council to discuss a proposal for an emergency mortuary at the old grandstand of Galleywood Race-course.

The buildings there had been inspected and were reported to be entirely suitable for the purpose, subject to various alterations. The Borough had been asked to make a provision for a hundred bodies and the Rural District for fifty. With this in mind it was agreed that cost of the adaptations together with the running costs should be divided proportionately between the two. Tenders for the necessary building work and the supply of the racks for corpses were sealed at the end of July 1940 with the builders Messers H.R. Barber (£310) and the Colchester Steel Construction Co. Ltd. (£105/11/-).

Friday 17th May 1940

EYEWITNESS ACCOUNTS: THE HOME GUARD

"To start off with we were very short on weapons too. In fact, much of our early drill was performed using broomsticks instead of rifles!"

As told to our our Special Correspondent

"After Dunkirk a message was put round the large local firms calling for men to volunteer for each firm's detachment of the Home Guard (then known as the Local Defence Volunteers). I worked at Hoffmann's so I joined the Home Guard there.

Our main job was to defend the factory in the event of an enemy attack. Whenever the air raid siren went off most of Hoffmann's workers used to go down into the air raid shelters, but those of us in the Home Guard had to rush over to our orderly room down Mill Lane and collect our rifles.

We'd load them with one round each, 'up the spout' as they called it, and then we'd go to our designated defence points all round the factory. Mine overlooked the railway goods yard, close to where I worked in J Department. Once the all-clear sounded we'd march back and form up in Mill Lane as a platoon where we'd present rifles and remove the live round from our rifles. Our sergeant used to look down their barrels to make sure they were clear, though I distinctly remember an occasion when one man left it 'up the spout' and accidentally fired the live round off. That took a bit of the brickwork out of the Social Hall! From then on we weren't allowed to have any live rounds.

When we first joined we had no uniforms or guns, only L.D.V. armbands, though after a while we were given our first guns. I was issued with a Thompson sub-machine gun - a 'Tommy gun'! It seems incredible now. Most of the men had Lee Enfields which were lovely light rifles. The army soon took then back to give them to the regular troops and we were issued ex-First World War Ross Rifles which were long-barrelled and quite heavy.

On the alternate Sundays when I didn't have to go to work I still had to undertake Home Guard duties such as shooting practice. The army used to pick us up in their big Bedford trucks and take us out to ranges at places like the Mersea marshes, Curries' Field near Moulsham Lodge, South Weald, an old gravel pit in Sandon and on an embankment somewhere along the Essex coast. I was quite a good shot and I became a member of the Home Guard's competition team. For that I was issued with my own rifle which I used to bring home to religiously 'pull through' every day or so to keep the barrel clean.

Eventually we were given army type khaki uniforms and boots. The trouble was that the uniforms didn't fit too well and were rough around the neck, so several of us went up to Frederick Hagger's tailors on the corner of Rectory Lane and Henry Road, and he altered them. After that we looked quite smart.

I was drafted into the Camouflage Unit where I was trained in how to make camouflage and on some Sundays we used to visit other Home Guard units to give demonstrations of this. On one occasion we were told to camouflage ourselves and hide in the hedges along the Bunny Walk between Victoria Road and Arbour Lane.

I went and hid in a ditch right by the footpath and as I lay there my father walked by on his way to All Saints' Church. I was so close that I could have put out my arm and touched his leg but he didn't even see me. If anything my camouflage was too good. A few minutes later a dog came by and thinking that I was a tree he did what he shouldn't. I got quite wet that morning, but I could say the camouflage was effective!

By 1941 the threat of invasion by Germany had practically gone, but the Home Guard was continued anyway.

We were working flat out at Hoffmann's, so for a lot of us the Home Guard became a light relief from work. We enjoyed it as it became like a 'social club' - you were with all your pals from work and there was great camaraderie. There were always interesting things to do. We used to take part in parades through the town and we attended courses at the Drill Hall in London Road where we were instructed in all sorts of things, like map reading and weaponry. For example, we were taught how to strip down a Bren gun.

In the latter part of the war we had to mount an armed night-time guard of the River Chelmer railway viaduct at the end of the goods yard. We had a wooden hut near the river and the fence was opened up so that we could straight through from the grounds of Hoffmann's. There were normally four of us on duty. We'd be there from around six in the evening till seven the following morning with a couple of hours on and a couple off.

After we finished I used to rush home by bike to Dorset Avenue, change out of uniform, have a cup of tea and get back to the factory to start work by 7.30 a.m. I was always pushed for time. Normally we had our bayonets fixed to our rifles and we'd take them off and put them into their scabbards on our belts as we marched back to Hoffmann's. That was quite a time consuming thing to do, so to save time I used to keep the scabbard and belt attached to my rifle and march back like that. It didn't look particularly professional but it saved time. Unfortunately one morning a regular army Captain came round to inspect us, out of the blue, and he was not too amused at this sight. Did he swear at me!

The railway engine drivers had their own hut nearby and there was usually a permanent pale of hot tea simmering away in there on a hot stove. How anyone could ever drink it, I don't know. You could have stood up a spoon in it.

One of the engine drivers, Mr. Scotchman, lived two doors away from me and quite often I'd see him in the goods yard and he would give me little bits of information about what he'd seen while driving his train. If there'd been a night raid on London and he'd driven up to Liverpool Street he'd tell how things were up there. On a bad night when there was a heavy raid on London you could see the flare from the fires there in Chelmsford.

At the end of the war I returned my rifle to a regular army guardroom which had been established in Roberts Adlard's building in New Street opposite Hoffmann's. I managed to keep most of my other equipment and I've still got a haversack full of memorabilia like my gas mask, manual on the Bren gun, forage cap badge, lapel badge, army issue maps and armbands. I enjoyed my time in the Home Guard, there was great comradeship there. "

George Brown

"The morning after Anthony Eden had announced that the Government was to start a home defence body. I, together with a colleague from County Hall who had been to school with me, went along to the Police Station in New Street to volunteer. After a few weeks a platoon, about fifty strong, commanded by Ernest Sorrell, was formed from the staff at County Hall. We were part of the 6th Essex Battalion Home Guard and our main duty was to mount a night-time guard for the building which contained the A.R.P. County Control Centre in the basement.

Our Sgt. Major was the County Hall keeper, Frederick Runcorn, who had been an R.S.M. in the Royal Fusileers and was a member of the Queen's bodyguard. In those days employees were either 'officers' or 'servants', so when we drilled in the County Hall car park, once a week after work, he would call out to us 'Gentlemen, attention' or 'Gentlemen, right turn'!

Initially we had no uniforms and only one L.D.V. armband for half a dozen volunteers. Our first uniforms were made of a denim type material. These didn't fit properly and made us look like barrage balloons. It was a fair while, perhaps a year or so, before we got better uniforms.

To start off with we were very short on weapons too. In fact, much of our early drill was performed using broomsticks instead of rifles. Eventually we were able to go to the Grammar School, which I'd only left a few months earlier, and drill using the Cadet Corps carbines which were relics of the First World War. This took place on the school playground. After that crates of rifles arrived from America. They too were of First World War vintage and included Winchesters, Lee Enfields and Remingtons, all packed in grease for protection. We had to clean them up using paraffin; it was a filthy job which made quite a mess.

Each night there were around eight of us on guard at County Hall. The younger members, like myself, who were waiting to be called up, tended to view the Home Guard in a transitory light. As a result we used to have all sorts of fun and games and do stupid things while on duty. One member was a chap called Reggie Clark who was expecting to go into the R.A.F. as an air gunner. He eventually became parliamentary agent for Tom Driberg, the M.P. for Maldon. One night we perched him on a revolving chair with his gun, on top of about six other chairs.

He was going round and round on this contraption in the middle of the night, making a good deal of noise, when suddenly the whole thing collapsed and his rifle broke in two. Needless to say there was an inquest the following day to find out how his rifle had come to be broken.

I left the Home Guard in October 1942 to go into the navy, though after six months I was given the chance to gain my discharge and to train for a technical commission at Dagenham Technical College. One of the conditions was that I had to rejoin the Home Guard.

Since I'd been trained in signals during my short time with the navy I was posted to the signals detachment whose headquarters were in premises at the corner of Rainsford Road and Broomfield Road. Our commander there was Lt. Pitts who worked at Christy's and lived in First Avenue. We used to go on patrols and there were often stories of Home Guardsmen being out along the River Chelmer in the early evening taking pot shots with their .303s at wild rabbits.

As far as I recall, and as the threat of invasion waned, the Home Guard just seemed to peter out. Eventually we had to hand our equipment in at the Drill Hall though I managed to keep my great coat with 'ESX 6' on the shoulders. I still use it to this day to lie on when I'm working under the car."

Les Appleton

ISSUED BY CHELMSFORD A.R.P.

AREA 31ST MAY 1940

Steps you should take in an air raid

If you are in or near your home when the air raid warning sounds stay indoors or get there at once and stay there.

Open all doors and windows unless a gas alarm is given, when they should immediately be closed. In either case at night make sure that the lights are extinguished.

Keep to the corners of the room you are inor go under the stairs.

Above all, don't go outside or even near windows to see what may be going on. Shell fragments may be falling.

Persons caught in the street when the air raid warning sounds should go at once to the nearest public air raid shelter:

Basement shelters	Accommodation
Public Library, Duke Street	140
Spaldings, High Street	150
Luckin Smith Ltd., High Street	60
R.D.C. Office, London Road	130
Shire Hall, Tindal Square	380
Freeman Hardy Willis, High Street	80
Congregational Church, London Rd.	400
Wenley's, London Road	60
Chelmsford Club, London Road	150
Trench Shelters	
Rear of Bell Hotel	900
Recreation Ground	1200

First Aid Post have been established at:
Chelmsford & Essex Hospital, London Road
St. John's Hospital, Wood Street
The Public Health Clinic, Coval Lane

After air raids relatives and friends of casualties will be informed as soon as possible and individual enquiries should be made at the Library, Duke Street where a Casualty Information Bureau will be established.

EYEWITNESS ACCOUNT: DUNKIRK

"In early June 1940 soldiers from the Royal Horse Artillery, who had escaped from Dunkirk, came to stay in Springfield."

As told to our our Special Correspondent

"In early June 1940 soldiers from the Royal Horse Artillery, who had escaped from Dunkirk, came to stay in Springfield.

Many of them had been wounded and were bandaged. Initially they were billeted in the Women's Institute hut, opposite the old Springfield School, though eventually they moved into Pendennis, which is a large verandahed house in Springfield Road between Stump Lane and Springfield Green. They remained in the area for several months and as young teenagers we became quite friendly with them. One of soldiers was a chap called Charlie Langley, who was a cook and came from Dover. Before I went to school he used to get me to visit my aunt's shop behind 'The Endeavour' to get whatever the soldiers wanted - things like Bisto and other groceries.

Later on Charlie came and lived with our family for a short time in our cottage at number 97a Springfield Road or 'Springfield Street', as we called it then. It was only a small place so Charlie had the upstairs and the rest of us used to slept downstairs. In the middle of one particular night his colleagues came and knocked him up to go out on duty because it was thought that Germans had started the invasion."

Eric Clark

GERMAN INVASION EXPECTED SOON

DEFENCES TIGHTENED - TOWN COUNCIL PLAYS ITS PART

AT THEIR MONTHLY meeting, members of the Council agreed to offer all possible assistance to the military by permitting the Borough's staff to help in the preparation of road blocks and barricades which were being set up as part of Chelmsford's anti-invasion defences. The move followed a request by Sir Will Spens, the Eastern Regional Commissioner.

In the town area particular attention was paid to defending the A12 Chelmsford by-pass. At the junction of Princes Road with Vicarage Road & Longstomps Avenue the defences included the erection of barriers made from lengths of angled steel on the roadside, the preparation and covering of placement holes in the roadway, and the construction of concrete anti-tank pyramid-shaped blocks across the open ground between the roads. The north-east corner of the junction was also home to a spigot mortar emplacement, while a similar structure was erected nearby in the south-eastern corner of Oaklands Park. The spigot mounting for the latter is still in existence. Another spigot mortar position was established between Moulsham Street and Princes Road, to the north-east of the roundabout. Anti-tank pyramids were also erected on the open ground around the Army & Navy roundabout, either side of Chelmer Road, and at the top of the hill either side of the old A12, London Road, Widford.

In other parts of the town spigot mortar positions were established in Coval Lane (opposite the old Burgess Well), in Broomfield Road (outside the shop at its junction with King's Road) and off Springfield Road (in

Brown's yard). Several pill boxes were built in the vicinity of Chelmsford's 'big three' factories, including one on the south side of Writtle Road (opposite Waterhouse Street) and one overlooking the River Chelmer adjacent the railway goods yard, and another on the island in the River Chelmer behind Hoffmann's.

To the east of the town elaborate measures were taken to prevent the landing of enemy aircraft. They included the erection of steel cables between poles across open ground - a particularly prominent feature on Baddow Meads, in fields to the east of Chelmer Road and in between the Moulsham Schools and Moulsham Lodge. Other obstacles placed in open ground included hurdles and up-rooted sign posts. Further afield, a chain of dozens of pill boxes skirted Chelmsford in part of a defensive line that ran across Essex.

Amongst other Council business members agreed to ask the County Council and Office of Works to camouflage the new extensions to St. John's Hospital. The new emergency ward block, which had received planning approval from the Council in June 1938, was white-walled, with a white roof and presented a very conspicuous bombing target from the air.

The Council also agreed to the use of the children's department of the Library as the area's Casualty Information Bureau. Mr. A.W. McClellan, the borough librarian, had consented to both act as the casualty officer and organise voluntary helpers to run the bureau.

It was also agreed to offer the German howitzer and field guns in Bell Meadow as scrap. They were trophies from the First World War.

Wednesday 29th May 1940

ROAD SIGNS ARE BEING REMOVED TO HINDER THE EXPECTED INVASION

At another busy Council meeting the Borough Engineer informed the members present that in accordance with instructions from the Ministry of Transport all the direction signs in the Borough had been removed as a measure to hamper the expected invasion.

Upon hearing this members asked him to remove those street nameplates which indicated the direction of nearby towns and villages in conjunction with the removal of all road signs.

The military authorities were reported to have requisitioned a small portion of a field near West Avenue, belonging to the Borough.

Wednesday 26th June 1940

HEINKEL BOMBER IS SHOT DOWN IN SPRINGFIELD ROAD

Narrowly misses houses and crashes at Bishopscourt

The remains of the Heinkel bomber which crashed in the grounds of Bishopscourt early on 17th June 1940. (Courtesy Essex Police Museum)

IN THE MOONLIT early hours a German bomber was shot down and crashed in flames in the grounds of Bishopscourt in Springfield Road. Three enemy airmen were killed, but there were no civilian casualties.

The aircraft had been one of around a hundred raiders, aided by a full moon, which had launched air attacks on targets throughout eastern England from late the previous evening. Seven of the bombers were shot down, two of them over Essex.

The aircraft that crashed in Chelmsford was a Heinkel He 111 H-4 of KG4 (number 2894, markings 5J + GA), which had been engaged over the Thames estuary by a Spitfire of 74 Squadron (Hornchurch) operating from Rochford Aerodrome. The Spitfire was flown by F.O. Adolph 'Sailor' Malan D.F.C., a South African who was to later command the squadron. The Heinkel was turned by A.A. fire, caught and then held by three or four searchlights which made escape impossible.

Malan approached the doomed aircraft, attacked from astern and closed to within fifty yards before firing a four second burst into it. Obviously damaged, the Heinkel broke away, spiralled downwards and with thick black smoke pouring from one engine it appeared over Chelmsford. It circled the town two or three times before crashing across the garden of Springfield Tyrells then Springfield Road itself, before coming to a halt in the grounds of Bishopscourt, home to the Bishop of Chelmsford.

One crewman of the Heinkel, Lt. E. Simon, managed to parachute to safety. He landed slightly wounded close to Writtle, and walked to a house along the Margaretting Road near Nathans Lane where he knocked on the door to be met by an astonished housewife. The local policeman was called and arrested Simon, who was taken to the Chelmsford and Essex Hospital to be treated to wounds to his arm. His three compatriots were not so fortunate. They failed to get out of the plane and were killed when it crashed. Two bodies were thrown clear of the wreckage and the third, who was the rear gunner, was found dead at his post. They were later named as Oblt.

H.-G. Corpus, Oberfw. W. Gross and Fw. W. Vick.

There were no casualties among people on the ground, though a major tragedy was avoided by a matter of feet when the aircraft just missed Springfield Tyrells. The house, which was run by Dr. Barnardo's as a training school, contained 54 people, of whom the majority were girls. It was unscathed but its boundary fence with Tyrells Close, a brick wall and wooden fence on top of it and numerous bushes and trees in the garden were all demolished. Very similar damage was caused in Bishopscourt where the burning wreckage of the aircraft ended up. The fire was quickly extinguished without incident.

Local rumour in Chelmsford soon put it that the Bishop himself had shot the Heinkel down with a shotgun he was known to possess. He had, after all, been an early recruit to the L.D.V.s. After the incident he was to subsequently receive a letter from a fellow Bishop congratulating him on his marksmanship!

Fittingly, the Bishop officiated at the joint funerals of the three German airmen in two days later at the Borough Cemetery.

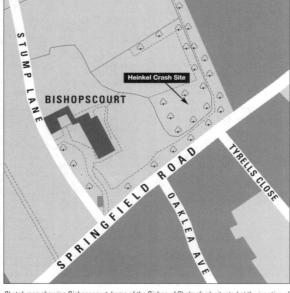

Sketch map showing Bishopscourt, home of the Bishop of Chelmsford, situated at the junction of Stump Lane and Springfield Road, scene of a dramatic aircraft crash on 19th June 1940 .(Author)

Another view of the remains of the Bishopscourt Heinkel in which three young Germans lost their lives in the first local aircraft crash of the war.

Wednesday 19th June 1940

EYEWITNESS ACCOUNTS: BISHOPSCOURT CRASH

"After a time the authorities found some more bits of a German's body, someone said it was a jaw with some teeth, so everyone was cleared out."

As told to our our Special Correspondent

"After the Heinkel had come down at Bishopscourt the same night I walked down to see it, along with my dad. We lived at 98 Springfield Road, near 'The Endeavour', so we didn't have far to go. It was bright moonlit night and by the time we reached Bishopscourt the plane was no longer on fire. We couldn't get right close but we were near enough to hear one of the blokes on the scene say something like 'Here's one dead bugger!' and someone else say 'Bloody good job'! Then we heard a woman say 'Well he is someone's son'.

Later I found out that when the surviving German parachuted from the Heinkel his boots had dropped off. My grandfather, William Carter, was a farmworker in Writtle and he'd found them out in the countryside and had handed them in to the police station. He never saw them again after that.

After work on the day following the crash I went back up to Bishopscourt to get souvenirs from the plane. By then the bits of wreckage that had been on Springfield Road had been pulled into Bishopscourt. There were long scratch marks left in the road from when the Heinkel had skidded across and they were there until well after the war. Hundreds of sightseers were swarming around the area. We were allowed a lot closer than the previous night and I managed to get quite a few mementos, including a German map of England with Chelmsford ringed in red. After a time the authorities found some more bits of a German's body, someone said it was a jaw with some teeth, so everyone was cleared out. The crashed plane had a smell all of its own, a horrible smell, I'll never forget that."

Gerald Carter

"One night as I was at home with my family in Gainsborough Crescent we heard machine gunning overhead and then the spent bullets as they fell on the sheds in the back gardens. A German plane was shot down by one of our fighters at the junction of Tyrell's Close and Springfield Road. At that time I was working as a V.A.D. nurse for the Red Cross at the Chelmsford & Essex Hospital where the one and only enemy airman to survive was brought in for treatment. He was taken into a small ward where he remained under guard."

Marjorie Wilks

"The air raid siren had sounded and I was at sitting indoors with my sister and her husband at home in Yarwood Road. I don't think we'd even got into the shelter when we heard the rat-a-tat-tat of machine gun fire in the sky above. Then suddenly there was a whoosh right across the roof of the house and the sound of debris dropping down. To our relief the plane, which turned out to be a Heinkel, went on to crash in the Bishop's garden in Springfield Road. For most of us it was our first real experience of war."

Jack Palmer

"My wife and I were patrolling in Springfield Road during the alert when we saw an aircraft approaching from the south-east, caught in the beam of a searchlight. It was evidently in trouble and had been hit. As it neared the town it was losing height and began circling. We sheltered in the passageway leading to the Gas Works and ran backwards and forwards in the passage as the plane circled three times, getting lower until eventually it landed in flames in the garden of Bishopscourt."

Gerald Hockley

"A chap that I once met had relatives who lived down by the 'Three Cups' in Springfield Road. He told me that one of them found a teddy bear from the crashed Heinkel at Bishopscourt. They thought it must have been the crew's lucky mascot."

Eric Clark

"During the night a Heinkel was shot down and had crashed in Bishopscourt, Springfield Road. By the morning the news had spread like wildfire so I, and dozens of others, went up to have a look. The wreckage was all roped off and there were police and air force personnel keeping the big crowds back. It was forbidden to take any wreckage, but us youngsters waited until the bobbies weren't looking and ducked under the ropes to get pieces.

I managed to pinch a small piece of fuselage, a few inches square and badly damaged, and I took it home as a souvenir. I wrote on it where I got it and what it was, but eventually it went the way of most things and my mother put it in the dustbin. Other kids got bits and pieces and there was a story of people having one of the Heinkel's wheels away.

We were in competition to get the best piece of crashed aircraft and if someone had an instrument he was reckoned to have done very well. Even if it was only a sort of a battered clock face it was considered worth having.

I can't recall any feelings of remorse or sorrow, whatsoever for the dead German crew, even though at that age I was sensitive to all those things. I suppose we'd been pretty well indoctrinated by then by the wardens, by the press and the Churchillian attitude and we took it for granted that the only good German was a dead one."

Ray Knappett.

"Whenever the air raid warning sounded I tended to listen until I heard something before venturing outside to have a look. For some reason you could always tell a German plane from one of ours by the droning, throbbing sound of its engines. Local people became experts at distinguishing them from friendly aircraft.

On that particular night, from my parents house in Patching Hall Lane, I heard the sound of a German plane which proved to be a Heinkel. I went out into the back garden with my father's First World War field glasses to see what was happening. The plane, which appeared to approach Chelmsford from the east, was picked up by the searchlights and once they got it they fixed onto it and passed it all the way along.

One of our fighters was up there too and it opened fire at the Heinkel which was set alight. As I watched, it circled the town once or twice obviously in trouble. Although the Heinkel was in the searchlights, the fire inside it was so fierce that it was brighter than them, and as a result I could clearly make out the shape of the plane's windows.

It eventually crashed in Springfield and I went over the next day to have a look at the wreckage. We were 'invincible' in those days and it was 'one up to us.'"

Les Appleton

"We heard that a German plane had come down in Springfield during the night and crashed by the Bishop's house. I was curious so I went up there to have a look, and saw the crew sitting in the wrecked plane dead. They were only young men. I thought 'They belong to somebody'."

Winifred Wales

"Alot of people went up to Bishopscourt to try to see the crashed German plane. Not many of us had ever seen one before and it created a great deal of interest.

At that age we didn't worry about the dead German crew, and to be honest, had we done so, we we'd probably have been pleased that they had been killed. I suppose it was a legacy of the First World War. When we were children we had been taught that the wicked Germans were 'the Hun' and our enemies."

George Brown

SAGA OF HOME AIR RAID SHELTERS

AT THE DAY'S Council meeting the increasing public concern over the lack of domestic air raid protection in Chelmsford was demonstrated when petitions were presented by residents of Weight Road and the Rainsford Lane Housing Estate, demanding the provision of some form of public air raid shelters in their neighbourhoods.

The Council had been unable to do anything of that sort so far in the war but things were set to change.

At the meeting the Borough Engineer, Vincent Willis, reported that the Government had given the Council new powers to provide domestic air raid protection within approximately 250 yards of the boundaries of Hoffmann's, Marconi's and Crompton's factories, the likely targets of German bombs.

Allowing for an average expenditure of £7 per house for blast walls or other brick shelters, the total estimated cost would be: 848 houses at £7 each = £5,936

The Borough Engineer went on to explain that at the time cement and bricks were practically unobtainable but the situation should gradually ease by the time permission for the scheme would be sought.

By the time of the Council meeting two months later, little progress had been made on the scheme. Members were told that the influential local branch of the A.E.U had written requesting that the Council expedite the scheme in the wake of continuing public anxiety. The Borough Engineer pointed out that the available cement supplies were sufficient for just 20% of the demand. It was further revealed that the Council would only be allowed to build shelters for a maximum of 10% of the town's population of around 35,000 people. As a result, members agreed to make representations to the Government to increase this percentage to a much higher level.

This failed to appease many worried people in Chelmsford. On Sunday 13th October, in an attempt to channel the public's concerns into positive action, a newly formed pressure group, the Chelmsford Citizens' Air Raid Shelter Committee (C.C.A.R.S.C.), held its first public meeting, ironically on the day that Chelmsford's Mayor was killed in an air raid. The meeting decided to organise a petition to press the Council to construct 'Haldane' type air raid shelters for the public.

The C.C.A.R.S.C. had been instigated by members of the local Communist Party. Its left-wing tendencies and vigorous campaigning style as it organised the petition over the forthcoming weeks were to lead to allegations that the Committee's real aim 'was to cause discontent among the workers and to weaken the Government'.

However, the campaign found widespread favour amongst all types of people in Chelmsford. On 15th November 1940 the Essex Chronicle published a letter from the Rector of Springfield supporting the C.C.A.R.S.C and appealing for an effort to be made to help those 'very small houses' which he suggested 'were not provided with as adequate air raid protection as those in bigger and more affluent homes'. His comments were given added pertinence by the previous night's horrific bombing of Coventry.

On 27th November 1940 the Council met, and received a deputation from the C.C.A.R.S.C. who submitted their petition of over 4,000 signatures, drawing attention to the inadequacy of air raid shelter accommodation in Chelmsford.

The C.C.A.R.S.C. wanted the immediate construction of 'Haldane' type reinforced concrete air raid shelters, designed to survive a direct hit from a 500 lb bomb, to house the whole of the population of Chelmsford at an estimated cost of £350,000. It also pressed for the provision of bunks to allow people to sleep in the Haldane shelters, the opening of all industrial, commercial and other communal shelters until the Haldane shelters were completed, the requisitioning of available premises for alternative accommodation for the homeless, and the setting up of communal feeding arrangements.

In response, the Chairman of the local Joint A.R.P. Committee, Cllr. Bellamy explained that the Council had done all it was permitted to do with regards air raid shelters under restrictions placed by the Government. He went on "Government support is coming, but they say that there are so many towns more vulnerable than Chelmsford. Chelmsford must wait its turn".

In the face of the C.C.A.R.S.C.'s demands and its obvious strong public support, the Council appointed a Domestic Air Raid Shelter Special Committee which reported back on New Year's Day 1941. It dismissed the call by the C.C.A.R.S.C. for large Haldane type shelters on the grounds of their cost and the Government's policy of discouraging the concentration of large numbers of people in small locations during air raids. Instead its recommendation that the Council proceed with the original scheme for blast walls and small shelters in locations within 250 yards of the 'big three' factories was adopted.

On 26th March 1941 the Mayor announced that the Government had given the green light to the scheme. Contracts to undertake the immense project were subsequently agreed with local firms.

Two months later the Council announced it was to seek permission to extend the scheme to include another 733 shelters and 468 blast walls in four other areas of the town.

The progress of the domestic air raid shelter building programme was as follows:

30th April 1941: Vicinity of Hoffmann's/Marconi's - 4 completed & 73 under construction (34 of those requiring roofs); Vicinity of Crompton's - 3 brickwork completed & 4 foundations laid

28th May 1941: 43 shelters completed, 35 the brickwork almost completed, 34 floor slabs laid, 5 blast walls nearly finished.

25th June 1941: Vicinity of Hoffmann's/Marconi's - 89 shelters completed, 26 almost complete, 20 floor slabs laid & 2 blast walls erected; Vicinity of Crompton's - 26 completed, 43 almost completed, 2 floor slabs laid & 7 blast walls erected..

27th August 1941: 214 shelters completed, 26 under construction, 7 blast walls erected.

29th April 1942: 367 shelters finished, 51 under construction.

Wednesday 31st July 1940

THE STRANGE CASE OF 'LORD HAW HAW' & THE SHIRE HALL CLOCK

The Essex Weekly News published a letter refuting propaganda claims recently broadcast by Lord Haw Haw that he knew the Shire Hall clock was two minutes slow. The correspondent pointed out that the clock had been without hands for some two years!

Friday 21st June 1940

NEW HALL TO BECOME A HOSPITAL

The County Council's Public Assistance Committee gave permission to the County's Emergency Committee to hire part of New Hall, Boreham as an emergency hospital. The building was to house patients transferred from Suttons Institution at Hornchurch which had been requisitioned by the Air Ministry. The transfer was subsequently carried out over the next couple of months and eventually provision was made for 280 beds, comprising 51 for sick male, 112 for sick female and 117 for other female patients.

Wednesday 26th June 1940

WATTLE HURDLES NEEDED

To prevent enemy aircraft landing

The Essex County Surveyor, Robert Buckley issued a statement requesting that members of the public urgently help to produce revetment wattle hurdles, 6' long by 4' high. They were needed in their thousands to be erected as obstacles in open fields to prevent the landing of enemy aircraft. The public were urged to 'Make a wattle once a day - this will keep our foe away'.

Wednesday 17th July 1940

BATTLE OF BRITAIN: FIRST LOCAL PLANE CRASH

R.A.F. HURRICANE CRASHES AT BATTLESBRIDGE

The Chelmsford district saw its first plane crash of the 'Battle of Britain'. Around 5 p.m. Hurricanes of 151 Squadron R.A.F. from North Weald Aerodrome were ordered to attack a formation of 38 Luftwaffe aircraft approaching from the east, intent on attacking Croydon Aerodrome.

They were intercepted and halted over Rochford and in the ensuing combat several R.A.F. aircraft were shot down or damaged. At 5.37 p.m. Hurricane P3940 was attacked by a Luftwaffe Bf 110 and crashed in flames and burned out at Tabriums Farm, Battlesbridge. The aircraft's Canadian pilot, Squadron Leader John Gordon, who had been wounded three days earlier, baled out badly burned and was admitted to Rochford Hospital.

Sunday 18th August 1940

Kingston Crescent & Gainsborough Crescent Raid: Monday 19th August 1940

FIRST CIVILIANS KILLED AS BOMBS FALL IN SPRINGFIELD RAID

POLICEMAN LOSES HIS WIFE, SISTER AND DAUGHTER

THE DAY SAW Chelmsford suffer its first civilian casualties of the war when three people were killed when a policeman's house was struck by a bomb in Gainsborough Crescent..

Shortly before 1.45 p.m. a Heinkel He 111, apparently on an armed reconnaissance mission, appeared without warning above the town.

Once over Springfield it released around 23 small sized high explosive bombs (H.E.s) and one or two incendiaries. The bombs were probably intended for the Essex Police Headquarters which stood at the north-western end of Gainsborough Crescent. However, they fell wide of their probable target and dropped in a line across Kingston Crescent and neighbouring Gainsborough Crescent. In the process they demolished two houses, left two others so badly damaged that they would require demolition and another twenty less seriously damaged. However, far more importantly, they left three people dead and six others injured, some seriously.

In Kingston Crescent the first four houses on the left from Sandford Road were damaged, with number 3 (Glendros) demolished and a slight fire caused. Its occupiers, Herbert and Audrey East were badly injured and were to spend months recovering in hospital. However, both were to recover and reach good ages; Herbert lived to be 87 whilst Audrey died in 1992, aged 100. The semi-detached neighbouring house, number 1, occupied by Ernest Windus, was damaged beyond repair.

In Gainsborough Crescent numbers 20 and 22, a pair of semi-detached police houses on its north-eastern side, were worst affected. One bomb struck number 20 and completely flattened the property. Its occupier Police Sergeant Albert Oakley had been in the kitchen preparing to go on duty at headquarters when the aircraft was heard overhead while the rest of his family were sat around the lunch table in the front room of the house. According to one report Sgt. Oakley went to the back door to look out for the aircraft, and as he did so a bomb from the aircraft passed over his head and dropped behind him in the middle of the house. Sgt. Oakley was flung into the garden by the explosion and escaped serious injury. The occupants of the front room were not so fortunate. Sgt. Oakley's wife, sister and daughter were buried under tons of debris, though remarkably his niece and his son, Gordon, who were also in the room escaped practically unscathed and were able to clamber out of the devastated house.

Rescue parties which rushed to the scene frantically began to clear away the debris to get to the three buried victims. The first to be recovered was Sgt. Oakley's 47 year-old sister, Alice Louise Oakley, of Brentwood who had been staying for a few days. She was rescued still alive but died soon afterwards at the Chelmsford & Essex Hospital. Eventually the other two casualties were recovered, both dead. They were Sgt. Oakley's 40 year-old wife, Ivy Beatrice Oakley, and their ten year-old daughter Gwendoline Marjorie Oakley. All three were subsequently buried in Brentwood on 24th August 1940.

At 12 Gainsborough Crescent a woman who was sheltering under the stairs lost her leg when she was hit by an unexploded bomb that penetrated the house. Nearby a man was reported to have been blown downstairs by the force of one explosion, but he escaped unhurt. At another house, a woman was holding a cup when the blast shattered it in her hand.

The road surface in Gainsborough Crescent was cratered by bombs and the gas, water, sewage and electricity utilities disrupted. Several small fires were reported but they were all quickly extinguished. The presence of some eight or nine unexploded bombs led to the evacuation of the neighbourhood while the Number 46 Bomb Disposal Squad dealt with them over the next five days.

The fire brigade, police and rescue services were quickly on the scene and were praised for their speed and effectiveness of their rescue work. One sour note, as far as the authorities were concerned, was the large number of sightseers who hampered some of the rescue work.

Bombs also fell in other parts of Chelmsford later in the afternoon, though fortunately they caused no further casualties. At Moulsham a stick of H.E.s fell in open fields. One landed in Warren Farm Field, another failed to explode in the grounds of St. John's Hospital and a further two were to explode the next morning - one at 6.30 a.m. midway between the Moulsham Schools and another fifteen minutes later in a field near Moulsham Lodge.

In the evening a delayed action bomb exploded at Avenue Road, Great Baddow, and caused slight damage to several houses, but no casualties. Among those affected were 'Elysium' & 'Xanthia'.

Monday 19th August 1940

EYEWITNESS ACCOUNTS: GAINSBOROUGH CRESCENT BOMBS

"Moments after the explosion Ted came running up the road for help from headquarters. We all rushed back to the heap of debris, which was all that was left of his house, and tried to dig his family out."

As told to our our Special Correspondent

"At the time I lived at number 40 Gainsborough Crescent. It was lunchtime, I was at home with my wife, and preparing for the 2 p.m. duty at the police headquarters where I worked on the police traffic patrols. At about half-one we were sat at the dining room table and had more or less finished lunch when, without warning, we heard the sound of bombs coming down.

It was obvious they were close by so we slid off our chairs and shot under the table for cover. Moments later several bombs exploded near to our house. One bomb fell on number 20 Gainsborough Crescent where a colleague of mine, Ted Oakley, lived. Ted was also due out on the 2 p.m. duty and like us he was home having lunch with his family. The bomb exploded in the middle of the house and brought it down on top of Ted's wife, daughter, sister and dog.

Afterwards Ted told us that he had been in the kitchen washing his hands at the sink when the bomb fell and had managed to get out the back door just as the house collapsed behind him. Moments after the explosion Ted came running up the road for help from headquarters. We all rushed back to the heap of debris, which was all that was left of his house, and tried to dig his family out. We were there most of the afternoon - it was a harrowing time and a terrible shock to us all.

As well as the bomb on the Oakleys' house there were also several unexploded bombs. One of them fell on number 12 Gainsborough Crescent and chopped off a woman's leg as she sheltered under the stairs there. All of us on our side of Gainsborough Crescent were evacuated out of our houses for nearly a week while the bombs were dealt with. We went to stay with a colleague of mine, Bill Jones, in Park Avenue."

Les Manning

"I was having lunch at my husband's home in Navigation Road when, at 1.30 p.m. or thereabouts, we heard a plane overhead. We went to investigate. The air raid siren had not sounded. Almost immediately we saw and heard bombs falling. My immediate thought was they were after the prison or the police headquarters.

As my family home was at number 29 Gainsborough Crescent we decided to go and seen where the bombs had fallen. We had a shock because the house opposite where my family and I lived had received a direct hit, and two time bombs fell plus one in Kingston Crescent. Two people were injured by these and a family was killed in Gainsborough Crescent.

My family (the Peagram's) had to be evacuated with many other families. As a result we were, of course, split up because being a large family we were placed with friends and relatives and so on. My parents and I went to stay with my husband's family in Navigation Road (Mr. & Mrs. Bertie Wilks)."

Marjorie Wilks

"It was lunchtime on a clear summer's day and I was at home sat around the table in our front (dining) room with my sister, mother, aunt and cousin, having just finished our meal. Then we heard a droning noise which I'd come to recognise as a German aeroplane - as a typical eleven year-old I'd become fairly expert at distinguishing our aircraft from the Germans by studying aircraft silhouettes and so on.

I rushed over to the bay window at the front of the house to see outside and as I looked up I could see a German aircraft coming from the direction of police headquarters. I shouted a warning to the family, something like 'It's one of their's!'. That is the last thing I can remember until I came round, actually under the table - how I got blown backwards from the window towards the bomb there is no telling! I never heard the sound of the bomb dropping, or even the house falling down. You can't really say that I was trapped, because I was able to pull away various bits and pieces of debris and crawl out to daylight.

There I found that our house had been totally destroyed and was reduced to a pile of rubble. Remarkably P.C. Shepheard's house next door was still intact, and apparently a newspaper reported that it didn't even have a broken pane of glass. The fireplace which backed onto his house was still there and I saw my cousin standing right beside it with her hands over her face. I got hold of her and we scrambled across the rubble to the road. Fortunately neither of us was injured - I didn't even have a cut even after clambering out over all the bricks and rubble.

The next thing I knew there were people shouting - a crowd of policemen had come out of headquarters and rushed down the road to start searching the debris for survivors. They took charge and one of them got hold of my cousin and I and took us a few doors down the road, I think to number 8, where someone invited us in and gave us comfort. My dad who had been in the kitchen getting ready to go on duty, had survived the bomb, and he stayed at our house to help with the rescue efforts.

A short while later there was an enormous panic when they discovered that some of the string of bombs had landed in Kingston Crescent, but had not gone off. That meant that we had to evacuate the area so they brought a police car down from headquarters and I was put in it and taken off to relatives of my father in Brentwood. My cousin was taken back to her family up Ipswich way. Of course I had nothing, no clothes nothing at all, so after a couple of days I was taken out shopping in Brentwood. While we were out another German bomber came over. As I watched it dropped bombs which I thought had fallen on where I was now living, but fortunately it turned out to be the next street.

It was at Brentwood that my dad told me that my mother, sister and aunt had all been killed. My mother and sister had been sitting nearest to the door to the hallway and were both dead when they were dug out. Apparently my aunt had left the dining room to go to the kitchen to warn dad when the bomb exploded near the hall.

She stopped all the shrapnel in her back which presumably saved dad. She was rescued alive and as she was being carried out on a stretcher she asked someone to wish my aunt, Gert Totterdell, a happy birthday. Although she was still conscious at that stage she died later in hospital.

My father had previously been stationed at Rettendon and through that he was able to get hold of fruit that my sister and I used to weigh up and sell from our house, making a bit of pocket money for ourselves. We used to keep the money in a bakerlite bowl on the mantle piece and I remember seeing that intact when I got out from under the table. However, once the site was cleared afterwards the money and bowl went missing - that has always griped me.

After the bombing I went back a few times to Gainsborough Crescent to see the site after it was cleared and I watched the house being rebuilt, but I never lived there again. I followed my father into the police and since retiring I frequently visit headquarters to attend functions, parking in Gainsborough Crescent. Then I often stop outside my old house and reflect on the bombing."

Gordon Oakley

The flattened remains of 20 Gainsborough Crescent where three people were killed in the lunchtime air raid of 19th August 1940. (courtesy Gordon Oakley)

Brockley Road Tragedy: Tuesday 20th August 1940

BOMBS AIMED AT GAS WORKS

Anger as again no siren sounds and an elderly lady is killed

AT 9.50 A.M. a lone Luftwaffe aircraft, believed to have been on armed reconnaissance, appeared without warning above Chelmsford and dropped some nine H.E.s and an incendiary bomb in the Navigation Road area, before it escaped unchallenged.

The likely target for the attack was the nearby Gas Works, but most of the bombs fell wide of there and hit residential areas and the canal banks. Casualties were surprisingly light - the attack left one person dead and four others injured. Some 69 properties were damaged in the attack, including two demolished and seven seriously damaged..

The fatality was 73 year-old Mrs. Sarah Ann Potham who was buried in the rubble of her home, 5 Brockley Road. She was well known locally and actively associated with the Chelmsford Sisterhood, Springfield Mothers' Union and Springfield Women's Fellowship. Her funeral was subsequently held 4 days later at Holy Trinity Church, Springfield.

Only one bomb hit the Gas Works, striking an above-ground tank containing prepared road tar. It passed through the tank and formed a crater in the ground below, into which about 3,000 gallons of tar were discharged from the tank. Men working in the vicinity escaped injury, though considerable damage was done to the adjacent tar plant.

One bomb fell onto the road surface in Navigation Road, opposite number 44, damaging the utilities, but just missing a 15 inch gas main. Meanwhile another fell onto the roof of numbers 35 and 36, while another demolished numbers 5 and 6 Brockley Road, killing Mrs. Potham. A slight fire was started at 7 Brockley Road. and a small gas main was fired. A dozen people from numbers 34 to 37 Navigation Road and fifteen others from numbers 4 to 8 Brockley Road were rendered homeless.

Another of the bombs fell on land between the Saracen's Head Hotel and the River Chelmer, narrowly missing some workmen. No one was hurt and damage was slight, though a crater was formed by the explosion. Mr. Porter, the enterprising manager of the hotel, charged the public a shilling each to view the scene. Such was the curiosity that he was soon to raise more than £100 which was later donated to the town's Flight of Fighters Fund which was to begin the next day.

At Bishopscourt the German aircraft had been observed approaching Chelmsford by the Bishop of Chelmsford's gardener. He rushed to tell the Bishop, who came outside, and watched the aircraft casually circle above Chelmsford, apparently looking for a target, before it released its bombs. Angered by what he had seen, the Bishop contacted the Mayor and together at 11.27 a.m. they sent a tersely worded telegram to the Minister of Home Security. It read "Solitary raider bombed this town yesterday and once today. Several lives lost. Strongly protest - no warning given. Signed Mayor and Bishop of Chelmsford".

The incident was to claim another victim some months later. On 14th July 1941 Mrs. Potham's 81 year-old husband, Thomas, travelled to Brentwood railway station. He was seen to put his head on the rail and calmly wait for a Shenfield to Liverpool Street train to strike him at 50 m.p.h. He died instantly and was subsequently buried alongside his wife.

Tuesday 20th August 1940

EYEWITNESS ACCOUNTS: NAVIGATION & BROCKLEY ROADS RAID

"My father could not move much because of his disability, but in the circumstances this was a blessing because he did not move from the kitchen. If he had gone into the living room it would have been a different story because the whole room was riddled with shrapnel."

As told to our our Special Correspondent

"It was about 9.50 a.m. and I was working the office (Luckin & Sheldrake) in Waterloo Lane when I heard the sound of a lone aircraft. I went outside and saw overhead what I assumed was a German plane, flying rather high in a south-easterly direction. I then heard bombs exploding and being an air raid warden I donned my helmet and cycled home to my sector (Navigation Road). There I found right in front of my house (number 44) a large crater extending from kerb to kerb. I looked up at the houses on both sides of the road and the fronts appeared undamaged to my surprise. Further along the road the roofs of numbers 35 & 36 had been hit by another bomb, while a third bomb had demolished the front of houses in Brockley Road. I cycled up to the wardens post in Weight Road to report the damage to Headquarters. Later I discovered that other bombs had been dropped in the vicinity of the gas works.

There had been no warning and, although this was normally a busy time for tradesmen and others in the street, fortunately no one seemed to have been about. Luckily my wife was away blackberrying in Boreham.

When I went into my house I found the window in the back room was blown out and a pile of soot had fallen down the chimney. Upstairs there was a large hole in the front bedroom ceiling and a large piece of the road surface had fallen in - fortunately between the bed, wardrobe and chest of drawers. Again the window facing the bomb was intact. Later I discovered that a piece of tarmac about two feet across and three inches thick had been blown right over the roof and had landed on the back lawn.

It appears that the bomb had penetrated the road for some feet, falling between two manholes and consequently the blast went straight upwards. In contrast the bomb falling on numbers 35 & 36 had exploded on impact and the blast had gone sideways and damaged many houses in the vicinity, breaking windows and leaving splinters of glass embedded in bedroom walls. Although the roofs of the two houses were severely damaged the bomb had not penetrated - in fact a member of the of the family evacuated the previous day from a house hit in Gainsborough Crescent was inside but sustained no injury. A woman was killed in Brockley Road when a bomb demolished a wall and she was buried."

Gerald Hockley

"There was a repeat of the previous day's events with another bombing incident, this time at about 10.30 a.m. Another lone raider made its way through and again there was no warning siren. This time it was my husband's home, no. 36 Navigation Road, that had a direct hit. In addition other bombs from the enemy plane fell in Brockley Road and in the fields adjacent to the gas works.

We had all gone out of the house for a short period that morning but my father was left in the house. We thought that he must either be killed or injured but he was very lucky. He could not move much because of his disability, but in the circumstances this was a blessing because he did not move from the kitchen. If he had gone into the living room it would have been a different story because the whole room was riddled with shrapnel.

In the event our two families had to find somewhere else to go as we were not allowed back into Gainsborough Crescent until the following Sunday because of the time bombs. My in-laws went with relatives and so did we while my parents went to friends in Widford. It was all very disturbing as there seemed to be very little organisation in those early stages of the war."

Marjorie Wilks

"After the bombing I remember going to Brockley Road to see the wrecked houses. By that time it had been made relatively safe, but the rubble hadn't yet been taken away and you could walk through the half-demolished walls. My mother was a friend of Mrs. Potham through the Mothers' Union and I can remember her feeling at least relieved that dear old Mrs. Potham hadn't suffered too much. We only lived a minute's walk away from Brockley Road and I used to go and do shopping for Mrs. Potham on occasions. She was an elderly, very unassuming, quiet, ordinary, friendly, pleasant lady - the very last sort of person you'd wish to see injured or killed."

Ray Knappett

"I was at the counter in the main Post Office when a small bomb fell behind the Saracen's Head. I heard a whistling as it came down, this being immediately followed by the explosion which sounded rather like the roller blind of a shop front being pulled down. There was no time to do anything and the blast literally lifted me up in the air half an inch and back down again. People in the Post Office didn't really know what had happened, but they knew it must have been something like a bomb."

Les Appleton

"I was at work in Hoffmann's one morning when I was told that bombs had dropped close to my parents' house in Navigation Road. I immediately rushed round there to see what had happened and check that they were alright. When I arrived I found that a bomb had fallen on number 36, home to Mr. & Mrs. Bert Wilks, just two doors from my parents'. The top part of the house was seriously damaged but fortunately Mr. & Mrs. Wilks had escaped unharmed. My father and mother, George and Hannah Brown of number 34, suffered from shock, but their house was too badly affected for them to stay there. They were very upset as it had been their home most of their married life. The army brought round a truck and loaded it with all their salvaged possessions and furniture. Most of that was brought round to my house in Dorset Avenue and my parents went and stayed with my sister in Springfield Park Avenue. My cousin, Will Locke, who had been lodging with my parents while he worked in Chelmsford, came to stay with us. It was quite a while before the house was repaired and they could return there. It was our first experience of seeing any bombing and it made me realise that the war would be at home as well as abroad."

George Brown

Battle of Britain:

DEFIANT DOWN AT BOREHAM: GUNNER FATALLY WOUNDED

During the afternoon the Luftwaffe attempted to bomb Hornchurch and North Weald Aerodromes. Aircraft from those missions were likely to have been responsible for the few incidents which occurred locally.

At 3.50 p.m. a single H.E. fell harmlessly in an open field at Brook Farm off Crows Lane, Woodham Ferrers. Twenty minutes later Defiant L6965 of 264 Squadron R.A.F., of Hornchurch Aerodrome was shot down in combat with Bf 109s of JG51 over its base, crashing at Boreham Hall, Boreham. The aircraft's pilot P.O. Richard Gaskell baled out slightly injured but Sgt. Air Gunner William Howard Machin, sustained fatal wounds dying later in hospital. Machin had only been with the squadron for two days and was buried at his home town cemetery in Handsworth, Birmingham.

Saturday 24th August 1940

LAUNCH OF FLIGHT OF FIGHTERS FUND

A public meeting, chaired by the Mayor, launched an appeal to raise £15,000 to buy a flight of three fighter aircraft in recognition of the gallant efforts of the R.A.F.

The fund got off to an excelent start and after two days it totalled £5,781/10/6, thanks largely to a donation of £5,000 from Mrs. J.H. Keene, the Galleywood philanthropist. The money, which was enough to purchase a Spitfire to be named 'Galleywood', was subsequently sent to Lord Beaverbrook, the Minister of Aircraft Production.

Donations continued to flow steadily and by 9th October 1940 it was reported to have passed the £10,000 mark, sufficient for the purchase of a second aircraft for the Chelmsford district, later named 'Chelmsford'.

At the monthly Council meeting in April 1941 the Town Clerk reported that photographs of the first two Spitfires had been received from the Ministry of Aircraft Production.

On 27th January 1942 the fund was formally closed down. Although the initial £15,000 target had not been reached Chelmsford had managed a very creditable performance; £14,219/11/5 had been raised after expenses, a figure per head of population that was twice the national average for similar schemes throughout Britain.

Wednesday 21st August 1940

THE BATTLE OF BRITAIN

INCIDENTS ALL AROUND THE CHELMSFORD DISTRICT

MESSERSCHMITT BROUGHT DOWN AT RETTENDON

2 crew taken prisoner

ON WHAT WAS one of the most heavily fought days of the Battle of Britain there was just one incident affecting the Chelmsford district.

At 4.25 p.m. the Hurricanes of 56 Squadron, North Weald were scrambled to intercept a raid of Heinkel He111 bombers of KG 53, escorted by Messerschmitt Bf 110s of ZG 26, enroute to bomb factories at Luton and Radlett in Hertfordshire. In the ensuing combat F.O. Innes Westmacott, flying Hurricane number 3018, engaged and shot down a stray Bf 110 over Brentwood. The aircraft, number 3496 with markings 3U + KP, was compelled to make a forced landing at Mill Hill Farm, Rettendon. It crashed practically intact, save for broken propellers and one or two pieces of detached fabric. Both crew members, Uffz. Rudolf Franke and Uffz. Willi Hubner, were taken prisoner by local air raid wardens.

Friday 30th August 1940

TWO HURRICANES BROUGHT DOWN NEAR CHELMSFORD

Around breakfast time, a force of 15 to 20 Dornier Do 17s of KG 2, escorted by Messerschmitt Bf 110s of JG 26 was intercepted by aircraft from North Weald Aerodrome's 56 Squadron over the Blackwater Estuary whilst returning from a raid on Debden Aerodrome.

In the ensuing dogfight four Hurricanes were shot down. One of them, number V7341 of F.O. Innes Westmacott, crashed into a field adjoining White Hart Lane, Springfield at 9.05 a.m. F.O. Westmacott, who had shot down an enemy aircraft the previous day at Rettendon, baled out badly burned and landed in a clearing amongst the trees between Blake's Wood and Colam Lane in Little Baddow.

He was rushed to Chelmsford & Essex Hospital but his injuries were such that he would not be able to return to his squadron until November 1940. Only one bomb from the raid appears to have been jettisoned within the Chelmsford district - an incendiary which was discovered during the day at the Rectory in Little Leighs.

In the afternoon another aircraft was brought down in the Chelmsford district. At 1.20 p.m. an unidentified Hurricane, possibly from 601 Squadron of Debden, came down a quarter of a mile the Chelmsford side of the Leylands, at Ray Farm, Ingatestone. The pilot was reported to have baled out unhurt.

Saturday 31st August 1940

HUGE DOGFIGHT FOUGHT ABOVE CHELMSFORD

THREE AIRCRAFT SHOT DOWN

At 9.45 a.m. a group of 54 Dorniers, escorted by around 80 Bf 110s, crossed the northern shore of the Thames Estuary intent on bombing North Weald Aerodrome.

The attack was pressed home successfully, but on its return flight the enemy force was engaged by Hurricanes of 1, 17, 46 249, and 257 Squadrons and Spitfires of 19 and 603 Squadrons. As a result a massive dog fight took place over mid Essex with numerous aircraft from both sides shot down.

An early casualty was Spitfire number X4185 of 603 Squadron, Hornchurch which was shot down off the Essex coast by enemy aircraft. Its pilot, P.O. Dudley Clark, baled out wounded and was admitted to the Chelmsford & Essex Hospital.

257 Squadron of Martlesham Heath suffered particularly badly. Around 10.40 a.m. its Hurricane number L1585 was shot down by a Bf 110 and crashed in flames at Parsonage Farm, Margaretting. The aircraft fell close to the brook and culvert which pass through the railway embankment, on the Ingatestone side of the stream. Its pilot, P.O. David Hunt, baled out badly burned and landed nearby at Brook Farm, Margaretting. He was rushed to Billericay Hospital and later transferred to the Queen Victoria Hospital, East Grinstead where he underwent surgery by the celebrated Archie McIndoe.

Minutes later Hurricane, number P3518, was shot down by a Bf 110 and crashed at Lodge Farm, Galleywood close to Killegrews. Its pilot, P.O. Camille Bonseigneur baled out but his parachute failed to deploy correctly and he was killed. Two other Hurricanes of 257 Squadron were damaged during the combat.

Also around 10.40 a.m., a Messerschmitt Bf 110 of ZG 26 (number 3310. markings 3U + EP) came down near Edwin's Hall in Woodham Ferrers. It had been shot down by F.O. Leonard Haines D.F.C. of 19 Squadron. The German airmen. Ltn. Manhard and Uffz. Drews baled out safely and were captured at Stow Maries.

As the massive dogfight was fought above Chelmsford the countryside below was littered with dozens of jettisoned bombs:

Chelmsford - 21 H.E.s and several incendiaries at Chelmsford Golf Course, gratuitously providing some new bunkers, 1 bomb east of 107 Galleywood Road near Tilekiln Farm, and 2 west of Galleywood Road on Thrift Farm land which caused damage to 114 and 122 Galleywood Road

Galleywood - 1 incendiary at Chaplin's (Bearman's) Farm, at Watchouse Lane where a cottage 'Lincoln' was slightly damaged and 3 incendiaries at 'Attwoods' in Well Lane.

Stock - 5 H.E.s including one unexploded at Greenacre Farm.

Roxwell - 3 incendiaries at Lord's End House and 11 at Skreens Road store hall.

Writtle - Incendiaries at Sturgeon's Farm where haystacks were set alight; 1 incendiary at Dawes Farm, 2 at Rollestones Farm, 6 at Oxney Green, 5 at Love Lane, 1 at Longmeads and 1 at Victoria Road.

Elsewhere: - 1 incendiary near Widford Rectory; 1 incendiary at Newney Hall, Newney Green; 2 incendiaries at Sandon Hall, Sandon; 2 incendiaries in a field south-east of Little Mascalls, Great Baddow; 1 incendiary at Rettendon Place, Rettendon; 1 at Smallholders Hall, South Woodham Ferrers: 2 incendiaries at Crondon Park, 4 at Fristling Hall, and 1 at Jackson's Farm. Stock.

Later in the day, around 3.15 p.m., 2 incendiaries were reported in Great Baddow. one at Deadman's Lane and another at the junction of Chelmerton and Dorset Avenues. All the fires caused by the day's incendiaries were soon extinguished without causing any serious damage or injuries.

Tuesday 3rd September 1940

HURRICANE SHOT DOWN AT WEST HANNINGFIELD

In mid afternoon Hurricanes of 73 Squadron, Debden, engaged Luftwaffe Ju 88s and Bf 109s above Burnham-on-Crouch. In the ensuing combat three Hurricanes were shot down, one crash landed and two others were damaged.

One of the former was number P3110 (markings TP O G), flown by P.O. Robert Rutter. It was shot down in a surprise attack by a Bf 109 at 3.25 p.m. as P.O. Rutter attempted to intercept the Ju 88s. His Hurricane crashed a quarter of a mile south-east of Steel's Farm, close to Seaman's Lane in West Hanningfield.

The plane was 'completely smashed'. P.O. Rutter had managed to bale out and was taken to hospital for treatment to a shell wound in his ankle.

Thursday 5th September 1940

TWO MORE HURRICANES BROUGHT DOWN

In the afternoon two Hurricanes were brought down in separate incidents near Chelmsford.

At 1.25 p.m. 25 year-old Ft. Lt. Denis Parnall was killed when his Hurricane, V6685 of 249 Squadron North Weald, was shot down by the A12 at Furness Farm, Furze Hill, Margaretting. He had engaged a Luftwaffe force heading for London near Gravesend.

Later on, at 5.40 p.m., Hurricane P3086 of 302 (Polish) Squadron crash landed at Sandon Lodge Farm, Sandon opposite 'Potash', having been damaged by debris from a Junkers Ju 88 it had just engaged in combat. The Hurricane's 30 year-old pilot Sgt. Edward Paterek was unharmed and the aircraft intact, save for a damaged propeller.

Wednesday 18th September 1940

1ST MAJOR RAIDS ON LONDON

HURRICANE CRASHES AT STOCK, SPITFIRE FORCED DOWN AT WEST HANNINGFIELD

THE DAY MARKED a turning point in the course of the war when the Luftwaffe launched its first major air raid on London.

The move was a significant change in tactics by Germany, which had previously concentrated on attempting to destroy the R.A.F. as its prelude to an invasion. It would later be regarded as one of Germany's biggest blunders of the war. The night blitz had begun and for many people it was to be the first of many sleepless nights.

A massive force of 348 bombers escorted by 617 fighters was launched on London. By 4.30 p.m. all 21 R.A.F. squadrons within 70 miles of the capital were in the air or under take off orders as they attempted to thwart the attack. Dozens of aircraft from both sides were shot down, with two coming down in the Chelmsford district.

At 5.00 p.m., at the height of the aerial combat taking place above the tidal length of the River Thames, Ft. Lt. Reginald Lovett D.F.C. of 73 Squadron R.A.F. Debden, was killed when his Hurricane (number P3234, markings TP O E) was shot down at Fritz Farm in Stock. As the stricken aircraft fell from the sky a game of cricket was in progress on Stock Common between Stock and Mildmay Ironworks. Players watched in horror as the Hurricane came plummeting towards them, but at the last moment it veered away to crash in the fields behind the Catholic School. After a pause, the cricket match continued. Ft. Lt. Lovett was 26 and came from Golders Green in London. Two days earlier he had survived being shot down over Burnham-on-Crouch by bailing out unhurt. He was an experienced airman having served in the R.A.F. since November 1935. He was later buried at Hendon Cemetery.

Around the same time several incendiaries fell on Danbury Common and started a few small fires which were quickly extinguished.

Around 5.35 p.m. Hurricane P3863, flown by Sgt. Alfred. Marshall of 73 Squadron Debden, was damaged in combat above Chelmsford by a Bf 110. The pilot was unhurt and managed to bring the aircraft down safely near Burnham-on-Crouch.

Ten minutes later Spitfire of 41 Squadron Hornchurch was compelled to make a forced landing midway between Tanfield Tye and Tinsley's Farms in West Hanningfield after combat over its home base. The aircraft, number N3266, was repairable and its pilot, Sgt. Ray Ford, was unhurt.

Saturday 7th September 1940

POLISH PILOT KILLED WHEN PARACHUTE FAILS AT BATTLESBRIDGE

On what would subsequently be celebrated as Battle of Britain Day, the Luftwaffe attempted one morning and one afternoon heavy air raid on London. Both were decisively repulsed by the R.A.F. though not without cost locally: around 3 p.m.

Ft. Lt. Tadeusz Chlopik was killed when his Hurricane, number P2954 (markings WX O E) of 302 (Polish) Squadron, was shot down in a surprise attack by German aircraft over North Weald Aerodrome. The 32 year-old baled out, but is believed to have been injured in doing so, and fell dead at Rawreth. His aircraft came down at Marks Farm, Battlesbridge and such was its impact that wardens there were unable to tell if it was a Spitfire or Hurricane. Ft. Lt. Chlopik was buried at the Sutton Road Cemetery in Southend.

Sunday 15th September 1940

MASSIVE UXB AT COUNTY GARDENS

At 1.55 a.m., on what was a moonlit night, a heavy calibre bomb fell unexploded at the old County Gardens off Rainsford Road, and in the process damaged nos. 11 and 12 School View Road. The device was jettisoned by a German aircraft which when it was intercepted by a British fighter above Chelmsford. The raider was reported to have been brought down near Harlow. The crew of three baled out, and were captured and taken to Chelmsford Police Station. The presence of the bomb led to the evacuation of the neighbourhood for some weeks. Once it was finally recovered the bomb was loaded on the back of a lorry and driven through the town to 'a safe place of demolition' in a convoy headed by a load speaker van warning the public to keep away.

Sunday 15th September 1940

SPITFIRE DOWN AT W. HANNINGFIELD

A large force of about 60 Bf 109s which had crossed the Kent coast around 11 a.m. were engaged by Spitfires from Biggin Hill and Hornchurch Aerodromes above the Thames Estuary and Medway towns. In the subsequent combat seven Spitfires were destroyed. One of them, number K9993 of 222 Squadron Hornchurch, was shot down and crashed at West Hanningfield, a quarter of a mile east of the church, opposite Linkhouse Farm. P.O. William Assheton managed to bale with slight burns and landed at Latchingdon. He was taken to St. Peter's Hospital in Maldon for treatment.

Friday 20th September 1940

EYEWITNESS ACCOUNTS:

"Two Spitfires, that was all, dived down out of the sky in between the German aircraft and opened up on them... they passed right through the formation, turned and came back up. Just as they did that all of the German aircraft turned in unison and flew back out towards the sea."

As told to our our Special Correspondent

"During the early part of the war my wife and I used to go for walks over the Meads with our white haired terrier dog, Skip. One afternoon we were by the lock at Barnes Mill (a nice spot in those days) and Skip was swimming in the river, when the siren sounded. I was a police officer, based at headquarters in Springfield, and whenever the siren went off I had to rush up there and report for duty. We yanked Skip out of the water and began running towards Springfield.

As we reached Sandford Road we saw two huge formations of German aircraft coming over from the Maldon direction, straight for Chelmsford. There were Dorniers and Heinkels and there must have been forty or more, making a hell of a roar. I said to my wife 'There's going to be a blitz on Chelmsford!'. The dentist Fraser Maguire, who lived in Sandford Road, saw us and he invited my wife into his house for shelter under the stairs. It was better than carrying on to our home in Gainsborough Crescent. Meanwhile I dashed on up to headquarters and watched the German aircraft continue their approach. As I did so two Spitfires, that was all, dived down out of the sky in between the German aircraft and opened up on them. Afterwards we were told that the Spitfires were flown by Polish pilots. They passed right through the formation, turned and came back up. Just as they did that all of the German aircraft turned in unison and flew back out towards the sea. Whether it was a test run on North Weald or what I don't know, but it was a sight that impressed me and one that I've never forgotten."

Les Manning

"1940 was a wonderful year weatherwise. The harvest at my father's farm, Newland Hall at Roxwell, was a very long drawn out one and lasted from the end of July right until the end of September. I spent much of that time in the fields helping the farmworkers and we saw no end of dogfights in the sky above us. The peak seemed to be around August when the Germans kept coming to try and get North Weald Aerodrome, and we weren't that far from there.

When a dogfight broke out work on the farm would stop. We'd unhitch the horses from the wagons and carts and keep hold of them to prevent them from bolting - they

weren't used to planes roaring past overhead. Then we'd stand enthralled, watching the planes fighting, not frightened for ourselves, but for the men who were fighting to save us. Everyone was aware what was going on - there was a terrific feeling of what a wonderful lot our pilots were - fighting and, in some cases, dying for us. We thought that we knew but we couldn't really tell the British and German planes apart-they were too high to see clearly. On one occasion we saw a plane shot down and crash towards Willingale so we all cheered. It turned out later that it had been one of ours, a Hurricane or Spitfire, and we felt a bit silly after that."

Leonard Menhinick

"One Sunday teatime, during the Battle of Britain, I was with a friend up near the Oasis, by Captain Bevington's house, when in the distance we saw a mass of German bombers appear over Danbury. We counted 42 of them travelling westwards, in formation and relatively low. We supposed that they were on their way to bomb one of our aerodromes. They altered course southwards and just then a single Spitfire came low across the sky from the west, turned and climbed right up into the middle of them. Within seconds he was shot down and crashed somewhere to the south-east. in the direction of Woodham Ferrers. There was no doubt about the pilot's bravery."

Eric Clark

"Along with a great friend of mine, Jack Eve, who alas was to die when his ship was torpedoed off Ireland, I was particularly keen on brass rubbing, long before it became a very popular pastime. The finest collection of brasses in England are in Cobham Church in Kent, so during the summer of 1940 we decided to travel there from home in Chelmsford. The only way to get there was to catch a bus down to Tilbury, get the ferry across the Thames and then another bus to Cobham. Off we set, but when we got to Tilbury there were large notices about it being prohibited to enter this zone etc. Of course we ignored them and duly went to Cobham. While we were there taking brass rubbings, we could hear the sound of machine gunning as the Germans and our planes fought the Battle of Britain above us. It was a

very moving experience and left a very deep impression on me. Whenever I see a brass or look at the rubbings I did then I reminded of that day."

Dennis Hance

"One fine morning we were out in the back yard behind our house, 97a Springfield Street, looking towards the Colchester direction watching a dogfight. The planes were so high that all you could see were little specks dodging about and their vapour trails. As we continued watching the planes mum noticed that one of them was coming down on fire. It was too far away to tell whether it was one of ours or a German plane. Our first thought was for the pilot but then we saw a white parachute open up after he'd baled out. As the plane descended it travelled towards us and soon we could see that it was a Hurricane. We weren't particularly worried, just curious as to where it was going to crash. It approached from the east, glided down across the A12, up-side-down, and disappeared out of view.

I knew that it had crashed somewhere along the railway line towards Boreham, so I ran out the back of the garden, up to the railway, and followed it to Pump Lane. There was still no sign of the plane so I crossed the railway bridge and ran along the other side of the railway, through an area we called 'the mountains' and up to White Hart Lane by the next bridge. As soon as I got there I could see the remains of the Hurricane in the first field to the north-east of the road. It had come low over the railway, across a field of stubble and ended up in the hedge at the furthest from the railway. The plane had been smashed to bits and, although the fire had gone out by the time I got there, I decided not to get too close. There were pieces of wreckage all over the field.

Later in the day I went back up to the crash site to have another look. By then there was a group of soldiers guarding the wreckage and a handful of other inquisitive youngsters. I think that the soldiers had come over from the fields towards New Hall where they were stationed. Fortunately they didn't stop us going up to the wreckage so we were able to take small pieces of the wreckage away as souvenirs."

Eric Clark

WOMAN KILLED IN RAID AT SOUTH WOODHAM FERRERS

In the afternoon the Chelmsford district suffered its first civilian casualty since 20th August 1940 when a dozen H.E.s fell on South Woodham Ferrers.

The bombs fell at 1.27 p.m. and demolished Ivy and Frank Reynolds' bungalow 'Sunnyside' in Albert Road. The couple, who were at home at the time, were buried as their home collapsed onto them. Despite the best efforts of the rescue services 30 year-old Mrs. Reynolds was found to be dead when she was recovered at 2.45 p.m.

Her husband sustained serious injuries and was taken to hospital along with one other person. Fortunately their six year old son was safe at school at the time of

the tragedy. Villagers were to later make a collection for him totalling £9/12/6 plus toys and clothes. The neighbouring bungalow was badly damaged and rendered unsafe, but luckily its occupier, Mrs. Sharman, had not been home when the bomb fell. One unexploded H.E. was found 100 yards south of the railway at Saltcoats Farm.

Mrs. Reynolds' funeral was held three days later at St. Mary's Church, Woodham Ferrers. The service was attended by a detachment of the local Observer Corps to whom Mr. Reynolds was attached. He was unable to be there but was reported to be 'making good progress' in hospital. Mrs. Reynolds is remembered on the Woodham Ferrers war memorial.

Wednesday 25th September 1940

BOMB DISPOSAL SQUAD IN THE WARS

It was an incident packed day for the Bomb Disposal Squads. At 9.07 a.m. a landmine exploded at No. 9 B.D.S.'s headquarters at 3 Phoenix House in London Road.

As a result one person was killed and fourteen others were wounded, eight seriously. Blast from the device damaged Phoenix House and its neighbour, no. 63a (Osbourne Place). During the day the squad was called in to deal with an unexploded parachute landmine at Powers Farm in Broomfield. The device was detonated, but unfortunately in the process three cottages and Scravels suffered considerable damage through the blast. Finally at 7.30 p.m. they blew up a mine at Boyton Cross.

Sunday 29th September 1940

EYEWITNESS ACCOUNT: PARACHUTE LANDMINE

"It was the sound of the wind in the chords of a parachute landmine."

As told to our our Special Correspondent

"We used to share an outdoor shelter with our neighbours, Mr. & Mrs. Sam Clark. During one night alert we were all sitting in the shelter which was in the back garden of 38 Gainsborough Crescent when we heard a swish noise from the sky above us. I immediately realised that it was the sound of the wind in the chords of a parachute landmine as it swayed to and fro. I've never felt so scared in all my life; I thought 'The bloody mine's going to go off any second, right by us', but fortunately it never did. What mystified me was that we never heard any result; I assume it must have failed to explode."

Les Manning

MILDMAY ROAD BOMBED

AT 11.07 P.M an H.E. bomb fell in the cul-de-sac part of Mildmay Road, beyond St. John's Road. The explosion damaged 43 nearby properties, including four seriously. Miraculously there was just one slight casualty, a warden who was cut by flying glass.

The device was probably dropped by one of a number of Luftwaffe aircraft which were briefed to carry out evening raids on London.

The fronts of four houses, numbers 150a, 152, 154 and 161

were wrecked by the blast. At no. 154 Stanley Finch, his wife and two children had been asleep in a downstairs room when the bomb exploded yards away, but all escaped injury. Their house was badly damaged though in the kitchen a basket of eggs was said to have survived unbroken. Next door, at no. 152, the damage was to a similar degree, but the house was unoccupied. It had only just been rented by a Southend family who had come intent on living in a 'safer town'! At no. 161, across the road, which was the staff residence for Palmer & Harvey Ltd.,

wholesale tobacconists, the damage rendered 11 people homeless, in addition to eight from the other badly damaged properties.

The aircraft also dropped an incendiary bomb that fell close to St. John's Vicarage in Vicarage Road. It was quickly smothered with sand by wardens from a local post. Other H.E.s were reported at Water Hall and Hammond's Farm in Little Baddow, and at Sturgeon's Farm in Writtle. Further afield an oil incendiary and H.E. fell at Sparrows End, Mashbury where slight fires were caused.

Friday 20th September 1940

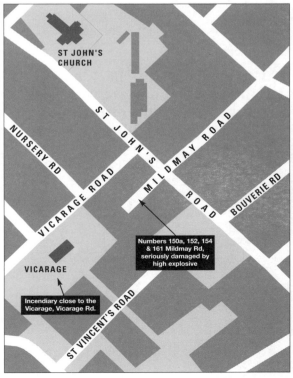

Sketch map showing the south-western end of Mildmay Road which was badly damaged by enemy action in the late evening of 20th September 1940. (Author)

MAYOR OF CHELMSFORD KILLED IN AIR RAID

Fluke German bomb in London Road scores a direct hit on his home, kills him and five others in a tragedy that shocks the whole of Essex

IN THE EVENING Chelmsford suffered its most serious incident of the war so far when a lone Luftwaffe raider dropped two bombs over the town.

At 7.30 p.m. one of these, a high explosive, scored a direct hit on Brierly Place (old number 52), London Road, the home to the Mayor and his family. The bomb passed through the building and exploded in its basement, 'collapsing it like a pack of cards'. Debris was strewn across London Road and caused its closure between Queen Street and Southborough Road.

The Mayor, his family and servants were at home and were thought to have been sheltering in the basement when the bomb struck.

The rescue services were soon at work on the scene and by 10.40 p.m. London Road had been cleared. However, it was not until 1.01 a.m. that the first casualty figures were received at the Police H.Q. - "Ten people involved (actually nine), two children recovered dead, three householders rescued but one injured, Mayor and Mayoress still unaccounted for". The dead children were the Mayor's grandchildren, 8 year-old Audrey Mary Thompson and her 14 month-old sister Deana Louisa Thompson. Their mother, Muriel who suffered serious injuries, was one of those rescued, along with a nurse and another daughter-in-law of the Mayor. By 5.31 a.m. a further two bodies were recovered, and by 11.50 a.m. another, the fifth fatality, was found. Rescue workers continued their search into Tuesday and in mid afternoon the remains of

The devastation of Brierly Place is clearly shown in this view of the Mayor's wrecked home. (Courtesy Essex Chronicle)

sixth body, a servant, were found.

The four adults killed were subsequently identified as the Mayor, 68 year-old John Ockelford Thompson C.B.E. D.L. J.P., his 78 year-old wife Emma, their 41 year-old son Lt-Col. Thomas Cloverley Thompson and Alice Maud Emery, also 41, who was a servant for the Mayor.

Apart from the victims in Brierly Place there were few other casualties though several residents did have remarkable escapes. Those people who were sat in 'The Manse' in London Road were showered with pieces of brickwork and mortar which were

brought down by the blast. The windows were said to have 'fallen in like the Niagara Falls but fortunately none of the occupants was hurt. In London Road a number of passers-by also had narrow escapes. One woman sustained a broken leg, another was blown off her bicycle by the blast and two men and two women pedestrians escaped serious injury by diving to the ground on hearing the whistling of the approaching bomb.

The second bomb, which was an oil incendiary, fell on the footpath in Moulsham Street, almost opposite Oaklands Park. It caused slight damage to some overhead telephone cables, but there were no additional injuries.The funeral service of the Thompsons was held at Chelmsford Cathedral three days later. Their five coffins were placed in the building overnight prior to the service. Their deaths had come as a great shock to the town and the Cathedral was filled to overflowing for the service which was conducted by the Bishop of Chelmsford and the Provost, the Very Rev. William Morrow. The congregation was swelled by a considerable number dignitaries from all over Essex and beyond. After the service the coffins were driven to the Borough Cemetery for burial, passing the remains of Brierly Place on the way. Large crowds lined the route. The mayor and his wife were buried in one grave and his son and grand daughters were buried in the one next to it.

Alice Maud Emery was also buried at the Borough Cemetery, on 17th October 1940. She had been a faithful servant to the mayor for more than a dozen years and was the youngest daughter of Mr. & Mrs. William Emery of 70 Waterhouse Street. She is remembered on the Writtle war memorial.

Sunday 13th October 1940

JOHN OCKELFORD THOMPSON C.B.E. D.L. J.P. 1872 - 1940

Alderman John Ockelford Thompson C.B.E. D.L. J.P., who was killed on 13th October 1940 when a German bomb demolished his home in London Road, was one of the best known and most respected men in Essex.

He was born in Springfield on 8th October 1872, the only son of the late Thomas Thompson. After an education at K.E.G.S. from 1883 to 1888 he followed his father as a journalist. In 1895 he married Emma Tanner and the couple were to have five sons. Following his father's death in 1908 until his own, Alderman Thompson was editor and part proprietor of the Essex Chronicle.

He was first elected to the Council in November 1907 as one of the members for the new Springfield ward. In same month he was raised to Alderman and served on the Council for the remainder of his life. In 1911 he organised Chelmsford's coronation celebrations .

In November 1916 he was elected Mayor for the first time. Subsequently he held the office in 1920-21, 1921-22, 1928-29, 1929-30, 1936-37, and 1939-40. On the occasion of his 68th birthday, the week before his death, he had accepted the Council's invitation to serve again in the forthcoming municipal year.

Much of his best work for the Council had been as Chairman of the Council's Education Committee, a position he had held since December 1921. He was also current Chairman of the Public Health Committee and been a County Councillor for the Chelmsford South Division for six years.

During the First World War he served with the Essex Volunteer Regiment initially as a private and later as an officer. He then went onto special coastal service with the Dorsetshire Regiment. After the war he was largely responsible for Chelmsford's War Memorial Fund, and during his mayoralty in 1920-21 and 1921-22 he took a great interest in the unemployed, for whom he started and carried on a fund.

He had held numerous other public appointments including; an Essex J.P. since February 1916, Chairman of the Chelmsford Bench of Justices, Deputy Lieutenant of Essex, Chairman of the Chelmsford

Brotherhood, President of the Essex & Suffolk Brotherhood Federation, Chairman of the Chelmsford District War Pensions Committee, Chairman of the Ministry of Labour Employment Committee, a member of the Essex Standing Joint Committee, a member of the Essex Federal Council of the League of Nations Union, Chairman of the Essex Discharged Prisoners' Aid Society, a member of the Essex Territorial Army Association, a member of His Majesty's Prison Board of Visitors, Chairman of the West Essex Building Society, Honourary Secretary to the Essex Association of the Treatment of Consumption, a Commissioner of Income Tax, Chairman of the Chelmsford Mutual Fund Association, and an appointed member Essex Agricultural Wages Committee. He was also a Freemason (Easterford Lodge), and a founder-member of the Old Chelmsfordian Lodge.

Since the outbreak of war the he had been a prominent figure behind the Flight of Fighters Fund and the local Air Raid Damage Funds Association. Indeed for the latter organisation he held membership card number one of the five hundred or so members.

He was awarded the C.B.E. in 1938 for his valued public services, having been received the O.B.E. for similar services in the First World War.

His recreations, in the little spare time he did have involved the open air and outdoor sports; he was, a past President of the Essex County Cycling & Athletic Association and Chairman of the Chelmsford Cycling Club. He was a life-long cyclist, and rode up to the time of his death a bicycle which he had used on tours through Switzerland and over the Alps. Between the wars he founded the Princes Marie Louise Bowling Club in the grounds of his Brierly Place home. The club was opened by the Princess when she attended and spoke at a rally of the League of Nations Union at Brierly Place. He was also a keen tennis player up until his sixties, a keen gardener and in his younger days had took part in amateur dramatics.

He was buried at the Borough Cemetery on 16th October 1940 and is remembered on the K.E.G.S. war memorial.

EYEWITNESS ACCOUNTS: MAYOR'S BOMB

> ## "My uncle took me back home via London Road and we went right past the remains of the house. I was so very frightened by what I saw and I can still remember the awful blackness which had been their home."

As told to our our Special Correspondent

"I was only four at the time but I can distinctly remember that afternoon. My uncle, Rodney Mead, cycled round to our house in Wood Street and took me to visit my aunt at their home in Nursery Road. While I was there there was a loud explosion as the bomb fell on the Mayor's house. My uncle took me back home via London Road and we went right past the remains of the house. I was so very frightened by what I saw and I can still remember the awful blackness which had been their home."

Sheila Wrenn

"The one night I particularly remember is when the Mayor's

house in London Road was bombed and nearly everyone inside was killed. I was at home in Braemar Avenue, which was no more than a quarter of a mile away, when I heard the bomb explode. It sounded as though it was a long way away - there was such a dull thud as it exploded well within the house. My uncle was staying with us at the time. He was always a bit clever and he reckoned that it must have fallen on Baddow Meads as the explosion sounded so remote. As a result we didn't bother to go out and have a look, and it was only the next day that we found out it had been so near to us."

John Plumtree

WAR WEAPONS WEEK

National Savings Drive

The day saw the start of 'War Weapons Week', a six-day campaign held throughout the Chelmsford district which aimed to encourage people and organisations to purchase National Savings certificates and bonds.

The money thus raised would be used by the Government to help pay for the armaments needed to win the war. In Chelmsford the intended target was £250,000 invested which, according to Cllr. Frederick Kearsley the campaign's honourary secretary, would be enough for a submarine to be named H.M.S. Chelmsford. To open 'War Weapons Week' a special parade was held in the town and a service at the Cathedral attended by the Bishop of Chelmsford, the Lord Lieutenant of Essex, Lt-Col John Macnamara M.P. and dozens of local dignitaries and members of all the wartime forces.

Sunday 27th October 1940

HOFFMANN'S NEAR-MISS

BOMBS JUST FALL WIDE OF WORKS

At 7.20 p.m. a stick of 16 H.E.s fell on farmland east of the River Chelmer between Springfield and Hoffmann's. It was the closest the Luftwaffe had come to bombing Hoffmann's vital ball and roller-bearing factory and its near neighbour, Marconi's. Fortunately no one was hurt though several properties suffered minor damage including Hoffmann's, where several holes were made in a garage roof, four window panes were smashed and telephone cables were severed. Other buildings that were damaged included 'Brambles' in Arbour Lane (today in Seven Ash Green), 2 Chelmer Place and nos. 57 & 63 First Avenue.

Friday 1st November 1940

BROOK END WARDEN COMMENDED BY KING GEORGE VI

The Essex Chronicle reported that Robert Crozier, a warden at Brook End Farm, Springfield had received a commendation from King George VI and a letter of congratulation from the Regional Controller, Sir Wil Spens. The recognition related to an air raid incident during August 1940 when an H.E. had fallen 'in a field' at the Sewage Works at Brook End. Mr. Crozier had dealt single-handedly with a run-away horse and had rendered valuable first aid to its rider who had been seriously injured in the episode.

Friday 1st November 1940

SPITFIRE CRASHES IN FLAMES IN LONDON RD

Pilot's remains found in wreckage

IN THE LATE afternoon a young Spitfire pilot, Sub-Lt. Arthur Blake of 19 Squadron R.A.F. was killed when his aircraft, number P7423 was attacked by a stray Bf 109 while on routine patrol near Gravesend.

His crippled Spitfire had travelled some twenty miles northwards before crashing in flames in London Road. It came down in London Road at 5.12 p.m., partially demolishing Oak Lodge (today no. 216), before ending up in the roadway.

The 23 year-old was one of 58 naval pilots on loan from to R.A.F. His remains were recovered from the wreckage and taken to St. John's Hospital. He was subsequently buried at St. Mary's Church in Langley near Slough.

Blake's aircraft had been on routine patrol over the south London/Kent area when it had been attacked by the Bf 109 returning from a daring and successful dive-bombing attack on North Weald Aerodrome.

London Road was blocked by the wreckage for a couple of hours but was re-opened at 7.35 p.m.

'Oak Lodge', which was occupied at the time by the 586 Army Field Company of the Royal Engineers, was badly damaged by the impact of the Spitfire. The front corner of the property, including a box room, scullery, cellar, w.c., coal shed and garage was completely destroyed with internal features, such as doors, walls and ceilings, badly damaged in the rest of the house. A small fire was started but that was soon extinguished. Outside, telephone wires and water mains were broken and the boundary wall with 'Fairleigh' was partially demolished. One chimney stack was severely cracked and the other partly demolished.

A modern day view of London Road at its junction with Moulsham Street. It was here that on 29th October 1940 a Spitfire crashed to the ground, having been shot down in combat with enemy fighters. The aircraft's 23 year-old pilot did not survive. (Author)

Tuesday 29th October 1940

SIDNEY TAYLOR IS NEW MAYOR

A SPECIAL MEETING of the Council appointed 67 year-old Cllr. Sidney Taylor as the new Mayor of Chelmsford in place of the late Ald. John Ockelford Thompson after Ald. Frank Fox turned down the invitation for the post.

Cllr. Taylor, who lived at 'Ardmore' in Rainsford Road, was the managing director of The Essex Weekly News and had previously served as Mayor in 1932-3 and 1933-4. He had an impressive family pedigree for the position of Mayor. His father, the late John Taylor, had been Mayor in 1890-1 and his brother, the late Ald. George Taylor, jointly held the record with Ald. John Ockelford Thompson of having been Mayor seven times. Cllr. Taylor had served on the Council since November 1930 and was well-known as a former president of the old Chelmsford Town F.C. supporters' club and current president of Chelmsford Athletic Club. Ald. Fox was appointed as the Deputy-Mayor, a position traditionally occupied by the outgoing Mayor.

Saturday 9th November 1940

WAR WEAPONS WEEK SUCCESS

Chelmsford's War Weapons Week ended, having raised a total of £231,565/12/10, with the biggest investment of £25,000 from the Pearl Assurance Company.

Saturday 2nd November 1940

PARA'MINES DROPPED

Just before 10 p.m. a pair of parachute landmines were dropped over Chelmsford. The first came down at Lawn Lane in Springfield and damaged at least 17 properties and the second prematurely exploded high above an area bounded by Moulsham Street, Princes Rd and Baddow Rd.

It was a lucky escape - had the device exploded nearer the ground there would undoubtedly have been extensive destruction and serious casualties. As it was, widespread minor damage, mainly to plate glass windows and roofs was inflicted to at least 35 properties in the area. No one was hurt.

Friday 15th November 1940

SIX KILLED AS SKINNERS LANE IS BLITZED

WIDESPREAD BOMBING TO THE SOUTH OF CHELMSFORD DURING THE EVENING

IN THE EVENING there were a considerable number of air raid incidents to the south of Chelmsford where enemy planes enroute, and returning from London, jettisoned dozens of bombs.

With so many bombs falling randomly over a large area, it was inevitable that sooner or later one would hit a property and claim some casualties. That is exactly what happened at 9.20 p.m. in a rainy Galleywood when an enemy aircraft, hidden by low cloud, released several H.E.s.

Two bungalows in Skinners Lane felt the full force of the resultant explosions which were felt some way off. The bungalows were demolished and half a dozen other properties in the vicinity suffered extensive damage.

Further afield, eight properties in the Borough also suffered damage from the incident; nos. 84, 103, & Stomps Garage in Galleywood Road; Tilekiln Farm; 4 Hylands Parade, Wood Street; two windows at Moulsham Infants School; 180 Baddow Road and 67 Vicarage Road. Skinners Lane was blocked by debris, gas and water mains were badly damaged and telephone and electricity cables were severed.

Rescue services were quickly on the scene and almost immediately rescued three people from the rubble and discovered two more who were dead. Others were believed to be trapped so efforts went on through the night to reach them. The rescuers, who were to receive widespread praise for their efforts, managed to recover the last of the victims by around 3 a.m.. Four people had been killed and five others injured, including two seriously.

Three of the dead lived at 'Rosedale' in Skinners Lane. They were 65 year-old George William Smith, his 55 year-old wife Alice Louisa Smith and 29 year-old Nellie Elizabeth Owers. Mrs. Owers was married to Walter Owers of Stepney in east London and had ironically moved from there to Galleywood 'to be safer'. She is believed to have been pregnant when killed.

The other victim was 70 year-old Elijah George Saveall of the adjacent bungalow 'Maylin'. He was well known and highly respected in the village, having spent his whole life there. For more than thirty years he had been associated with the Galleywood Methodist Church and for many years he had been a gardener for Mr. P. Buckton until illness had forced his retirement 12 months previously. Mr. Saveall was married with a son and daughter and his daughter was one of those people injured in the bombing and detained in hospital.

Sadly the four who died at Skinners Lane were not the only fatalities. Mr. & Mrs. Smith's 13 year-old adopted daughter, Nellie Lodge, was to die as a result of her injuries the next day at St. John's Hospital and on 2nd November 53 year-old Charles Herbert Francis was to succumb to his wounds at the Chelmsford & Essex Hospital. Mr. Francis had been injured at 'Rosedale'. He was a veteran of the First World War and worked for the transport department of the Chelmsford Co-op.

All the victims' funerals took place at St. Michael's Church, Galleywood, with the building filled to capacity on each occasion. The first funeral was Mr. Savaell's, held on 4th November, followed by Mr. & Mrs. Smith's, Miss Lodge's and Mrs. Owers' on 6th November, and finally, Mr. Francis' on the 7th November. All six are remembered on the Galleywood war memorial at St. Michael's.

As well as the bombs in Skinners Lane another fell close to Rose Cottage in Watchouse Road where a gas main was ruptured, but fortunately no one was hurt.

The first incident of the evening had been at 7.15 p.m. when two H.E.s and an oil incendiary caused some damage to orchards and farm buildings at Great Sir Hughes in Great Baddow. The same farm was damaged three and a quarter hours later when a further five H.E.s and two oil incendiaries fell and caused more damage to sheds, windows and fruit trees. With over thirty craters in the area difficulty was experienced in detecting fresh ones.

At 7.30 p.m. a small bomb fell in the hedge at the side of Swan Lane in Stock, about half a mile from the B1007. Although the road was covered in mud thrown up by the explosion, the carriageway escaped undamaged. Soon afterwards seven H.E.s fell nearby, 50 yards north of the Hawkin's Wood. Another single H.E. also fell in the village at Brook Farm, between Stock Road and Greenacre Lane.

Further to the west, at 7.40 p.m. three H.E.s and two oil incendiaries fell in open fields at Colleybridge and Ewan's Farms in Radley Green. The bombs failed to explode until 9.15 a.m. the following morning when they blew out windows at Colleybridge Farm. Also around 7.40 p.m. two H.E.s fell in the vicinity of Hylands Park.

At 8.00 p.m. H.E.s fell close to Coptfold Hall in Margaretting, damaging outbuildings, whilst an unignited oil incendiary fell in a field near Adelaide Cottage, Swallows Cross Farm in Mountnessing. Half an hour later four H.E.s plus one unexploded fell at Brazil's Farm in Woodham Ferrers. At 9.15 p.m. two H.E.s near Great Mascall's in Great Baddow inflicted slight damage on the farmhouse.

Wednesday 30th October 1940

ESSEX POLICE H.Q. BOMBED

Police Officers killed: Aircraft crash follows at Stock

TWO POLICE OFFICERS were killed and over fifty properties damaged when a string of bombs fell across Springfield at around 7.20 p.m.

Following an air raid siren, a number of German aircraft had appeared in the night sky above Chelmsford in the early evening. One of the enemy raiders was captured by the local searchlights and targeted by intense anti-aircraft fire. As the pilot took violent evasive action to escape, his aircraft released the stick of bombs that fell in a line from police headquarters to fields adjoining Chelmer Road.

The first high explosive bomb blew up on the gravel forecourt of police headquarters almost directly beneath the clock and only a few yards in front of the main building. Although sand bagging around the ground floor absorbed much of the blast t two officers on armed guard duty by the main entrance were caught in the open close to the bomb. P.c. Alexander Simpson Scott, aged 27, was killed instantly, whilst his colleague, 29 year-old D.c. Maurice George 'Dixie' Lee was grievously wounded and was to die shortly afterwards at the Chelmsford and Essex Hospital.

Blast from the device caused extensive superficial damage to the roof, windows and ceilings throughout headquarters. The protective sandbagging was dislodged and corrugated steel sheets and other debris thrown across the courtyard. An early assessment reported that not a single window at headquarters had survived unscathed. The time of the explosion was eerily recorded by the headquarters clock which was stopped by the blast at 7.17 pm. Nearby dozens of houses in the adjacent residential areas also suffered from the explosion.

Another high explosive device from the stick of bombs landed on the lawn of the Chief

Bomb exploded here, killing two policemen

Photograph of Police Headquarters taken the morning after a German bomb had exploded there, killing two police officers. (Courtesy Essex Police Museum)

Constable's garden opposite to the room where the Chief Constable and his wife were reported to have been eating dinner. Fortunately they escaped serious injury, though their house was badly damaged.

At least half a dozen more bombs fell across the police sports ground and bowling green. Surprisingly one of the devices, which landed close to the footpath across the sports ground and about 100 yards from Sandford Road, failed to detonate. It was to remain dormant for almost a year until it exploded one Sunday morning almost a year later (28th September 1941). Fortunately this belated incident failed to cause any significant damage or injuries.

A further three H.Es, fell into a field 400 yards south-east of Dukes Farm and 17 more were reported in the vicinity of the A12 Chelmer Road (Chelmsford bypass). As a result, eight houses on the road's eastern side closest to Dukes Cottages suffered minor damage from the blast. A crater in the road surface resulted in traffic being reduced to one lane pending its repair. A warden,

George Goodenough, from one of the damaged houses was slightly injured and a number of sheep were killed in nearby meadows.

Further a field incendiaries were dropped at Boreham, 400 yards south of Boreham Hall and across the River Chelmer in Little Baddow, near the Church and Gibbs Farm. No damage or injuries were reported.

Within minutes of the bombing at police headquarters reports were arriving there suggesting that an enemy aircraft had crashed at Stock, a third of a mile north of the church, an incident perhaps related to the raid. However, at 8.30 p.m. an updated report described the aircraft as 'an R.A.F. Defiant, completely destroyed and still burning'. Two unburnt bodies were found fifty yards from the wreckage and the revised crash location given as half a mile s.s.e. of Ramsey Tyrells, with the crash having occurred at 7.15 p.m. Further searches around the crash site led to the discovery of a third body at 9 p.m., some hundred yards from the aircraft which was consequently believed to have been an R.A.F. Blenheim.

Saturday 16th November 1940

EYEWITNESS ACCOUNTS: POLICE HQ BOMBS

"It was a shock to my brother in law ... 'Blimey!' he said, 'We don't have 'em drop like that in London!'"

As told to our our Special Correspondent

"The first bombing incident I can remember once I'd become a warden was one weekend in November 1940 when my brother-in-law came down to visit us from Hanwell. He was also a warden so that particular evening he offered to come out with me on my round during an air raid alert. As we were out in Springfield Park Road a German bomber suddenly appeared overhead and dropped a stick of about sixteen small bombs.

As soon as we heard them whistle we dived to the ground for cover. I remember my brother-in-law frantically searching his pockets for a rubber he carried with him - you were supposed to put it between your teeth so that even if you were knocked out by the blast or whatever you'd still be able to breath!

The bombs fell outside our sector, across the Police Headquarters, where two policemen were killed, and into the fields nearby. It was a shock to my brother-in-law who had never heard so many bombs go off so quickly after one another. 'Blimey!' he said, 'We don't have 'em drop like that in London!'. After the plane went we got up off the ground and continued our round."

Jack Palmer

"At that time I lived at 40 Gainsborough Crescent, a house on a corner just behind the police headquarters. It was evening and dark. I was at home when a lone raider appeared overhead and jettisoned a stick of bombs as it flew off towards the coast.

At the time I didn't know the extent of the damage but afterwards I saw that the first bomb had come down on the edge of the lawn and drive at the front of the police headquarters buildings. Another three or four others had gone off on the police sports ground to its rear, leaving large holes.

The first bomb landed practically at the feet of of two police officers who had been standing up against a sandbagged enclosure at the entrance to the building. They were both killed and the sandbagging wrecked. There was a damn great

big hole in the drive and lawn, and all the headquarters buildings suffered superficial damage."

Les Manning

"At 24 I married Alex Scott and we were to have eighteen months of wedded bliss. He was an all round sportsman who was loved by all, a policeman based at headquarters where he was a wireless operator on the cars.

The war was on and for a holiday we went to Chigwell to stay with his mother and father. After that we went on to Grays to a pal of Alex's from the Police Headquarters. When we returned to Chelmsford he had to go on duty. That was the last I saw of him.

That afternoon I went to the pictures to see a film but instead I slept through it. Going home, I felt something was wrong. During the evening a policeman came and told me that Alex had been killed. He took me to my mother who lived nearby.

I went to bed and did not wish to get up. My brother came in and kept worrying me to go down stairs and eventually I did. I had such a caring family, eight brothers and sisters and, of course, I can't forget my loving parents.

Alex's mother asked if he could be buried at Chigwell so that is where he lies today.

The next thing was to get me out. My brother-in-law and sister nagged me to go dancing with them and gradually I started to go out again. The only thing to do when you lose someone is to get out again as soon as possible. It helps.

A few months later I joined the W.A.A.F. and left Chelmsford. I was a wireless operator, as I had learned Morse code in the guides.

I was so pleased when Alex was remembered at the memorial service at the Police Headquarters last year. He was the love of my life and I've shed a few tears writing this. I still feel his presence sometimes, watching over me. When I look at his photograph I ask, 'Why did it have to happen?'."

Myrtle Scott

COUPLE DIE IN UPPER BRIDGE RD

AT 2.30 P.M. A lone enemy aircraft dived out of the clouds above Chelmsford and dropped several H.Es, apparently aimed at Crompton's factory in Writtle Road.

They fell in the vicinity of the junction of Upper Bridge Road and Bradford Street, where as a result, two people were killed and some 34 properties were damaged, including three that were demolished. The water, gas and sewage utilities were all broken, telephone and electric cables severed, and both roads strewn with wreckage.

The fatalities occurred at 28 Upper Bridge Road where 70 year-old, retired bricklayer, Edmund Roper lived with his 61 year-old wife Emily. Their house was

demolished and the couple buried under tons of debris. Rescue parties promptly on the scene first recovered the body of Mrs. Roper and soon afterwards found her badly injured husband. He was to die soon after reaching hospital. The funeral service for the Ropers was subsequently held at St. John's Church, Moulsham six days later with interment at the Borough Cemetery.

Next door to the Ropers' house, 27 Upper Bridge Road, occupied by Mr. A. Salmon was also demolished. Number 26, home to Mrs. E.E. Allen, had its front portion and contents severely damaged. In fact the main structure was so badly affected that demolition was thought to be necessary.

Round the corner at 1a Bradford Street the house and its

contents were totally destroyed, though miraculously its occupiers, Mrs. Bannister, her 12 year-old daughter and an eight year-old evacuated boy all escaped serious injury. On hearing the enemy aircraft Mrs. Bannister had rushed the children and herself under the stairs as seconds later the bomb demolished the house around them. All three were rescued by the A.R.P. services and taken to hospital suffering from shock and minor injuries. A member of the Auxiliary Fire Service was also taken to hospital.

Rescue work at the incident was complicated by the presence of three suspected unexploded bombs. Other H.E.s were believed to have fallen nearby in the vicinity of Writtle Road, though no casualties or damage were reported there.

Thursday 21st November 1940

EYEWITNESS ACCOUNT: UPPER BRIDGE RD

"I'd always thought that bombs used to come down pointing towards the ground but this one fell perfectly level.."

As told to our our Special Correspondent

"It was a grey afternoon with thick low cloud. I was working with an 'old boy' up on what used to be Robinson King's glass factory in Writtle Road, opposite the Cherry Tree. Crompton's had taken it over to be used as a canteen and I was up on the roof fixing new battens ready for re-tiling on one of the buildings near the road.

While we were up there we heard a plane above the clouds. From the sound of it it was obvious it was a German one, so the fella I was working with climbed down sharpish and went for shelter. I was less concerned for my safety and

stayed there listening to it as to it circled round a time or two. As I looked up suddenly I saw a bomb plummeting out of the clouds to the north of the factory. I'd always thought that bombs used to come down pointing towards the ground but as I watched this one it fell perfectly level. I could see it wasn't coming towards me so I ran further up the roof to get a better view of it. I watched it come down on houses a few hundred yards away in Upper Bridge Road. There was a loud explosion and debris flew right up into the sky."

Norman Hume

EYEWITNESS ACCOUNTS: DOREST AVENUE BOMB

"The bomb made a big crater in the road and large pieces of concrete from it were blasted for quite a distance - one lump came down on a friend's house in Baddow Road.."

As told to our our Special Correspondent

"My wife, Edna, and I had just arrived back at our home, 35 Dorset Avenue, one evening when there was a loud explosion outside. A bomb had fallen further up our road, between Chelmerton Avenue and Beehive Lane, outside houses belonging to Mr. & Mrs. Mayes and Mr. & Mrs. Martin.

The blast caused minor damage to our house, we lost a few tiles and several of our windows were shattered, but neither of us was hurt. Our dog, a cross-bloodhound, heard the bang and ran to the front door, thinking that the noise was someone there. He was showered with glass from the lead light in the door and we had to pick the pieces out of his coat afterwards.

The bomb made a big crater in the road and large pieces of concrete from it were blasted for quite a distance - one lump came down on a friend's house in Baddow Road. Luckily no one was hurt though several people had pieces of shrapnel fall on their beds and they were badly shaken.

Most of the houses in Dorset Avenue had their windows blown in and debris made holes in their roofs. The gas main was set alight and we could see its flare out of the window, but because it was dark we had no idea how serious the damage was until the next morning.

Even today there are one or two legacies from when the bomb fell. Mr. Rippon's former house in Chelmerton Avenue, 'Little Paddocks' has got different colour roof tiles from when they were replaced after the bomb and there is still a slight dip in the Dorset Avenue where the crater was filled in."

George Brown

" I was working up on the roof at Crompton's, making blackout shutters to put over the skylights, when a bomb came down in Dorset Avenue. I was sent over there to do first aid repairs on some of the houses which had been badly damaged by the blast.

In one of them I went into the living room and there was a large hole in the ceiling with a huge lump of concrete, which had been blasted from the road, wedged in it. Bits of debris and parts of the bed, linen, and mattress from the room upstairs had been pushed though bedroom floor by the concrete and were left squashed around it.

Luckily the people in the house had hidden under the stairs when the bomb had fallen. Had they been in bed they would have been crushed."

Norman Hume

AMAZING ESCAPES AS BOMBS FALL IN DORSET AVENUE

At 10.45 p.m. several H.E.s, including a delayed action bomb, fell in the vicinity of Dorset Avenue in Great Baddow. One bomb which struck the roadway left a crater 20 feet across and hurled large pieces of concrete from the road some distance in all directions. Several residents had narrow escapes from serious injury though there were only two slight casualties caused.

The bomb fell directly outside the home of Mr. & Mrs. C.G. Windey who were in their air raid shelter in a room at the back of the house. Neither of them heard the bomb go off. The first they knew of it was when they heard debris raining down and water began trickling through the ceiling from a fractured pipe. One piece of concrete came through the roof their house and ended up rested on the ceiling above them. At a nearby house Mr. & Mrs. C.E. Martin also had a narrow escape from serious injury. They had been asleep in their bedroom as the bomb fell, and knew nothing of it until Mr. Martin awoke to see a hole in the ceiling above him. He got out of bed and discovered that a huge piece of concrete, weighing nearly half a ton, had been blasted through the roof, had crashed through their bedroom, before striking their bed and landing on the floor beside it. Surprisingly no crockery or window panes had been broken. At another house Mr. & Mrs. J.W. Taylor also had a remarkable escape. They had been asleep downstairs when debris from the road passed them by inches. So close was a piece of concrete that it pulled the eiderdown off their bed.

All the public utilities were affected and around eighty houses in the vicinity suffered some degree of damage from the blast and debris. The presence of the delayed-action bomb forced the temporary evacuation of around 150 residents. Repairs to the road were eventually completed on Christmas Eve.

Sunday 1st December 1940

STOCK CHURCH HIT BY PARACHUTE LANDMINE

FRIDAY THE 13TH turned out to be an unlucky day for Stock Church. At 7.25 p.m. a parachute landmine, one of a pair dropped on the village, fell in the churchyard thirty yards to the east of the building. It exploded and damaged the Church so badly that it as to be rendered useless for almost a year.

Stonework on the south side and the rear was torn away, the nave roof was blown off, all the stained glass was destroyed, the organ made useless, the famous wooden tower was shorn of its shingles, its foundations unsettled, and the bells became unhinged with their mediaeval mechanisms smashed. The Rectory nearby, occupied by the Rev. C. Austen, was also badly damaged and many cottages in the vicinity lost their windows. In the graveyard several gravestones completely disappeared in the explosion and many of those that were left were broken. Fortunately no one was reported to have been injured in the incident.

For some time afterwards services had to be held close by at the private chapel at Lilystone Hall, home of Lord Perry, the head of the Ford Motor Company in Britain. As the chapel was not fully licensed part of the church was still used for funerals and marriages. The Church was eventually re-opened on 12th October 1941.

The second parachute landmine fell on the Ingatestone road, 150 yards from Stock Wash but it failed to explode and disintegrated harmlessly in the road.

Friday 13th December 1940

SHRAPNEL KILLS MAN AT NEWNEY GREEN

63 year-old farmworker, Ernest George Warren was fatally injured in the back by shrapnel in the yard of his home at Moor Hall Cottages, Newney Green by an H.E. which fell at 6.22 p.m. between the farmhouse and farm buildings at Moor Hall.

Five people in the house escaped injury, but Mr. Warren was to succumb to his injuries two days later.

German aircraft involved in the air raid on the capital were most likely responsible for this, the last local incident of the year as the evening saw a major air raid on the City of London in which the Guildhall, six Wren Churches and numerous other historic buildings were destroyed. The attack engulfed most of the 'square mile' in a huge fire which was to become known as the 'Second Great Fire of London'.

Investigations the morning after the raid by Mr. G.A. Deal, the A.R.P. warden of Jubilee Farm, revealed that the fatal piece of shrapnel had passed through an apple tree, one side of a corrugated shed, a basket of onions hanging inside the shed, out the other side of the shed, hit a brick wall and had then struck the unfortunate Mr. Warren.

Mr. Warren had lived in Newney Green for many years and had toiled on the land for practically all his life, having spent the previous 11 years working for John Shanks at Moor Hall. Prior to that he had been employed for several years by James Christy at Warren Farm in Writtle.

Mr. Warren left a widow, three sons and four daughters. His funeral was held at All Saints' Church in Writtle on 4th January 1941. He is commemorated on the village's war memorial.

Sunday 29th December 1940

TRAIN 'GUNNED'

At 10.05 a.m. a lone enemy aircraft was reported to have dropped from the clouds and machine gunned a moving train in the vicinity of the Writtle Road railway bridge. The train continued its journey and no one was hurt.

The police, who had received no reports of German aircraft over the district, subsequently investigated the incident and were to conclude that the gun fire had been 91 rounds fired by units posted to defend 'Messers Hoffmann's factory'.

Monday 6h January 1941

BOMBS BY THE TULIP PUB

At 7.10 p.m. H.E.s fell in the vicinity of Church Lane in Springfield, close to The Tulip P.H. A total of 28 properties were damaged as a result, including Tulip Cottage in Church Lane which was demolished. There, a woman and two children were trapped in the collapsed property but were rescued thanks to the bravery of Police Sergeant Harry Warnes who crawled through the wreckage to free them. They were taken to the Chelmsford & Essex Hospital to be treated for shock and minor injuries. For his actions Sgt. Warnes was subsequently given a commendation, published in the London Gazette on 11th April 1941, which spoke of 'his disregard of immediate danger of falling debris' and his 'great promptitude'.

Sunday 12th January 1941

UNUSUAL INCIDENT AT DANBURY

The Essex Chronicle reported on an unusual incident that had recently occurred in Danbury. Two soldiers, L/Bdr. Gloves and Gnr. Phelps of the Royal Artillery, were standing at a bus stop in the village, awaiting a bus to take them to Clacton on leave.

As they waited a large saloon car, driven by a chauffeur, drew up and a middle aged woman beckoned the men. Gnr. Phelps stepped forward and the woman handed him a packet and said 'Please take this laddie, it's a present for you and your friend'. Rather surprised, the gunner thanked the lady and the car drove off. The soldiers opened the packet and, to their amazement found that it contained £150 in £1 notes.

Accompanying the money was the following letter; 'For a soldier serving his country, today's my son's birthday. He was killed early in the war and the money would have been used as his birthday present. Use it laddie. God bless you, a broken hearted mother'. The astonished soldiers just had time to relate their good fortune to comrades when their bus came along.

Friday 14th January 1941

AIR TRAINING CORPS

The days saw the official formation of Chelmsford's Air Training Corps, to be known as 278 Squadron Air Training Corps. So far 160 boys had applied to enroll in the organisation which was to be commanded by Ft. Lt. Frank Holder M.C. of Lane's End, Church Lane in Springfield. He had served as a Flying Officer in the Royal Flying Corps and had been a member of the Council since December 1939.

Saturday 2nd February 1941

COUNCIL TRIBUTE TO HEROS

At the monthly Council meeting the Mayor gave his congratulations on behalf of the town to Council employee George Paverley of Dorset Avenue, Great Baddow, who had been awarded the recently introduced George Medal, and to local firemen Sub Officer Joseph Warren and Leading Fireman Frederick Keen who had both been awarded the O.B.E. (Civil).

The firemen's awards were in connection with the recent large fires caused by enemy action at industrial premises in Thames Haven and Thames Wharf in the south of Essex.

In the relevant incident the valve of a tank containing 6,000 tons of benzene was alight at the low extremity of a big container and was burning furiously. A thirty foot extended ladder was put up against the side of the tank and Warren and a colleague from the Ilford Auxiliary Fire Service. ascended the top of the tank and opened a manhole there, thus realising some very dangerous and highly flammable fumes.

The pair inserted a 'swan-neck' to enable water to be poured into the tank. When this was done Keen mounted the ladder and packed wet sacking around the manhole to prevent any more fumes from escaping. A second 'swan-neck' was placed in position but Keen found that fumes were still escaping and ascended the ladder to pack more wet sacking around the manhole.

The tank was leaning over to one side and. in the event of the spirit overflowing, it would have poured onto the burning valve, thus igniting the whole tank and endangering the lives of many people. Warren and Keen had both joined the A.F.S. before the war as part-time members, and had gone full-time at the outbreak of hostilities.

Two other Chelmsford firemen, Chief Officer Alfred Norman and Leading Fireman H.W. Youell, had received the King's commendation for gallant conduct on the same occasion and had the event recorded in the London Gazette. A considerable amount of Chelmsford Fire Brigade's equipment had been lost or totally destroyed in fighting the fires, though most had subsequently been replaced.

Mr. Paverley, a 51 year-old road roller and compressor driver within the Council's Highways Department, gained his award in relation to his gallantry on two occasions when he assisted the B.D.S. in the removal of unexploded bombs. Firstly Mr. Paverley worked a pneumatic drill compressor to cut through a concrete floor, and then excavated 10 feet down to the foundations of a house to reach the bomb. On the second, he worked a pneumatic drill down to two unexploded bombs of an exceptionally large calibre, 18 feet below ground.

The bombs had been dropped during an air raid incident near School View Road on 15th September 1940. He then drove, at considerable personal risk, the steam roller which dragged the bombs out from the ground. The official account of the incident spoke of his cheerfully and willingly accepting the great risk involved. Mr. Paverley had worked for the Council for some 21 years.

Wednesday 29th January 1941

3 BOMBS HIT MARCONI'S

SEVENTEEN WORKERS KILLED ON NIGHT SHIFT
DOZENS OF OTHERS HURT

IN THE EARLY hours Chelmsford suffered its most serious air raid of the war so far when 17 workers at the Marconi Wireless Telegraph Co. Ltd.'s New Street factory were killed in a skilled attack.

A red air raid warning had sounded the previous evening at 11.24 p.m. but all was quiet until 2.22 a.m. when an enemy Junkers Ju 88 approached the town.

Eyewitnesses saw the raider clearly in the almost full moonlight, as it dived to within a few hundred feet of roof tops, released two bombs, circled and dropped two more, before rising rapidly and escaping towards the coast. The aircraft had in fact come so low that those who had seen it thought it likely to hit the Cathedral spire.

Initially it was known that two of the bombs which were dropped had scored direct hits on Marconi's, whilst another went astray and struck residential properties in Marconi Road which ran along the northern side of the factory.

Obvious target

Marconi's was an obvious target for the Luftwaffe. The New Street factory carried out vital work for several Government departments - designing, testing, developing and producing wireless instruments for the Admiralty, Air Ministry, Ministry of Supply and the Crown Agents.

Of the factory's 3221 workers, some 390 were engaged on the night shift at the time of the raid. They had been on duty since 8.15 p.m. the previous evening and were due to finish at 7.30 a.m., with the day shift taking over fifteen minutes later.

The air raid warning had interrupted work of the two hundred or so employees in the machine shop The men there had taken shelter behind an internal blast wall, whilst the women had gone to the strong rooms below the main office building.

The bombs that hit Marconi's fell at the western end of the main factory building. One, thought to have been a 250 kg. DH H.E., exploded in the centre of machine shop which occupied the southern half of the building. Another, a 500 kg. DH H.E., fell on its northern half, through the first floor carpenters' shop and detonated on the floor of the SWB8 transmitter erection shop beneath it.

This bomb ignited a drum of cellulose in the carpenters' shop and the fire rapidly spread across debris into the neighbouring paint spray shop. There dope was ignited and several men, who had survived the initial explosions, were trapped behind a blast wall and killed by the fire before rescuers could reach them. The fire was eventually brought under control by 5 a.m., though not before flames had spread to Ridley's flour mill in neighbouring Townfield Street. Damage

there was extensive with a very large number of roof slates lost, timbers charred and internal linings destroyed.

The bombs and the resulting fire killed 17 men at Marconi's. A further 20 were seriously injured and 18 others slightly hurt.

Unexploded bomb

During the day, whilst clearing up operations continued at the factory, a worker reported hearing tapping sounds from beneath the debris of the wrecked paint spray and transmitter erection shops.

Immediately, workmen with crowbars and shovels began frantic attempts to locate the source of the sounds but despite their efforts no one could be found and it was decided to terminate any further rescue work as it was concluded that anyone still buried would be dead by then.

On the following day, Saturday 10th May, the large pile of debris was cleared and somewhat alarmingly the source of the tapping sounds was clear to be seen by all - a third 500 Kg DA H.E. bomb, lay there unexploded but still ticking. Its serial number Ex 536 could be clearly seen. The Bomb Disposal Squad was immediately called in and the factory and surrounding streets were evacuated.

Such was the nature and position of the device that the B.D.S. were forced to detonate the bomb where it lay. A warning was put out to this effect, and at 10.30 a.m. on Monday 12th May the bomb was exploded in situ. Further damage was inflicted to the paint shop, a temporary substation which had been hastily erected after the initial bombing, and to dozens of other buildings nearby. There were no further casualties.

Damage was confined mainly to the machine shop, SWB8 transmitter erection shop, carpenters' and paint spray shop, though blast had affected other parts of the factory, notably to the roofs of the turret lathe shop, instrument shop and, to a lesser extent, to the office buildings and winding shops.

Production badly affected

Productivity at Marconi's was badly affected by the bombs. An immediate assessment of the damage suggested that production would be reduced by a quarter for four weeks, but after the explosion of the third bomb this was reduced further.

In the month or so before the raid production at the factory had stood at around 90,000 productive man hours per week. In the week of the bombing, ended 11th May, it was only 51,340 man hours and the following week it had slumped further to 37,427 man hours.

After that production was to gradually improve up to 76,371 hours by the week ending 22nd June. The improvement was pos-

sible through a combination of the use of existing facilities elsewhere and the sub-contracting out of work to other firms. A duplicate shop had already been built in London, so some of the more urgent contracts were handled there.

The worst affected shop was probably the machine shop where around 60% of the machines were damaged and few could be restarted during the first week after the bombing. By 25th May 10% were working, and by 8th June, 40%. - by then rebuilding and extension works had begun and all of the original floorspace re-occupied.

Work in the carpenters' shop was transferred to a large shop lent by Crompton's with some work sub-contracted out to other companies. Eventually the shop was permanently rehoused in an old store building.

The paint shop was temporarily housed in the open air, though by October work was continuing in small sheds. Help was also provided by Crittall's and others through sub-contracting. The SWB8 transmitter erection shop was temporarily based in a garage in New Street (perhaps Hadler's). By 3rd August production there was to rise to 25% of normal and by November the shop was able to return to re-built premises at the main factory.

Following the air raid the German News Agency claimed that 'crews of two German bombers, under the command of Lt. Kloss, penetrated as far as Chelmsford where they bombed a ball-bearing factory and caused very heavy destruction'. Apparently the Germans had mistaken Marconi's for its near neighbour Hoffmann's.

Sketch map showing the Marconi factory in New Street, subject to a serious air raid on 9th May 1940 which left 19 people dead. (Author)

HEROIC RESCUE ATTEMPTS

The incident was attended by five ambulances, two sitting case cars, two stretcher parties, two rescue parties, the fire brigade, wardens, police, Home Guard, and 74 Company Royal Engineers who helped clear debris from Marconi Road. Once again people owed their lives to their gallant efforts.

One off-duty member of a rescue party was 59 year-old James Ellis Grimwade. On hearing the bombs fall he had left his Regina Road home for Marconi Road and bravely and skillfully helped to rescue four victims, despite the grave dangers posed by the partially demolished buildings around him.

For his efforts Mr. Grimwade was subsequently awarded the British Empire Medal (Civil Division). It was not the first time he had received such recognition. After service in the South African War, Mr. Grimwade had fought in the First World War in France with

distinction and had received the Queen's Medal with four clasps. For many years he had been employed by the Council as a labourer and at the outbreak of the war he had put his building expertise to good use by volunteering for civil defence duties. He was one of the men who had undertaken the difficult task of extricating the victims of the bombing of the late Mayor's house in October 1940.

Lt. F.B. Shaughnessy and W.J. Hodgson of Marconi's Home Guard detachment, F Company 6th Battalion Essex Home Guard, subsequently were to have their names drawn to the attention of army commanders for gallantry in connection with the rescue of seven fellow employees.

Twenty year-old Rover Scout Gordon Morton carried out valiant work at the scene of the bombings as a worker with the ambulance service. He was subsequently awarded the Scouts' Gilt Cross for courage and resource for his part in the rescue work.

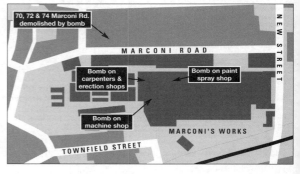

TWO NEIGHBOURS KILLED IN MARCONI RD

THE FOURTH BOMB, a 250 Kg. H.E., narrowly missed the Marconi works and fell onto houses in Marconi Road, where two people received fatal injuries.

A terrace of six houses near the junction with Bishop Road suffered most as a result, with three demolished (nos. 70, 72 & 74) and two others damaged beyond repair (nos. 76 & 78). The sixth house, no. 80, was seriously damaged as were five others (nos. 62, 64, 66, 68 & 82). The combined effects of blast from all four bombs affected around 375 other properties within a quarter of a mile radius with damage mainly confined to windows, doors, roofs and ceilings.

At 72 Marconi Road two people were trapped in the rubble.

One of them, Frank Coe, was rescued practically uninjured, but his landlady, Mrs. Hannah Whybrow was killed. She was married to former builder Sidney Whybrow and they had three daughters. Her funeral service was held at Holy Trinity Church, Springfield on May 15th.

Next door to Mrs. Whybrow's house, at number 70, lived an elderly married couple, Martha and Charles Ernest Ray. They had been asleep in a downstairs room when the bomb had struck and were buried under tons of debris.

Both were eventually rescued alive, but Mr. Ray was to die as a result of his injuries in hospital twelve days later. He had retired from Hoffmann's just six months prior to his death, having held the record for the longest service

with the company - he had worked there since its opening in 1899. His funeral service was held at All Saints' Church with burial at the Borough Cemetery. Mr. Ray's wife escaped with a broken arm and other injuries but was to die within a couple of years.

At 66 Marconi Road Mr. & Mrs. Alfred Bates and their two daughters were saved from serious injury by the prompt call of their son, Edmund, who shouted out a warning of the approaching just in time. Mrs. Bates and the daughters rushed into the cupboard under the stairs for shelter, whilst her husband and son dived underneath a table. Although their house was seriously damaged, all escaped unharmed and Edmund was able to go off on A.R.P. duties soon afterwards.

The Marconi Raid: Friday 9th May 1941

EYEWITNESS ACCOUNTS: MARCONI RAID

"Minutes later we heard the roar of an aircraft passing directly overhead and then a couple of damn great bangs - we never heard the bombs whistle. Then soot and debris came into the shelter, and the dust went up my nose and choked my lungs."

As told to our our Special Correspondent

"In the early days of the war Marconi's had proper underground shelters built. The snag was that whenever the sirens sounded everyone would go to the shelters and no work would be done - and frequently with no enemy planes around Chelmsford.

To solve this the authorities introduced an imminent danger warning, so that we could carry on working after the siren until there were enemy aircraft in the local vicinity, at which point the factory's alarm bells would sound. By then of course it would be too late to go to the shelters and at first we used to get under our benches when they sounded, not that they were going to do much good!

Later on the firm provided better protection for us when it built a blast wall that ran the length of the factory inside the building, parallel to an ordinary wall. Together the walls created a corridor, about six feet wide, in which we could shelter. It was covered with a corrugated iron roof that prevented debris from falling on top of us.

I was working at Marconi's on the night that it was bombed. There were two warnings that night - the first sounded while we were in the canteen for a break so we went into the underground shelters. After a time the all clear was given and we returned to our benches before the alarm bells went again.

The second time I went into the corridor shelter along with most of the other men. Minutes later we heard the roar of an aircraft passing directly overhead and then a couple of damn great bangs - we never heard the bombs whistle. 'Oh God' I thought, 'We've been hit!' Then soot and debris came into the shelter, and the dust went right up my nose and choked my lungs.

As the air cleared I looked down the factory and saw flames leaping up from where the bombs had exploded, less than a hundred yards away. I said to a colleague, who was in a first aid party with me, 'There's trouble down there mate' so we started to go towards where the bombs had hit to see if we could help.

As we did we heard the plane returning to make another attack, so the pair of us turned and dived back to where we'd come from - throwing ourselves on the ground for cover. Immediately afterwards there was a third awful bang and the plane made off. We found out later that two bombs had exploded in the factory and a third had hit a house in Marconi Road.

The casualties were dealt with by first aiders and other civil defence people. They took the injured to a new building at the top of the factory yard which had been set aside for casualties. The works ambulance was based there too.

Most of the factory's roof had been destroyed by the bombs - you could see the moon shining through. There was no way that we could do anymore work that night so we were sent home and told to report back in the morning.

Alot of the men were annoyed that there had been no anti-aircraft fire - there was a four barrelled Lewis machine gun mounted on top of Marconi House, but that was only manned by the soldiers during the daytime. Had it been so during the night they would probably have got the German bomber.

In the morning we began tidying up the mess left by the bombs. I went back to my bench to sort my gear out and noticed that there was a groove on the underside of the shelf above my bench that looked as if it had been cut by a special chisel. Apparently it had been caused by a piece of shrapnel which had gone right along there and was embedded in the wall - right where my head would have been.

Word got round that another bomb had been found ticking in the debris. We were out of Marconi's as quick as anything - in fact I was even reported missing for a time because I didn't have time to get my bike!

After that, clearing up continued and temporary roofs were quickly put up so that we could get back to work. Moral was not affected by the raid - we'd known that Marconi's was a target for the Germans and I suppose at that time we accepted things and just got on with the job which we knew was important."

Jack Palmer

"I was working nights at Hoffmann's. My section faced head on to New Street at the corner with Rectory Lane, and during the alert I sheltered under the concrete stairs near the outside entrance to Rectory Lane with one or two colleagues. While we were there we heard the sound of one or two planes overhead, apparently circling the town.

At the time I thought that they were ours, but after a short time there was a thump as one of them dropped bombs on Marconi's, just down New Street from us. I got up to the door and looked out to see the reflection of the fire at Marconi's in the windows of the tall office building at Hoffmann's, though at first, from what I saw saw, I thought Hoffmann's was on fire.

After the raid rumour spread that the Home Guard on the factory roof couldn't fire at the bomber because if they had they'd had been firing into the town - the plane was that low. A chap I worked with used to say that the droning noise made by a German bomber used to sound like 'Where do want it, where do you want it?'"

Bill Wilson

"I had five brothers, four of whom served in the army. The fifth, who was medically unfit, worked at Marconi's all through the war. After the bombing of the factory they were clearing things up and he was handed an object and told to take it up to Galleywood racecourse to the old main stand - the object turned out to be a severed leg of one of the bombing victims and the racecourse was where all the the bodies were being taken."

Eileen Hance

THE MARCONI VICTIMS

THE BOMBING of Marconi's claimed the lives of 17 workers on the night shift, with all except John Smith dying at the factory. The youngest was aged 29 and the eldest 62, with the majority coming from the Chelmsford area.

A memorial service, conducted by the Provost William Morrow, was subsequently held at the Cathedral in their memory. It attracted a large congregation including representatives of Marconi's, the Home Guard, Police, Civil Defence Services and local dignitaries. The seventeen victims at the factory were as follows:

Harold Walter Beavers
He was the 38 year-old son of Eliza and the late George Bevers and married to Isabel Bevers of 60 King Street, Maldon.

George Cousins
Aged 57, he was a member of F Company, 6th Battalion Essex Home Guard - Marconi's Home Guard detachment. He was married to Nellie Cousins of 117 Springfield Park Road and was buried at Holy Trinity Church, Springfield.

Cecil Vall Roberts Cutts
He was married with three young sons and lived at 6 Council Houses, Maldon Road in Hatfield Peverel. He was a native of Maldon but had spent the last twenty of his forty years in Hatfield Peverel. His funeral took place at Hatfield Peverel.

David Easton Davidson
Aged 39, he was married to Louisa Davidson with two sons and two daughters. He was a quiet man and lived at Shellow Bowells near Willingale. His funeral was held at Shellow Bowells Parish Church on 17th May.

Charles Thomas 'Tom' Franklin
He was married to Jessie Franklin of 9 New Road, The Hamlet in Coggeshall and had a daughter and son. Aged 46, he was buried at Coggeshall Cemetery on 14th May.

Alfred Howard Griggs
Aged 28, he was the second son of the late Mr. A & Mrs. Griggs of Witham and had been married for nearly two years to Joan Griggs, the daughter of Mr. & Mrs. P. N. Smith of 16 Nelson Road. He lived at 'Oaklyn' in Moulsham Drive and prior to working at Marconi's had worked for eight years for the stonemasons Messers J.B. Slythe of London Road. He was a member of Marconi's Home Guard and was buried at the Borough Cemetery on 16th May after a funeral service at St. John's Moulsham.

Harold Joseph Harvey
Aged 41, he had lived in Chelmsford nearly all his life and was the son of the late Mr. & Mrs. Harvey of Coval Lane. He was married to Dorothy Harvey of 4 Ockelford Avenue with one son and one daughter. He was a veteran of the First World War, having seen service then with the 5th Essex Regiment. His funeral service was held at the Rainsford Road Methodist Church on 16th May, with burial afterwards at the Borough Cemetery.

Hector Francis Head
Aged 27, he was married to Rose Head of 21 Cherry Garden Lane in Maldon. They had a four year-old daughter. His funeral service was held at the Elim Tabernacle in Maldon on 14th May, with burial afterwards at Maldon Cemetery.

Victor Arthur Joslin
Aged 31, he was the son of Mr. W.A. Joslin and came from Pleasant Place, Great Tey near Colchester.

Cyril Edward Maggs
Aged 25, he was the son of William Maggs of Ystrad, Rhondda in Wales. He had lived at 25 Valentine Way in Silver End with Mr. & Mrs. Maison for the previous seven years and prior to joining Marconi's had worked for Crittall's. His funeral took place at Cressing Church.

Herbert Joseph Pearce
Aged 42, he was the son of Jessie Pearce of Clacton and married to Violet Pearce of Olive House, Berkeley Road in Clacton.

William Henry Scotchman
Aged 62, his wife lived at The Firs in Galleyend. They had three daughters. His funeral was took place on 16th May at St. Michael's Galleywood, where he is remembered on the village's war memorial.

Benjamin George Reed
Aged 31, he lived at 20 Rochford Road. Prior to working at Marconi's he had been an Eastern National bus conductor for ten years. He was buried at the Borough Cemetery on 15th May after a funeral service at St. John's Moulsham.

John Kenneth Smith
Aged 19, he was the youngest man killed in the air raid. He was rescued from Marconi's with serious injuries but he died in the Chelmsford & Essex Hospital later the same day. He was the nephew of Mrs. A. Frost and lived at 1c Marlborough Road, and was engaged to Peggy Gooday. His funeral was held on 14th May with a service at St. John's Moulsham preceding burial at the Borough Cemetery.

George Frederick Vowles
Aged 32, he was the son of the late Alfred and Grace Vowles and lived at 10 Belle Vue. He had been in Chelmsford some four years, previous to that he had spent time in Canada and the west of England. He was a bachelor and member of the A.R.P. services. His funeral was held on 13th May with a joint service with that of fellow victim and close friend, Harry Woods at St. John's Moulsham, followed by burial at the Borough Cemetery.

Sidney Victor White
He was married to Mrs. E.H.M. White of 70 Brownings Avenue with four sons. Aged 46, he had spent all of his life in Chelmsford. He was buried at the Borough Cemetery on 15th May.

Harry John 'Pearce' Woods
Aged 27, he was the eldest son of Alice and Harry Woods of Eye in Suffolk. He had been married for four years to Ethel Woods, the daughter of Mr. & Mrs. H.S.G. Chilvers of Upper Bridge Road. They lived at 'Harwin', 31 Fourth Avenue and had a young daughter. His funeral was held with that of close friend George Vowles on 13th May with burial at the Borough Cemetery following a service at St. John's Moulsham.

HEINKEL SHOT DOWN OFF BEEHIVE LANE

4 CREW BALE OUT

AROUND 12.35 A.M. an enemy Heinkel He 111 H-5 of I/KG28 was shot down by a night fighter and crashed in flames into an apple orchard behind Strathcote Cottage, Beehive Lane in Great Baddow.

The four crewmen, Lt. O. Kruger, Uffz. K. Schrey, Gefr. Lindenmayer and Uffz. O. Gauernack, baled out seconds before impact and were rounded up and taken to Chelmsford Police Station as p.o.w.s. Two had come down in a field adjoining a Mr. Scott's house, another came down on Mr. Selby's house on the Stock Road near the Ship Inn and the remainder landed at Crondon Hall near Margaretting Tye.

Sunday 11th May 1941

DANBURY CHURCH WRECKED

DANBURY CHURCH was severely damaged around 2.30 a.m. by a high explosive bomb that landed just six yards from the east wall, leaving a crater several feet deep.

The east of the building was badly damaged and many graves in the churchyard were obliterated. All the stained glass and leaded windows were blown out, including the two beautiful east windows.

A great deal of masonry was dislodged and parts of the east and north walls were demolished. The roof was also badly damaged. However, the church's west end and tower survived practically unscathed and in the morning the flag of St. George could still be flown from the flagstaff.

Inside the church much of the woodwork was damaged and the alter was covered in debris. Superbly carved white marble angels had been thrown across the chancel, whilst the alter covers lay torn in the rubble.

Many of the pews were covered in broken glass, brass ornaments had crashed to the floor, but a bible remained unscathed on the lectern save for a coating of dust. The church organ was wrecked as was the vestry. A small fire which had broken out in the chancel was soon extinguished by the Rector & firemen who rushed to the scene.

Many properties near the church were damaged by blast, including The Griffin P.H. and a wardens' post.

Repairs to the wrecked church were to take months to complete. In September 1943 it was reported that the semi-demolished south-eastern corner had been screened off, the roof retiled, indoor timbers repinned, walls replastered and new windows put in. By then £300 from a restoration fund had been used to repair furniture and other items not covered by various government grants.

Tuesday 20th May 1941

Coval Lane Carnage: Wednesday 21st May 1941

SINGLE BOMB KILLS SIX IN COVAL LANE FLATS

SLEEPING VICTIMS BURIED UNDER TONS OF DEBRIS

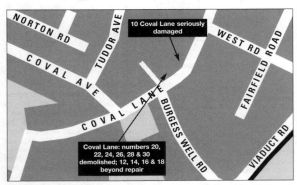

Sketch map showing the Coval Lane area where six people were killed in a night raid in the early hours of 21st May 1941. (Author)

SIX PEOPLE were killed as they slept when an enemy aircraft glided noiselessly from a great height and dropped a single heavy calibre bomb onto a block of flats in Coval Lane.

What the intended target may have been is unclear. The resulting explosion at 12.50 a.m. demolished one of four blocks of ten flats on the road's western side. Sleeping residents, many of them elderly, were buried in the debris.

The rescue services, consisting of three stretcher parties, four ambulances, a sitting case car, police wardens and fire brigade were quick to arrive on the scene. Five seriously injured and three slightly injured people were rescued from the wrecked flats. However, five bodies were recovered and a sixth was to die in hospital later. Some 244 properties in the area suffered some degree of blast damage.

At 18 Coval Lane 57 year-old Ester Meggy was killed in her flat. She was the younger daughter of the late Andrew and Eleanor Meggy. Her father had been a well-known local solicitor formerly in practice with Francis Stunt. Miss Meggy had come to live at Coval Lane following his death at their home in London Road. She was buried at the Borough Cemetery on 24th May.

At number 22, 78 year-old Lucy Emma Coulcher was killed in her flat. She was a spinster and daughter of the late Mr. R.W. Coulcher. Her funeral service was held at the Cathedral five days later with burial at the Borough Cemetery afterwards.

Two people were killed at 26 Coval Lane. They were 39 year-old Winifred Gowen and her nine year-old son, Barry John Gowen. Mrs. Gowen's husband Arnold was called to the scene from work at Hoffmann's and waited for an hour before being told that his wife and son had been recovered

dead. Mrs. Gowen was the only daughter of Robert and the late Sarah Farrant of Braintree. Her son was a pupil at the Victoria School and a keen boy scout. They were buried six days later at Braintree Cemetery.

At 28 Coval Lane 38 year-old Winifred Kate Stokes was killed. She was the daughter of George and Daisy Stokes of Howe Street and had worked for many years at Messers J.G. Bond in the High Street. She had been an active worker for the Cathedral for many years. From the same flat 69 year-old William Howard was recovered alive but died shortly afterwards in the Chelmsford & Essex Hospital. The two victims were buried at the Borough Cemetery on 25th May after a funeral service at the Cathedral.

Other residents were more fortunate. Albert and Ellen Barritt of 24 Coval Lane were dug out alive by rescue services, having been buried in the remains of their home for several hours. They were both taken to hospital suffering from shock, cuts and bruises and were released three days later. Mrs. Barritt then went to stay at her sister's house at Manor House in Great Baddow but suffered a relapse and was to die on 29th May. Her funeral service was held at the Baddow Road Congregational Church on 23rd June with interment at St. Mary's Church in Great Baddow.

Despite the large number of deaths in the Coval Lane incident and that at Marconi's two weeks earlier, none of the emergency graves, which had been dug in the Borough Cemetery for such contingencies were required.

The Coval Lane bombing would prove to be Chelmsford's last major bombing incident for more than a year. Indeed there were to be just three more occasions when bombs would fall on the whole Chelmsford district in the rest of 1941. The worst of the nightly raids on Britain were over at last.

Wednesday 21st May 1941

INVASION EXERCISES CONTINUE

Despite Germany's apparent decision to postpone the invasion of Britain and instead concentrate on the Russian front, invasion defence preparations continued. In Chelmsford a large military exercise was held with local members of the Home Guard defending the

town from regular soldiers representing the invading Germans. The attackers were beaten off and military chiefs who watched the exercise were said to have learned valuable lessons. Heavy 'casualties' were inflicted by both sides with a fierce battle centred around the Shire Hall.

Sunday 6th July 1941

GROOM AGED 95 - HIS FIFTH MARRIAGE

An unusual wedding took place at Chelmsford Registry Office when 95 year-old Alfred Seymour, a retired farmer of Wheelers Farm in Little Waltham, married his housekeeper, 63 year-old widow, Helen Wood. It was Mr. Seymour's fifth marriage. His fourth wife, whom he had married when aged 78, had died three years previously.

Wednesday 18th June 1941

MORRISON SHELTERS FOR CHELMSFORD

At the monthly Council meeting it was revealed that Chelmsford had been designated as one of the areas that were to be issued with the new Morrison indoor air raid shelters.

They were to be free to people whose occupations were compulsorily insurable under the National Health Insurance Act and to those households with an income of less than £350 per annum plus £50 for every third or more school child. A limited number of the Morrison shelter was also to be made available for purchase at £7 each by householders not covered under these conditions.

Wednesday 25th June 1941

SALVAGE TO BEGIN OF CHELMSFORD'S RAILINGS

An official notice in the day's local papers announced that the Council intended to requisition unnecessary iron and steel rAilings,gates, posts, chains, bollards and stiles throughout the Borough for salvage purposes in compliance with new Ministry of Supply orders.

The objects would be used as scrap for war production. Exceptions were to be made for safety reasons, the prevention of cattle straying, and for objects of special artistic merit or historic interest. Owners would be permitted a two week period in which to appeal against their property being taken.

Over the next five months an exhaustive survey would be carried out to ascertain the location of suitable objects throughout Chelmsford prior to the removal of any of them for scrap.

Friday 26th September 1941

HUNDREDS OF WAR WORKERS COMING

AT THE MONTHLY Council meeting the Chief Billeting Officer reported that a large number of war workers were to be transferred to Chelmsford to work in the 'big three' factories.

As a consequence some 14 properties were under consideration for requisition to help accommodate them. Following a Government request the Council agreed to appoint a temporary canvasser in order to prepare a list of the available lodgings in the town.

Wednesday 28th May 1941

EYEWITNESS ACCOUNT: BEING A WARDEN

"According to the booklet that we were all given as wardens the main aim of a warden was 'to advise and help his fellow citizens in the sector to which is allotted in all the risks and calamities which might follow from air attack, and to form a link between them and the authorities for reporting air raid damage and calling aid when required'."

As told to our our Special Correspondent

"In 1938, around the time of the Munich crisis, the Government wanted volunteers for the air raid wardens service. I felt that I ought to being something useful on that front so I duly joined up at Chelmsford police station.

According to the booklet that we were all given as wardens the main aim of a warden was 'to advise and help his fellow citizens in the sector to which is allotted in all the risks and calamities which might follow from air attack, and to form a link between them and the authorities for reporting air raid damage and calling aid when required'.

After joining we all undertook a course of training which comprised of lectures and practical demonstrations. We were trained in a wide variety of subjects including; anti-gas precautions, the local A.R.P . organisation, fitting of respirators (gas masks) to the public, the principles of the air raid warning systems, protection against high explosive bombs, methods of dealing with incendiaries, the Auxiliary Fire Service, relations with the police and public, message writing and reporting, equipment at the wardens posts and elementary first aid.

Demonstrations of fire fighting techniques were given to us by a police inspector at the field adjoining the Police H.Q. In the meantime the ladies, including my wife to be, were assembling gas masks, not only for adults, but for children and babies, at the Victoria School in Victoria Road. By the time war started we were all set.

Each warden was allotted to a particular wardens post and in my case I was sent to one in Great Baddow, not far from my home in Longfield Road. The post was situated between the village hall and brewery, in a room adjoining a pub somewhere along the Southend Road. It served an area or sector around it of about 500 people, and throughout the district there were dozens of other sectors each with their own wardens post.

I was one of a handful of wardens allotted to the post, and we used to man it on a rota basis. Our senior warden was Mr. Brumwell of Tabors Avenue, who was responsible for organising the manning of the post and the supervision of the wardens there. Above Mr. Brumwell there was a Head Warden, responsi-

ble for a group of several post and at the top, above him was the Chief Warden, head of the local organisation.

Each warden was given a steel helmet, a gas mask, a whistle and armlet saying 'Warden'. We had to return all the gear after the war but I've still got the armlet as a memento. As well as our own equipment the post was supplied with other bits and pieces like torches, whistles, a first aid box, some anti-gas equipment and hand rattles which were for warning of a gas attack - thankfully we never had to use them.

Our main duty as wardens was to clear the streets of people during air raid alerts. Once the action warning had been given by the sirens we had to put on our helmets, take our whistles and leave the post to check that no one was still outside. We'd blow on the whistle to warn any one who had not taken cover at the siren. One warden would stay at the post during this time, ready to answer the phone or send in reports. If I was at home during an alert I used to go out into the garden or walk up and down my road in case anyone was still out in the open.

On one occasion I can remember one a chap, a friend of mine who I was at school with, came out of his house to have a look during an air raid alert. I didn't recognise him at the time and i shouted to him to get under cover. He retorted "Mind your own bloody business!'. Since then I've often reminded him and his wife about that - it was jolly funny. I suppose that in those early days we, of course, took the job seriously, but on occasions we were in a way a little overbearing, though I can't remember the public being too awkward about it.

If bombs were dropped during the alert period our job was to send a message to our superiors giving them details so they could call insistence if need be. Fortunately for me no bombs fell in our sector until after I left the wardens in November 1940 to go into the army. Looking back, in many ways I think that the people in Chelmsford ran into more danger that most of us who left to go into the army."

Gilbert Torry

BRITISH RESTAURANTS FOR CHELMSFORD

THE DAY SAW THE OPENING of Chelmsford's first British Restaurant by the Mayor, Cllr. Sidney Taylor in premises in Moulsham Street, opposite St. John's Church, which had formerly been used by Messers Walls as an ice cream depot.

A further two British Restaurants were to subsequently open in the town, one in Rainsford Lane and the other at Tunman Mead (off Victoria Road). Their origin can be traced back to December 1940.

On the last day of 1940 over a hundred local authority delegates from all over Essex attended a conference in Chelmsford where it was revealed that the Government intended to introduce Communal Feeding via a county-wide network of 'Community Centres for Feeding', (later to be known as British Restaurants).

The benefits of Communal Feeding were seen as three-fold: firstly, it was more economical and practical to feed large numbers of people than for people to individually cook their own meals at home; secondly, the centres would facilitate feeding arrangements in the event of a heavy air raid; and thirdly, it would lead to the development of an organisation capable of dealing with food shortages during and after the war had finished. Funding for a Communal Feeding scheme would come wholly from the Government with a town the size of Chelmsford would require three Centres.

In response to the conference the Council appointed a Communal Feeding Special Committee to formulate a scheme for the provision of British Restaurants in Chelmsford.

It quickly identified three premises in the town which would be suitable for the establishment of British Restaurants: Rainsford Senior School for the northern portion of the town; Trinity Road School for the Springfield portion of the town and the Wall's Ice Cream Co. building in Moulsham Street for the southern portion of the town.

At the Council meeting on 26th March 1941 members were informed that proposals for its first British Restaurant in Moulsham Street had been sent to the Ministry of Food for approval. However, the proposed sites at the Trinity Road and Rainsford Senior Schools were facing opposition from the education authorities.

It was not until the end of May 1941 that the Council finally received ministry sanction to begin to adapt the former Wall's premises in Moulsham Street as Chelmsford's first British Restaurant.

Bureaucracy had dogged the project for several months, much to the dismay of members of the Council and public alike. The Borough Engineer immediately invited tenders for carrying out the alterations to the premises and a month later that of £447/10/- from Messers W.J. Wade was accepted. Meanwhile the locations of the town's other two proposed British Restaurants had still to be determined.

Progress appeared at last to be being made on additional British Restaurants. Despite persistent opposition from local education bodies, members of the Council decided to seek Ministry of Health and Board of Education approval for the establishment of the second and third British Restaurants at the Trinity Road and Rainsford Senior Schools. However, as a contingency the Borough Engineer was instructed to prepare plans to adapt Mrs. Hayes' jam factory in Rainsford Lane into a British Restaurant.

A month later the Communal Feeding Committee reported that the establishment of the British Restaurants proposed at the Trinity Road and Rainsford Senior Schools were abandoned after it was reported that the Board of Education vetoed the plans, so the Borough Engineer was instructed to seek other sites.

Finally on 16th September 1941, some nine months after its establishment had initially been suggested, Chelmsford's long delayed first British Restaurant was opened by the Mayor in Moulsham Street.

According to subsequent reports in the local press the Mayor and his colleagues enjoyed a meal at the restaurant. However, eyewitnesses told of the party being dressed in dinner suits and making their way off to an alternative, more salubrious, venue for dinner!

Had they dined at the British Restaurant they could have enjoyed the menu for the first meal consisting of; soup with bread at 2d, meat and vegetables at 7d, apple tart at 2d, and a cup of tea for a penny. The restaurant employed a manageress, two paid assistants and volunteers from the W.V.S.

The first day saw a total of 148 meals served and 117 cups of tea drunk. This was to increase and by the end of the year an average of around 280 meals were to be served there each day. At the opening ceremony the Mayor revealed that the official approval had been received to spend an estimated £1,091/14/2 to establish the second British Restaurant in premises in Rainsford Lane. Conversion work was to be carried out by Messrs H. Potter (William Sharp) Ltd. at a cost of £443 with the food preparation equipment being supplied by the Ministry of Food.

Chelmsford's second British Restaurant was opened by the Mayor five months later on 24th February 1942 at the converted premises in Rainsford Lane, opposite Primrose Hill, which had formerly been Mrs. Hay's jam factory.

Seating was provided for 168 people and the building would be open for business from 12 noon to 2 p.m. weekdays, giving a capacity for over 500 meals per day. The first day's customers totalled 124, but this was to climb over the next few weeks to an average of around 230 by early March 1942 and 329 per day during the last week of March 1942.

Subsequently the Ministry of Food informed the Council that its head catering advisor rated the Rainsford Lane British Restaurant to be the best in the whole country in terms of quality of the cooking and menus. This success led to frequent lunchtime congestion and pleas were made for the public to try and use the British Restaurants out of these rush periods.

In September 1942 the the Borough Engineer was instructed to investigate possible sites for the provision of a third British Restaurant, in the Springfield area. Unlike the first two no cooking would be done on site. Instead food would be sent from a Ministry of Food sponsored Cooking Centre in Witham which was set to open shortly.

Eight days later he reported that there were no existing buildings suitable for conversion but that three potential sites had been identified where a prefabricated building could be erected - in Trinity Road, Tunman Mead in Victoria Road and Wharf Road.

In October 1942 the Council opted for the Tunman Mead site (now Riverside car park) and the Borough Engineer was instructed to submit plans and estimates for a British Restaurant on that site to the Ministry of Food for its consideration. At the end of December 1942 the Council voted to submit these to the Ministry whilst tenders would be sought for the building's erection..

At the end of April 1943 approval was received for the provision and equipping of the third British Restaurant at Tunman Mead at a cost not exceeding £2,265/0/10, and the Council quickly sealed a contract with Messers Henry Sharp (William Potter) Ltd. who rapidly undertook the necessary work and on 9th August 1943 the premises were opened by the Mayor.

The new premises were open from noon till 2 p.m. weekdays and between 5.30 p.m. and 7.30 p.m. for meals for billeted war workers. Its opening was somewhat marred by a shortage of staff meant that the Mayor and two other Councillors helped serve customers.

Poor patronage by war workers and a failure to find a solution to the shortage of staff led to the evening meals provision being withdrawn in mid September 1943. However, daytime usage was satisfactory with around 1,800 meals served per week in its first month of opening.

In April 1944 the Council was informed that the half millionth meal had now been served in Chelmsford's British Restaurants.

The Moulsham Street and Rainsford Lane restaurants continued to turn in a healthy surplus, but that at Tunman Mead was continuing to run at a loss.

With that in mind the Council embarked on negotiations with Ministry of Food with a view to adapting the Restaurant so that it could become a self-contained facility with cooking could done on site. Ministerial approval for the plan was received in September 1944.

Despite the ending of the war in August 1945 the Government decided to keep the country's British Restaurants open. On 17th September 1946 the one millionth meal was served at Tunman Mead to a Marconi employee, Mrs. G.C. Sheppard of World's End Cottage in Little Baddow.

Eight days later members of the Council were informed that the restaurants would pass to their control from the Ministry of Food in March 1947.

Tuesday 16th September 1941

SECRET HYDROGEN PLANT OPENS AT THE GAS WORKS

Gas for Barrage Balloons

AT THE GAS WORKS a top secret hydrogen gas manufacturing plant was put into regular production for the first time on 1st January 1942. It had been undergoing trials since 11th December 1941. The plant, which had been built amid great secrecy by the Air Ministry, was intended to produce the gas for both domestic and overseas barrage balloons.

Moves to establish the plant had begun during the summer of 1940 when the Council was approached by Viscount Ridley, the Director of Hydrogen to the Air Ministry with regard to the possibility of manufacturing balloon hydrogen for the Ministry. The Council approved the proposal and agreed to lease a site occupied by disused plant and a small disused gasholder for storage.

In May 1941 the Ministry's contractors cleared the site, repaired the Council's gasholder and began to erect plant for the manufacture, purification, compression and storage of one million cubic feet of hydrogen per week. Two additional gas holders were constructed and to provide the additional blue water gas and steam which were required for manufacture, the Ministry installed an additional water gas unit and steam boiler. Entirely unskilled labour was recruited locally and trained, 15 men being eventually employed in hydrogen making alone.

In February 1942 the plant was handed over to the Gas Works management from the contractors and it continued the manufacture of hydrogen until the end of September 1944. The compressed gas was removed in cylinders by R.A.F. personnel billeted on site, with the normal supply for the first two and a half years averaging 240 cylinders per day. In June 1944 the requirements of D Day, when the balloon barrage was carried overseas, followed by their deployment against the V-1s, created the need for greatly increased production. With difficulty and for a limited period, production was increased from 1 million to 1.75 million cubic feet of hydrogen without any serious problems until the position eased in September 1944. During the whole period 127.5 million cubic feet of hydrogen were manufactured, the content of 7,082 barrage balloons, requiring 214 million cubic feet of water gas and over 10,000 tons of steam. The Council was paid £3,124 for running the plant which produced hydrogen valued at £22,105.

Sunday 1st January 1942

WARSHIP WEEK IN ESSEX

THE CHELMSFORD DISTRICT INVESTS WELL OVER £750,000

Throughout Essex the day saw the start of Warship Week, the latest National Savings campaign. Warship Weeks had been held in other parts of the country since 18th October 1941 and were to continue until March 1942.

The public was encouraged to invest in the Government's Savings Bonds, National War Bonds, Defence Bonds and Savings Certificates and thus raise sufficient funds to pay for the construction of war ships for the Royal Navy. Chelmsford and its Rural District had been set a target of investing £240,000 and if the target was met then two corvettes, H.M.S. Corianda and H.M.S. Cyclamen, would be officially 'adopted' by the Borough and Rural District.

In Chelmsford the bonds and certificates could be purchased from any bank, post office, warship selling centre or any one of dozens of street savings groups that had been set up since the war started. Additionally, selling centres were opened at the Duke Street H.Q. of the local Savings Committee, 36 High Street, Messers Bonds in the High Street and the Rural District Council Offices in London Road. To help publicise the event a week long programme of events was to be held around the town and a totaliser erected outside the public library.

By the end of the week it would be clear that Warship Week was going to be a success, though its magnitude was a great surprise when the total invested in National Savings was subsequently revealed - £770, 710/7/9, over three times the target figure. The 33,142 people in the Borough's contributed £536,274/18/9, an average of £16/3/7 per head, whilst the Rural District's population of 34,062 had invested £234,435/9/- at £6/17/7 per head. Overall the average investment per head was £11/9/4

The Borough's total was swelled by a £100,000 investment from Marconi's which was handed over by its boss, Admiral H.W. Grant. Workers there had already raised some £20,000 in the previous year for an R.A.F. bomber. Of the Rural District's parishes the top three investors were Ingatestone & Fryerning with £55,044, Boreham & Springfield Rural with £48,354, and Danbury with £21,534. The best investments measured per head of population were Boreham & Springfield Rural at £28/3/-, Ingatestone & Fryerning at £23/9/-, and Good Easter at £14/4. The worst figures for both counts were for Runwell which invested a meagre £558 at 9/3 per head.

The various fund raising and publicity activities of Warship Week accrued a profit of £647/10/10, of which £500 was subsequently donated to Mrs. Churchill's Aid to Russia Fund.

The huge success of Warship Week would mean that it was likely that the Admiralty would have now offer Chelmsford a more important ship to adopt than the two corvettes initially allotted to the Borough and Rural District.

Saturday 14th February 1942

'JUDGE TINDAL' VANDALISED

According to the Essex Chronicle during the previous week a prankster, later to be revealed as a Hoffmann's employee, had poured white paint over the head of Judge Tindal's statue in Tindal Square. Apparently, although the judge had been decorated before, it was the first time he had been painted.

Friday 2nd January 1942

COUNTY COUNCIL LETTER GOES UP IN FLAMES

At the monthly meeting of the Council the County Council was reported to have written requesting that it should not have to surrender any of its railings for scrap purposes. The Mayor informed the meeting that the County Council's would receive the same consideration as everyone else, and furthermore he instructed the Borough Engineer to put the County Council's letter on the fire!

Wednesday 28th January 1942

REQUISITION OF RAILINGS BEGINS AT LAST

In Chelmsford the requisition of unnecessary iron and steel railings and other street furniture was finally begun.

Symbolically the first railings to be taken were those from the Mayor's house 'Ardmore' in Rainsford Road, followed by those at nearby Admirals' Park. Unfortunately, within days the Council was to receive many complaints about the poor state sites were being left in, once contractors had taken the salvaged metals.

Tuesday 12th March 1942

CHELMSFORD TO ADOPT HMS HARDY

IN THE WAKE of the huge success of Chelmsford's Warship Week the Admiralty announced that the Borough was to 'adopt' a destroyer, subsequently revealed to be H.M.S. Hardy.

The famous 1,565 ton vessel had been completed in December 1936 and on 10th April 1940 she had been driven aground by gunfire during an attempt to recapture Narvik Fjord from German control. The ship's commander, Captain B.A.W. Warburton-Lee who was killed in the attack as posthumously awarded the Victoria Cross, the first of the war, for his actions that day. The corvette H.M.S. Cyclamen, one of two corvettes which had initially been intended to be adopted by jointly by the Borough and Rural District was now to be adopted solely by the latter

.Thursday 19th March 1942

HOME GUARD EXERCISE: TRAGEDY AS WOMAN IS KILLED IN EXPLOSION

DISASTER IN NAVIGATION RD

AN EVENING EXERCISE being undertaken by members of the 6th Battalion of the Essex Home Guard went disastrously wrong when an unexpected explosion claimed the life of one civilian bystander and injured fourteen other people, some seriously.

For the exercise several Home Guards were briefed to capture numbers 36 and 37 Navigation Road, a pair of empty houses opposite Brockley Road which had been damaged by enemy action during August 1940. At 8.45 p.m. a Home Guard placed two 'smoke bombs' on the road surface, one a regulation army type and the other, a homemade device. The former functioned correctly, but the latter, made from an old tin can failed to do so. After around thirty seconds it suddenly and unexpectedly exploded with devastating results. Mrs. Louisa Rolfe, aged 61, of 29 Roman Road was struck in the chest by flying fragments of the device as she stood outside number 35 Navigation Road, the home of her daughter Winifred Harrhy. Her injuries were so severe that she was to die the following day at the Chelmsford & Essex Hospital.

A number of children who had been playing in the street and members of the Home Guard were struck by shrapnel. Those detained in hospital included Kathleen Fisher aged 15 of 58 Navigation Road, Frank Joslin aged 10 of 5 Hill Crescent, Derek Saville aged 14 of Wharf Road, and the following members of the Home Guard; Major William Nield aged 51 of Little Dunmow, Captain Frederick Scheidweiler aged 54 of Longfield Road in Great Baddow, 2nd Lt. James Low of Grassmere, Links Drive, Sgt. John Anderson aged 25 of Bouverie Road, Sgt. Joseph Eve of Galleywood, Pte. Christopher

Anthony of 17 Mildmay Road, Pte. John Bicknell aged 60 of Widford Road, and Pte. Laurence Ketley of 30 Vicarage Road.

Four others were allowed home after treatment including Police Sgt. Harry Warnes of Elm Road, who had been commended earlier in the war for rescuing a mother and her two children from a bomb damaged house.

The wife of one of the injured Home Guards was reported to have been less that sympathetic to his injuries. On being told that his arm had been smashed she was said to have snorted and replied 'Serves him right, playing soldiers at his time of life'!

The blast damaged several properties in the vicinity including numbers 17, 18, 19, 22, 35 and 41 Navigation Road.

Subsequently the inquest into Mrs. Rolfe's death was to return the verdict of accidental death. It appeared that the second 'smoke bomb' had in fact been an improvised high explosive mine, thought to have been one of many home made by members of local Bomb Disposal Squads from materials salvaged from dismantled German bombs.

The device had lain in the Home Guard store for some time. It had not been clearly labelled and had been presumed it to have been a harmless smoke bomb.

Mrs. Rolfe's funeral service was held at St. John's Moulsham on 9th May with her interment at the Borough Cemetery afterwards. Sadly that was not the end of the tragic episode. Mrs. Rolfe's 66 year-old husband Frederick was to return to his carpenter's job at Hoffmann's on 18th May but a day later he was discovered dead at work, his skull having fractured in a fall down stairs. He had been depressed since his wife's death and his inquest was to record a verdict of accidental death.

Tuesday 5th May 1942

7 SONS IN ARMY

According to the Essex Chronicle 67 year-old John Crozier of West Avenue had seven sons in the army; three were with the R.A.S.C. in the middle east, 32 year-old Cpl. Ernest, 29 year-old Cpl. Arthur and 23 year-old Pte. Harry; 25 year-old Albert was also in the R.A.S.C., 34 year-old Gunner Fred was with the Royal Artillery in west African, 21 year old Sgt. Douglas was with the Queen's Regiment, and the youngest, 19 year-old Gunner Frank, was with an A.A. (searchlight) company.

Friday 20th March 1942

SHELTER PROGRESS

At the monthly Council meeting members were informed on the progress of air raid shelter provision in the town. 367 domestic surface shelters had now been finished with 51 under construction. 2,345 of the 2,374 Morrison shelters which had been ordered had now been delivered, giving a shelter accommodation to 8,108 residents.

Wednesday 29th April 1942

WOMEN WAR WORKERS CAMPAIGN

A two week campaign to get every available woman in Chelmsford into war work was launched during the day.

Women were sought in four main categories; full time work at a war work factory, part time work at a war work factory, to replace younger women in their full or part time job, or to look after war workers' children. The event, which had been organised by the Ministry of Information on behalf of the Ministry of Labour and production ministries, saw the opening of a War Job Exhibition and information bureau at Wenley's store in London Road. It was to be hailed as a great success by the organisers, with over 500 women registering for war work, and another 75 with children ready to start once the Council's three nurseries were opened.

Saturday 23rd May 1942

DUKE OF KENT IN SURPRISE VISIT TO COUNTY TOWN

King's brother's first visit since opening the by-pass in 1932

The day saw a surprise visit to Chelmsford by Prince George, the Duke of Kent, who had last visited the town just over ten years to the day previously.

On that occasion he had toured local factories, the museum and officially opened the town's first by-pass, part of which was named Prince's Road in his honour. During the day's unpublicised visit the Duke was driven around the town in a camouflaged Rolls-Royce. He visited Hoffmann's where he opened a factory extension, Crompton's, the Chelmsford & Essex Hospital , the N.F.S. Fire Station in Market Road and the ambulance station at Widford Lodge.

BRITISH RESTAURANT FOR GREAT BADDOW

Another set to follow in the Writtle before the end of the year

The Rural District Council opened its first British Restaurant and cooking centre at the former County Council highways depot at Bell Yard, at the junction of Bell Street and Great Baddow High Street.

Thursday 11th June1942

JEHOVAH'S WITNESS IMPRISONED FOR HIS BELIEFS

At the Chelmsford Petty Sessions a Gloucester Avenue man was sent to prison for three months for refusing to carry out civil defence duties or farm work, in contravention of his registration as a conscientious objector.

In his defence the man stated that he was a full time minister of the Ministry of Jehovah God and his vow of consecration prevented him from undertaking those duties. In the coming months several more Jehovah Witnesses were imprisoned in other parts of Essex for similar offences.

Friday 12th June1942

MAKING A BEE LINE FOR THE SHIRE HALL

Two swarms of bees, belonging to Dr. J.T. Whitely of London Road, caused a considerable disturbance when they swarmed on a pair of 'keep left' bollards outside the Shire Hall during the day.

The police were called in to warn pedestrians and motorists to pass carefully until the doctor and his assistants were able to entice the bees into boxes and take them away. The operation took more than an hour and was watched by a large, curious crowd. It was one of a number of instances of bees swarming reported in Chelmsford throughout the week.

Monday 1st June 1942

NEW HOME GUARD ANTI-AIRCRAFT BATTERY FOR CHELMSFORD

BRIGADIER H.A.D. Murray, commander of the 37 A.A. Brigade, today received War Office authorisation to form two Home Guard anti-aircraft batteries, one at Colchester and the other at Chelmsford.

They were to be set up using existing troops of 171/61 A.A. Z Battery Royal Artillery, a regular unit then deployed at Lexden Lodge and Writtle plus Home Guards transferred from their usual battalions. Each battery would consist of 64 anti-aircraft rocket projectors, and would be manned by eight separate shifts of 178 men - a total of 1,428 men. The Chelmsford battery was to be established at the Recreation Ground and was officially designated the 211 (101 Essex Home Guard) Rocket Anti-Aircraft Battery. Major H.G. Moore MC, of 'Plantations' in Stock, and commander of the village's of the Home Guard was appointed Battery Commander and immediately set about recruiting men aged up to 60 to serve with the battery,. Enrolment was to be on Tuesday and Friday nights at Lancaster House in Mildmay Road.

Tuesday 7th July 1942

CATHEDRAL RAILINGS TAKEN FOR SALVAGE

Enhances the look of the churchyard

The Cathedral's railings had finally begun to be removed for scrap during the week, and according to the Essex Chronicle, this had greatly enhanced the churchyard. Remaining railings around certain tombs in the churchyard were set to be taken shortly. All told some 2,000 feet of railings would be taken from the site, weighing 2 tons, 13.5 hundredweight.

Friday 17th July 1942

LUFTWAFFE MOUNTS DARING RAID ON HOFFMANN'S WORKS

3 BOMBS HIT FACTORY: 4 WORKERS KILLED: BOMB KILLS COUPLE IN RECTORY LANE: 500 PROPERTIES DAMAGED

AROUND 6.15 a.m., a lone Dornier Do 217 performed a precise and daring low level daylight attack on the Hoffmann Manufacturing Company's works in New Street and Rectory Lane. The aircraft dropped four bombs, three of which hit the factory, killing four men. The other bomb landed on houses in Rectory Lane, killing an elderly couple.

The Dornier took advantage of low-lying cloud which enabled it to approach Chelmsford undetected. Significantly no siren had sounded and no anti-aircraft fire was directed at the aircraft.

Once above the town the raider circled for several minutes, and with its target located it began a final low-level bombing run on Hoffmann's. It was a technique that the Luftwaffe had successfully employed on recent similar raids on Rolls Royce at Derby and Lockheed Hydraulics at Leamington Spa.

The aircraft approached the factory from the south-east over Victoria Road and the railway embankment, and with machine guns blazing it released four 500 Kg SC high explosive bombs before making off into the clouds. Three of the bombs scored hits on Hoffmann's, whilst another went astray and exploded amongst residential properties in Rectory Lane.

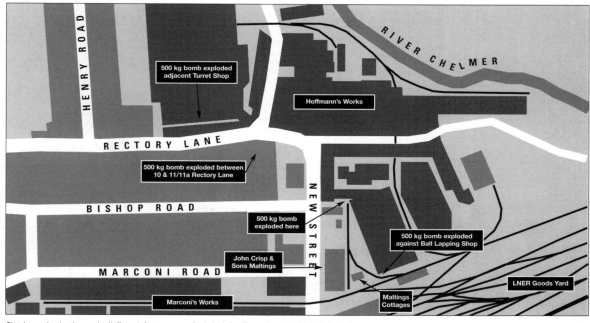

Sketch map showing the massive Hoffmann's factory, scene of a daring Luftwaffe attack on 19th July 1942. (Author)

First Bomb - Hits Hoffmann's Ball Lapping Shop

The first bomb to be dropped fell short of the factory and first struck a tarmac surface in the L.N.E.R.'s goods yard.

It then ricocheted off the ground, leaving a score mark 7 feet by 3 feet, and passed through both sides of a covered railway wagon at a height of about ten feet above the rails.

It continued in the air for a distance of some 241 feet and and exploded against the external wall of the Ball Lapping Shop of Hoffmann's, just below ground level.

The Ball Lapping Shop was a single storey building, situated towards the New Street end of the boundary with the goods yard - behind the site of the modern-day Texaco petrol station. It had brick walls and a north light steel roof with its glazing replaced by asbestos sheets for blackout purposes.

The detonation of the bomb brought down 78 feet of the external wall and collapsed four roof trusses, with the damage confined mainly to the south-western corner of the shop.

The blast completed lifted three open railway wagons off the rails in the goods yard and destroyed a length of track which was subsequently replaced by the morning of 21st July. A telegraph pole and wires belonging to the

L.N.E.R. also needed replacing. A pair of semi-detached cottages, 1 & 2 Maltings Cottages, were both seriously damaged by the blast. They were located between the Ball Lapping Shop and the back of John Crisp & Son's maltings (site of Texaco garage) which stood in New Street directly opposite Marconi Road.

Second Bomb - Kills two and starts a fire within Hoffmann's

It struck the corner of the fan house superstructure on the roof of the Ball Lapping Shop, and broke and dislodged a five feet by two feet lump of reinforced concrete. It then passed through and demolished a parapet brick wall, was deflected and travelled parallel with the western wall of the building before it detonated at ground level at the north western corner of the Ball Lapping Shop at its junction with a two storey building which was square on to New Street.

From its initial impact point the bomb had travelled some 117 feet and descended about 39 feet from the roof of the fan house superstructure.

The explosion caused the first floor concrete floor to collapse, killing two workers and seriously injuring two others. One man's body was recovered badly burned from fires which had probably been caused by the ignition of paraffin and other oils used in the ball machines.

Hoffmann's fire brigade was summoned by the works spotter and the fires in the troughs of the machines were extinguished in around two minutes with foam

extinguishers. Some debris and rags which were also set alight were extinguished using water from the factory. Chelmsford's N.F.S., who were called to the fire at 6.15 a.m., reported the situation under control half-an-hour later and had returned to base by 8 a.m.

Third Bomb - Couple die after Rectory Lane home is struck

The third bomb initially penetrated the corner of a building, which is believed to have belonged to the timber merchants Brown & Son Ltd. - it stood in New Street, adjacent to Hoffmann's and directly opposite Bishop Road.

The bomb struck the building some seven feet above the ground, ricocheted off an adjacent concrete drive and in the process left its tail fin caught in some iron railings fronting New Street. It then crossed New Street diagonally, passed over the eighteen feet high premises of the builders' merchants, Roberts Adlard & Co. Ltd., on the northern corner of Bishop Road and New Street before it finally fell and detonated in the passageway between numbers 10 and 11/11a Rectory Lane. The bomb had travelled some 326 feet from its initial impact point.

The explosion, which occurred below ground level, left a crater 32.5 feet deep in the clay soil. In the process four dwellings were demolished, nos. 9, 10, 11 & 11a Rectory Lane, and a further four either side of them, nos. 7, 8, 12 & 12a, were damaged beyond repair.

The bomb claimed the lives of an elderly married couple, 61 year-old Walter Richard Vernon and his 59 year-old wife, Laura, who were trapped when the explosion demolished their end-of-terrace home, number 10 Rectory Lane. Both were recovered alive by civil defence staff, but Mrs. Vernon died shortly afterwards and her husband was to succumb to his injuries a day later at the Chelmsford & Essex Hospital.

Mr. Vernon, a wood machinist at Marconi's, had spent his whole life in Chelmsford. He had been employed by the company for over 32 years. The couple was cremated at the City of London Crematorium and their funeral services were held at Holy Trinity on 25th July.

Adjacent to Mr. & Mrs. Vernon's house stood a pair of recently-built semi-detached houses, each containing two flats, numbers 11, 11a, 12 & 12a Rectory Lane. They were owned by Rex Taylor who lived at 7 Rectory Lane, but who was serving in the forces at that time.

The bomb detonated only three feet from from number 11, a ground floor flat, which was occupied by Mr. L.J. Rout, his wife Phyllis and their young daughter Norma. On hearing the approaching German bomber all three had rushed into their Morrison shelter in the smaller bedroom at the back of their home. Although the bomb demolished the building around them and the shelter was displaced some six feet across the room, bouncing three times in the process, it was undamaged and its occupants escaped with minor injuries. They were rescued within minutes.

Mrs. Wood who lived in the flat above them, number 11a, also

escaped with her life, although she was injured as was Horace Seyfang of no. 8.

Fourth Bomb - explodes adjacent Hoffmann's Turret Shop

The fourth bomb, which was the only one which did not ricochet from its initial impact point, scored a direct hit on Hoffmann's directly opposite nos. 24 & 25 Rectory Lane.

It passed through the nine inch external brick wall of a cycle shed, which formed the factory's boundary wall, through the shed itself, across a short stretch of open ground and into the single storey Capstan Shop of the Turret Shop.

The bomb then detonated at, or just below, ground level in the outside wall of a brick surface air raid shelter which had be built in the shop. The explosion flattened the shelter, demolished some forty feet of the shop's wall and brought down a large area of its roof.

Blast also seriously damaged eighteen houses on the southern side of Rectory Lane which faced the factory. Two men were killed as a result and three others had narrow escapes. They had been running towards the shelter when the bomb struck and were blown back by blast. After-wards they were to find that the shelter had been obliterated, as they surely would have been had they reached it.

More news from raid on page 20

Target Hoffmann's: Sunday 19th July 1942

WE WERE LUCKY, IT COULD HAVE BEEN FAR WORSE

Fortunately at the time of the attack no regular shift was on duty at Hoffmann's so casualties were substantially fewer that may have been expected - dozens would have been killed in the shelter alone.

At 11.05 a.m. Hoffmann's control reported that all employees had been accounted for. Four were known to have been killed, four others had been taken to hospital whilst numerous others had been taken to the works first aid post off Bishop's Hall Lane.

Three of the dead were Irish labourers, over fifty of whom had been brought to the country to work at Hoffmann's since the start of the war. They were: James Aloysius Brennan, aged 27, who lodged at 7 Chapel Place. He was the son of Mr. & Mrs. James Brennan of Rathgar in Dublin;

Daniel Gannon, aged 29, who lodged at 7 Sixth Avenue. He was the son of Daniel and Isabela Gannon of Dublin; and Walter Patrick Moffatt, aged 25, who also lodged at 7 Sixth Avenue. His parents were Robert and Elizabeth Moffatt of Cabra in County Down. His wife, Mary, lived in Dublin.

The three Irishmen were buried at the Borough Cemetery on 25th July. Their coffins spent the previous night in the Church of Our Lady Immaculate in London Road. A requiem mass was held there prior to interment.

The fourth victim at Hoffmann's was 40 year-old Charles Richard Brett, son of the late Mr. T.F. Brett and husband of Violet Brett of Nubian Lodge, Oakhurst Drive in Wickford. He was a former honourary secretary of the South East Essex Goat Club and was subsequently buried in Wickford. He had been employed

in the building and decorative trade in the town.

Among those injured at the factory was John Hilton, aged 54, who suffered a machine gun bullet in his left foot and Beatrice Bainbridge. Moral at Hoffmann's after the attack was said to be good, despite the fatalities.

Apart from the six people known to have been killed as a result of the raid, the exact number of casualties is difficult to establish. According to a report at 6 p.m. by Chelmsford's Casualty Officer 5 people had been killed, 4 men and 7 women had been admitted to hospital (including Mr. Vernon who was subsequently to die there), plus 23 others slightly injured. Those injured included Eunice Griffiths of 33 Rectory Lane, Mrs. Bullard of 29 Rectory Lane, Leslie Metson and a Mrs. Hill.

Photograph of a Luftwaffe scale model of the New Street and Rectory Lane areas, viewed from the 'west'. It was used to help bomber crews familiarize themselves with their intended targets of Hoffmann's and Marconi's works. (Courtesy of The General Electric Company plc)

THE COUNTY TOWN'S REACTION

CONTINGENCY plans for dealing with the incident appeared to work well, with the civil defence and rescue services widely praised for their efforts.

Amongst those in attendance were two rescue squads, three ambulances, two stretcher parties, three sitting case cars, , one mortuary van and the N.F.S. A rest centre for bombed out families was opened at the North Avenue Congregational Church.

Its first arrivals was a family of four who were received at 9.10 a.m. It finally closed at midday with arrangements having been made for the billeting of all those made homeless in the raid.

An early visitor to the bomb damaged areas was the Mayor who promised angry residents that there would be an inquiry to find out why no sirens had warned of the attack and why the anti-aircraft defences at Hoffmann's had failed to open fire on the German bomber.

BLAST DAMAGE & STRAY SHELLS

AROUND 500 properties in the vicinity of the bombs suffered some degree of damage, with the blast causing its customary strange effects.

One corrugated shed was reported to have been blown over three hundred yards onto the roof of a house, whilst the famous Hoffmann's clock, which stood above the Turret Shop's entrance, had its face blown away whilst, remarkably, its glass covering remained in place.

Stray cannon shells fired by the German aircraft were discovered in several locations on the Boarded Barns Estate, including at West Avenue and at 18 Eastern Crescent.

At the latter, a shell exploded in the scullery, though fortunately no one was hurt.

Sunday 19th July 1942

THE DAY AFTER: GERMAN RADIO CLAIMS HOFFMANN'S BOMBED

The German News Agency reported 'An important industrial works near Chelmsford was heavily bombed yesterday by German bombers on armed reconnaissance'.

Direct hits to factory buildings were claimed in the bulletin which was also repeated on Berlin Radio.

Monday 20th July 1942

HOFFMANN'S PRODUCTION SEVERELY DEPLETED

The raid successfully disrupted the production of the vital ball and roller bearings at Hoffmann's.

Initial assessments suggested that manufacturing would need to be stopped for about three days in the Turret, Ball Lapping and Roller Lapping Shops, pending salvage and clearing-up operations.

Fortunately losses of bearings were relatively small, confined to those in the course of machining. Salvaging them was, however, a time-consuming operation as the force of the explosions had flung them considerable distances in all directions.

An initial estimate expected a 20% loss in overall production in the five or six week period following the raid. This was illustrated in figures detailing the value of Hoffmann's total production output. In May 1942 this had been £344,103, in June £362,087 and in July £350,102. However, the August 1942 figure was to turn out to be just £249,877, though by September it was to recover to £343,848.

Hoffmann's was particularly susceptible to a loss in production by air raid damage because the manufacture of bearings required the use of tailor-made machines which were very difficult to replace. Additionally, manufacturing required a dust and debris-free environment - exactly what a bomb would prevent.

In the Ball Lapping Shop 16 of the 162 machines there were damaged, but only one of them beyond repair. In the Roller Lapping Shop 32 of the 95 machines were similarly affected.

Fortunately Hoffmann's maintenance staff were able to repair the vast majority of them by the time building repairs were completed at the end of 1942.

Those repairs were to cost around £49,000, though an additional £17,000 was expended on two small extensions to the factory's buildings, one close to the site of the second bomb and the other in the vicinity of the fourth, alongside Rectory Lane.

The contractors for the repairs and extensions were Messers V.G. Selwood & Co. of 86 Broomfield Road, who carried out work to east side of Broomfield Chase, and Messers F.J. French, who carried out the work on the factory premises on the west side of the road.

Ironically some good was to come of the demolition of several properties in Rectory Lane by the one stray bomb. In September 1942 Hoffmann's arranged to lease the sites of numbers 7, 8, 9, 10, 11, 11a, 12, & 12a Rectory Lane for the duration of the war. The ground was cleared of rubble and the company erected bicycle sheds on the land which were to remain until the land was returned to its owners in April 1947.

Modern day view of houses in Rectory Lane, close to corner with New Street,. These properties replaced several destroyed on 19th July 1942. (Author)

EYEWITNESS ACCOUNTS: HOFFMANN'S RAID

"I shouted to my dad 'There's a Dornier!' 'Don't be so stupid' he said. Seconds later there was a loud bang as bombs exploded at Hoffmann's."

As told to our our Special Correspondent

"There were Bofors guns mounted on buildings around the town, including on the roofs of the Marconi College in Arbour Lane and on top of County Hall. This Sunday morning an enemy plane flew over Chelmsford very low and dropped some bombs on Hoffmann's.

The gunners must have been able to see the plane very clearly, but people reckoned that they didn't open fire because they hadn't got an officer or someone there to give them the order to do so. They had to stick to the rules and regulations."

Kenneth Smith

"Early one particular Sunday morning I was laying in bed with my mother when all of a sudden we heard the sound of a plane coming over our house in Victoria Crescent. I looked out of the front window and watched as a single German plane, all painted black, passed right over us in the direction of the Grammar School.

I shouted to my mum "That's a

German plane!' We jumped out of bed just as the siren went and ran down to the shelter outside. The plane returned and dropped some bombs on Hoffmann's."

Betty Pryke

"After the raid on Hoffmann's I went up to look at the clock in the Turret archway. All the guts of the clock were blown out, but like a miracle the glass front was left intact. For years since the war I've told people about that clock."

Bill Wilson

"That particular Sunday morning I was lying in bed at home in Springfield when I heard an aircraft. I looked out the window and to the south-east I saw a low flying Dornier Do 217E approaching the town.

There had been no air raid warning or gun fire. I shouted to my dad 'There's a Dornier!' 'Don't be so stupid' he said. Seconds later there was a loud bang as bombs exploded at Hoffmann's."

Gerald Carter

WARTIME NURSERIES FOR CHELMSFORD

First opens in Corporation Road

AT 3 P.M. on Saturday 1st August 1942 the Mayor, Cllr. Sidney Taylor, formally opened Chelmsford's first wartime nursery in newly erected premises on the southern side of Corporation Road, opposite Woodland Road.

The nursery, which had a capacity for eighty children in four classes (ages 0-1. 1-2, 2-3, 3-5), was to be initially available for public inspection for the following week, prior to the admission of its first children nine days later. It was open 7 a.m. to 7 p.m. on weekdays and 7 a.m. to 1 p.m. on Saturdays, with parents charged one shilling per day for each child. Subsequently further wartime nurseries were opened in London Road and Waterloo Lane.

Efforts to provide the nurseries were but a part of the Government's larger campaign to increase production at the country's vital war work factories. Since most young men had left the factories to join the armed forces emphasis had been placed on recruiting hundreds of thousands of women to take their places. The provision of nurseries was seen as a vital step that would enable mothers of young children to work, either full time or part time.

In Chelmsford moves to provide nurseries had began in November 1941 when, in response to instructions from the Ministry of Health, the Council appointed a new Sub-Committee to urgently investigate the establishment of wartime nurseries in the town. The costs of the nurseries, which were to be of a prefabricated design, would be borne by central Government.

A month later the Sub-Committee reported that it saw 76 and 90 Broomfield Road as ideal locations for the wartime nurseries. Unfortunately the military were not prepared to vacate either building and so the matter was put into the hands of the Maternity & Child Welfare Committee. It subsequently drew up a shortlist of proposed locations that was put before the Council in January 1942.

The committee recommended the adoption of a site on vacant land between the Library and Rainsford House which had formerly been used as a tennis court, and a plot of land in Corporation Road opposite Woodland Road that formed part of the King's Road Playing Field. After due consideration the Council opted for the latter site. The necessary Ministry of Health approval for the scheme was received a few days later. The building consisted of prefabricated sections that would create a single storey nursery 80' long by 18'9" wide, with a wing and air raid shelter.

At the end of February 1942 the Council gave further thought to sites for a second and third nursery. After considering locations adjacent Rainsford House, in Oaklands Park and in the London Road area, it opted for providing nurseries on land adjoining Crompton's Social Centre in Writtle Road and at the old brewery site in Victoria Road. The proposals were then sent to the Ministry of Health for its consideration.

A month later the Council received a deputation, consisting of Mrs. Norton, Mrs. Roberts, Mr. & Mrs. Whitehead and Mrs. Slade, who were campaigning for the provision of day nurseries and school meals in Chelmsford.

The Council was able to inform the deputation that plans were already advanced on both fronts; at the same meeting the Council accepted a tender of £2,784 from Messers Jesse Gowers Ltd. to carry out the construction of the Corporation Road nursery. Meanwhile it was revealed that the Ministry of Health official had rejected the Council's latest favoured sites for additional nurseries; adjacent Crompton's Social Centre and off Victoria Road. However, he had identified two alternative locations; one in Waterloo Lane, next to the old R.D.C. offices and the other at 59 London Road, on allotments near South Lodge.

The sites both found favour with the Council and on 29th April 1942 it accepted tenders valued at £1,775 each from Messers A.J. Arnold and Messers F.J. French to erect the nurseries in London Road and Waterloo Lane respectively. Both contracts were then formally sealed, along with that for the Corporation Road nursery. An architect, Mr. E.P. Archer, was employed to adapt the prefabricated buildings to each of the three sites' needs at a fee eventually totalling £348/16/4.

The Corporation Road nursery took took its first children on 10th August but at the Council meeting on 26th August and subsequent meetings, throughout the autumn and winter, attendances at the nurseries were reported to have been disappointing. Controversy was stirred up when the Deputy-Mayor, Alderman Fox, accused the nurseries as 'being a waste of money'.

The London Road and Waterloo Lane nurseries, each accommodationing 40 children, were opened on 31st August 1942 and 28th September 1942 respectively. The latter was enhanced by paintings of Disney cartoon characters by art students at the Mid Essex Technical College.

All three nurseries remained open for the duration of the war, though today, only that in London Road survives. The Waterloo Lane site is now occupied by Aquila House,while that in Corporation Road has been redeveloped for housing purposes.

Saturday 1st August 1942

AMERICAN SERVICEMEN NOW IN CHELMSFORD

The local press reported that American servicemen had begun to arrive in Essex and published the first in a series of articles entitled 'Americans in Britain - advice on how to get on with us'.

Over the coming weeks problems were to arise when many of the servicemen who visited Chelmsford in the evening for entertainment missed the last buses back to their bases. With the town already suffering an acute accommodation shortage many were forced to sleep in the open air.

Friday 14th August 1942

HALIFAX SHOT DOWN AT STOCK

AT 3.45 A HALIFAX bomber of 76 Squadron R.A.F., from Middleton St. George Aerodrome near Durham, crashed into a turnip field three hundred yards north-east of Fristling Hall near Stock.

The aircraft had been critically damaged by two German fighters off the Dutch coast and had passed over very low before exploding on impact. Six of the seven Canadian and American crew managed to bale out before impact, with pilot remaining at the controls until the plane was away from a built up area. The seventh man, the upper mid gunner had already sustained fatal wounds and his body was subsequently discovered in the wreckage. His colleagues parachuted safely to ground in Stock, Canfield, Willingale, the Roothings and one in the grounds of Newland Hall in Roxwell. One was reported to have landed in a road, another in a barley field, one in a haystack and the three others in cornfields. Fortunately none was seriously hurt.

Saturday 1st August 1942

HOME GUARD ROCKET BATTERY MOVES TO 'THE REC'

THE 211 (101 Essex Home Guard) Rocket A.A. Battery officially moved to its operational site at the Recreation Ground from Writtle.

It had held its first training session just two weeks earlier. The Home Guards were under the command of Major H.G. Moore M.C.

A large section of the 'Rec' had been requisitioned for 'protective measures' with a diversion of Seymour Street to Coval Lane cycle path to the railway side of the lake. The Rocket Battery now consisted of 12 officers and 803 other ranks, three-quarters of whom were workers at the town's 'big three' factories.

Additionally, a small number of regulars from the Royal Artillery would serve as instructors with fire control directed by R.A. officers. Cooking facilities were to be provided by the A.T.S. The Rocket Battery's headquarters had been established at Lancaster House in Mildmay Rd.

Saturday 23rd August 1942

YANKS MONOPOLISE TALENT SHOWS

AT THE CORN EXCHANGE the weekly talent competition, part of the regular dance evening, was won by an American serviceman from Kansas, the only male in the eight entrants.

The Corn Exchange dances were to prove increasingly popular with the newly-arrived Americans, with the next four talent competitions all won by their servicemen.

Tuesday 25th August 1942

HIGH ALTITUDE BOMBER ATTACKS TOWN

Six weeks after the Hoffmann's raid another precision attack was attempted on Chelmsford on what was a bright sunny day with a few high clouds.

At 3.20 p.m., without an air raid warning or anti-aircraft gunfire, a Junkers Ju 86P approached Chelmsford from the east at about 29,500 feet. It circled the district and made a single bombing run from the north-west to south east, releasing one high explosive 250 kg screamer type bomb before making off eastwards.

The device was apparently aimed at the Gas Works but missed its target and crashed through the slate roof of Baddow Road warehouse premises of the builders Messers Trigg & Moore. The bomb broke up on impact with a roof beam and fortunately failed to explode. Even so the building (number 37) was badly damaged and two people slightly hurt as a result.

The No. 13 Bomb Disposal Squad was called in and evacuated the immediate area, closing Baddow Road between Mildmay Road and Goldlay Road. The Ritz Cinema was evacuated, services at the Baddow Road Congregational Church were concluded and the Sunday School was halted.

It was not until eight days later that the remains of the bomb were declared safe, the roads reopened and residents allowed to return to their homes. Apart from destruction at Trigg & Moore's, the only damage was a few broken windows at numbers 62, 64 and 66 Baddow Road. Part of the bomb's screamer was found a mile away.

The bombing had come during an inspection of Chelmsford's Air Training Corps by Air Chief Marshall Sir William Mitchell, commander of the London Region of the service.

Sunday 30th August 1942

U.S. RED CROSS TO TAKE OVER SARACEN'S HEAD HOTEL

THE ESSEX CHRONICLE revealed that the American Red Cross was to take over parts of the Saracen's Head Hotel in the High Street for use as a hostel for American servicemen who were visiting Chelmsford.

The premises would subsequently be known as the 'American Club'. Since the Americans' arrival in Essex during the summer many had found accommodation hard to come by, and it was hoped that the new hostel would go some way to solving this problem. The Saracen's Head would provide sleeping accommodation for 30 men in unoccupied bedrooms, whilst the dining hall and kitchen would be able to provide around 300 meals per day. Another facility looked upon with interest by some Chelmsfordians was a trouser pressing service. Since considerable reconstruction works had been completed at the Saracen's Head in 1941 only two bars had been open, and these were expected to continue so as a separate entity from the hostel. Meanwhile, plans were well advanced for converting 193 Springfield Road in to a Y.M.C.A. hostel. There was still, however, a considerable shortage of similar facilities in the town for women.

Friday 16th October 1942

'HITLER'S COFFIN' PASSES THROUGH CHELMSFORD

A huge boiler was transported through Chelmsford inscribed 'Hitler's coffin - very urgent'.

Wednesday 14th October 1942

AT LAST - A FULL SCALE INVASION EXERCISE

OPERATION ADON TAKES PLACE

Chelmsford's long awaited invasion exercise, code named 'Adon', was held over two years after the greatest threat of an invasion!

The enemy, represented by units of the Essex Regiment, was said to have made seaborne landings around Clacton and Walton and was to attack Chelmsford enroute for London.

Overnight, the attacking forces were imagined to have conducted a heavy bombardment of the town, destroying all water main supplies, blocking several main roads, and destroying ambulances and mortuary vans. Neither defenders nor attackers were said to have established air superiority. With the scenario set up the exercise began in earnest with an early morning dive bombing raid by the invading forces, represented by R.A.F. aircraft.

Once the raid had finished the attackers entered the northern and eastern outskirts of Chelmsford and were engaged by the defending units of the 6th Battalion Essex Home Guard, who fought 'gallant delaying actions'. A second aerial attack was then made in which one dive bomber 'crashed' onto the roof of Messers Luckin-Smith's grocery shop no. 76 High Street.

The aircraft was in fact a model with reality created through the ingenious use of thunderflashes and B.B.C. sound effects recorded during the London Blitz! Two of its crew were 'killed' whilst the 'pilot' was captured by the Home Guard. Rest centres were opened and people played the part of casualties.

Sunday 18th October 1942

THE LUFTWAFFE PAYS HOFFMANN'S ANOTHER VISIT

4 WORKERS KILLED, 6 SERIOUSLY INJURED, 59 OTHERS HURT

FIVE OTHERS KILLED BY STRAY BOMB IN HENRY ROAD

THE PREVIOUS DAY had seen an exercise in which Chelmsford had suffered an imaginary air raid. Today a lone enemy aircraft made a very real attack on the town, with Hoffmann's bombed once again, exactly three months to the day after the previous attack. on the factory.

Throughout the morning around thirty German bombers had mounted missions on targets all over East Anglia. At 10.59 a.m. one of these aircraft, thought to have been a lone Dornier Do 217E, approached Chelmsford from the east at an altitude of around a thousand feet.

Low level attack

Taking advantage of low cloud and poor visibility, typical of a misty autumn morning, the aircraft dropped to around a 150 feet to make a bombing run on Hoffmann's approximately along the line of one of the factory's railway sidings.

Almost immediately Hoffmann's light machine defences opened up on the raider, but other army posts were unable to fire their Bofors guns at the aircraft because of its extremely low altitude - the gunners would have been firing in the direction of nearby buildings and people.

The Dornier was able to release two 500 Kg SC high explosive bombs on the works, with delayed actions of about twenty seconds, and machine gun the ground. With its bombs released the aircraft turned north-eastwards, circled to the north of Chelmsford and made off due east towards the coast, apparently unscathed. Those on the ground were not so fortunate.

Bomb hits works

One of the bombs scored a direct hit on the factory. It penetrated the roof and exploded in the recently completed Cage & Assembly Shop, (part of Hoffmann's 'C factory', to the north of Rectory Lane).

The other bomb deflected off the factory's roof and exploded amongst houses in neighbouring Henry Road. Four people died as a result of the bomb at Hoffmann's and another five were killed at Henry Road. Dozens more were injured.

The Hoffmann's bomb entered the factory through the roof of the Turret Shop at a very flat trajectory. The building was of single storey construction, steel framed, with north lights, covered on both slopes with polite and sheeted out with an inner lining of board for heat conservation. Having penetrated the roof the bomb struck two RSJs, severing them from RSJ stanchions at one end, bent them and then travelled through the brick wall dividing

the Cage and Turret Shops. It then passed over internal air raid shelter 9c and exploded on the concrete floor in the centre of the Cage and Assembly Shop, level with the 11th of the 17 parallel bays from the Rectory Lane end of the Shop. Detonation was after a delayed action of about twenty seconds, the explosion leaving a crater some fourteen feet across by six feet deep, filled with debris.

Extensive damage

The blast destroyed practically all of the Shop's roof, some 20,000 square feet's worth, and further disrupted a large area of the Turret Shop's roof. Considerable damage was inflicted on the building's steelwork, but fortunately none collapsed.

The brick wall which divided the two Shops considerably relieved the blast effect on the roof of the Turret Shop. Stanchions and RSJs were perforated and bent, and around 150 feet of the outside western wall of the Cage and Assembly Shop was demolished. This ran parallel and immediately behind the gardens of houses on the eastern side of Henry Road.

Two timber offices, which stood above internal air raid shelters 26c and 27c, were set ablaze and demolished after being set alight by hot fragments from the bomb. Several other small fires which broke out amongst the debris of timber, paper and clothing were promptly tackled by Hoffmann's Fire Brigade. All the fires were put out within ten minutes using some thirty to forty soda-acid extinguishers. The N.F.S. stood by but their services were not required.

The Cage and Assembly Shop was where the cages for ball bearings were manufactured, and where the ball bearings' constituent components were brought together from the factory's various departments for assembly. The Shop had chiefly contained considerable stocks of finished and part-assembled bearings, bullet cores and projectile points. Those bearings which escaped damage during the raid were ruined afterwards by rain that fell through the roof and from water used to fight the fires. Fortunately the nearest machine to the explosion was over sixty feet away, and as a result only eight of them were damaged. Hoffmann's staff were able to repair all of those within a month.

Production badly affected

The explosion rendered the Cage & Assembly Shop out of action and consequently this led to a serious disorganisation in production. As a temporary measure the damaged roof was cov-

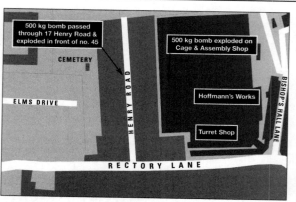

500 kg bomb passed through 17 Henry Road & exploded in front of no. 45

CEMETERY

500 kg bomb exploded on Cage & Assembly Shop

HENRY ROAD

Hoffmann's Works

ELMS DRIVE

Turret Shop

BISHOP'S HALL LANE

RECTORY LANE

Sketch map showing Henry Road and the Hoffmann's works which were bombed in a daring daylight raid on 19th October 1942, exactly three months after an almost identical raid on the works. (Author)

ered in tarpaulins whilst clearing up operations were begun, but it was not until around 2nd November that the output of finished bearings could be restarted. On 7th November production was to reach 25% of normal with full production expected at the end of

November.

Damage in the neighbouring Turret Shop had been minimised by the brick wall that divided it from the Cage & Assembly Shop. Only two machines were affected and they were subsequently repaired and back in action by

mid January 1943. Production was not too seriously reduced in the Turret Shop and by 9th December it was to return to 98% of normal.

The bombing was later calculated to have resulted in the loss of production of around one and a half million bearings or six weeks production at the factory. This was a huge amount, roughly equivalent to the combined output for two weeks of all the bearings factories in the country. - all from a single bomb! The financial loss to the company was estimated to be £13,000 in loss of machinery and plant and another £45,000 for work in progress.

Structural repairs to the factory were carried out speedily and were completed by the start of January 1943.

HOFFMANN'S CASUALTIES: FOUR MEN KILLED

THE HOFFMANN'S bomb resulted in the deaths of four men, with a further six seriously injured, and 43 men and 16 women slightly hurt.

Three local men killed

Of the four men killed as a result of the bombing only one died at the scene, having been caught by the blast outside a shelter.

He was 35 year-old Albert Radley, the son of Alfred and Annie Radley of 7 Steamer Terrace, and married to Ivy Radley of 72 Brownings Avenue. He had worked in the factory for more than twenty years, and as well as being an civil defence worker he was one of the longest serving members (since 1929) of the Chelmsford branch of the St. John's Ambulance Brigade. He was the leader at their Westfield Depot and a first aid party leader at Hoffmann's. Mr. Radley was buried at the Borough Cemetery on 24th October, following a service at All Saints' Church in King's Road.

Edward Charles Miller, aged 41 and a foreman at the factory, received serious shrapnel injuries as he stood at the entrance to one of the air raid shelters. Despite being rushed to the Chelmsford and Essex Hospital he was to die there seven days later. He was married to Mrs. M.K. Miller of 8 West Avenue with a young son. Mr. Miller had spent all his life in Chelmsford and had worked at Hoffmann's for nearly a quarter

of a century. His funeral was held at All Saints' Church in King's Road, followed by interment at the Borough Cemetery on 31st October.

Another victim, believed to have been caught in the open, was 64 year-old Frederick Walter Birt who lived almost opposite Edward Miller at 13 West Avenue. He is thought to have been buried under rubble and was to die two days after the bombing at the Chelmsford & Essex Hospital. He was married to Anne Birt with two sons, One of them, Cpl. W.H. Birt R.A.S.C. was a p.o.w. in German hands. Mr. Birt was a native of Martlesham in Suffolk but had lived in Chelmsford some 22 years. His funeral was also held at All Saints' Church in King's Road, on 27th October with burial afterwards at the Borough Cemetery.

Roof worker killed

The final victim at Hoffmann's was 28 year-old Denis Wyatt. He was one of a group of outside contractors from the Tentest Fibreboard Company who were working on the roof of the Cage & Assembly Shop when the bomb fell. He was seriously injured, along with two colleagues, and was to die the same day in the Chelmsford & Essex Hospital. He was the son of Mr. & Mrs. E. Wyatt of Streatham with a wife, Mrs. P.J. Wyatt, and young son living in East Dulwich. At the time of his death he was residing with his mother at 'Hartest Villa' in Beehive Lane, Galleywood. His

funeral was held at St. Michael's Church, Galleywood on 24th October. He is remembered on the village's war memorial there.

Excellent civil defence arrangements

Casualties would have been far higher but for the excellent civil defence arrangements at the factory.

At 10.57 a.m., two minutes before the bomb fell, roof spotters had given the take cover warning, and as a result the majority of employees had managed to make it to the air raid shelters. However, the bomb fell close to several of the shelters, and the 59 people slightly injured were occupants of four of them; shelters 9c, 26c, 27c and 19c. Shelter 9c, which stood forty feet east of the bomb, adjacent to the dividing wall with the Turret Shop, was practically demolished by the explosion.

Miraculously its concrete roof slab was failed to fall onto its occupants despite the severe blast damage to its brick walls. Five of those seriously hurt were occupants of shelter 27c, which was only twenty feet south of the bomb, and on which the wooden offices stood. It suffered serious damage at its northern end. The other two shelters were less seriously affected. One man running towards them was said to have had his trousers torn off by the blast.

Hoffmann's Hit Again: Monday 19th October 1942

DEVASTATION IN HENRY ROAD

FIVE KILLED BY BOMB THAT BOUNCED OFF FACTORY ROOF AND PASSED THROUGH A HOUSE

Of the two bombs aimed at Hoffmann's the second, a 500 kg SC high explosive, deflected off the roof of the Cage & Assembly Shop at Hoffmann's and continued westwards over a back garden and into the rear of number 17 Henry Road.

The property was a two storey 'L' shaped terraced house, built in 1922 and stood on the eastern side of the road.

The bomb entered the house's back bedroom and in the process it demolished the room's side and back walls and window. It then passed into the middle bedroom, demolishing its window and external wall, before continuing through the bedroom floor and the ceiling of the rear downstairs room. From there it passed through the partition wall into the front downstairs room, where it struck the side of the property's Morrison shelter.

David Alan Westrip, a ten year-old boy, had just taken cover inside the shelter, whilst a man, believed to have been his father, David, was just about to get inside too. The latter was holding onto the Morrison's side curtain when it was struck with such force that the shelter and its occupants were carried though the front of the house at high speed.

In the process the front bay window and wall below it were completely torn out by the bomb and shelter, which then travelled some sixty feet across the road and into the front Garden of number 45 Henry Road. There the bomb finally detonated and the shelter was hurled back towards number 17 by the explosion. Its frame finished up twisted and mangled in the road, whilst its top plate was flung up into the front bedroom of number 17.

David Westrip (junior) was left lying in the road with severe injuries to his legs which were badly crushed and broken. The man with him had a remarkable escape. He had been clinging onto the Morrison's side curtain and had felt the curious sensation of flying through the air. After the explosion which rendered him unconscious he awoke to find himself among the wreckage of the houses on the west side of the road, and managed to get up suffering only from a cut on his back and bruises. Realising that he was not seriously hurt, he went to the aid of the boy who was then rushed to the Chelmsford & Essex Hospital.

Despite the valiant efforts of surgeons, who amputated both his legs, David Westrip was to die later in the day. He was the only child of David and Florence Westrip, formerly of 42 Longfield Road in Great Baddow, and a member of the 3rd Chelmsford Boys Brigade. He was a pupil at Trinity Road School and was buried at the Borough Cemetery on 24th October.

The bomb's detonation in the front garden of number 45 caused widespread destruction. Five houses were demolished outright (numbers 42 to 46), another nine were damaged beyond repair, a further six were seriously damaged and dozens more slightly so.

There was a human cost too. In addition to David Westrip a further four people lost there lives as a result of the bomb, with two others seriously injured and two slightly.

At 45 Henry Road, immediately outside of which the bomb exploded, one person was killed. He was 25 year-old Andrew Fenwick Menzies, and is thought to have been a war worker lodging there with Cyril Joslin. Mr. Menzies was the son of Mr. & Mrs. James Menzies of Hallyards, Meigle in Perthshire. He was subsequently buried in his home village on 24th October.

Next door at number 44 Elizabeth Locke was killed, having been buried in the wreckage of her home. She was a 57 year-old widow. Her husband Cpl. H. Locke of the Grenadier Guards had been killed in the First World War. Her funeral was later held at the Borough Cemetery on 23rd October.

Their 25 year-old son Dennis Wilfred Locke was also caught in the explosion and was to succumb to his injuries in a Braintree hospital on 29th October. Due to ill health he had been unable to work for the previous five years, having formerly been employed at Marconi's. His funeral was held on 3rd November.

The remaining fatality was 28 year-old May Ellen Wrenn, who was killed at the back of her home, number 43 Henry Road. She was the daughter of Charles and Ellen Smith of Bailey's Farm in Mashbury and was married to Robert Wrenn, a Hoffmann employee. Her eight year-old son Bernard was buried in the rubble with his mother but her body shielded him from much of the debris. He was nevertheless badly injured and was to spend the next couple of months in hospital recovering from his injuries. Mrs. Wrenn, who was pregnant when killed, was later buried at the Borough Cemetery on 24th October.

The death toll at Henry Road would have been higher, save for the speed, skill and courage of the civil defence staff, aided by a platoon of soldiers who had been passing along Rectory Lane when the bombs fell. Many residents had once again been saved from serious injury by their Morrison and surface air raid shelters. Among those reported injured in the incidents were Harry E.A. Chaplin, Ernest Lodge, Florence Locke, George Farnsworth, Stella Whitley, William Cousins, Albert Herbert, and Claude Edgar-White.

The North Avenue Congregational Church was opened as a rest centre for the bombed out and homeless during the afternoon, and was to remain so until noon the following day, by which time all the homeless would be billeted out.

Early visitors to the devastation were once again the Mayor and his wife.

EYEWITNESS ACCOUNTS: HOFFMANN'S RAID

"Our foreman, Ted Miller, was stood by the entrance to our shelter and saw all of us inside safely when the bomb struck.....Poor old Ted was hit by the shrapnel and died afterwards."

As told to our our Special Correspondent

"I was at work in Hoffmann's when the take cover warning sounded, so we all went down into the shelters, and we were there when the bombs were dropped on the factory.

Later I heard that a friend of mine, Bill Richardson, who was only about 14, had been pulling a truck load of wheels, around Hoffmann's when the German bomber appeared. Like any sensible person as soon as he'd heard the plane he let go of the truck and the whole thing tipped over and broke a load of the wheels, which were components for our aircraft.

Afterwards the governor had him in his office and gave him a right telling off, saying that because he'd broken the wheels all our Spitfires wouldn't be able to fly and that he'd gone and lost the war for us. Poor old Bill believed it all and he was in tears.

Workers at the factory weren't happy after the raid about the defences and that's when they began to demand barrage balloons for the town."

Gerald Carter

"I was a pupil at the grammar school and on this occasion we were up in the old hall, listening to a rehearsal of a Shakespeare play. The hall was in semi-darkness with the blue roller blinds down over the windows and only the stage lit for the production. The character on stage playing Falstaff (with a pillow stuffed up his jumper) had just quoted the immortal words I am as strong as a lion' when the alarm bell rang, denoting that there was an immediate emergency. He and everyone else rapidly dropped to the floor for cover.

I was at the back of the hall, where I could play the fool without being seen. I was sat on the floor, leaning next to the grand piano. With my instinct for self preservation I slid under the piano for shelter though unfortunately for me in the rush a chap called 'Gorky' Sylvester, the big drummer in the band, the tallest boy at the school and wearer of hobnail boots, slid from his place on the piano and put his foot in my face. It was a rather painful experience to say the least!

We'd hardly hit the floor when a stick of bombs were dropped on Hoffmann's and Henry Road, less than a quarter of a mile away. I remember as the bombs fell we heard them whistle, then explode and a few seconds later the blinds wafted out with effects of the blast. Once the aircraft had gone we all got up again and continued the rehearsal.

We had a fairly good idea where the bombs had landed and the conjecture was that it was Hoffmann's. Confirmation of this soon filtered through the school grapevine and afterwards I went to try and have a look. I cycled down to Rectory Lane and looked up into Henry Road which had been closed off to the public. There was wreckage and debris all over the road and a lot of dust - it looked horrific."

Ray Knappett

"I was at work in a recently-built part of Hoffmann's when a lone raider approached. As there had been no air raid warning we had not gone in the shelters, but fortunately the soldiers who were on guard at the factory heard the plane coming so they gave the take cover warning. Afterwards we heard that the soldiers were reprimanded for giving us the warning without word from Colchester, which was what they were supposed to do!

They saved our lives because most of us managed to make it to the shelters that had been built inside the factory. Our foreman, Ted Miller, was stood by the entrance to our shelter and saw all of us inside safely when the bomb struck. The explosion brought the roof down and blasted shrapnel and debris everywhere.

Poor old Ted was hit by the shrapnel and died afterwards. After the bomb had gone off there was some panic as none us knew what to do and there was no-one to tell us what to do. I was with a girl who had two sisters working in other parts of Hoffmann's so I went out of the shelter with her to look for them and check they were alright.

As we were making our way through the debris someone shouted 'He's coming back again, take cover!'. There was no way that we could go back to the shelters so we kept going, but luckily it was a false alarm. As we made our way out I remember passing a huge tank full of a spirit used for washing the ball-bearings. I remember thinking 'Supposing that catches fire!'. After we'd got out of the factory we were in a bit of a daze with the shock of it all and wandered off into town."

Mary Bateman

"I was aged eight and I lived with my mother and father at 43 Henry Road. On the morning of that particular raid I was at school at the Victoria School in Church Street, just behind the Cathedral. When the air raid siren went, my mother, who had been shopping in Chelmsford, came to the school and picked me up. Parents were allowed to take their children home during alerts as our school had no air raid shelters.

First of all we went to my grandmother's house in Railway Street, where my mother collected her shopping which she had left there earlier. We didn't stay long as my mother was expecting her sister, Ivy, at our house that morning, so we walked home to Henry Road. In the event aunt Ivy missed her bus from Brentwood and was an hour late into Chelmsford. As things turned out that delay probably saved her life.

When we reached home we went into the house and dropped the shopping off. Then we went out the back door and were going to head for a neighbour's, two or three doors away towards Rectory Lane, to use an underground shelter in their back garden that they'd built themselves. We'd always gone down there as it had seemed safer that our brick surface shelter which stood in our back garden.

Just as we got outside our back door a bomb must have exploded at the front of numbers 44 or 45 Henry Road. The strange thing was that I never heard any sound of the explosion.

Our house was demolished and my mother and I were buried under tons of debris. What has always stayed in my mind is seeing the single German bomber going away from me, climbing to the west right above the tower of the Church Cemetery Chapel which stood directly behind our garden. I don't remember the debris falling on me or feeling any pain. The next thing that I can recall is looking up, with dust in my eyes, and seeing daylight, I suppose as the rescuers had managed to uncover me. Then it went dark again as more rubble covered me again.

Eventually they got me out, though I don't remember anything else happening until I came round in a lighted room at the Chelmsford & Essex Hospital where I had been taken. I had serious injuries to both legs, my left arm and my head, and as a result of the bombing

I lost all the memories of my childhood up to that day. My father, who had been working in Hoffmann's when the raid happened had known nothing of our house being hit until he had come home for dinner. He used to visit me in hospital during the evenings and was the only father that they let into the ward.

I was in hospital until around Christmas 1942. The night before I came out my father revealed to me that my mother had been killed in the raid. Her body had lain over me in the rubble and had saved me from more serious injury or even death. According to my grandmother my mother's body didn't have a mark on it.

Afterwards my father told me more about what had happened after the bombing. Practically all our possessions had been destroyed in the house and just about the only thing left standing had been our own air raid shelter which we used to store things in. Sadly most of what was in there and had escaped damage by the bomb was stolen that morning - thieves took a bicycle, a kiddie's push car and all my father's fishing tackle. My father told me that our neighbour at number 44, Dennis Locke who was an invalid, had been found at the top of his garden still in his bed where it had been blasted.

He seemed to have escaped without a scratch, but kept asking for his mother who looked after him. He died once he heard that she had been killed. I got on well with Dennis. He was very good with his hands and had built me a magnificent fort which my friends and I used to play with. That was destroyed in the bombing, but while I was in hospital my friends at school saved their money and bought me a new toy fort with aeroplanes and soldiers.

It was put on display in Spalding's shop window in the High Street and I was given it when I came out of hospital. The Essex Chronicle and the Evening Standard wrote about me and took photographs of the fort. One lady, whose son had been killed in a raid, saw the articles in the newspapers and arranged to meet me. She had wanted her boy's toys to go to a good home so she gave them to me.

After leaving hospital I went to live with my mother's parents at Bailey's Farm in Mashbury. It was a year or more before I was able to start school again, and in the meantime my aunt would push me around the village in a wheelchair. I've stayed at the farm ever since.

On the anniversary of the bombing in October 1992 I thought to myself that's fifty years I might never have had."

Bernard Wrenn

SCHOOL MEALS INTRODUCED

THE DAY SAW the introduction of school meals for the first time at several of Chelmsford's elementary schools.

Efforts in Chelmsford to provide school meals can be traced back to January 1942 when the Chief Education Officer informed a meeting of the Council that a recent Board of Education circular had attached the highest importance to the provision of school meals - primarily out of the necessity to maintain a high standard of nutrition for children with many mothers now having to take up war work.

After much discussion on the matter the Council appointed a new ten man committee to investigate the matter and it agreed to carry out a census of parents to ascertain the likely demand for school meals.

Two months later, in March 1942, the Council meeting received a deputation consisting of Mrs. Norton, Mrs. Roberts, Mr. & Mrs. Whitehead and Mrs. Slade, who were campaigning for the provision of both day nurseries and school meals in Chelmsford. The deputation argued that both measures would help to enable more women to take up war work and help those women already engaged in such work.

The Council was, however, able to point out to the deputation that progress had already been made. It was revealed that the census of the views of the parents of Chelmsford's 3,588 school children had now been completed. Some 3214 replies had been received of whom 982 said that they were in favour of midday school meals and that their children would regularly use the facility.

With that in mind the Council voted to go ahead with the provision of school meals along the basis of a scheme which had been drawn up by the Borough Engineer. It proposed that the meals would be cooked at a Ministry of Food cooking depot at The Retreat in Witham and then delivered to all the Borough's schools except St. Peter's, Victoria Mixed & Infants and Friars Schools where demand was too small. Incidentally the cooking centre had originally been established for emergency use in the event of a heavy blitz on Chelmsford.

On 29th July 1942, at the monthly Council meeting, the Chief Education Officer reported that Government's Board of Education approval had been received for the Council's arrangements for school meals. Over the summer the cooking centre was equipped and staff recruited, and on 19th October 1942 after much debate the

Council finally agreed to fix the price of school meals at five pence each with the scheme to begin a week later.

Initially around 990 meals were served each day to children at the Council's schools. However, by the following summer a combination of complaints over the quality and quantity of the meals and late deliveries of the food from Witham led to a decline to around 630 meals per day, somewhat less than the Board of Education's target of meals for 75% of Chelmsford's 3,200 school children. The Board of Education was aware of the deficiencies in the service and draughted new legislation calling for an expansion and improvement in the standard of school meals throughout the country. It could now supply, erect and equip complete kitchens and canteens for schools free of charge if requested to do so by local authorities.

In July 1943 the Council discussed the implications of this at some length and then instructed the Chief Education Officer to apply to the Board of Education for the provision of; one central kitchen and dining hall to provide 1,000 meals per day at the Moulsham Schools; one kitchen and dining room at Rainsford Senior School to provide 1,000 meals per day for pupils at the school and King's Road School; one canteen kitchen to provide 150 meals per day at the Trinity Road School; and one canteen kitchen to provide 150 meals per day at the Catholic School.

There were no further developments on the matter until December 1943 when the Chief Education Officer told the Council that an inspector sent to assess the Council's proposals had intimated that the Board of Education would initially approve plans for the provision of 1,000 meals per day in Chelmsford. The Council discussed the offer and agreed to establish one 500 meal kitchen on a site at Moulsham Senior School to the west of the boy's school, to serve all departments at the Moulsham Schools; and another on a portion of King's Road Playing Field adjoining Dixon Avenue, then under military occupation, to serve the King's Road and Rainsford Senior Schools. Board of Education approval for the plans was subsequently received by May and July 1944 respectively.

However, when the Board gave its approval to the King's Road kitchen it warned that construction work was likely to be delayed by the transfer of labour and materials to areas that were affected by the V-1 attacks. This prediction was to prove accurate and it was not until the end of the war that the canteens were finally established.

Monday 26th October 1942

BARRAGE BALLOONS ARRIVE TO PROTECT CHELMSFORD

DESIGNED TO PREVENT REPETITION OF HOFFMANN RAIDS

The day saw R.A.F. Fighter Command request a reconnaissance to be made of Chelmsford for the location of possible barrage balloon sites. Number 30 (Barrage Balloon) Group R.A.F. subsequently ordered two of its officers to visit the town to carry out the work.

The matter was treated with some urgency and at noon on the 30th October 1942 Squadron Leader L.P. Bonnet arrived in Chelmsford and set about the task of identifying potential barrage balloon sites. He was joined the next day by Squadron Leader A. Blande D.S.O. who dealt with details regarding the administration and accommodation. Their assignment was completed on 4th November and a report sent to their superiors.

The report described the Luftwaffe's usual method of attack on the Chelmsford's main targets, Marconi's and Hoffmann's. Raiding aircraft would approach the town from the north-east, follow the railway line at about three hundred feet in a south-westerly direction before swerving off and dropping to make a final bombing run on the factories.

The commander of the 37 A.A. Brigade, which was responsible for Chelmsford's anti-aircraft defences, had explained that the usual very low altitude of the enemy aircraft meant that most of the local light anti-aircraft guns, mounted high on buildings in the town, could not be used against the raiders - that would require the guns to fire downwards and towards other buildings and people. In effect there was at that time no defence against determined low-level raiders.

The Squadron Leaders recommended that three flights of ten, ten and eleven balloons should be used to prevent such low-level attacks on Chelmsford. The necessary 31 sites for the balloons and additional H.Q. sites had been identified without too many problems. Chelmsford town centre was reported as having more potential locations than was customary in similar towns that they had visited., Accommodation was to prove a greater problem and all the balloonists would have to billet in tents or caravans, though

these were eventually replaced by Nissen huts. Operational instructions would come via R.A.F. North Weald from Number 11 Fighter Group. Hydrogen for the balloons was to be obtained from the top secret plant at Chelmsford Gas Works, and any balloon repairs were to be undertaken by R.A.F. Felixstowe. Work on the Squadron's vehicles would be carried out at the R.E.M.E. workshops in Broomfield Road.

The R.A.F.s Number 30 (Barrage Balloon) Group quickly adopted the Squadron Leaders' proposals; Number 993 (Barrage Balloon) Squadron, which had been assembled at Horsham St. Faith Aerodrome in Norfolk just six months earlier, was directed to Chelmsford to form the barrage. The Ipswich barrage was ordered to be non-operational at 2 p.m. on 3rd November. Subsequently the first balloonists arrived in Chelmsford at 11.30 a.m. on 4th November. The first balloon was inflated within three hours of that, and at 9.50 p.m. that evening all thirty one sites were in operation. The barrage was code named 'Bertie'.

The Squadron's H.Q. was soon established at 'The Priory' in Writtle with additional accommodation nearby at 'Ratcliffs' in The Green. Each of the three Flights also had their own H.Q.s in Chelmsford.

The balloon barrage provided an effective deterrent to the Luftwaffe's low-level raids on Chelmsford until the end of January 1944 when Number 993 Squadron left the town to be deployed as part of the preparations for the Normandy invasion. On its removal from Chelmsford the Squadron consisted of 16 officers and 388 other ranks.

The Barrage Balloons were initially deployed as followed:

SITE 1   Waste ground on the west side of the southern end of Waterhouse Street.
SITE 2   South corner of field off Rainsford Lane immediately north of Site 14.
SITE 3   Grass plot just behind 23 Ash Tree Crescent.
SITE 4   Grass space immediately west of railway viaduct & south of River Can.
SITE 5   North-east corner of field west of Rainsford Lane, opposite number 79.

SITE 6   East corner of Admiral's Park.
SITE 7   East end of K.E.G.S. playing field opposite junction of Rectory Lane.
SITE 8   Plot of land north of Corporation Road between numbers 54 and 63.
SITE 9   South-east corner of football ground opposite 161 Broomfield Road.
SITE 10   Vacant site on north side of Second Avenue, opposite number 74.
SITE 11   Garden plot 130 yards north of Bishop's Hall Mill.
SITE 12   West side of field east of Arbour Lane.
SITE 13   Railway side of field north of Springfield Green, opposite Whittles Hall Farm.
SITE 14   150 yards down west side of field off Arbour Lane, next to 10 Upper Arbour Lane.
SITE 15   Bomb site next to number 80 Marconi Road.
SITE 16   Grass space between railway lines, immediately west of Cramphorn's building in Goods Yard.
SITE 17   Centre of field south of railway and west of Arbour Lane.
SITE 18   North-east corner of Driver's ironyard in Victoria Road.
SITE 19   Open space north side of Duke Street, opposite number 67.
SITE 20   Grass plot at west end of Swimming baths.
SITE 21   Small paddock in grounds of Tower House.
SITE 22   North-west corner of Recreation Ground between Park Road & railway.
SITE 23   South-east corner of car park between cattle market and River Can.
SITE 24   Land at the end of Brockley Road.
SITE 25   Ritz (Odeon) Car Park in Baddow Road.
SITE 26   Piece of land 100 yards north of New Writtle Street, opposite Anchor House.
SITE 27   Plot of land south and behind Lower Anchor Street, opposite Queen's Head P.H.
SITE 28   Plot of rough grassland in Moulsham Drive, opposite St. John's Road.
SITE 29   Crompton's social hall.
SITE 30   North end Oaklands Park, opposite Hillside Stores.
SITE 31   North-west corner of field at the junction of railway and Moulsham Street.

Thursday 29th October 1942

COUPLE IN SUICIDE PACT

At a house in Lyme Street, near St. Pancras in London, a landlady discovered the bodies of a Chelmsford couple lying side by side in bed, having been poisoned by the gas fire in their rented room.

They were Aircraftsman Frederick K. Reed, aged 29, married and a former Chelmsford bus driver, and 36 year-old Edith Gasiorowski. The inquest into

their deaths was to conclude that they had taken their own lives whilst the balance of their minds had been disturbed. The couple had become close companions whilst working together at Eastern National and had begun renting the room in June 1942 under the false names, Mr. & Mrs. Evans. The day before their deaths they had apparently made a trial attempt at poisoning themselves using the coal gas fire.

Monday 30th November 1942

CLEANER DISCOVERS MOTHER AND TWO CHILDREN MURDERED IN GALLEYWOOD ROAD HOME

WHEN MRS. IRENE WHIPPS of Moulsham Drive arrived to clean at 148 Galleywood Road (later re-numbered after the war) she discovered that the four occupants were dead.

They were Stanley Worrell, aged 42, his wife Doris, aged 40, and their children Michael, aged eleven and Diana, aged seven. A

note was found addressed to the coroner and another to a friend of Mr. Worrell's, Mr. E. Alston. Subsequent police investigations were to reveal that Mr. Worrell, a £800 a year chemistry teacher and head of the junior department at the Mid Essex Technical College, had been in financial difficulties and, following a meeting with the college's governors, was facing dismissal on account of

£75 of college money found in his possession. At the inquest into the family's deaths it was concluded that Mr. Worrell had knocked out his wife, a teacher at the Moulsham Schools, with a blow to the jaw, chloroformed his children and then killed all three and himself with potassium cyanide. They were later buried at the Borough Cemetery on 17th November.

Wednesday 11th November 1942

EYEWITNESS ACCOUNTS:
BARRAGE BALLOONS

"He'd never seen anything like it. 'is it always like this?' he asked."

As told to our our Special Correspondent

"I was working at Hoffmann's at the time, but those of us in the Air Training Corps were given the day off to help show the barrage balloonists to their various sites in Chelmsford.

We were taken by coach up to Hatfield Peverel where we met the convoy of lorries with their barrage balloons on the back. Each member of the A.T.C. was assigned a different lorry to direct, so we climbed in the cabs with the drivers to show them the way. I had to take mine down Bishop's Hall Lane to a site by the allotments behind Hoffmann's.

We reached New Street around midday and of course all the Hoffmann workers were pouring out for lunch. Most of them were on bikes and they used to fill up the whole street and tear down it like bats out of hell.

The driver had to stop the lorry to let them all pass. He'd never seen anything like it. 'Is it always like this?' he asked me. It was a good day for me because as soon as we were done I got the rest of the day off."

Gerald Carter

"Chelmsford had a ring of barrage balloons. Normally they were kept at about a hundred feet up but when the siren went they were immediately put up quite high.

At Hoffmann's where I worked there were one or two of them in the grounds, including one near the old house on the island in the River Chelmer to the north of the main factory buildings. The crews were stationed there permanently so we got to know them quite well.

When there were thunderstorms it was quite exciting because if the crews didn't lower them quickly enough the barrage balloons used to get struck by lightning. They'd explode and come down in flames.

I used to think that the barrage balloons just attracted the German planes because they knew that the military would only place them at important targets."

George Brown.

BOYS CLUB HAS SALVAGED 761 TONS OF PAPER

The Essex Chronicle reported that the Chelmsford Boys' Club had recently produced its annual report which had revealed that in the past year it had salvaged 761 tons of paper, up from 636 tons the previous year.

Of that 223 tons had come via the Council and the rest collected door-to-door or from the Boys' Club depot. Since the outbreak of the war the club had salvaged 2,111 tons of paper. In recent weeks the Club had provided emergency sleeping accommodation for up to 20 American servicemen per night at its premises.

The paper also reported that Chelmsford was suffering from an acute shortage of bicycle lamp batteries. Their scarcity was due to a heavy demand by the military.

Friday 27th November 1942

RECREATION GROUND: EXPLOSION KILLS TWO SOLDIERS AND A LOCAL BUILDER

Involved in preparing Home Guard Rocket site

SHORTLY BEFORE 11 a.m. an explosion at the Recreation Ground killed two soldiers and one civilian man, and injured another five who were carrying out construction work in connection with the establishment of the new Home Guard Rocket Battery.

Afterwards it would emerge that the explosion occurred when the men discovered a pieced of galvanised iron tubing, eight to ten feet long and two and a half inches in diameter, lying amongst weeds beneath a nearby broken wall. The tubing, which bore no distinguishing marks, appeared to the men to be an old water pipe with one end sealed with wax and the other with a wooden plug. A pipe was required through which cables could be threaded and the tubing seemed to be the perfect for the job. One of the soldiers cleared the wax away with a penknife and a brown substance, said to resemble a bread roll, fell out. An attempt to force the cables through the pipe failed and as a second attempt was made the pipe suddenly exploded. 23 year-old Driver Walter James Wilkinson from Ealing and 62

year-old clerk of the works Robert Gladstone Moore of 'Louiseville' in Baddow Road were killed outright by the blast. A large piece of human flesh was blown 200 yards to the north and descended onto barrage balloon site 22 in the north-west corner of the Recreation Ground. This grisly object was later removed by personnel from the Rocket site. A third man, Sgt. Robert Henry Orris, aged 21 from Gillingham, was rushed to hospital but he died a few hours later from his injuries. Those injured included C.S.M. Alfred Batchelor, aged 46, of Sutton., L/cpl. Robert Price, aged 21, and 31 year-old Signaller Christopher Slennett of Walthamstow.

At the subsequent inquest verdicts of accidental death were recorded for all three men. The inquest also revealed that the innocent looking piece of tubing which had exploded had in fact been a makeshift weapon known as a 'Bosche Bump' similar to that which had claimed the lives of five people in Ramsden Heath at the end of October 1942. During the invasion scare of 1940 thousands of the devices, packed with

gelignite, had been hurriedly made ready for use against the invading Germans. In May 1941 the War Office had ordered their withdrawal and most were dumped into the North Sea. However, not all had been collected and some had remained in Home Guard and army stores, not clearly marked and easily mistaken for scaffold poles. The coroner was scathing in his criticism of the army's laxity and told the inquest that he would bring the matter to the attention of Chelmsford's M.P forthwith in order that strong representations could be made by him to the army to ensure that there was no repetition of the incident.

Mr. Moore, the civilian killed by the explosion, was married with one son. He was well known in the local building trade and was a brother to Maurice, the Moore in Messers Trigg and Moore of Baddow Road. In his younger days he had played football for Chelmsford Swifts and was a keen angler. His funeral service was held on 17th December, with a service at Baddow Road Congregational Church preceding burial at St Mary's, Great Baddow.

Friday 11th December 1942

'PSYCHIC' WOMAN FINED £10 AFTER PREDICTING THAT WORKS WOULD BE BOMBED

PREDICTION LED TO ABSENTEEISM

A fifty year-old woman appeared at the Chelmsford Petty Sessions and pleaded guilty 'to publishing statements likely to cause alarm and for doing an act likely to interfere with the performance of essential services'.

She was fined £10 with £1/4/6 costs and was told that only her excellent character had saved her from going to prison. The court heard that during September 1942 four young factory girls from one of Chelmsford big firms had visited the woman who was regarded locally as a clairvoyant and fortune teller. She told the girls that the factory would be bombed between 1.45 and 2 a.m. one night in October 1942, though the girls would be unharmed. The prediction was repeated at another meeting on 7th October and as a result a rumour spread around the factory that it would be bombed imminently. The works manager, Thomas Hughes, told the court that as a result of the scare absenteeism had increased and production of vital war supplies had been affected.

Friday 11th December 1942

OUTLOOK ENCOURAGING SAYS CHELMSFORD'S M.P.

BUT HARDER TIMES AHEAD

IN HIS REVIEW of the year, published in the Essex Chronicle, Col. John Macnamara M.P., reported that although the outlook was encouraging, there were still harder times ahead and that the difficult task of defeating the Germans still remained.

He praised the recently published Beveridge Report on social

security and looked ahead to post-war Britain when he hoped that people would no longer fear old age, bad health or unemployment. He wrote 'Never again do we wish to witness this wicked spectacle of people idle through no fault of their own'. Locally it was rumoured that Col. Macnamara had impressed the Prime Minister in the House of Commons and was set to be given a new military command.

Friday 18th December 1942

ONE THOUSANDTH BABY BORN AT DANBURY PARK

Gifts from the Queen

IN THE BALLROOM at Danbury Park the Bishop of Chelmsford christened the thousandth baby to be born at the wartime maternity hospital which had opened on the opening day of the war.

The baby was Elizabeth Taffs, the daughter of Violet and L.A.C. Arthur Taffs R.A.F. of Brentwood. A letter of congratulation and gifts including two nightdresses, a blanket, a knitted coat, booties, socks, shoes, soap powder, coats, dresses and a dressing gown, sent by Queen Eliza-beth, was presented to the family. The baby was named Elizabeth after the Queen.

Sunday 31st January 1943

ROAD SIGNS REAPPEARING AROUND THE COUNTY

The Essex Chronicle reported that over recent weeks around fifty road signs had been re-erected in parts of Essex outside the Metropolitan Police area and in excess of twenty miles from the coast.

The work had been carried out by the County Council's Surveyor's Department in conjunction with the Ministry of Home Security and the Chief Constable. Signs throughout Essex had been removed during the summer of 1940 as a precaution to prevent them providing assistance to the expected invading German forces. Around Chelmsford six signs had already re-appeared, including one at Ash Tree Corner, Little Waltham, the junction of the A130 and A131.

Friday 12th February 1943

SPITFIRE HITS CHELMSFORD BARRAGE BALLOON CABLE

AT 12.50 AN unidentified Spitfire collided with the barrage balloon cable at site 10, at an altitude of 800 feet.

The aircraft was seen to make off in a south-easterly direction, gradually losing height. Its fate is unknown.

The collision followed a spate of incidents involving barrage balloon cables colliding with, and damaging, buildings all over Chelmsford in recent weeks.

Thursday 14th January 1943

BARRAGE BALLOONS SHOT UP BY RAIDER

At 10.57 p.m. a lone enemy aircraft dived from a considerable height over Chelmsford and fired about 20 rounds of cannon at the barrage balloons, which were at 4,500 feet, before rising rapidly and hurrying off under A.A. fire . The roof and guttering of 1 Burns Crescent was slightly damaged by the gunfire or shrapnel. Heavy A.A. fire was heard to the south-west of Chelmsford.

Wednesday 20th January 1943

ROCKET BATTERY NOW READY FOR BUSINESS

At the Recreation Ground the 211 (101 Essex Home Guard) Rocket A.A. Battery was operationally manned for the first time, some seven months after its establishment had been given the green light. The first men on duty were of Number 1 Relief, commanded by Captain E. Mead. The other seven reliefs were to follow in rotation.

Monday 1st February 1943

AMERICAN RED CROSS CLUB OPENS AT THE SARACEN'S HEAD

AT THE SARACEN'S HEAD Hotel the American Red Cross' American Club opened for the first time as a hostel for American servicemen.

In other parts of the country around 50 similar clubs, employing 5,000 English women, had already opened with another 25 set to do so soon. Since plans for the facility at the Saracen's Head had first been revealed in October 1942 over 150 women had volunteered to work there, many of whom were said to be young and good looking. Anglo-American relationships were obviously managing quite nicely!

Monday 22nd February 1943

A Near Miss: Wednesday 3rd March 1943

HEAVY RAID ATTEMPTED ON CHELMSFORD

Fortunately bombs fall mainly in rural areas
It could have been far worse

THE EVENING BROUGHT widespread bombing all over the Chelmsford district, reminiscent of the early Blitz period some two and a half years previously.

In the event a heavy A.A. defence and the town's barrage balloons prevented any bombs from hitting their targets in Chelmsford, with most of the bombs falling in rural areas around the town. No serious casualties were caused and damage was minor.

Around 35 German bombers crossed the English coast, intent on bombing London, though a number of them were briefed to attack the Chelmsford factories of Marconi's, Hoffmann's and Crompton's.

The siren sounds

The Chelmsford sirens sounded the alert at 8.12 p.m. and within three minutes the first enemy raider appeared at between 10,000 and 12,000 feet travelling westwards. It was followed by a steady stream of around ten aircraft which passed over at long intervals.

The bombing began at 8.30 p.m. when an H.E. was reported to have fallen harmlessly into a field east of Littley Park Farm near Ford End.

Around 9 p.m. three ABB 500 incendiary containers fell into a field immediately south of Lower Stock Road in West Hanningfield. One device exploded and burned out on impact and set a hedge alight. The other two burst on impact with no spread of incendiaries. Nearby in Stock an unexploded bomb fell into a field at Crondon Park to the north-west of the house, whilst around twenty SD2 'Butterfly' anti-personnel bombs, from an AB23 container, fell on King's Head Farm, Brook Farm and Greenacre Lane.

New Hall Hospital, Boreham targeted

About the same time the German bombers made a concerted attack on New Hall in Boreham, though fortunately most of the bombs fell to the north-west of their target. A total of six 50 kg Phosphorus bombs were dropped in the vicinity; three fell into fields to the south-west of Park Farm, Boreham, two fell into fields to the south-east of Hill Farm, Broomfield, and the other into a field south of Belstead Hall Farm, about 200 yards from a searchlight station. Two ABB 500 incendiary containers were dropped; one fell on Nabbott's Farm and burst on impact, but although the incendiaries ignited there was no spread; the other container was found by a warden close to Pratt's Farm Lane, Little Waltham. Approximately sixty 1 kg incendiaries from the latter fell in a line north-east to south-west, over an area of about a thousand square yards, consisting of fields to the northern side of New Hall and the grounds of the building. Thanks to the vigilance of staff at New Hall none of the incendiaries were able to cause serious damage. Two other unidentified bombs fell between Park Farm and Channels.

To the south-west, around 9 p.m. seven or eight flares were reported to have been seen to fall into a field 250 yards east of the G6 Wardens' Post at Loves Green.

South of Chelmsford

At 9.10 p.m. eight 50 kg H.E.s fell in a line running south and south-westwards for 400 yards from Park Lodge on the west side of Writtle Road in Margaretting. Two of the bombs fell in the garden of a bungalow and practically demolished it and severed overhead cables. One man suffered shock, two women received superficial cuts and a boy had cuts inflicted to his head. None of them was seriously hurt, though they were detained at St. John's Hospital for observation.

Park Lodge was slightly damaged by the blast from the third bomb, whilst the other five exploded in fields & ditches.

Five minutes later a further four 50 kg H.E.s fell nearby, into a field between Southwood Farm, Writtle and the south-western corner of Hylands Park. Each device made a shallow crater around ten feet across by three feet deep.

Around the same time a pair of 500 kg H.E.s fell near Buttsbury Church; one into a field between Buttsbury Hall Farm, Stock and the River Wid, leaving a crater 44 feet across by 7 feet deep, and the other into Fincham's Field, close to Stock Lane. The latter left a water-filled crater 42 feet across. A pair of ABB 500 incendiary containers fell nearby: one into the River Wid, just to the south of the bridge on the Ingatestone to Stock Road (exploded on impact with no spread), and the other in a field belonging to Buttsbury Hall Farm. Incendiaries, but no container, also fell further south in fields belonging to Elmbrook Farm. They failed to spread or ignite.

At 9.20 p.m. four 250 kg H.E.s fell in fields at Peatlands Farm in South Woodham Ferrers, whilst two 500 kg H.E.s fell nearby on Midford's Smallholding and Radford's Smallholding. Two cottages were damaged, along with overhead electric cables. Minutes later four 50 kg H.E.s fell harmlessly on Marsh Farm, South Woodham Ferrers, close to Clements Green Creek. A fifth bomb fell unexploded into the Creek. Further west, four 250 kg H.E.s, plus one which failed to explode, fell on Hayes Farm, Battlesbridge, between the River Crouch and Fenn Creek.

To the west

Meanwhile to the west of Chelmsford, between 9.20 p.m. and 9.30 p.m. a pair of 500 kg H.E.s fell 70 yards apart in a field at Colleybridge Farm near Radley Green. They left craters 31 feet across by 6 feet deep and 36 feet across by 5 feet deep and inflicted blast damage to buildings up to 150 yards away.

Around the same time an unclassified H.E. fell in the middle of the A414 to the north-west of Boyton Cross. Blast from the bomb slightly damaged Hill Farmhouse and telephone wires in the vicinity. The road would remain closed until repairs could be completed the next day. Meanwhile an ABB 500 incendiary container was dropped at 'Dukes' in Roxwell. The device opened in mid air and incendiaries fell scattered over an area 150 yards by 60 yards. Some farm buildings were set ablaze but the fires were soon extinguished by the Home Guard. Another ABB 500 incendiary container and an unclassified bomb fell at Bailey's Farm near Roxwell. The container burst on impact and spread incendiaries for about 60 yards. Around a 100 incendiaries fell at Chalk End Farm, where one haystack was destroyed. To the north, a pair of ABB 500 containers, each holding a hundred and twenty incendiaries, fell scattered on open ground, a mile long and one hundred yards wide, running west to east at Pipers Farm to the north of Good Easter. A small percentage which failed to ignite were taken to the farm for storage, pending their disposal by the authorities.

The all-clear was sounded by Chelmsford's sirens at 9.53 p.m.

Rocket Battery in action for first time

The raid saw the first firing in anger of the Recreation Ground based Home Guard Rocket Battery, manned on the occasion by number 6 relief. Although a passing enemy raider was engaged no hit was recorded and the Battery was plagued by a number of misfires. There was very heavy A.A. fire reported to the south and south-west of Chelmsford.

Meanwhile in east London a major tragedy occurred during the raid when 173 people were crushed to death on a staircase as they rushed into an emergency air raid shelter in the recently completed, but unopened, Bethnal Green Underground Station. Ironically the rush had been partly due to a Rocket Battery, similar to Chelmsford's, firing for the first time in nearby Victoria Park. The panic had been induced when the Battery fired its first salvos - the terrifying noise was mistaken by many of the victims as that of deadly parachute landmines.

Wednesday 3rd March 1943

TRAIN MACHINE-GUNNED AT SOUTH WOODHAM

At 7.28 a.m. the Chelmsford sirens sounded an air raid warning. Two minutes later the 0709 train from Southminster was machine-gunned by an enemy aircraft some three hundred yards east of South Woodham Ferrers Station.

Although the locomotive and carriages were were hit by the gunfire, fortunately no one was hurt. The aircraft was likely to have been one of two dozen Fw 190s which operated over Essex during the morning and carried out an air raid on Barking and Ilford where 43 people were killed. Some of the aircraft are thought to have attempted an unsuccessful attack on the factories in Chelmsford. The all-clear was sounded at Chelmsford at 8.04 a.m.

Two of those killed in Ilford were 38 year-old Arthur Wilson and his 37 year-old wife Chrissie, who died when their house received a direct hit. Mrs. Wilson's mother, Mrs. R.W. Burton, lived at 9 St. John's Green in Writtle and a week later Mr. & Mrs. Wilson were buried at the village's All Saints' Church.

Friday 12th March 1943

200 WOMEN WAR WORKERS COMING TO CHELMSFORD

THE ESSEX CHRONICLE reported that beginning in the next week around two hundred young women were to arrive in Chelmsford from Leicester and Bedford to work in the town's war work factories.

The Chief Billeting Officer appealed for householders with any spare accommodation to come forward and contact his office in the Vestry Hall in New Street, so that the women could be housed. He warned that compulsory billeting powers were available to him should the public's response not be sufficient. The Government was seeking a 20% increase in production at the factories.

Friday 19th March 1943

PHOTOGRAPHIC RECORD NEEDED OF CHURCHES

The Essex Chronicle reported that the church authorities sought the help of amateur photographers to help record the county's churches in case they should be damaged by enemy action. Locally both Stock and Danbury Churches had already been wrecked by bombs.

Friday 19th March 1943

TWO WEEK BOOK SALVAGE CAMPAIGN BEGINS

The day saw the start throughout Essex of a two week long drive to salvage old books at the behest of the Ministry of Supply. Paper products were vitally important in the munitions industries.

In the Borough the Ministry had set a target of two books from every person, a total of some 65,000 of them. Subsequently this to prove easily achievable , with 213,588 books eventually collected by the end of the fortnight, over three times the target, and the highest figure per head in Essex. Of those, 2,500 were donated to blitzed libraries, 1,000 to children and some 17,000 to soldiers, with the rest going for recycling. In the Rural District the target of 70,000 books was subsequently beaten by over 10,000 items. The paper drive followed a similarly successful salvage drive the previous year which had netted 21,053 tons of paper, 15,280 tons of metals and 12,271 cwt. of bones in Essex.

Saturday 3rd April 1943

STRONG WINDS CAUSE CHAOS

13 BALLOONS BLOWN AWAY

GALE FORCE winds of between 50 and 60 m.p.h. caused thirteen of Chelmsford's 31 barrage balloons to brake away from their moorings.

Those affected were at sites 2, 4, 6, 7, 9, 12, 14, 17, 18, 21, 23, 27, and 31. Meanwhile those at sites 3, 5, 13, 16, 22 and 24 were all damaged whilst storm bedded and two balloonists were injured at site 3. Several balloons were shot down whilst others drifted away. Fortunately little damage was caused, though some was reported at numbers 10, 12 & 16 Queen Street and 171 Springfield Road. All the missing balloons were quickly replaced. In Beehive Lane, Great Baddow, a great elm tree belonging to Mr. T. Chaplin was brought down across the road, just missing an Eastern National bus full of passengers.

Wednesday 7th April 1943

CHELMSFORD ON FIRE

Town punished in massive Luftwaffe incendiary raid

2 PARACHUTE LANDMINES, 80 HIGH EXPLOSIVES, AROUND 1800 1 KG INCENDIARIES ARE DROPPED ON THE COUNTY TOWN - BUT NO ONE DIES

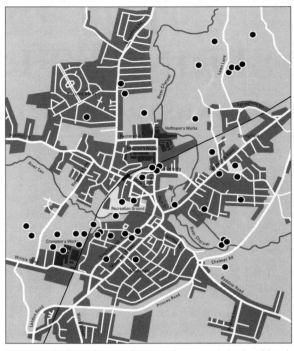

15th April 1943 Fire Raid on Chelmsford. The symbols ● represent the locations of the main bombing incidents. Miraculously, despite the large number of incidents no was killed during the raid. (Author).

AFTER TWO RECENT, largely unsuccessful, attempts to bomb Chelmsford the Luftwaffe returned to the town in the early hours to mount the heaviest raid of the war so far, with incendiaries its preferred weapon.

Conditions were not ideal for bombing - their was 50% cloud cover above 8,000 feet, and a little low cloud. However, the moon was three-quarters full and there was a south-westerly breeze of 7 m.p.h. that would help fan any fires that were started.

Raiders approach

The first sign of impending trouble was the previous evening at 11.40 p.m. when a purple warning was given to the Chelmsford area as around eighty German aircraft were tracked approaching the Essex coast. They included Ju 88s of KG6 based at Beauvais, Creil and Cormeilles, and Do 217s of KG40 from Gilze Rijen and of KG2 from Eindhoven and Coulamniers.

At 12.07 a.m., the Chelmsford air raid warning was sounded as two hostile and one friendly aircraft were detected flying from the Boreham direction, apparently guided by the main Chelmsford to Colchester railway line. The town's barrage balloons remained close hauled, whilst searchlight beams were illuminated to the south and west. Simultaneously anti-aircraft defences open fired, with gun flashes and shell burst seen to the south, south-east and south-west of Chelmsford.

Target flares dropped

At 12.21 a.m. the first enemy aircraft appeared directly above Chelmsford and three minutes later the order was given to the raise the town's barrage balloons to 4,500 feet as a defensive measure. The aircraft was soon accompanied by another hostile and a friendly aircraft. Within a

few minutes, at 12.29 a.m., the raiders began to drop the first of around thirty target marker flares which were to be used as guides by the main bombing force.

Defences open fire

Almost immediately the Arbour Lane Bofors gun site was detailed to extinguish the flares. It was quickly overwhelmed so all the Bofors sites went into action against them. Bombs soon followed the flares as more enemy raiders appeared to proceed over the town from an easterly and south-easterly direction, turn and make their bombing runs from the north-east. The Arbour Lane Bofors site was to eventually fire 208 rounds at the bombers, whilst its counterpart in Henry Road fired 167 rounds.

At 12.30 a.m. the Home Guard Rocket Battery in the Recreation Ground, manned on this occasion by number 1 relief, began to engage the enemy force overhead with the launch of its first salvo.

Communications cut

Around the same time the town's civil defences suffered a critical blow when a firepot fell in front of the Rosebery Hotel in Springfield Road and put approximately two hundred telephone lines out of action, including the military's G.O.R. lines and those to most of the local defences. Thereafter general communications had to be relayed by messenger, a time consuming and unreliable method.

One result of this was the failure of the decoy site at Graces Walk, Little Baddow to go into action until after the raid had finished. Another was the serious breakdown in the organisation and control of the N.F.S., a situation which was to be a major talking point in Chelmsford after the raid. The disruption of telephone communications caused considerable delays in the attendance of firemen and appliances at many

of the town's fires.

The frustrations of those who watched their properties go up in flames were subsequently exacerbated by the knowledge that many of the fire crews stationed in villages throughout the neighbouring Rural District received no call for their assistance - assistance that would have proven extremely helpful in the circumstances. Reports were also to later emerge that at some fires Fire Guards, and even children, had to use stirrup pumps for nearly an hour before the N.F.S. arrived. They were said to have been greeted by ironic cheers.

At 12.47 a.m. the Home Guard Rocket Battery fired its second salvo. By then it was clear that the German bombers were managing to bomb from a comparatively safe height, under the high level explosions of the Home Guard's rockets, and above the low level defences of the barrage balloons, local Bofors and machine gun batteries. Additionally, the perimeter of the balloon barrage was found to be not far enough from the primary targets of Hoffmann's, Marconi's and Crompton's - the raiders were seen to be banking steeply in order to successfully throw their bomb loads into the centre of the town.

Bombs miss targets

Fortunately, however, for Chelmsford most of the bombs either fell wide of the town's factories or failed to explode and no major damage was caused to any of Chelmsford's nine 'Key Points'. Many of the incendiary firepots and ABB incendiary containers were dropped from too low a height, so that in most cases they failed to open in order to spread their loads effectively -the devices simply exploded on impact and the incendiaries burned themselves out. Accurate bombing was further hampered by the failure of many of the target marker flares to function adequately as they too were dropped from too low an altitude. Even so

Chelmsford was brightly illuminated throughout the raid.

An intelligence assessment was to subsequently report that had the German bomber released their loads from a greater height then Chelmsford would have suffered far more seriously with fires 'continuing for many days afterwards'.

Extensive damage but no fatalities

Even so by the time the last bombs fell at 1.15 a.m., and the all-clear sounded thirteen minutes later, Chelmsford had suffered extensive damage in the Springfield Road and Broomfield

Road areas, with 28 fires reported in the Borough comprising one 'serious', four 'medium' and 23 'small'. Miraculously no one was killed in the raid and there was just one serious injury and a dozen slight casualties of whom seven were detained in hospital. By 2.45 a.m. two rest centres were opened up under the homeless persons scheme - one at the Trinity Road School catered for 43 people, and the other at the Catholic Church Hall catered for 31 people.

The quantity of bombs delivered on Chelmsford was estimated to have been: 2 parachute landmines, 80 H.Es, 16 areas of incendiaries and around 1,800 1 kg incendiary bombs.

EYEWITNESS ACCOUNT: A.A. DEFENCES

"In the end house, nearest the tower, there lived an old lady and she complained because of the bad language they were using."

As told to our our Special Correspondent

"In the early days of the war the military erected a number of anti-aircraft towers around Chelmsford. One concrete one was built at the back of Hoffmann's and another, made of steel girders, was constructed at the bottom (eastern) end of Yarwood Road on a site now covered by garages and the back gardens of some houses in Chelmer Road.

The tower was about as high as a house, 12 to 14 feet square, and was topped by a flat platform on which the Bofors gun was mounted. It was never camouflaged. The Bofors was just like a machine gun only it used to fire clips of five shells instead of bullets.

It was manned by a group of around a dozen soldiers who worked in shifts and used to live in a hut built beneath it. They'd climb up a ladder to get to the gun. The people at that end of the road got to know them quite well, inviting them in for

tea and that kind of thing .

On the night of the fire raid the soldiers at the tower weren't exactly happy with the bombing. They were really hammering at the planes, and calling the Germans everything under the sun. In the end house, nearest the tower, there lived an old lady and she complained because of the bad language that they were using - the gun barrel was nearly red hot and she was more concerned about their swearing than the bombing!

When the tower was dismantled at the end of the war my brother-in-law got hold of some of the steel gusset plates from the tower and made a garden path from them at his house, 5 Yarwood Road. Although the path's not there anymore there are still about half a dozen of them lying flat between the pavement and front garden there."

Jack Palmer

THE FIRE RAID: SPRINGFIELD BADLY HIT

BOMBS ALL OVER DISTRICT

THE SPRINGFIELD area of Chelmsford was particularly badly hit during the raid.

Bombs fell in residential neighbourhoods as well as in rural areas.

Around Lawn Lane

Two 500 kg H.E.s fell in the large field to the west of Lawn Lane, one in the north-east corner of the field near Lawn Lane Lodge and the other in the south of the field, close to the present day junction of Waveney Drive and Meon Close.

The former left a large crater 35 feet across by 10 feet deep and the latter, one 32 feet across by 5 feet deep.

A total of 34 of the 1 kg type incendiary were reported to have fallen around Springfield Hall. Nearby, a group of several bombs fell harmlessly in a line north-easterly to south-westerly across a grass field on the eastern side of Lawn Lane that was part of the Springfield Place Estate.

Today some of the field has been redeveloped as Torquay Road, Burnham Road and the Boswells School playing field. The bombs included six 50 kg phosphorus types, two 50 kg firepots and one unexploded H.E. of an unknown size. A seventh 50 kg phosphorus bomb fell in the next field to the east, close to the present day junction of Dartmouth Road and Bodmin Road.

Meanwhile, further south a single 250 kg SC H.E. fell between Arbour Lane and the River Chelmer in William Seabrook & Sons orchard, just 300 yards due east of Hoffmann's. It left a crater 24 feet across by 7.5 feet deep and seriously damaged one property, The Bungalow. Around Arbour Lane itself, 38 of the 1 kg incendiaries were counted, and were believed to have represented the contents of one half of an ABB 500 container.

Dukes Farm

To the east, a string of ten 50 kg firepots, including one suspected to have been unexploded, fell in a line north to south across land belonging to Dukes Farm.

Two of the devices were in a small field directly to the north-east of the farm itself, whilst the remainder were in the next field, immediately east of the A12 and north of the farm. The area was also struck by one ABB 500 device which contained 120 of the 1 kg type incendiaries.

String of bombs across Lionmede Park

Several bombs, apparently aimed at the Essex Police H.Q. fell across the eastern half of Lionmede Recreation Ground, Sandford Road and into the grounds of the prison.

Lionmede Recreation Ground was struck by four unexploded 50 kg firepots, one 50 kg phosphorus bomb which left a crater 14 feet across by 6 feet deep, and four 50 kg firepots which left a craters of 11 feet across by 3 feet deep, 11 feet across by 4 feet deep, 12 feet across by 3 feet deep, and 11 feet across by 4.5 feet deep respectively.

Sandford Road

Another 50 kg firepot and an ABB 500 device, containing 120 incendiaries, fell on 24 Sandford Road, home to Reginald Baverstock, starting a fire that burned the house down along with its semi-detached neighbour, number 26, occupied by Frank Goddard. Mr. & Mrs. Baverstock were trapped in their blazing, smoke-filled house with their front door wedged shut by the heat and explosions.

A neighbour, Bertie Bond from number 43 across the road, who was on Fire Guard duties, shouldered the door open to rescue the choking couple. Another 50 kg firepot struck the roof of a house on the southern side of Sandford Road, broke on impact with the main portion of the device bouncing through the prison wall before exploding some 30 feet inside it.

The house was slightly damaged by a fire that was quickly put under control. In addition, a total of 66 of the 1 kg type incendiaries were subsequently counted in the vicinity of Sandford Road.

Fire at Old Court

A few hundred yards to the west of these bombs one 50 kg firepot scored a direct hit on the County Surveyor's Offices at Old Court, off Arbour Lane. The resultant fire badly damaged the premises which were the former Essex Police Headquarters.

West of Springfield Road

The area around and including Chelmer Place was struck by five 50 kg phosphorus bombs and three unidentified H.E.s. Two of the phosphorus bombs and one H.E. fell in open land between Tower House and Chelmer Place, with the phosphorus bombs both leaving craters 2.5 feet across by 3 feet deep.

The remaining three phosphorus bombs fell onto properties in Chelmer Place, one scoring a direct hit on number 15. They were accompanied by the other two unidentified H.E.s which fell close by. Chelmer Place and St. Anne's Place had to be evacuated as a result.

Further south an ABB 500 device, which exploded on impact and burned out, fell 233 feet west of Springfield Road and 44 feet north of Victoria Road.

MAJOR FIRE AT THE PRISON

Chelmsford Prison in Springfield Road was badly affected by 1 kg incendiaries, with a almost 50 counted on its grounds and 32 within the prison walls.

Initially the devices were successfully extinguished by prison staff aided by good conduct prisoners, using stirrup pumps and sand, and little fire damage occurred.

Prison Governor's House destroyed

While work was being concentrated on protecting the prisoners' buildings incendiaries started a fire at the Governor's House, between the prison and Trinity Church. The prison's trailer pump was sent to deal with the blaze, with water drawn from the prison's own static water tank.

However, when between four and six incendiaries hit the two storey stores and manufacturing premises sited at the south-western corner of the prison the pump was quickly redirected and the Governor's house left to burn. The fire destroyed it and all its contents lost. Subsequently he would be accommodated at 'Berberis' in Roxwell Road.

Stores & manufacturing building ablaze

The stores and manufacturing building formerly housed women prisoners, but had been converted in 1937 to provide ground floor storage space for maintenance and A.R.P. equipment, and a second floor store which contained components necessary for the manufacture of brushes, brooms, mail bags and prison clothing.

Fire broke out in the roof, which soon collapsed and flames spread throughout the first floor and down to the ground at the south-eastern end of the building. With the situation at the prison rapidly becoming out of control efforts were made to telephone the N.F.S., but these failed because the phone lines were down. A cyclist was successfully sent to the nearest N.F.S. station in Springfield Road to summon assistance. Unfortunately, by the time the N.F.S. arrived the stores building was well alight and little could be done to save it, so efforts were concentrated instead on preventing the fire spreading to the neighbouring administration and prisoners' buildings.

Water supply problems

The N.F.S were seriously hampered by the breakdown of a 5,000 gallon mobile water carrier and an inadequate mains water supply - lines had to set up to draw water for fire-fighting from the River Chelmer some 470 yards away.

The fire was eventually brought under control around 4 a.m., almost three hours after it had broken out. By then the store building was extensively damaged with the roof completely destroyed and the walls only surviving owing to their thickness.

Much of the building's contents, including around 8,000 mailbags, 877 jackets, 830 pairs of trousers, 38 overcoats and thousands of brushes, were badly damaged by fire and water and very little proved salvageable afterwards.

"By the time we got there it was well ablaze."

As told to our our Special Correspondent

"At the time of the raid I was one of the wardens based at the post in Springfield Park Road. We were patrolling the estate when we were called to a house in Springfield Park Avenue, between Hill Road and Springfield Park Parade. Incendiary bombs had hit a garden shed which contained a couple or three gallons of paraffin.

By the time we got there it was well ablaze and although the incident wasn't as serious as if it had been a house we still had to get the flames out quickly as they made a damn good target for other bombers that were still overhead. When we tried to phone headquarters for assistance but all the lines were down - we couldn't get a messenger through because the town was a bit hectic at that particular time, so in the end we managed to get the fire out ourselves using stirrup pumps and buckets of water.

There were many other fires all over Chelmsford but we never really knew much about them. In those days people didn't wander about too much and we tended to keep to our own sector. Even so, I do remember cycling to work at Marconi's the next morning when New Street was like a skating rink because of all the melted fat from the suet factory which had been burned down during the raid."

Jack Palmer

HOLY TRINITY CHURCH IN NEAR MISS

INCENDIARIES WERE spread outside the prison, with a total of over 80 of the 1 kg types falling on Holy Trinity Church and graveyard, the neighbouring Trinity Road School and its grounds.

The school was prevented from burning down by the actions of two residents from Hill Road, Percy Thacker and Mr. W. Ward. Mr. Ward was the son of Cllr. Frank Ward who along with his fellow Council members was to thank the men for the actions at the Council meeting at the end of May 1943. Meanwhile six more 1 kg incendiaries fell in Springfield Park Avenue.

To the south, a 50 kg firepot scored a direct hit on 27 Navigation Road. The house was set ablaze but the fire was soon reported to be under control.

ROSEBERY HOTEL DESTROYED

Owner's Anger

A 50 KG FIREPOT that scored a direct hit on the Rosebery Temperance Hotel at 209 Springfield Road, started a fire which destroyed the premises and a neighbouring property - A. Lloyd's confectionery shop at number 207. Both properties were owned by Wenley Ltd.

A 10 inch gas main was fractured and set alight, and Springfield Road was blocked as a result.

Fortunately the hotel's residents were either outside or in a shelter to its rear when the bomb struck. However, as the fire began to take hold the hotel's distraught proprietress, Mrs. G. Digby, went back inside to see what she could save.

Police Sgt. Warnes and Senior Warden J. Sutterby followed her in and persuaded her to return outside and wait for the N.F.S.

Subsequently, in a letter to the Essex Chronicle, Mrs. Digby was to complain that the N.F.S. took at least 35 minutes to arrive at the fire, by which time her hotel and her livelihood had been destroyed.

She complained further that when the fire brigade did turn up they appeared not to know where the closest hydrant was. Her irritation was understandable - the nearest fire station was only a few hundred yards away at 169b Springfield Road, just beyond the Victoria Road junction. Ironically the breakdown in N.F.S. telephone communications, which was responsible for the delay, had also been caused in part by the bomb that destroyed hotel.

The Fire Raid: Thursday 15th April 1943

DOZEN LARGE BOMBS JUST MISS THE GAS WORKS

A GROUP OF A dozen large bombs, perhaps intended for the Gas Works, fell close to the junction of the River Chelmer and the Springfield Basin stretch of the Chelmer & Blackwater Canal.

They included a pair of 250 kg H.E.s and a 50 kg phosphorus bomb that fell in meadowland immediately to the north of the canal. The H.E.s left craters 25 feet across by 6 feet deep and another water-filled one that had a diameter of 24 feet. A second pair of 250 kg H.E.s fell on the peninsular between the the canal and the River Chelmer. One left a crater 21 feet across by 6 feet deep, while the other failed to explode. It fell on land recently purchased for the extension of the Gas Works, just 20 feet from an 18 inch gas main that served the southern part of Chelmsford.

After the raid the unexploded device was tackled by a bomb disposal squad who were to work on the site for over two months but were unable to locate the bomb. Eventually the work had to be abandoned owing to the flooding of the ground in late summer and autumn.

It was not until the summer of 1944 and after several more months of difficult excavation that the bomb was eventually located, around 25 to 30 feet underground and less than eight feet from the gas main. On 26th July 1944 it was safely removed by the Royal Engineers.

The two 250 kg H.E.s were accompanied by another seven 50 kg phosphorus bombs and 120 of the 1 kg type incendiary bombs. Their container is believed to have struck Chelmer Road and bounced into an adjoining field, having blown out about nine feet of 12 inch gas main. Fortunately the gas was not ignited.

The only damage at the Gas Works was self-inflicted. The hydrogen plant was put out of action by a fragment of an A.A. shell that pierced a small hydrogen relief holder, and the largest gasholder was pierced by another A.A. shell which passed through both sides near the crown and rapidly emptied the holder.

Luckily the gas did not catch fire. Blast also badly damaged one end of the retort house and a fragment of shrapnel entered an overhead water tank and partially emptied its contents into the yard below. Nearby the barrage balloon at site 25 (in the Ritz car park) was also damaged by A.A. fire and had to be bedded and replaced by a reserve balloon after the raid had finished.

PARACHUTE LANDMINES FALL EITHER SIDE OF HOFFMANN'S

ELDERLY WOMAN SEVERELY BURNED IN SECOND AVENUE

One enemy bomber dropped pair of parachute landmines over the town. Their intended target appears to have been Hoffmann's, but the factory was spared as they fell wide of their target, one to the south-east and the other to the north-west.

The former detonated in a field 253 feet north of Victoria Road and some 350 feet east of Regina Road, a site more recently occupied by the Staples superstore.

The explosion left a crater 41 feet across by 9 feet deep and caused widespread blast damage to dozens of properties within a three hundred yard radius. 'Ellton' in Victoria Road was seriously damaged though repairable.

The other parachute landmine exploded above houses, 32 feet south of Second Avenue and 243 feet east of Broomfield Road. The blast demolished four properties, left six others damaged beyond repair and caused considerable damage to hundreds of houses up to 300 yards away.

The worst affected properties were numbers 2, 4, 6 & 8 Second Avenue which were demolished and number 10 which was damaged beyond repair. Opposite them, on the northern side of the road, numbers 1, 3, 5, 7 & 9 were also damaged beyond repair. At number 5 a 70 year-old widow, Mrs. Alice Johnson, was badly burned and was the raid's most severely injured casualty. In neighbouring First Avenue numbers 1, 3, 5 & 7 were seriously damaged, as was number 130 Broomfield Road. A man was subsequently charged for looting from 1 Second Avenue.

A pair of ABB 500 containers fell nearby, one falling in Swiss Avenue and another in First Avenue. At the former, all 120 of the 1 kg type incendiaries burned out in their container, whilst a further 153 from the latter fell in Swiss Avenue, Corporation Road and Broomfield Road.

CHAOS IN NEW STREET

NEW STREET, the home of both Hoffmann's and Marconi's was naturally badly affected by enemy action, though remarkably neither of the large factories suffered serious damage. Instead neighbouring properties suffered most with large fires set at the in a former school used as a store and in a suet factory.

Railway goods yard

The closest bombs to Hoffmann's were two 50 kg firepots and a cluster of 14 of the 1 kg type incendiaries that fell on the L.N.E.R. goods yard adjacent to the factory.

Neither firepot failed to cause any significant damage, whilst the incendiaries only caused slight damage to a little used siding in the centre of the yard. A number of railway trucks were partially damaged by fire. At Hoffmann's some damage by blast was caused to the blackout and production was subsequently slightly affected for two nights. Two small fires, caused by incendiaries, were quickly extinguished and the damage caused was negligible. A further 27 of the 1 kg devices fell to the north of Hoffmann's on the Henry Road allotments.

One ABB 500 container opened high above New Street and spread 142 1 kg incendiaries over the area around the Victoria Road cross-roads, including Marconi's, Archer's Suet Factory and the former Victoria Girls & Infants School.

Damage at Marconi's was only minimal with one 1 kg device striking the drawing office's roof and another falling on a bicycle shed. Both were quickly dealt with by the company's bomb disposal officer. A similar device penetrated the roof of the rear wing of the factory's two storey high canteen & club premises and came to rest in the roof trusses. Fire quickly spread via a ceiling to an adjacent glazed partition and to the floor. However, prompt action by a Fire Guard confined the damage to just a small part of first floor. The canteen below was unaffected.

Suet factory destroyed

Archer's Suet Factory was housed in three adjoining buildings on the eastern side of New Street, directly south of the railway embankment. Six of the 1 kg incendiaries struck the western end of the office building, penetrated the roof, and started a fire which grew extremely rapidly and spread down from the first floor. The 68 year-old Fire Guard on the premises was unable to cope with the situation and called for the N.F.S. as the whole of the factory quickly became engulfed in flames. He suffered from shock and a suspected stroke. The first fire pump on the scene came from Marconi's brigade and was quickly joined by another from Hoffmann's, four from the N.F.S aided by personnel from barrage balloon site 18 in Driver & Ling's scrapyard behind the factory. They fought the fire with water obtained from a hydrant, a steel pipe running along the bottom of the railway embankment from the River Chelmer and a 100,000 gallon static water tank. It took 80 minutes to get the fire under control and despite their efforts the factory was gutted save for a single storey annexe and a small portion of the north-western corner of the premises closest to the railway bridge. The factory had contained around 30 tons of fat in bulk, another 50 tons in 265 oak barrels, 180 trays of fat being processed and an additional 70 to 80 tons in packing mats. Much of that went up in flames and a large quantity of melted fat poured in to New Street to create a large slippery pool that was to linger for days afterwards.

However, around 1.5 tons of shredded suet and 52 tons of fat were subsequently salvaged, along with five lorry loads of damaged cartons and paper. The blaze ended production at the factory but afterwards arrangements were made with another firm, Messers Wilkes & Lewis of St. Albans, to carry on its work.

250,00 ball bearings ruined

Just to the south of Archer's factory three of the 1 kg incendiaries passed through the slate roof of the former Victoria Girls & Infants School which had already been damaged by blast earlier in the raid. The property was being used by Hoffmann's for the storage of around half a million finished ball bearings ranging from 0.25 to 16 inches in diameter. The bombs were immediately tackled by two Fire Guards who were on the premises, but the fire got out of control and the N.F.S. were called to deal with it. Structural damage was mainly confined to the building's roof and some storage racks. However, around half the bearings, around £27,000's worth, were damaged by a combination of the fire and water used to extinguish it, and only 10 to 15% of the reminder proved salvageable. Fortunately none of the bearings was awaiting urgent delivery. Five other 1 kg incendiaries fell in a garden at the rear of the school

Banana store

An unknown number of the 1 kg incendiaries fell onto Denham & Archer's 'banana store' premises next door to the Y.M.C.A. in Victoria Road The building was shared by Marconi's, who used it as a store for wireless components, and by Messers Bond's for the storage of furniture. It was of a single storey shed type construction and the incendiaries damaged about 40% of its roof. Marconi's lost almost £7,000's worth of stores but there was no direct effect on production as the firm was able to draw on other stocks from other premises it had acquired shortly before the raid.

Nearby, 21 of the 1 kg type incendiaries fell on a house called Ellton in Victoria Road. The house was seriously damaged along with two hairdresser's premises.

EYEWITNESS ACCOUNT:

"The firebomb had come through the bedroom ceiling and gone into the mattress on the bed which had been set alight."

As told to our our Special Correspondent

"I used to live with my parents, Mr. & Mrs. George Ainsworth, at 36 New Street. It was one of a terrace of three little houses on the west side of the road between the railway bridge and the junction with Victoria Road.

Directly opposite us was the Victoria Girls & Infants School, and between that and the railway line stood a house and then Archers' Suet Factory. We were fairly near to the railway, Marconi's and Hoffmann's, so if any attempt was made to bomb them then we felt the repercussions. In fact we were bombed on three occasions, the most memorable being in the early hours of 15th April 1943.

When the raid began we were in the brick air raid shelter which we had in the back garden. It had been built by the Council and we used to share it with our neighbours. My father would never go in and used to stand outside instead. The Germans dropped many incendiaries scattered around the vicinity of our house.

Some hit the suet factory across the road and set that ablaze and another came through the roof and into the main bedroom of our house. Luckily it didn't hit anyone but it started a fire. The fire brigade turned up to fight the fire at the suet factory so someone went over there to tell them about the fire that had been started in our house. The firemen said that they couldn't do anything to help as they had to deal with industrial fires before they could tackle domestic ones. So instead we set up a line of buckets. My father was one of those gregarious sorts of people, and every time he had a bucket of water passed to him he'd stand and chat. We'd have to say 'Come on dad!'.

The firebomb had come through the bedroom ceiling and gone into the mattress on the bed which had been set alight. We were managing quite well at putting the fire out with the buckets of water and thought that if we could get the mattress out of the window then it would be alright.

Then all of a sudden there was the sound of wood splintering downstairs. The firemen had come over and smashed down the front door with their axes! They came in and all crowded up the stairs and into the bedroom and quickly put the fire out, though sadly we did lose the family bible. The trouble was that they had the melted suet from the factory all over their boots and had trod it over the carpets. The firemen caused more damage and more mess than the firebombs had themselves!.

After the raid what always amazed me was gawping people, who'd pass by on their way to work at Hoffmann's or Marconi's. Some of them would really come and glare through the windows to see what the damage was like inside, even though we were still living there."

Eileen Hance

The Fire Raid: Thursday 15th April 1943

CHELMSFORD TOWN CENTRE: THE CATHEDRAL IS 'SAVED' BY TEENAGE FIREWATCHERS

Unusual view of the Cathedral which was struck by several incendiaries during the Fire Raid of 15th April 1943. Fortunately the prompt actions of fire watchers prevented its destruction. (Author)

IN THE TOWN CENTRE the most serious incidents were around the Cathedral precincts. Some 79 of the 1 kg type incendiaries fell in the vicinity of the Cathedral.

One of the devices struck part of the roof on the north side of the building, burned furiously and started a small fire that threatened to spread and cause more serious damage.

Fortunately three members of the Cathedral's Fire Guard, 18 year-old Dennis Hance, 17 year-old John Copsey and 15 year-old Albert Pearce, promptly and successfully tackled the device and were subsequently praised for having saved the Cathedral from destruction.

Dennis was the son of Mr. & Mrs. Edward Hance of 57 Coval Lane and was a server at the Cathedral. John was also a server and the son of Mr. & Mrs. John Copsey of 101 West Avenue, whilst Albert, who was the Cathedral's head choir boy, was the son of Mr. & Mrs. Albert Pearce of 30 Cramphorn Road.

Meanwhile other 1 kg incendiaries damaged the roof of St. Mary's Lodge in Cottage Place. The building was used by Marconi's as auxiliary work rooms. A further two of the devices fell on Rose Brothers motor car garage situated in premises to the rear of the Lion & Lamb P.H. in Duke Street.

A suspected 50 kg phosphorus bomb fell in the grounds of the Market, close to the River Can, and several small incendiaries were said to have fallen on the Home Guard Rocket Battery in the Recreation Ground, where one lodged itself in a rocket store and had to be removed by a member of the Home Guard.

EYEWITNESS ACCOUNT: SAVING THE CATHEDRAL

> **"The story was in the local papers and also got through to the German press and the Illustrated London News. I've still got a German newspaper with an article about the incident and photographs of us.."**

As told to our our Special Correspondent

"During the war I was member of the Cathedral choir and, like many people associated with the Cathedral, I also undertook fire watching duties.

The fire watch used to be based at the Cathedral Vestry in New Street, which was within two hundred yards of County Hall, on top of which was the air raid siren, Being so close, you were able to sleep there because the siren would wake you up, and if need be you could then go to the Cathedral roof to fire watch.

On occasions there would be only one of us on duty, sometimes three or four. From the Cathedral you had a wonderful view - I can remember watching the sky glow from the oil refineries burning down on the Thames. I'd sometimes sit at the east end of the Cathedral roof, put my legs around the cross which is still there and hold on, rather like a jockey.

I belonged to the a very good youth group at the Cathedral, the Young People's League, or Y.P.L. To be honest a number of us lads found it very convenient to be fire watchers because we could go to the Y.P.L. club on a Wednesday evening, see our girlfriends home afterwards and our parents never knew what time we'd got home because we 'd drop in the Cathedral afterwards for fire watching duties overnight!

On the night of 14th to 15th April 1943 I was on fire watch duty with a couple of mates of mine, John Copsey and Albert Pearce. After the sirens had gone off we left the vestry as usual and went up to the Cathedral roof. As we watched a small incendiary came down on the roof, though it took us two or three minutes to locate where it had landed. Eventually we discovered it had ignited on impact with the north aisle roof.

The device was two or three inches in diameter, slightly conical in shape, with a flange at the back. We had all been trained how to deal with incendiaries using a stirrup pump. John, who was always a far more enterprising young man than me, got hold of the stirrup pump nozzle - I was the charlie in the middle operating the pump, and poor old little Albert was running up and down the ladder with buckets of water.

Despite spraying water on the incendiary for about five minutes it was still burning and, to be honest, we'd got a bit fed up with it. We had been warned in training that in theory some incendiaries contained a bit of gunpowder and could explode but John eventually went over to it, kicked it and it went out.

The story of us 'saving the Cathedral' is quite well known because about the time of the event the Government felt that there was a need to give the Fire Guard some publicity and a boost. As a result the B.B.C. was told to do a feature on it. The three of us lads on duty were invited to Cannon's Restaurant in Duke Street where we met a scriptwriter from the B.B.C.

She turned up with a little yappy dog. We told her our story and she duly wrote a script which exaggerated the incident. A few weeks later the feature was broadcast on the radio, I believe on a Monday evening, about 7-7.30 p.m. on the Home Service. The amusing thing was that some relations of my mother got in touch with her afterwards and said 'How lovely it was to hear the story about Dennis. We knew it was him because he's got such a nice posh voice!'. Actually it was not me at all - the three of us were played by paid up actors in London.

The story was in the local papers and also got through to the German press and the Illustrated London News. I've still got a German newspaper with an article about the incident and photographs of us. The Cathedral Chapter felt that they'd better do something about it too, so they gave us about £15 each, which was a lot of money in those days.

I used it to buy three architectural books and the Provost, an old Irishman the Very Rev. W.E.R. Morrow, wrote a thank you message inside them in his slightly shaky handwriting. After the war I followed a career in architecture and town planning and am now retired and lecturing. John became an accountant and is now retired and living in the west country. Albert became a jobbing builder, but alas died in early 1993.

The three of us regarded the whole event as a bit of a laugh, bearing in mind tat it hardly took half a bucket of water to put the incendiary out. Basically it was the need to give a boost to the Fire Guard that made the story so well known."

Dennis Hance.

EYEWITNESS ACCOUNT:

> **"It became more and more churned up. The stink was terrible, I can still smell it now - like an old fish pan."**

As told to our our Special Correspondent

"The morning after the raid I walked to work at Hoffmann's from my lodgings in Upper Bridge Road. I remember walking up New Street and a long time before we reached the suet factory there was greasy, melted fat stretched all along the road.

In those days New Street was very narrow by the railway bridge with very small pavements. Well of course hundreds of people who worked at Marconi's or Hoffmann's like me had to go that way to get to work and as we all trod on the melted fat it became more and more churned up.

The stink was terrible, I can still smell it now - like an old fish pan. It lasted on the road and pavements for months afterwards before it was all eventually worn away."

Joan Taylor

INCIDENTS IN MOULSHAM

To the south of the River Can there were further incidents in the Moulsham area.

Two ABB 500 devices, each containing 120 of the 1 kg incendiaries, fell between the river and Chelmsford City F.C.'s New Writtle Street stadium and these were dealt with by the Home Guard.

London Road

Several bombs fell in London Road in the vicinity of the New Writtle Street cross-roads. They comprised of three unexploded 50 kg firepots that fell in the grounds of the Chelmsford Club, a 50 kg phosphorus that fell opposite, in the garden of 'Yverdon', and another 50 kg phosphorus that scored a direct hit on Mansard House where flats 1 and 2 were gutted by fire.

A suspected 50 kg phosphorus incendiary was also reported to have fallen in the front of the London Road Cemetery, whilst two 50 kg phosphorus bombs dropped in the vicinity of Moulsham Street - one in St John's Nursery in St. John's Road (today site of Mews Court) and the other in Moulsham Street itself where the rear of number 136 and its roof were damaged.

Meanwhile a pair of unexploded 50 kg firepots fell in the back gardens of numbers 13 and 15 Upper Bridge Road. Another unexploded device was also reported in the garden of 67 Upper Bridge Road, while a 50 kg unexploded phosphorus fell to the rear of 6 Baker Street.

The railway

Further to the west a total of four incendiary devices fell on or near to the London & North Eastern Railway that ran along the eastern perimeter of Crompton's Writtle Road factory site. One 50 kg firepot landed on the L.N.E.R. some 1,925 feet north of the Writtle Road railway bridge and 44 feet east of the railway. Nearby two ABB 500 incendiary container fell near the railway and both exploded on impact with their contents burning out harmlessly. one 1,500 feet north of Writtle Road and 44 feet east of the railway, an identical container that fell 20 feet nearer the railway bridge and 80 feet east of the railway lines.

The fourth bomb was a suspected unexploded 50 kg phosphorous device which fell between the rails some 525 feet north of the railway bridge, and directly outside one of the main Crompton buildings. Trains on the line were disrupted until the bomb could removed. An identical bomb struck the footings of the east wall of the factory's electric power building, though fortunately damage was only slight and was confined to the wall.

Four bombs fell on land to the north of Crompton's. They comprised of a 50 kg phosphorus bomb, 60 feet north of the last house in Crompton Street, and one H.E. of an unknown type and two suspected 50 kg phosphorus incendiaries in the field to the west of the Crompton Street to Seymour Street public footpath.

Waterhouse Lane

A pair of 50 kg phosphorus bombs fell into a field immediately to the west of Waterhouse Lane, close to barrage balloon site 2 and the modern day junction with Forest Road. One of the devices set a gas mains alight. Two balloonists from the site, L.A.C.s Leadbetter and Sharp received slight burns to their feet in tackling one of the bombs. The crew had been on a deployment exercise at the time of the raid and their barrage balloon was bedded. A string of three suspected unexploded 50 kg incendiaries dropped harmlessly into another field a quarter of a mile further west. The land was part of the Skegg's Farm estate and today lies close to the junction of Forest Road and Abbess Close. A total of four ABB 500 devices, each containing 120 of the 1 kg type incendiaries, fell other on land also belonging to Skegg's Farm.

RURAL AREAS AROUND CHELMSFORD ALSO HIT

CHELMSFORD'S RURAL District did not escape the attentions of the Luftwaffe, with bombing incidents occurring at Boreham, Springfield, Little Baddow and Great Baddow, Battlesbridge and Woodham Ferrers.

Boreham

At Boreham an attempt was once more made to bomb New Hall - despite its use as an emergency geriatric hospital. The Luftwaffe aimed a pair of parachute landmines and four 250 kg H.E.s on the building. Although it escaped any direct hits one of the landmines fell in its grounds close to the rear of the east wing.

The explosion left a crater 34 feet across by 9 feet deep and inflicted substantial blast damage to the wing. Several patients were buried in the rubble, but miraculously none were hurt. The hospital's electric plant was destroyed, putting water supplies out of action and impairing cooking facilities to such a degree that the hospital's master, Mr. R. Clark, called for the evacuation of 250 patients as soon as possible.

The other landmine floated down and detonated opposite 1 and 2 Park Cottages. In the process it damaged both properties beyond repair and left a crater 24 feet across by 9 feet deep.

The four 250 kg H.E.s fell in a line north-east to south-west in open fields to the east of Plantation Road and north-west of Culverts Farm. Each device left a crater around 20 feet across by 6 feet deep. Another ten 50 kg phosphorus bombs and an ABB 500 incendiary container fell to the north of Brick House Farm.

The Boreham area was illuminated by a total of six half ABB 500 containers, seven complete ABB 500 containers and three groups of 36 of the 21 leaf type incendiaries that fell in open fields around the village. Three of the ABB 500s that fell to the north-west of Roman Road and a fourth that fell north-west of the L.N.E.R. failed to scatter their complements of 120 of the 1 kg type incendiaries.

However, seven scattered groups of the devices were reported - four north-west of the L.N.E.R. contained 58, 107, 34 and 72 of the 1 kg types respectively, whilst three others to the south east of Roman Road contained totals of 100, 131 and 86 of the 1 kg types.

Springfield Parish

At Springfield fifteen 50 kg firepots fell close to the 415 H.A.A. Battery's 'Charlie B' anti-aircraft site, between Old Lodge Farm and the avenue leading to New Hall. The battery, incidentally, fired 97 rounds during the course of the raid. Meanwhile, to the south-east, ten 50 kg firepots fell in fields to the north-east of Lonebarn Farm.

At Little Baddow a single suspected 500 kg H.E. fell unexploded into Blakes Wood.

Great Baddow

Further west, a pair of type C parachute landmines was dropped over Great Baddow. One of the devices exploded in a ploughed field 100 yards north-east of Spalding's (Whitehouse) Farm, on a site between Baddow Road and Chelmer Road that has since been covered by the Great Baddow By-Pass.

The explosion left a crater 40 feet across by 20 feet deep, badly damaged the buildings at the farm and caused widespread minor damage to buildings in Baddow Road. The second parachute landmine fell in a paddock to the rear of the Blue Lion Inn, about 250 yards east of the eastern end of Dorset Avenue. Dozens of properties in the vicinity were also damaged by blast.

To the east of the village, Manor Farm suffered from a total of nine 50 kg phosphorus bombs and two ABB 500 devices each containing 120 of the 1 kg incendiaries. Fortunately the incendiaries failed to spread from the container. Meanwhile, further south a string of four 500 kg H.E.s fell in open fields to the west of Great Sir Hughes. The biggest crater was 46 feet across by 15 feet deep, and the smallest, 31 feet across by 6 feet deep.

Further afield four H.E.s fell at Hayes Farm, Battlesbridge and another was reported at Woodham Ferrers.

POSTSCRIPT TO THE RAID

At least three Luftwaffe aircraft deployed in the raid were shot down. They crashed outside the Chelmsford district in the Thames Estuary, at Bockings Elm and Layer Breton respectively.

Following the raid Berlin Radio was to claim that a heavy raid had taken place on Chelmsford and 'in the large industrial works located at the northern exit of the town many heavy bombs exploded. Fires were started which spread rapidly. The local ball-bearings factory was hit with particular strength.'

At 4.46 p.m. on 16th April 1943 the Chelmsford sirens sounded as three enemy aircraft flew over the town at 25,000 feet, making distinct vapour trails. They then turned south-eastwards and made off over Kent at 360 m.p.h. The aircraft are believed to have been Fw 190s on a reconnaissance mission to assess the damage made by the previous day's raid.

Thursday 15th April 1943

EYEWITNESS ACCOUNT:

"The crater was huge, big enough to put a double-decker bus."

As told to our our Special Correspondent

"One night during an air raid a parachute mine came down on a paddock in the grounds of 'Noakes Place' no more than two hundred yards from the back of our Dorset Avenue house. In those days Noakes Place was owned by Dr. Lyster. It was a large building off the southern side of Baddow Road, near Tabors Hill.

I was at home at the time and the blast was so strong it was if someone had picked up the house and put it down again. Luckily no one was hurt, though two of Dr. Lyster's horses were panicked and ran off across the fields. They were recaptured later in Vicarage Lane.

Afterwards my wife and I went over to have a closer look. The remains of the parachute had stopped up a large tree and the crater was huge, big enough to put a double-decker bus in. A neighbour of ours, Mr. Carr, climbed right down to the bottom and he looked about an inch tall. It made me shudder to think what would have happened had it fallen nearer to our house.

In no time at all the crater filled with water and it made a large pond. Children used to paddle on the edge, but after the war it was filled in as it was thought too dangerous. The paddock became part of the Recreation Ground and houses were built all around on what had been fields during the war. You can still just make out where the mine came down - there is a slight dip in the ground near to the ends of the back gardens of houses in Rothmans Avenue."

George Brown

EYEWITNESS ACCOUNT:

"The trouble was our poor old landlord used to suffer from wind."

As told to our our Special Correspondent

"At one time during the war I used to lodge with a workmate of mine, Janet Bacon, at 20 Upper Bridge Road. The house had an indoor Morrison shelter. Whenever the air raid siren sounded our landlord, who worked with us at Hoffmann's, would call out 'Come on Joan, come on Janet, you've got to come down to the shelter - you're our responsibility'.

The trouble was that our poor old landlord used to suffer from wind - he'd come from the pub, eat bread and cheese with pickled onion! Well you can imagine it - our landlord and his wife, and Janet and me all laying in the Morrison shelter with him getting the wind something terrible! Sometimes I thought I'd rather take my chances outside the shelter during a raid!"

Joan Taylor

BOREHAM AIR RAID WARDEN KILLED BY ACK-ACK SHRAPNEL

BETWEEN 12.15 A.M. and 1 a.m. a lone raider was thought to have been responsible for a number of incidents confined to rural areas to the east and south of Chelmsford.

At 12.15 a.m. two unexploded H.E.s fell into the mud bank of the River Crouch near South Woodham Ferrers. Fifteen minutes later an H.E. was reported in a field near Little Seabrights, Great Baddow, another in open fields at Roxwell and one more in Shot Field, Rettendon Place. No one was hurt though fourteen houses were superficially damaged at the last incident.

At 12.40 a.m. fragments of an anti-aircraft shell fell at Stocks Cottages in Waltham Road, Boreham. They struck and killed 54 year-old air raid warden Alfred Edward Cole.

His was the first civilian death in the Rural District since Christmas 1940 when Ernest Warren had been fatally injured at Newney Green. Mr. Cole was married with three sons and employed as a farm worker. He was subsequently buried in the village on 24th April.

Twenty minutes after Mr. Cole was injured four H.E.s fell in a meadow 450 yards south of Little Mascalls Farm in Great Baddow. At the same time three others fell in a field opposite Riffhams in Danbury and a suspected A.A. shell fell into a ploughed field behind Franklin's butcher's shop in South Woodham Ferrers. No one was reported hurt.

Saturday 17th April 1943

DOCTOR'S DAUGHTER KILLED BY RAMPAGING COW THAT ESCAPED FROM THE MARKET

INCIDENTS OF RUNAWAY animals were not uncommon in Chelmsford but the day saw an example that was to have tragic consequences.

At Chelmsford Market a cow belonging to a Great Waltham farmer, Arthur Pyne, broke lose as it was being led to the auction ring. It charged through two eight feet high wooden doors and ran into Market Road, Tindal Street, the High Street and into Springfield Road, and in the process charged and narrowly missed many people.

Once in Springfield Road it found its way into the garden of number 196, home of Dr. Robert Pitts. As attempts were made to corner the cow it panicked and struck Dr. Pitts' only daughter, Mary Sedgwick. She fell and hit a stone step, sustaining a serious injury from which she was to die nine days later.

Friday 7th May 1943

INQUIRY INTO FIRE SERVICE FAILURES IN FIRE RAID HELD IN PRIVATE

A two day N.F.S. enquiry was begun to investigate public complaints about its inefficiency and delay during the air raid on Chelmsford on 15th April. At its conclusion a confidential report, which was thought to have praised the work of the firemen but recommend an alternative system of 'calling' them to incidents, was sent to the Home Office for its delectation.

Tuesday 4th May 1943

WORK ON NEW AERODROME AT BOREHAM BEGINS

Construction of Boreham Aerodrome was begun by the U.S. Army 861st Engineer Aviation Battalion. Consisting of about 560 men, it had arrived at Greenock in Scotland, two days earlier on board the liner Queen Elizabeth.

Thursday 13th May 1943

EYEWITNESS ACCOUNT:

"A typical American would be sitting on a chair, reading a book, smoking a cigarette or cigar with his rifle lying on the ground beside him."

As told to our our Special Correspondent

"In the war if you wanted to go anywhere the only thing to do was to go by bike or walk. We used to cycle, in twos or threes all around the Chelmsford district and one of our favourite destinations was Boreham Aerodrome.

When construction was begun we saw the first signs of access being restricted. I remember seeing American soldiers by the roadside on guard duty. A British guard would, if on duty, be either standing or walking around with his gun, but the Americans were far more relaxed. A typical American would be sitting on a chair, reading a book, smoking a cigarette or cigar with his rifle lying on the ground beside him.

As you rode by he'd give you a nonchalant wave, say "Morning chum", and if you spoke nicely you might even get a piece of chewing gum or candy off him.

On one occasion a chap over there told us that the Marauders the Americans flew from there were considered to be very dangerous aircraft. He reckoned that if your plane was hit you hadn't a chance of using a parachute because the Marauders were so designed that if you jumped out the tailplane caught your head and chopped it off!"

Les Appleton

CHELMSFORD IS BLITZED

Biggest raid of the war leaves more than 50 people dead

ALMOST 1,000 MADE HOMELESS

The 14th May 1943 Chelmsford Blitz: The symbols ● represent each major incident location. (Author)

IN THE EARLY hours Chelmsford experienced what was to prove to be its heaviest air raid of the war. In a sharp attack that lasted for just over an hour, the Luftwaffe dropped a large number of H.E.s, incendiaries and parachute landmines which caused extensive damage to residential, commercial and industrial properties and led to the deaths of around 50 people.

Perfect conditions

Weather conditions were almost perfect for the raid. The previous day had been sunny and warm, and the fine weather had continued overnight with good visibility enhanced by bright light from a moon that was just over its zenith. There was just a slight south-westerly breeze.

The first indication that trouble was on its way came at 1.46 a.m. when the approach of 44 Do 217's of KG2 and 41 Ju 88's of KG6 towards the Essex coast led to the order being given to raise all of Chelmsford's barrage balloons to 4,500 feet. Five minutes later a bright flash was seen in the sky to the south-west of the town. Three minutes after that, at 1.54 a.m., Chelmsford's air raid sirens sounded the alert and a minute later the crash warning was given

Target flares dropped

The Luftwaffe was not long in coming. Within two minutes of the crash warning the first of an estimated 15 to 20 enemy aircraft were heard over Chelmsford. Pathfinder aircraft from the force dropped several clusters of red, green and orange target marker flares. Almost immediately they were engaged by the local Bofors guns sites of 403 Battery Light. Anti Aircraft. Troop A were to fire 196 rounds during the course of the raid and Troop C a total of 208 rounds.

Guided by the flares, the main

bombing force approached the town at an altitude of around 7,000 to 8,000 feet. The aircraft made their bombing runs from the south-west to north-east, apparently aided by the railway, and dived down to just above the barrage balloons to release their loads. Some unconfirmed reports suggested that they had travelled north to south before turning to make their bombing runs.

Rocket battery

Around 2.05 a.m. the Rocket Battery at Writtle fired its first salvo at the enemy bombers, just as the first bombs began falling on Chelmsford. It was to fire many times during the course of the attack. The raid rapidly developed over the next half an hour with dozens of incendiaries and H.E.s raining down on the town.

It had passed its peak by 2.30 a.m., though ten minutes later one of the bombers was seen to drop to about 3,000 feet, pass through the barrage and drop three bombs in quick succession, comprising of one in King Edward Avenue, another in Duke Street and one on the Telephone Exchange Garage.

Over 3000 properties damaged

By the time the aircraft departed for the coast Chelmsford had been struck by some 44 H.E.s, 6 parachute landmines, 25 unclassified devices, and 312 kg of incendiaries in 8 areas. Over three thousand properties were damaged in the Borough. The worst affected areas were the town centre, particularly around the railway station, Rainsford End, Boarded Barns, Moulsham and Widford. A total of 18 fires were started, though most were of a minor scale, with the worst at the Drill Hall in Market Road. In contrast to April's heavy raid the N.F.S. reported no problems with Chelmsford's water supply.

During the raid nine sets of baskets at the decoy site at Graces Walk, Little Baddow were

MARCONI'S POTTERY LANE WORKS FLATTENED

lit in an attempt to draw some of the bombing away from Chelmsford. Unfortunately the Luftwaffe pilots were not deceived, probably because of the brightness of the night, and consequently not one bomb fell within two miles of the site.

4 raiders shot down

The Luftwaffe lost at least four aircraft involved in the raid. They comprised of a Do 217 which was shot down by A.A. fire at Bawdsey in Suffolk, a Ju 88 that made a forced landing at Great Barton near Bury St. Edmund's and two other Do 217s that were shot down over the North Sea.

Factories escape

Despite the widespread nature of the bombing the Luftwaffe once again failed to cause significant damage to the town's important industrial targets. Of Chelmsford's nine 'Key Points' only Marconi's in Pottery Lane was seriously damaged, whilst of the remainder, Crompton's and Hoffmann's suffered only slight damage. Springfield escaped relatively unscathed, though further afield there were incidents at Great Baddow, Broomfield and Boreham, with heavy loss of life at the latter.

Thunderstorm

At 2.45 a.m., just after the raid ended, the first flashes of lightning were seen and rumbles of thunder were heard as a storm very suddenly came in a sky which had previously been practically clear of any cloud.

The order was given for the majority of Chelmsford's barrage balloons to be bedded down but several were struck by lightning. At 3.16 a.m. the Royal Observer Corps post in Great Baddow reported that it was raining hard. Seven minutes later Chelmsford's sirens sounded the all-clear.

IN THE NORTHERN part of Chelmsford the most serious incidents were caused by a pair of parachute landmines that were aimed at Marconi's Pottery Lane factory.

The factory consisted of a group of nine various sized, single storey buildings. They were sited in the centre of a 10 acre field with access via its north-east corner from Pottery Lane. To the south of the field lay Eves Crescent, to the west was Brownings Avenue and to the

north lay Sunrise Avenue.

One parachute landmine landed on open ground in the centre of several of the factory's buildings. It left a crater 31 feet across by 8 feet deep. Blast demolished three buildings immediately to the south of the explosion - the boiler house, the women's lavatory, and the newly completed, and as yet unused, testing shop. Further south the new assembly shop, comprising of four adjacent 30 feet span Nissun huts, was less seriously damaged - the Nissun

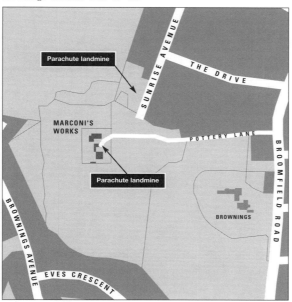

MARCONI'S WORKS

Parachute landmine

Parachute landmine

SUNRISE AVENUE

THE DRIVE

POTTERY LANE

BROOMFIELD ROAD

BROWNINGS

BROWNINGS AVENUE

EVES CRESCENT

Sketch map showing Sunrise Avenue and the isolated Marconi Pottery Lane works which were wrecked by a pair of parachute landmines on 14th May 1943. Since the war Sunrise Avenue has been extended across the site to join Eves Crescent. (Author)

hut nearest the bomb was partially collapsed, but damage to the building's contents were surprisingly light as the construction had a cushioning effect on the blast and debris. The thunderstorm that broke out immediately after the raid caused further water damage to exposed pieces of equipment and components that had been spared by the explosion, though a considerable amount of salvage was subsequently possible as most sets were only partially damaged. An air raid shelter situated close to the Nissun huts escaped undamaged.

To the north of the explosion, the old experimental station which had been used for testing until shortly before the raid, was badly damaged with several walls and its roof collapsed. Fortunately the building protected the air raid shelter and canteen, immediately to the north from much of the blast. Towards Pottery Lane the men's lavatory building and the timekeeper's hut both lost all their glass, doors and required new roofs and south walls.

Despite the destruction there were no casualties, primarily because there was no shift working at the time of the incident. There were only 15 people on site for testing work and all had taken shelter in the factory's dual purpose canteen and air raid shelter.

The site had been home to the company's Testing Station, but recently had been adapted as a dispersal from the company's main New Street works for the assembly and testing of wireless components for CR100 anti-submarine devices and receivers for all the services. Some 70% of its output was intended for the Admiralty, with the remaining

30% split evenly between the Ministry of Aircraft Production and Ministry of Supply. Its normal complement was of around 150 operators, working a day shift only, producing 100 sets a week at a cost of £48/10/0 per set. The factory had only been completed on 9th May 1943, and full production had yet to be attained.

In the week following the raid temporary arrangements were made for the assembly of the CR100 sets at New Street whilst repair work was begun. By the end of May 1943 work would be transferred to Waterhouse Lane, prior to a permanent dispersal to the Bettawear brush factory in Romford from mid-August 1943. It was subsequently estimated that the incident had resulted in the loss of about 100 of the CR100 sets.

The second parachute landmine aimed at Marconi's Pottery Lane facility fell to the north-east of the factory. It detonated on grassland 144 feet south of the last bungalows on the western side of Sunrise Avenue, leaving a crater 31.5 feet across by 8.5 feet deep.

Blast from the device caused widespread damage to local properties. On the western side of Sunrise Avenue the last two homes, numbers 34 & 36, were demolished, while number 32 was damaged beyond repair and numbers 18, 20, 22, 24, 26, 28 & 30 were seriously damaged. On the road's eastern side numbers 13 & 15 which faced the site of the explosion were demolished while numbers 17 & 19 were damaged beyond repair and number 21 seriously damaged. Around the corner, 11 & 21 The Drive were also thought to have been so severely damaged that demolition was necessary.

BARRAGE BALLOON SQUADRON IN THE THICK OF IT

Three Balloonists Killed near Cricket Ground

THE R.A.F.'S 993 SQUADRON was badly affected by the raid and the subsequent storm. Three balloon operators from C Flight were killed, and another three were less seriously injured and taken to hospital.

The three balloonists were killed when a 250 kg SC H.E. exploded within the compound of 993 Squadron's barrage balloon site 26, some 273 feet north of the east end of Chelmsford City F.C.'s New Writtle Street stadium. The dead men were L.A.C. L.S. Hall, L.A.C. H. Hunt and L.A.C. H. Telford.

11 balloons lost

Eleven of the squadron's balloons were lost - six were destroyed by lightning as follows: site 22, north-west corner of the Recreation Ground, at 2.45 a.m.; site 21, paddock at Tower House,

Springfield Road, at 3.30 a.m.; site 30, Oaklands Park, at 3.25 a.m., site 7, K.E.G.S. playing field, at 3.27 a.m.; site 23, south-east corner of Corporation Car Park, at 3.27 a.m.; and site 11, near Bishop's Hall, at 3.28 a.m.

Three other losses were caused when balloons were struck and destroyed by A.A. splinters as follows: site 9, football ground south of First Avenue, at 2.20 a.m.; site 2, Waterhouse Lane, at 2.30 a.m.; and site 25, Ritz Car Park, at 2.40 a.m.

Enemy aircraft collides with balloon cable

There were two breakaway balloons: the first occurred at site 12, a field opposite Springfield Hall Lodge in Arbour Lane, around 2.20 a.m when an enemy aircraft collided with and severed the balloon's cable - the balloon and some 1,400 feet of cable were

carried away in the wind. The second occurred at 2.34 a.m. when site 26, north of New Writtle Street and opposite Anchor House, suffered a direct hit from a 250 kg H.E.

Billet damaged

In other incidents the billet at site 19, opposite 67 Duke Street, was badly damaged by blast, as was the hut at site 23, in the south-east corner of the car park between the cattle market and River Can. The latter site had to be evacuated due to the presence of delayed action bombs.

All the balloon casualties were replaced by 10 p.m. on 14th May, save for site 26 which was to be relocated to a site north-east of the Army & Navy roundabout, and site 27, off Lower Anchor Street, which had to be evacuated because of a delayed action bomb.

Friday 14th May 1943

EYEWITNESS ACCOUNTS: POTTERY LANE BLASTS

"The blast blew in the glass from my bedroom window, along with the blackout shields which my father had made, and I awoke to find them on my bed."

As told to our our Special Correspondent

"Our house was number 37 Patching Hall Lane, a semi-detached property on the southern side of the road between Sunrise Avenue and Broomfield Road.

During the war my parents used to sleep in the Morrison shelter which was in the living room. I never went in that, as I was determined to sleep in my own bed which was upstairs in a back bedroom. I was woken when a pair of parachute landmines exploded a few hundred yards away above the Marconi premises at the top of Pottery Lane.

The blast blew in the glass from my bedroom window along with the blackout shields which my father had made and I awoke to find them on my bed. My parents, who didn't like me sleeping upstairs, were worried that I'd been injured but fortunately I was unhurt. Every window in the house was broken by the blast, but we didn't lose the slates off the roof since, unlike practically every other house in the lane and in

Sunrise Avenue. Ours was one of only two pairs that were slated. Those roofs didn't come off but all the tiled ones did. The reason was that slated roofs needed every slate to be nailed whereas the tiled ones were nailed down less frequently with intermediate tiles hooked onto one another. That enabled the blast to get under them and lift them all off."

Les Appleton

"The morning after the Pottery Lane factory had been hit by the landmine Marconi's asked for volunteers to go and help clear up. I was one of those that went along, There was a massive crater and all we seemed to do was throw anything we could into it - even completed radios because they were damaged, anything to fill it up. It was amazing what went into the crater and what is still buried there today!"

Jack Palmer

The Chelmsford Blitz: Friday 14th May 1943

BOARDED BARNS AND RAINSFORD:
CHILDREN DEAD IN KING'S RD FIRE
PARK AVENUE AND HOME SCHOOL WRECKED BY 1 TON BOMB

On the western side of Chelmsford the worst incidents were on the Boarded Barns Estate, where two children were killed, in Park Road, where the Home School was badly damaged, and in Sunningdale Road.

Boarded Barns was hit by a string of thirteen bombs, comprising of six 50 kg phosphorus (including three unexploded), six SBC 50 kg firepots and one unclassified unexploded device, that fell in a line across King's Road, Park Avenue, Swiss Avenue, Dixon Avenue, Corporation Road and Cooper's Row.

Children killed

One of the 50 kg phosphorus devices fell at the footings of 111 King's Road, the last house on the road's southern side. It caused structural damage and started a fire which led to deaths of nine year-old Alan Judd and his two year-old sister, Beryl.

At least five other people were injured in the incident. Another 50 kg phosphorus device landed on the roof of 15 Park Avenue, and caused slight structural damage to the house, but no fire. Two of the SBC 50 kg firepots fell in Park Avenue.

The first exploded in the centre of the footpath outside number 11d and fractured an 18 inch trunk gas main which was set alight for several yards. The fire was not extinguished until 10.30 a.m. later that morning when workmen managed to cut off the gas supply from either side.

The second firepot fell opposite number 16 and damaged a sewer. Further to the east, a third firepot struck 91 Swiss Avenue and started a fire which gutted the house. The property's occupants, who were sheltering in their Morrison, are believed to have escaped unharmed.

Pensioner killed

In Dixon Avenue an unclassified device fell in the back garden of number 25, some 100 feet from the road. Nearby, 67 year-old Alfred Offord was killed at his home, 30 Dixon Avenue. Across the road, a fourth firepot fell to the rear of number 7, while a third phosphorus device fell next door, behind number 8.

A fifth firepot fell harmlessly behind the two houses onto the King's Road School playing field. It was accompanied by two unexploded 50 kg phosphorus devices. A sixth firepot landed in the garden of a Corporation Road house which adjoined the playing field. It caused a small amount of structural damage, but no fire. Meanwhile a sixth 50 kg phosphorus device fell harmlessly to the rear of 1 Cooper's Row, some 315 feet from its junction with Broomfield Road.

Home School and Park Avenue wrecked

Considerable damage was caused by a 1,000 kg SC H.E. that exploded on the Essex Home School's recreation ground, 60 feet east of Park Avenue and some 500 feet south of the Home School itself.

The explosion left a crater 27 feet across by 4.5 feet deep and caused extensive damage to the Home School and several houses in Park Avenue that stood opposite it.

The school's headmaster, Reginald Fish, considered the building uninhabitable and was to request the Home Office's advice regarding its evacuation.

On the western side of Park Avenue two houses, numbers 36, & 38, were demolished. Seven others, numbers 32, 33, 34, 35, 37, 39 & 40, were damaged beyond repair, while numbers 26, 27, 28, 29, 30, 31, 41, 42, 43, 44 were seriously damaged.

On the eastern side of the road the worst affected house was number 11, immediately to the south of the bomb, which was also seriously damaged.

Sunningdale Road

To the west, an unclassified H.E. fell to the rear of 40 Sunningdale Road, home to the Rev. B. Vaughan Pryce. The device left a crater 38 feet across by 8 feet deep and seriously damaged the house.

Nearby, one SBC 50 kg firepot and an unexploded 50 kg phosphorus bomb fell on allotments and grassland, immediately north-west of Rainsford Senior School - today part of the school's playing field.

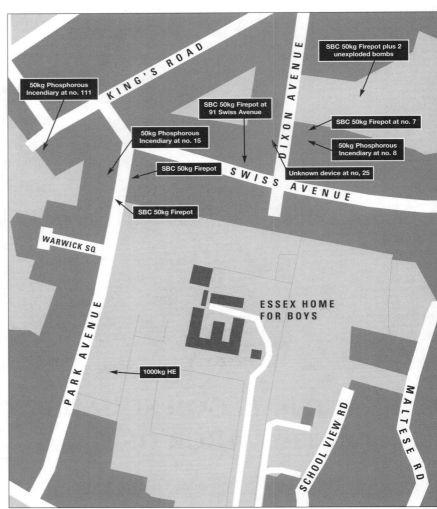

Sketch map showing the Park Avenue, Swiss Avenue and Essex Home School areas which were heavily bombed during the raid. (Author)

Numbers 40 to 35 Park Avenue, severely damaged by a one ton bomb that fell in the Essex Home School's recreation ground. (Taken from the book 'Changing Chelmsford' by John Marriage)

Modern day view of the rebuilt Park Avenue properties shown in the left photograph. In early 1996 the Home School playing field site was turned into a housing estate. (Author)

Friday 14th May 1943

The Chelmsford Blitz: Friday 14th May 1943

NINE KILLED BY PARACHUTE LANDMINE IN VICTORIA CRES.

Dozens of homes demolished or wrecked beyond repair

A PAIR OF PARACHUTE landmines, apparently intended for Marconi's, narrowly missed the factory and struck residential areas.

One fell to the north-west of the factory and scored a direct hit on 8 Victoria Crescent. The explosion there led to the deaths of nine people, the highest total from any incident within Chelmsford during the raid. Two others died when the other device exploded off Townfield Street.

The brunt of the blast from the Victoria Crescent landmine was felt by the terraced houses on the road's western side, with numbers 2, 4, 6, 8, 10, 12, 14 & 16, demolished. All the dead came from those properties: Gertrude Byford and her daughter Bessie Byford were killed at number 4; Lilian Arnold and her daughters Margaret Arnold & Lilian Taylor died at number 10; and George & Sarah Newman and their children Alfred & Elsie Newman were killed at no. 14.

Several of those killed are believed to have been burned alive after being trapped in their Morrison shelters. Five other people were reported to have been injured in the incident.

The remaining six houses on the western side of Victoria Crescent, numbers 18, 20, 22, 24, 25 & 28, were seriously damaged. Across the road numbers 1, 3, 5, 7, 9, 11, 13, 15, 17 & 19 were damaged beyond repair, while the last six houses, numbers 21, 23, 25, 27, 29 & 31, were seriously damaged.

In the streets close to Victoria

Crescent, blast seriously damaged 17, 18, 19, 20, 21, 22, 23, 24, 25, 26, 27, 28, 29, 30, 31 & Homeleigh Cottage in the northern portion of Glebe Road; and 94, 96, 98 & 100 Marconi Road.

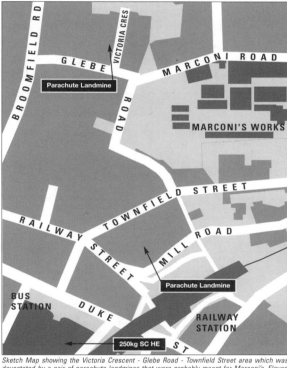

Sketch Map showing the Victoria Crescent - Glebe Road - Townfield Street area which was devastated by a pair of parachute landmines that were probably meant for Marconi's. Eleven people were killed by the two devices. (Author)

Modern day view of the rebuilt Victoria Crescent, viewed from Glebe Road. During the Chelmsford Blitz the first eight properties on the left where demolished by a parachute landmine. (Author)

Modern view of the rebuilt Victoria Crescent, looking towards Glebe Road. It was here that nine people were killed in the worst single incident of the Chelmsford Blitz. (Author)

EYEWITNESS ACCOUNT: VICTORIA CRESCENT

"A fire had broken out and they must have all been burned alive. My father and Mr. Ashford went out of our shelter to see what they could do, but the rest of us were told we'd got to stay where we were - I suppose as they didn't want us to see anything. As we waited there we could still hear the screams for help, it was dreadful."

As told to our our Special Correspondent

"I lived at 19 Victoria Crescent with my father, Percy Hagger, my mother and two brothers. Ours was an end of terrace house about half way along the eastern side of the road. At the time of the raid I was almost 16 years-old.

As soon as the siren sounded we got out of bed and rushed to the brick shelter which stood in our back garden. We shared it with our neighbours from number 17, Mr. & Mrs. Ashford, and they joined us in there too. The shelter was quite crowded. It had bench seats along each side, a wooden door and was normally lit by candles. It was my turn on a Saturday morning to clean it out and I was always worried by the spiders that used to live in there!

Almost immediately after we got into shelter the bombing began and it was quite horrendous. We were really scared as we knew that the Germans would be trying to bomb Marconi's just round the corner from us. As we sheltered suddenly there was a huge explosion as a landmine fell almost

directly opposite our house on the other side of Victoria Crescent.

My dad was standing against the shelters door and he was blown right to the back of the shelter with the door by the blast. He was shaken up but not seriously hurt. From outside we could hear terrible screams from people calling for help. At the time we didn't know what had happened but afterwards we found out that the people across the road had been trapped in their indoor shelter by the rubble from their house as it came down all around them.

A fire had broken out and they must have all been burned alive. My father and Mr. Ashford went out of our shelter to see what they could do, but the rest of us were told we'd got to stay where we were - I suppose as they didn't want us to see anything. As we waited there we could still hear the screams for help, it was dreadful. We were all crying and shaking and worrying to death what was outside.

That really shook us up. It was almost daylight by the time we came

out of the shelter and then we could see what damage had been done. We walked around and had a look at the devastation. The parachute from the landmine laid across Marconi's wooden fence which ran along Glebe Road. All the houses on the opposite side of Victoria Crescent had been demolished between Glebe Road and the passageway almost facing ours.

On our side of the road all the frontages were down as far as our house, which was wrecked and too dangerous to go into. Even so, my parents went upstairs to see if they could save anything but there was little that they could and the house was too badly damaged to live in anymore.

I went to see a friend of mine, Jean Redgwell, who lived round the corner at 94 Marconi Road. Her family had all been shaken up but they were unhurt. Their house was too badly damaged and they had to go and live with relatives in Hatfield Peverel afterwards.

During the morning the Salvation

Army or W.I. set up a canteen in Glebe Road outside Marconi's and we went there to get cups of tea and some food. None of us had anything to wear apart from our nightclothes so we went to the Women's Institute shop in Broomfield Road, next door to King's the dentist's, and they fitted us all out with clothes.

My parents got in touch with my uncle who owned our house and lived at The Wheatsheaf in Hatfield Peverel. Late in the afternoon he brought an open-back lorry down and we managed to load it with what furniture and possessions we could salvage from our house.

We couldn't actually go into Victoria Crescent so we took all our stuff out the back of the house and through the passageway into Marconi Road. My mother had a piano which she prided and the landmine had blown it into hundreds of pieces that were scattered all over the street. She picked them all up and we put them on the lorry too. After the war she got someone to put it all back together

again. Once it was loaded we all went off on my uncle's open lorry back to Hatfield Peverel and we lived there with my aunt and uncle for a while. We couldn't stay there all that long so eventually mum and dad got us a council house in Springfield Park Avenue.

Our house in Victoria Crescent wasn't rebuilt until a couple of years after the war had ended. We went back then but we didn't like it afterwards - it wasn't the same as before. We had been brought up in that house and had got used to it as it had been, but when it was rebuilt they did it differently.

There needed to be a bathroom and because there were three of us children living at home they had to put the bath where the old kitchen was with a table top over. In fact the style of the rebuilt house was really horrible. We called them 'Gerry-built' - talk about utility!"

Betty Pryke

The Chelmsford Blitz: Friday 14th May 1943

MARCONI NEAR MISS:
SECOND PARACHUTE LANDMINE FLATTENS TOWNFIELD STREET

ELDERLY COUPLE ARE KILLED

THE SECOND OF the pair of parachute landmines which narrowly missed Marconi's New Street works fell between Townfield Street, Chapel Place, Mill Lane and Railway Street.

It detonated directly behind 46 & 47 Townfield Street and 1 & 2 Mill Road, leaving a water-filled crater 35 feet across.

The explosion caused a considerable amount of damage to nearby buildings in the four surrounding streets, but inflicted only two fatalities, an elderly couple, George & Agnes Bonner, who were killed at their terraced home, 46 Townfield Street. The property was demolished by the blast along with its immediate neighbours, numbers 45 & 47.

The remaining 11 houses on the south-eastern side of the road, numbers 35, 36, 37, 38, 39, 40, 41, 42, 43, 44 & 45 were all damaged beyond repair. Opposite them, all 25 properties in the terrace from number 1 The Royal Steamer P.H. to number 25 The White Horse P.H. were seriously damaged. Beyond Glebe Road the remaining nine houses, numbers 26 to 34 Townfield Street were damaged to a similar degree.

As the raid was raging Mrs. Felton, who lived in Townfield Street, was rushed to Danbury Park Maternity Hospital where she gave birth to a daughter, Valerie.

The whole block formed by Townfield Street, Chapel Place, Mill Road and Railway Street was subsequently purchased after the war by the Council for use as a car park.

In the southern part of Glebe Road numbers 1, 2, 3, 4, 5, 6, 7, 8, 9, 10, 11, 12 & 13 were seriously damaged. All nine houses and the Mission Hall in Chapel Place were also so severely damaged that demolition was deemed necessary. It was a similar story in Mill Lane where numbers 1 & 2 were demolished outright, and numbers 3, 4, 5, 6, 7, 8, 9 & 10 were damaged beyond repair.

In Railway Street the worst affected property was number 16, occupied by the haulage contractor William Smith, and number 17 both of which stood between Townfield Street and Mill Lane. The pair were damaged beyond repair. Eight others in the road, numbers 9, 10, 11, 12, 13, 14, 15 and Rose Brothers' garage, were seriously damaged as were all ten houses in Steamer Terrace.

EYEWITNESS ACCOUNTS: TOWNFIELD STREET AREA

"Suddenly there was a terrific bang which turned out to be a landmine... It demolished practically the whole of Mill Road... My cousin, who had been at the top of the road, came into the shelter and said to us 'Well you haven't got a house anymore!'"

As told to our our Special Correspondent

"I had been on duty the previous evening at the Y.M.C.A. in Victoria Road where I worked as a volunteer in the canteen which was used by a lot of servicemen. After I finished I walked up to my sister-in-law's at 2a Highfield Road. My brother was in the army and they had a baby so I was staying with her.

During the night we heard this dreadful bombing and we knew that the town was being badly hit. I became very worried because my parents lived in New Street and their house was very close to Marconi's, Hoffmann's and the railway which the Germans were bombing. They weren't on the phone so I told my sister-in-law that I wanted to go and see if they were alright.

I started walking but when I got down near the railway station they wouldn't let me through because part of the railway station and the bus station had been bombed. So instead I had to walk up Broomfield Road and down Glebe Road.

By then I realised I couldn't walk in the pair of high heels I'd been wearing, so I took them off and went barefoot. As I walked down Glebe Road and by Marconi's I could see the area had been badly hit. There were fires everywhere, ruined buildings, ambulances, firemen and rescue personnel. Seeing all the destruction, my apprehension grew about what I was going to find when I actually got to my parents' home in New Street. When I eventually reached there, to my great relief I found my mother and father and family were all safe and unharmed in the shelter."

Eileen Hance

"At the time of the raid I was aged 26 and was living with my mother, Ada Copsey, and my cousin, Leslie Dawson at 10 Mill Road. Leslie had come from Lowestoft to live with us when he'd got a job at Marconi's. My father, Sidney Copsey, had died earlier in the war. Our house was a rented, three bedroomed terrace cottage which stood facing the railway embankment. As you looked at the front of it, to the left were numbers 9 to 1 Mill Road going towards Railway St., while to the right was a passageway and then the side of 9 Chapel Place. Chapel Place led off Mill Road at right angles and then went off up to Townfield Street, opposite the junction with Glebe Road. Further down Mill Road there was Ridley's Mill and then the back of Marconi's factory.

The previous day had been gor-

geous - very hot and sunny. In the evening I had been on a Young People's League walk all around Springfield and back down Bunny Walk. The night was very warm, which was just as well because most of our household ended up running about in our pajamas! We'd all gone to bed and were woken by the sirens.

We got up and I went out in the back garden to see what I could see. My mother remained indoors for a while, but then she decided to go to the brick and concrete communal shelter, in the back garden of 8 Chapel Place, which we shared. I stayed in our back garden and stood watching the searchlights in the sky above. At that time there was no gun fire, but after a while I decided to join my mother in the shelter. I don't know why I did - perhaps it was some instinct that drove me there, because I'd never bothered to go into the shelter before. I usually roamed about in the garden, looking up, but if I'd stayed out there I should probably have been hit by shrapnel or something and killed.

After a while we could hear the sound of bombs coming down and it was obvious to us that it was a heavy raid. Occasionally we'd hear the rockets firing in the Recreation Ground and that was a comfort to us. In the shelter it was rather funny because there was an elderly lady who had a glass eye, and in the middle of the air raid she looked at me and said 'Peggy, is my eye in straight?'!

Suddenly there was a terrific bang which turned out to be a landmine that had fallen at the top of Mill Rd. near Railway St. It demolished practically the whole of Mill Rd., including our house and all the houses in Townfield St. that backed on to them. My cousin, who had been at the top of the road, came into the shelter and said o us 'Well you haven't got a house anymore!'.

The noise from the explosion deafened him for some weeks afterwards. The rest of us were unhurt We got outside to see what had happened. Our house was still standing, but was very badly damaged. I went inside to have a look around and get some clothes to wear. The chairs had splinters of metal in them, there was dust everywhere, and it smelt horrible. We had an outside loo and water was pouring out of that. In the distance we could see the explosions as ammunition at the Drill Hall went up.

The police and rescue people

came along quite quickly to help us. Next door there was a very old lady and her daughter, and they carried them out. At first we didn't really know what to do with ourselves, so we went across the road and sat on the embankment and just waited. We managed to get our portable radio so we listened to that.

The first people who came in the morning to give us some comfort were, of course, the Salvation Army who arrived with a food van to dole out tea and food. Soon after that the gas man came down, went in what was left of our house and emptied the gas meter. We had a lot of sightseers come round, and that was horrible. They were all wandering down the road and I blew my top at a couple who were snooping around our house. Someone else took my cousin's bicycle from the embankment and he had to go to the police station to get it back. That was not all - later on when we'd left someone took all the coal from our indoor coal place!

My cousin and I managed to salvage a fair amount from our house but we smashed a lot of things which we couldn't pack and objects that weren't really necessary, such as our expensive china. As it turned out we needn't have, because our district visitor, Mrs. Sharp, sent for men from her husband's business, Henry Potter Ltd. builders of Fairfield Road. They came down with their lorry and collected all our stuff and took it to be stored at their workshops.

I went to report that we were bombed out at an office in Threadneedle St. We hoped to be rehoused but that never happened, though the social services assessed the damage at our property and we got £86 compensation in the end.

The morning after the raid my mother went to stay with her sister's-in-law who lived at 29 Victoria Road. When we went there I said to my aunt 'We've been bombed out!'. She replied "Oh we've had a window broken!". My cousin and I were invited to stay with Mr. & Mrs. Hance in Coval Lane, and did so for about six weeks. Eventually we got rooms in a house in South Primrose Hill where there was a table shelter. We would sleep on mattresses on the floor under that. Surprisingly I was not afraid of being bombed again, but ever since the raid I have never like loud noises."

Peggy Brown

Wartime view of the damage inflicted by the Townfield Street parachute landmine. In the foreground is Mill Lane and in the distance, running left to right, is Townfield Street itself. (Battle Over Essex)

Salvage work under way after the the Chelmsford Blitz. Despite the 'wartime spirit' incidents of looting of bombed properties were reported. (Battle Over Essex)

The Chelmsford Blitz: Friday 14th May 1943

EYEWITNESS ACCOUNTS: TOWNFIELD STREET AREA

"The blast knocked the whole of the shelter over, but we were saved by the wooden sleepers which protected us from the blast and shrapnel."

As told to our our Special Correspondent

"My father, William Smith, ran a haulage business with premises on the north side of Railway St., between Townfield St. and Mill Rd. He had a large yard there, and next to that was a long narrow house called 'Langlands' (number 16), that went off Railway St. along one side of the yard. As you stood in Railway St. facing the house, Rose Brothers' garage was to its left towards Townfield St. and to the right was my father's yard which was behind a long brick wall, and then 17 Railway St. which was on the corner with Mill Rd.

Langlands was a large house and it was home to my father, mother, brother Ken, myself and my husband Jack. When the sirens went we were all in bed - my husband and I were up on the top floor while my parents and my brother were sleeping downstairs as my mother wouldn't go upstairs. When the Bofors guns opened up and I quickly jumped out of bed, but my husband said 'I'm not getting out of bed, not til I hear anything'. I told him 'You're getting out of bed now', and he did!

We ran down the top landing and the second landing, then into the hall where I grabbed the dog's lead that was hanging there and I pushed the dog, Trixie, into my mother's arms for her to take.

I was worried about my cat, Panda, who used to sleep in a big locker up in the shed at the top of the yard so I went to open the back door to go and get her - I worshiped that cat. By then the flares had begun to come down so my husband wouldn't let me out to get her. As we stood there a neighbour, Miss Seabrook, began knocking at the door. She had run round from number 17 where she lived with a nurse midwife, Annie Carter. We let her in and the six of us made our way to our shelter.

The shelter was in a large room at the far end of the house. Mr. McShane, the vet who owned the house before us, had used the room as his surgery and we had it as a little cafe. The shelter itself was in the far end of the room and it had been built by my father from wooden railway sleepers. It was square shaped and had been thought so interesting that some people came from the War Office to photograph it. Inside there were little stools to sit on but no lighting.

We'd been inside the shelter for only a few minutes when there was this terrific explosion right behind our house as a landmine exploded. We hadn't heard it falling as it was on a parachute. For a split second I though 'This is it!. We were all terrified. The blast knocked the whole of the shelter over but we were saved by the wooden sleepers which protected us from the blast and shrapnel. We were all shaken but none of us was hurt though my father's woollen jacket was slashed across the back as if someone had tried to get at him with a knife.

We stayed in the remains of the shelter until it was almost daylight when the rescue people finally reached us and helped us out. My brother had managed to get out before us and had gone to the Co-op. bakery across the road. We were taken to the Coval Lane Rest Centre where we were given cups of tea. The Salvation Army were very good and gave us all spare clothes to wear - all I'd got on before then was the red nightdress that I'd gone to bed in.

My father was anxious to go back to the house to get hold of some money that he'd taken out of the bank the day before to pay some bills. We rushed back as soon as we could, and it was a good job we did because there were people looting the place. My father damn near killed them. Eventually we found the money, buried under some bricks. My mother had been in a state too because her false teeth had been left behind when we'd gone to the shelter, but we also managed to find them.

Our lovely house had been practically demolished by the landmine and we'd lost almost everything. There was no way we could live there. There was a big cupboard in the kitchen and my mother had a set of every glass there was. When I saw it I thought 'Oh good, we can save that!' as it seemed alright, but as we touched it the whole lot crumbled and we couldn't save any thing.

Outside in the yard there was a huge crater which had filled with water from a burst water main. It looked like a swimming pool and the rescue people didn't go near it as they couldn't tell how deep the water was. There had been my father's lorry and a 32 seater coach parked in the yard overnight that was used to get people o work - that was completely smashed to pieces. There had also been no end of bicycles in the shed where Panda had been, including my brand new one, but they and the shed had been obliterated by the terrific blast.

We used to have an outdoor shelter and some chickens in a run but we never saw no more of them after. A brick wall had stood at the back of the yard and behind that was Thomas Moy's coal yard which had its entrance off Townfield St. The blast had knocked the wall onto a horse which was trapped by its back legs. The police had to shoot it to put it out of its misery.

Three days later I was at the front of the house with my husband trying to see what I could salvage when I heard the sound of a cat meowing. We didn't think that it could be Panda because we hadn't seen her since before the raid and we thought that she had been killed.

Anyway we pulled all the bricks and debris away and there was the little face of my cat and she was alright. I would have lost anything bar that cat. The blast from the landmine must have taken her from the shed right across the yard and into Railway St. She wasn't injured at all, just absolutely terrified and afterwards whenever she heard a plane she would panic.

After the raid my mother and brother went to Writtle to stay at her mother's while my father, my husband and I went to live with a friend's in another part of the village. At first my father wouldn't stop in the house at night until he gradually got his nerve back. After a few days he met a friend of ours, Fred Smith of Steven's Farm in Chignall St. James. Mr. Smith offered us a cottage on his farm to live in so we moved there. My father had lost his lorry and my husband was too ill to work so we had no means of income, only living on the bank.

To get some money we used to go pea picking, potato picking and things like that . Eventually someone told us that there was a bungalow in the village which had got evacuees from London in it.

They couldn't stick the country any longer and they were going back to London dead or alive. My father went quick round the council offices and told them about the bungalow and they allowed him to take it. It was in a filthy state but we cleaned it up and stayed there for the rest of the war.

When the war was over my father went back to the council and asked them what would happen about our home. After the raid the whole square bordered by Townfield St., Chapel Place, Mill Rd. and Railway St. had been cleared of the bombed buildings and levelled by the council.

They told him to draw up plans and we could have our house rebuilt, but they changed their minds and told us that they wanted the land for a car park. Eventually, after a lot of fighting the council built us a new house in Mill Rd., called Townfield House. It was almost opposite the footpath tunnel under the railway to Victoria Rd., and father started up his business there again.

When the Townfield St. car park was rebuilt as a multi-storey one our house was in the way and was the only one that had to be demolished."

Winifred Wales

"After the air raid sirens went my family made our way to our shelter which was in a room at the back of our house, 16 Railway Street. My father had built wooden sleepers around it to give it extra strength. We'd been in there between a quarter and half an hour when suddenly there were clouds of dust and soot as a parachute landmine exploded just behind the house. We were so close to the explosion that I never heard a thing.

The single storey room collapsed around us and the timber was cracked open by the blast. If we hadn't have had that I reckon we'd all have been killed. I a daze my first thought was to get out of the shelter. I clambered out over the rubble and broken glass, looked around and made for the Co-op. bakehouse across the road which was built like a fortress. I went in there and I thought I was seeing ghosts when I saw the bakers there all covered in flour. The rest of my family joined me later and we all went to the First Aid Post in Coval Lane.

All of Chelmsford's barrage balloons had been up that night. Some were struck by lightening and were brought down as a big thunderstorm came on during the raid. I reckon that drove the German planes away, otherwise we'd have really had it that night. That storm probably saved Chelmsford.

Later in the morning we went back to have a look, Although much our house was still standing, most of it was in such a bad way that it was too dangerous to go in. We heard that some people were trapped in their houses in Mill Road, just round the corner from our house. I went over there to see if I could help.

There was a brick shelter outside on of the houses with an emergency exit where the bricks fell away. I went inside - it was dark and as I peered around I put my hand on something wet. I thought 'It's blood!', so I rushed outside quick as anything and looked at my hand which was covered in paint.

Afterwards I asked one of the chaps, when he had been rescued, 'What have you got in your shelter?'. 'Oh' he said, 'I store my paint in there'. I replied 'You frightened the life out of me!'.

Kenneth Smith

BOMB SCORES DIRECT HIT ON TOWN'S BUS STATION

Many buses destroyed

A view of the bus station in Duke Street which was devastated by a 250 kg bomb. (Courtesy Blitz Then & Now)

A 250 kg SC High Explosive bomb scored a direct hit on Eastern National's Duke Street Bus Station. The explosion and subsequent fire seriously damaged the building and destroyed 13 buses.

The device penetrated the centre of building's roof and then detonated against a lattice girder. The blast demolished a 64 feet long stretch of the rear wall down to within a few feet of the ground and left the remainder badly damaged.

Fire spreads to homes

The Bus Station's roof was entirely stripped of its glass but the offices along the Duke Street frontage escaped serious damage. A fire broke out in the south-eastern corner of the building when hot fragments penetrated the lubricating oil store.

Flames quickly spread and destroyed 15 vehicles parked inside the Bus Station, a collection of around 250 tyres and all of the tyre fitting equipment.

All seven houses in East Road, which ran behind the Bus Station, suffered serious damage from a combination of blast and flames from the fire. Another four properties in Duke Street were seriously damaged by the bomb; numbers 28 The Plough Hotel, 29 Chelmsford Dry Cleaners, 30, & 32 Newcombe's cycle shop. Debris forced the closure of the road's entire length.

15 buses destroyed

The Bus Station had housed some 43 buses, including three that had been converted into ambulances, one staff car and a Tilling's van. Of the buses, 15 were totally destroyed, 20 had extensive damage to their bodies and slight to their chassis, while the remainder suffered minor damage.

Three large N.F.S. pumps were sent to deal with the fire and their crews took around an hour and a half to get the blaze under control. There were only two slight casualties - a Mr. Lockwood who suffered shock and back injuries when he was caught by the blast just outside the Bus Station's air raid shelter, and a fireman who sustained cuts whilst damping down afterwards.

Despite the loss of so many buses Eastern National was able to resume most of its normal operations by midday, including all essential factory services.

Draughty journeys

For many people the journey to work was on buses entirely lacking glass, with gashed panels and roofs, and their interiors littered with debris. Certain town services could not be run because of air raid damage in other parts of Chelmsford. Eastern National's surviving fleet was augmented by eight buses drawn from Messers Tilling's of Westcliff, and from Eastern National's other depots; 14 from the striking Gray's depot, 3 from Colchester, 6 from Luton & Bedford, and one from Hitchin. Following its experiences in the raid the company was to implement an increase in the dispersal of its vehicle fleet.

In a postscript to the incident - on 9th August 1943, Reginald Baker, a 37 year-old fitter from Queen Street, was injured when a bomb he had discovered at the back of the Bus Station exploded in a vice while he was examining it. Mr. Baker was a Senior Warden! Later, in April 1946, Mr. Oliver, a bus driver who lived at 4 East Road, was to discover a suspected unexploded bomb in his back garden. It was believed to have also been a remnant of the raid.

The L.N.E.R. down line was blocked at Chelmsford Station by debris from the Bus Station and the signal box was damaged by blast. However, there was no serious effect on essential rail traffic.

The Chelmsford Blitz: Friday 14th May 1943

VICTORIA ROAD AREA:
MANY BUILDINGS HIT

Hawkes shop, YMCA and telephone exchange all badly damaged by bombs

The Victoria Road area was the struck by several devices which caused serious damage to property, but fortunately not to life.

YMCA demolished

One 250 kg H.E. scored a direct hit on, and demolished, the Y.M.C.A. in Victoria Road. The building would not to be completely rebuilt until 1956. Blast from the bomb also seriously damaged Sam's Coffee bar opposite the Y.M.C.A. (today's Back-Inn-Time) and its neighbours, Tindal Cottage and St. Mary's Lodge in Cottage Place. The latter was being used by Marconi's as auxiliary work rooms.

Middle of the road

A 250 kg bomb fell at the junction of Duke Street and Victoria Road. It detonated in the road and inflicted serious damage to several nearby properties, an N.F.S. water pipe and telephone cables.

To the east of Victoria Road, 27 Duke Street, occupied by the dentist Frederick Jones, was seriously damaged, while to the west, Hawkes' confectionery shop at number 27a was practically demolished, and the County Motor Works' garage, workshop & flat, The Cottage and the L.N.E.R. Stationmaster's House were all seriously damaged.

On the opposite, southern, side of Duke Street numbers 64, 65, and Cannon's Restaurant were also seriously damaged, as were offices in the neighbouring Prudential Building on the corner with Market Road (today's Victoria Road South).

Telephones disrupted

Another 250 kg H.E. exploded on the Telephone Exchange garage roof, 90 feet west of Cottage Place and 90 feet north of its junction with Legg Street.

The garage was partly demolished, but despite the disturbance the Exchange was able to maintain essential services, even though public calls were disorganised.

Blast from the bomb affected several nearby properties; immediately to the north of the Exchange, 15 & 16 Cottage Place were both damaged beyond repair, and numbers 9 & 10, which stood opposite the Telephone Exchange on the northern corner with Legg Street, were seriously damaged.

Two views of the Y.M.C.A. in Victoria Road which received a direct hit from a 250 kg. bomb. (Courtesy Blitz Then & Now and Battle Over Essex)

COUNTY HALL IN NEAR MISS

But two killed nearby

TWO PEOPLE WERE KILLED by bombs that fell in the vicinity of County Hall

A 250 kg H.E. fell close to County Hall, 45 feet south of Duke Street and 248 feet from Market Road (today's Victoria Road South), causing considerable damage in the vicinity.

It demolished several small assembly shops, belonging to the County Council's Land Agent's Office and numbers 74, 75 & 76 Duke Street.

A middle-aged lady, Ellen Dowsett, was killed at the office premises of number 74. Next door, number 75, housed Flexman's radio specialists premises while number 76 was occupied by the optician Philip Parkes. Following the raid Mr. Parkes was to relocate his business and share with Loveday & Wilson at their High Street practice.

Two other properties, 70 & 71 Duke Street, occupied by Hilliard & Ward and Stunt & Sons respectively were seriously damaged. All the stained glass windows on the Cathedral's southern side. were destroyed by the blast.

To the west, Arthur J. Arnold's building contractor's premises in Market Road (today Victoria Road South) were damaged beyond repair, while to the south a number of properties were badly affected in King Edward Avenue. There, the W.V.S. depot at number 2 was seriously damaged, while the house at number 3 was demolished, and the Baptist Minister's home at number 17 seriously damaged.

Further along King Edward Avenue another 250 kg H.E. scored a direct hit on the rear portion of number 10, a two storey brick dwelling on the south side of the road. The device killed Ida Machell at her home, number 9. The blast left numbers 9, 10 & 11 all so severely damaged that demolition was thought necessary, while numbers 12 & 13 were seriously damaged.

Hello boy, hello boy!

Number 11 was occupied by Cecil Bocking, a chiropodist and an Inspector in the Special Constabulary. After the raid he was searching through the ruins of his house when he heard a voice calling 'Hello boy, hello, boy!' from beneath the rubble. Somewhat startled, he dug through the debris and discovered his 20 year-old African Grey Parrot still alive and unharmed save for a covering of dust and plaster. Mr. Bocking had assumed that the bird had been killed.

Elsewhere, an SBC 50 kg firepot fell 68 feet to the north of Duke Street and some 80 yards north-west of the junction with Threadneedle Street, leaving a crater 6 feet across by 2 feet deep. The device seriously damaged Sycamore Cottage and was accompanied by unexploded device which fell 128 feet north of Duke Street and 207 feet from its junction with Threadneedle Street.

A view of the junction of Victoria Road and Duke Street where a bomb caused extensive damage to Hawkes Brothers' shop. (Taken from the book 'Changing Chelmsford' by John Marriage)

Another view of the bomb damaged junction of Duke Street and Victoria Road. The site was redeveloped in the 1980s as Saxon House. (Book of Chelmsford)

M.E.T.C., DRILL HALL & THE 'REC' HIT

Considerable damage was inflicted in the Park Road area with the Mid Essex Technical College (M.E.T.C.) and Drill Hall the worst effected buildings.

One 250 kg H.E. exploded just 10 feet from the southern end of the 1938 vintage commerical block and workshops at the M.E.T.C. (today's university). The building, which housed laboratories that had been requisitioned by the War Office, suffered serious damage for a distance of 50 feet from its southern end. The explosion also damaged three houses in Park Road beyond repair, numbers 19, 20 & 21. Another seven, numbers 22, 23, 24, 25, 26, 27 & 28, were seriously damaged.

A pair of SBC 50 kg firepots fell onto the Drill Hall in Market Road to the rear of those houses. One struck a roof coping and exploded on the flat roof of the eastern building while the other fell in the north-western corner of the Drill Hall's courtyard, close to the ammunition dump. The latter device started a fire which spread to the dump and resulted in an inevitable series of huge explosions when stores of small arms, ammunition and grenades caught fire.

Damage at the Drill Hall was described as serious and debris

fell scattered all over the Home Guard's Rocket Battery in the Recreation Ground, immediately to its south.

The Rocket Battery had an eventful night. Early in the raid a bomb splinter put the its radar out of action and hardly had the crew repaired it then it was once more put out of action.

After that the Battery fired by improvised barrage with only one definite misfire, but 79 rounds not fired through drill faults. Sgt. Lewis and two other men who were manning the Battery's Lewis gun had a fortunate escape when a bomb that fell at their feet failed to explode. The Battery's Sgt. W.G. Eve was later awarded a certificate of meritorious service for smothering an incendiary.

The Recreation Ground itself was also struck by a stick of five small unclassified devices. One fell 100 feet east of the railway and 20 feet north of the River Can; a second landed 750 feet east of the L.N.E.R. viaduct and 100 feet north of the river; the third and fourth fell 20 feet north of the river, and 175 feet west and 50 feet west of the boundary with the Market respectively; while the fifth fell on a tennis court 168 feet from the boundary with the Market and 90 yards north of the river. The refreshment rooms were damaged by blast.

Friday 14th May 1943

The Chelmsford Blitz: Friday 14th May 1943

BOMBS EAST OF THE REC

Four SBC 50 kg firepots and three unexploded devices fell immediately to the east of the Recreation Ground on land now occupied by Bellmead and High Chelmer.

One firepot landed on one of several buses dispersed parked in the open air in the Corporation Car Park, approximately 30 feet east of the boundary with the Recreation Ground and 173 feet north of the River Can. A total of eight buses were lost as a result of the fire and blast, including four that were gutted and another two which were burned out. The second, third and fourth firepots fell in the Corporation Car Park, 184 feet east, 190 feet east and 222 feet of the Recreation Ground boundary and 100 feet, 42 feet and 163 feet north of the river respectively.

Of the unexploded bombs; one fell in the Corporation Car Park, 152 east of the Recreation Ground boundary and 110 north of the River Can; a second fell 80 feet north of the river, directly in line with Threadneedle Street; and a third fell in Bell Meadow, 108 feet east of Threadneedle Street 138 feet east of the right angle bend in the road.

EIGHT DIE AS HOMES HIT IN LOWER ANCHOR ST.

Rescuers commended for their brave efforts

AT LOWER ANCHOR STREET a 250 kg H.E. scored a direct hit on number 22, an old terraced house on the road's northern side between The Orange Tree and The Queen's Head P.H.s. Eight people were to die as a result of the explosion.

On that side of the road the bomb demolished numbers 21, 22, 23, 24 & 25, while numbers 19, 20 & 26 were damaged beyond repair, and numbers 13, 14, 15, 16, 17, 18, 27, 28, 29, 31, 32, 33, 34, 35, 36 were seriously damaged.

Across the road the explosion seriously damaged numbers 89, 90, 91, 92, 93, 94, 95, 96 & 97 which stood opposite the scene of the bomb.

At number 19 the bomb claimed the lives of William & Mary Judd. The couple's 11 year-old daughter, Doreen, was trapped in the remains of the property for a considerable time afterwards. She was eventually rescued via a cellar by Senior Warden Brett, formerly the head gardener for the late Mayor, John Ockelford Thompson. Mr. Brett was subsequently praised by the Regional Commissioner for his efforts.

Three people died at number 22 - Sidney & Cissie Westrip and their lodger Gwendoline James. The Westrip's baby daughter, June, was to die later in hospital from her injuries. At number 24, a married couple, Henry & Joan Smith were also killed.

Meanwhile Robert Wilson, from number 20, was badly injured and had to spend several weeks in hospital recovering. On his discharge he was to discover that looters had stolen several items from his bombed home, including a lino, utensils and a jacket.

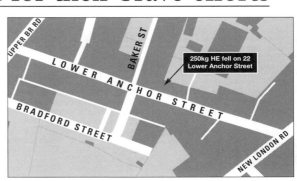

Sketch map showing Lower Anchor Street where eight people were killed by a 250 kg. bomb during the 'Chelmsford Blitz'. (Author).

NEW WRITTLE STREET AREA

BALLOONISTS KILLED

Five bombs, comprising of two 500 kg H.E.s, one 250 kg SC H.E., one 50 kg H.E., and one unexploded, fell between the River Can and New Writtle Street. The 250 kg device killed three R.A.F. balloonists.

One of the 500 kg H.E.s fell in a hedge running westwards from the County Cricket Ground to the River Can near the footbridge into the Recreation Ground. It detonated some 235 feet west of the Cricket Ground and in the process created a crater 50 feet across by 12 deep. A 5 inch water pipe was also damaged.

The other 500 kg device fell 142 feet north-east of the first, on a tennis court some 40 feet from the river. Its crater was 44 feet across by 12 deep, with a mound of returned earth standing some 6 feet high in the crater.

The 250 kg SC H.E. exploded within the compound of barrage balloon site 26, 273 feet north of the east end of Chelmsford City F.C.'s New Writtle Street stadium.

Three barrage balloonists were killed as a result of the explosion; L.A.C.s Arthur Telford, Leslie Hall, and Thomas Hunt. Another three, L.A.C.s H. Potkins, F. Ashworth and H.F.L. Hobson were taken to hospital.

The bomb left a crater 20 feet across by 5 feet deep, while the balloon was lost and the winch badly damaged. Blast from the device seriously damaged seven masionettes in a nearby cul-de-sac - numbers 8, 9, 10, 12, 13, 14 & 16 Hayes Close.

Meanwhile, the 50 kg H.E. fell in the middle of the County Cricket Ground, 120 feet from the southern boundary and 100 feet from the eastern one. No significant damage was caused apart from a shallow crater 7 feet across by 1.5 feet deep.

The unexploded bomb landed between the River Can footbridge and Seymour Street, some 54 feet south of the bridge. The bombs were accompanied by an ABB 500 incendiary container which deposited 63 of the 1 kg incendiaries across London Road, the Chelmsford & Essex Hospital, County Cricket Ground and River Can. One of the incendiaries is believed to have started a fire which badly damaged E. Palmer's carriers yard, which was located in premises in New Writtle Street behind the Select Cinema. Others set alight and caused serious damage to Eastern Automobile's London Road premises and to the neighbouring building occupied by the coachbuilders, A. Young & Sons.

To the west

On the western outskirts of town, five unclassified devices fell in a line, south-west to north-east. across the fields from Writtle Mill (beside Writtle Road) towards Waterhouse Lane.

One detonated on the edge of the River Wid's Mill Race, near Writtle Mill. Blast from the explosion demolished a wooden store shed on the edge of the crater, and seriously damaged a brick store house 70 feet away, along with a detached cottage a hundred yards away.

The second device fell 110 feet along a hedge that ran northwards from the north-east corner of the gravel pit behind South View Cottages, Writtle Road. Since the war the site where the bomb exploded has become part of the Hylands School playing field.

A third fell in the middle of the ploughed field immediately to the north-east of the same gravel pit, and the fourth, close to the north-eastern corner of the same field.

A fifth, unexploded, bomb fell harmlessly into the allotments immediately west of Waterhouse Lane, 100 yards south of Ash Tree Crescent.

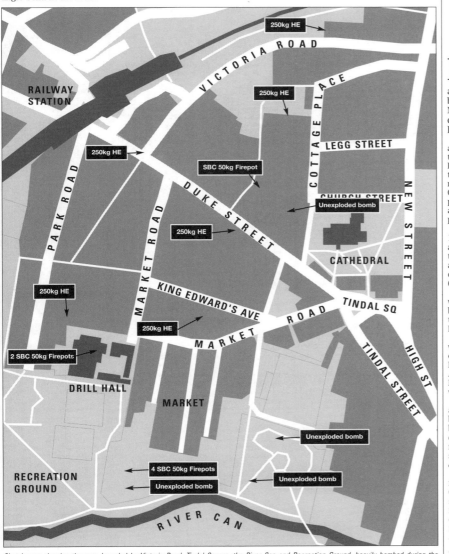

Sketch map showing the area bounded by Victoria Road, Tindal Square, the River Can and Recreation Ground, heavily bombed during the Chelmsford Blitz. (Author).

COUPLE DIE IN UPPER BRIDGE ROAD BOMBING

9 houses destroyed, 2 others beyond repair

A 250 KG. BOMB struck the tarmac pavement outside 109 Upper Bridge Road, close to the corner with Cherry Garden Lane. The explosion, which left a crater 9 feet across by just 2 feet deep, led to the deaths of two people and caused extensive destruction.

Houses flattened

On the eastern side of Upper Bridge Road, numbers 109, 110, 111 & 112 were demolished, number 108 was damaged beyond repair and numbers 100, 101, 104, 105, 106 & 107 seriously damaged.

Across the road, 113, 114, 115, 116 & 117 Upper Bridge Road were all demolished, while number 118 was damaged beyond repair and numbers 119, 120, 121, 122 & 123 seriously damaged.

The fatalities occurred at number 115, where Ernest Dale died along with his daughter Vera Willis. Nearby, at number 117, 84 year-old Ernest Cass was rescued from his wrecked house by his grandson Mr. P.G. Cass.

Gas main fracture

The explosion cracked the gas main in Upper Bridge Road and water from the adjacent water main entered and flooded the whole of the mains in the local area - some 281 properties were affected and the water was not cleared until 18th May.

Men from the Colchester Gas Company were to make an invaluable contribution in helping the Chelmsford Gas Undertaking's men to restore supplies at this, and numerous other incidents, caused during the raid. The Council was to subsequently pay the Company £30/12/9 for the cost of their assistance.

Blast damage at Crompton's

Blast from the device swept across the L.N.E.R, and badly damaged the offices at Crompton's.

However, the general production of electric motors, switchgear, instruments and generators at the factory was not affected.

Post-raid view of houses at the southern end of Upper Bridge Road, damaged by a 250 kg bomb that fell on the pavement outside number 109. Crompton's factory is in the background. (Courtesy Blitz then and Now)

Modern day view of the rebuilt houses at the southern end of Upper Bridge Road as seen from the Writtle Road railway bridge embankment. (Author)

OLD MOULSHAM BADLY AFFECTED

HOUSES STRUCK: 7 PEOPLE DEAD

The residential area between Baddow Road and Lady Lane was particularly badly affected by a string of nine bombs plus incendiaries, perhaps intended for the Gas Works, that fell in a line between Mildmay Road and Lynmouth Avenue.

5 die in Goldlay Road

Two 500 kg H.E.s fell between Goldlay Road and Lynmouth Avenue, close to Baddow Road. One scored a direct hit on 45 & 46 Goldlay Road, and killed five people.

shelter just 30 feet from the lip of the crater escaped undamaged. Further south three 1 kg incendiaries struck 61 and 62 Goldlay Road. Number 62 was gutted while number 61 had its roof destroyed by the ensuing fire.

2 killed in shelter

.In Lynmouth Avenue a pair of 250 kg H.E.s that fell either side of the road caused considerable damage.

One detonated in the tarmac pavement on the road's eastern side, outside number 36, home to Leslie Clark the Borough's Deputy Registrar of Births & Deaths.

Grove Road respectively. No fires were caused in the former three roads, but at the latter one caused a fire in a bed that was extinguished by a warden.

Mildmay Road

The vicinity of Mildmay Road and Rochford Road was struck by four SBC 50 kg firepots and one unexploded bomb.

The latter struck the rear of 18 Mildmay Road, a single-storey brick dwelling. It rendered the property damaged beyond repair, while its neighbour, number 16, and number 22 were seriously damaged. The device was accom-

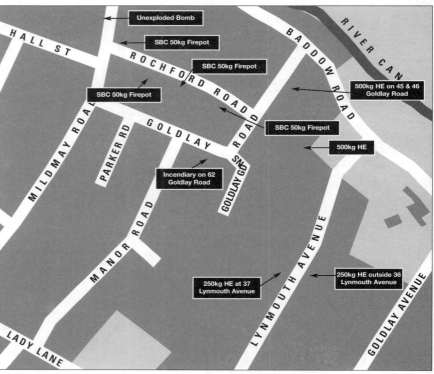

Sketch map of Chelmsford showing the Mildmay Road - Goldlay Road - Lynmouth Avenue area where several bombs fell in the early hours of 14th May 1943, killing seven people. (Author).

Three people died at number 45, a site now covered by the west-bound lane of Parkway. They were a middle aged married couple, George and Florrie Simms, and Lily Lidbetter whose husband ran a furnishing business at 45 Baddow Road.

At 46 Goldlay Road two widows were killed, Alice Snow and Elsie Gledstone. The bomb left numbers 45, 46, 47 & 62 damaged beyond repair, whilst numbers 48, & 61 were seriously damaged.

The other 500 kg H.E. fell near to the boundary of an orchard and garages that lay between the back gardens of houses in Goldlay Road and others in Lynmouth Avenue.

The device left a crater 45 feet across by 16 feet deep, totally demolished five small garages and seriously damaged 65 Lynmouth Avenue. One surface

The explosion left a crater some 17 feet across and demolished numbers 32, 34 & 36, left numbers 30, 38 & 40 damaged beyond repair and numbers 26 & 28 seriously damaged.

The second 250 kg H.E. exploded across the road at number 37, just twelve feet from a brick surface shelter. An elderly woman, Elizabeth Baker, who was in the shelter, was killed when the wall nearest the bomb collapsed on her. Her husband, Charles Baker, was to die from his injuries a few weeks later.

The bomb left a crater 19 feet across by just 2 feet deep and left numbers 31, 33, 35, 37, 39 & 41 damaged beyond repair, while number 43 was seriously damaged.

Meanwhile, another four 1 kg incendiaries fell in Lady Lane, Bouverie Road, Roman Road and

panied by four 1 kg incendiaries that fell at the western end of Rochford Road.

Meanwhile an SBC 50 kg firepot scored a direct hit on 21 Mildmay Road, a one storey property on the northern corner of the junction with Rochford Road, opposite The Woolpack P.H.. The device ignited a small gas main and started a fire that rendered the property uninhabitable and threatened with demolition.

A second SBC 50 kg firepot fell at the bottom of the garden of 21 Rochford Road and failed to cause any serious damage, though a shelter, a dozen feet from where it fell, was cracked by the vibration.

The other two SBC 50 kg firepots landed in the back gardens of numbers 30 and 31, but neither caused any fire or significant damage.

The Chelmsford Blitz: Friday 14th May 1943

Modern day view of garages between Goldlay Road, Lynmouth Avenue and Parkway. During the Chelmsford Blitz a 500 kg bomb fell here. An identical device killed 5 people in Goldlay Road. (Author)

Modern day view of the western side of Lymouth Avenue. A 250 kg bomb fell at number 37, killing 2 people and left the house and four neighbouring properties damaged beyond repair. (Author)

Modern day view of houses on the eastern side of Lynmouth Avenue. Here a 250 kg bomb exploded on the pavement outside number 36, demolishing it and two other houses. (Author)

SPRINGFIELD ESCAPES

IN MARKED CONTRAST to the fire raid a month earlier the Springfield area suffered comparatively little from the Luftwaffe's attentions.

Two unexploded devices fell on farmland, one either side of the track leading from Springfield Hall to Lawn Lane Lodge.

Parachute landmines

To the south of the track, one of a pair of parachute landmines exploded in a field close to the present day junction of Waveney Drive and Tamar Rise, leaving a crater 31 feet across by 8 feet deep.

The second of the devices fell on open ground between the River Chelmer and Arbour Lane, just north of William Seabrook & Sons' orchard and 200 yards to the north-east of Hoffmann's. It created a huge crater 55 feet across by 18 feet deep. At Hoffmann's damage was confined

to broken glass, asbestos roof sheets and the blackout. No devices actually fell within the factory's perimeter and production on the night shift was subsequently affected for one night only.

River Chelmer

However two suspected ABB 500 containers fell nearby on marshy ground just north of the River Chelmer and only about 400 feet north-east of the factory. Their loads of 1 kg type incendiaries were spread harmlessly over open ground. Many of the devices were thought to have subsequently been taken away by souvenir hunters.

Further east, a single 50 kg firepot fell in the grounds of Bishopscourt, 30 feet from Springfield Road and 210 feet from Stump Lane. The bomb failed to cause a fire or any damage.

THE RURAL DISTRICT: BROOMFIELD

BROOMFIELD CHURCH SERIOUSLY DAMAGED

The Chelmsford Rural District area received around 17 tons of bombs, comprising of nine 50 kg H.E.s, twenty SBC 50 kg firepots, one 50 kg phosphorus bomb, five 250 kg H.E.s, fifteen 500 kg H.E.s, four 1,000 kg H.E.s, seven parachute landmines (including one unexploded), and 12 unclassified (including seven unexploded).

The majority of them fell between Broomfield and Boreham, though a unknown number of H.E.s are thought to have fallen in Great Baddow.

Broomfield was struck by six parachute landmines, two 500 kg SC H.E.s, two 250/500 kg SC H.E.s, ten SBC 50 kg firepots, and four AB 36 containers.

Starting to the west of the village, ten SBC 50 kg firepots fell scattered about a wheat field to the south-west of Priors Farm. They were accompanied by the two 250/500 kg SC H.E.s.

Further to the east, one 500 kg device fell in a bean field at Parsonage Farm, some 500 feet from the farmhouse, while another exploded in Broomfield Churchyard. Both left a shallow crater 25 feet across by 4.5 feet deep.

The Eleventh Century Church, with its distinctive round tower, was very seriously damaged by blast and fragmentation.

Many stained glass windows were lost, its roof was stripped of tiles and its interior devastated by pieces of masonry, brick, glass, timber and tiles. Outside dozens of gravestones were shattered and mature trees reduced to ugly stumps.

Despite the damage villagers, assisted by Boy Scouts, were able to clear the building of debris sufficiently to enable the wedding of L/Bdr. Alfred Franklin and Kathleen Freeman to go ahead there on 15th May 1943.

An early assessment of the Church suggested that repairs would cost about £2,500 including £650 for the organ. The damage was such that services had to subsequently be transferred to Broomfield School, and it was initially thought that it would not be possible to return to use the Church until the end of 1943.

Four ABB 36 containers fell at Broomfield Hall, immediately to the south-west of the Church. Although they spread and set fire to several barns Broomfield Hall was saved from the flames.

Five of the parachute landmines came down on land to the east of the River Chelmer in the vicinity of Back Lane, and the sixth fell to the west, close to Mill Lane.

One exploded in a turnip field belonging to Pratts Farm, south of Pratts Farm Lane and west of Belsteads Farm. It created a crater 30 feet across by 6 feet deep.

The second fell unexploded in a gravel pit three hundred yards to the south. It was subsequently dealt with by members of a Royal Navy bomb disposal squad. The third came down on the edge of a

Broomfield Church which was badly damaged by a 500 kg bomb that fell in the churchyard to the north of the building in the early hours of 14th May 1943. (Author)

gravel pit 300 yards south-west of Channels Farm and left a crater 25 feet across by 5 feet deep.

The fourth exploded in a gravel pit to the north-east of the junction of back Lane and Belsteads Farm Lane, making a crater 28 feet across by 7 feet deep.

The fifth came down in a field at Stubbing's Farm, immediately east of Belsteads Farm Lane. It left a crater 23 feet across by 5.5 feet deep and inflicted serious damage to a pair of semi detached two storey cottages. 150 yards away, and to Channels Farmhouse, some 200 yards away.

A 1,000 kg H.E. exploded a few hundred yards to the south-east, in the farm's Blue Post Field. It left a crater 60 feet across by 8 feet deep and fell close to the searchlight site between Belstead Hall and Channels.

To the west, the sixth parachute landmine exploded in Windmill Field, immediately to the south of Mill Lane and close to Broomfield Mill. The explosion left a crater 28 feet across by 6.5 feet deep and seriously damaged three detached brick dwellings.

Meanwhile further to the south, a string of half a dozen H.E.s, comprising of two 250/500 kg SC types, two 500 kg SC types and two 50 kg SC types, fell between the River Chelmer and Little Waltham Road, to the east of Broomfield Mill.

The 250/500 kg H.E.s fell 40 yards apart in a wheat field at Hill Farm, close to the River Chelmer. The bombs left craters 38 feet across by 11 feet deep and 43 feet across by 12 feet deep respectively. To the south-east, the 500 kg H.E.s fell 50 feet apart in a wheat field of Marriage's Farm - blast from them destroyed wooden outbuildings 30 feet from one of the bombs.

They formed craters 33 feet across by 8 feet deep and 41 feet across by 12 feet deep respectively. The 50 kg devices fell further to the south-east, either side of the Little Waltham Road.

To the south, and just into Springfield, a parachute landmine exploded above a wheat field at Grays Farm. A brick built, thatched cottage, just 30 yards from the explosion, was damaged beyond repair. The device left a crater 27 feet across by 7 feet deep.

GREAT BADDOW

100 HOUSES DAMAGED

AN UNKNOWN NUMBER of H.E.s caused widespread damage, but no serious casualties, in the vicinity of Beehive Lane in Great Baddow.

Warden's Post F1 reported that 50 properties had been damaged in Beehive Lane & Dorset Avenue; Post F2 reported that 25 had been similarly affected in Beehive Lane, Loftin Way & Avenue Road; Post F3 reported one had been damaged in Beehive Lane; and Post 4 reported 16 had been similarly affected in the Dorset Avenue extension, Chelmerton Road & Baddow Road.

TEENAGER KILLED AT WIDFORD

At Widford a string of five bombs appears to have been aimed at the A12 bridge over the L.N.E.R.

One 50 kg SC H.E. fell between the railway and Links Drive, some 120 feet down the latter. Across the railway an identical device fell to the rear of 65 Widford Road, injuring four people.

One of them, 17 year-old Gerald Blundell, was to subsequently die from his injuries. Other 50 kg SC H.E.s fell in a hedge on the western side of Widford Chase and in a ditch 44 feet north of the A12 and 310 feet west of the railway. A fifth, unclassified device, fell nearby into the ploughed field 200 feet north of the A12 and 110 feet west of the railway.

NEW HALL HOSPITAL BOMBED

AT LEAST 11 ELDERLY PATIENTS DEAD

Post-raid views of New Hall at Boreham whose bombing on 14th May 1943 led to the deaths of 11 elderly people. (Courtesy Essex Chronicle)

BOREHAM WAS BOMBED with a particular intensity with the Luftwaffe returning once again to target the 270 bed New Hall Emergency Hospital. Two of the H.E.s scored direct hits on the building and caused at least eleven fatalities.

The bombing commenced with the dropping of a container of 1 kg incendiaries, followed ten minutes later by nine H.E.s, comprising of three 250 or 500 kg SC H.E.s, three 50 kg H.E.s and two large unidentified H.E.s.

As soon as the raid began the able bodied patients from the top floor had been led into the basement shelter while the infirm remained asleep in their beds. Around 20 of the Hospital's staff were outside on Fire Guard duties when the incendiaries began falling around them.

Of the 1 kg type incendiaries, 34 were subsequently counted in the grounds of New Hall, and a further 19 in the fields up to Walter Hall. As they burned out they served as target markers for the H.E.s which fell close by.

One 250/500 kg SC H.E. exploded in the grounds of New Hall, 238 feet west of the west wing and left a crater 46 feet across by 12 feet deep. A second, unidentified, device fell 72 feet further south, forming a crater 38 feet across by 10 feet deep. A 50 kg H.E. fell 17 feet north and 53 west of the west wing, leaving a crater 12 feet across by 4 feet deep.

Nearby one 250/500 kg SC H.E. fell 100 feet from the north side of the west wing, level with the centre of the wing. The explosion left a crater 46 feet across by 14 feet deep and caused slight blast damage to the building. Meanwhile, a pair of 50 kg H.E.s exploded to the south; one fell 16 feet from the west wing and 80 feet to its south, leaving a crater 23 feet across by 3 feet deep, while the second fell 40 feet from the wing and 80 feet to the south, leaving a crater 12 feet across by 4 feet deep.

Direct hit on wing

The worst damage and all of the fatalities was caused by a 250/500 kg SC H.E. which scored a direct hit on New Hall near the main entrance to the courtyard. An area of the wing some 30 feet by 52 feet was destroyed by the bomb and some 20 elderly people were trapped in the wreckage.

A second direct hit was caused by an unidentified H.E. which struck the wall of the west wing in the inner courtyard and then penetrated a six inch concrete surface before exploding and tearing up concrete for a radius of 20 feet. Blast from the bomb demolished up to 50 feet of the wing's frontage.

Staff and other patients quickly rushed to the wrecked wing and were joined by Policemen and Wardens in the rescue and recovery work which was to last for 48 hours. During that time several people were dug out alive, including 92 year-old Mrs. Caroline Hamshire, and 89 year-old Kate Cloake who was blind and rescued uninjured.

Elderly Casualties

The first casualty report, sent to Essex Police H.Q. some seven hours after the raid, gave a total of 23 casualties at New Hall, including 5 fatalities and 10 serious. However, a final report on 19th May 1943 spoke of 71 casualties, including 7 fatal, 25 admitted to hospital and 39 minor. The seven elderly people who died at New Hall were Angelo Clarke, Thomas Farrow, Sophia Gersen, William Holmes, Phillipa Hook-Newman, William Mason and Frederick Wilson.

Four of those admitted to hospital were to die later. They were Sarah Cooper, William Hill, Frederick Middleton and Mary Poulter. The majority came from south-west Essex and had been evacuated to New Hall from the Suttons Institution at Hornchurch early in the war. Among the survivors was Mrs. Emma Ritcher from Rainham, who was to stay in hospital until April 1946 when she died at Stisted Hall Hospital aged 100 years and 10 months.

After the raid patients were transferred to other hospitals throughout Essex - the last few would eventually leave New Hall on 14th September 1943 when the building was re-occupied by nuns. By then one of the craters in the ground had filled with water and had been stocked with roach, apparently thanks to the activities of local schoolboys!

Bombs in fields

To the south of New Hall an 500 kg SC H.E. fell in a pea field to the east of the drive leading up to New Hall from Roman Road, to the north-east of the New Hall railway signal box. It left a crater 19 feet across by 4 feet deep on land that belonged to the Fordson Estate. The bomb was accompanied by three unexploded devices.

To the south-west three 250/500 kg SC H.E.s fell; one in a pea field and the other two in a potato field on Hodges Farm, either side of the drive. They left craters 33 feet across by 8 feet deep, 31 feet across by 9 feet deep and 29 feet across by 8 feet deep respectively. An unclassified device fell in a neighbouring beet field immediately to the west. Nearby 415 H.A.A.'s site close to Old Lodge Farm escaped unharmed and was able to fire a total of 81 rounds at the enemy bombers during the raid.

Half a dozen bombs, comprising of two 250/500 kg SC H.E.s, three SBC 50 kg firepots and one unidentified device, fell in fields to the north-east of New Hall, between Bull's Lodge, The Grove and Duke's Wood. The 250/500 kg SC H.E.s exploded 50 yards apart in a field that was part of the Fordson Estate leaving craters 33 feet across by 10 feet deep. They were accompanied by the unidentified bomb which fell some 200 yards to their east and left a similar sized crater. Meanwhile, the string of three firepot devices fell to the east of Mount Maskell on land that formed part of the Air Ministry's Boreham Aerodrome estate. They failed to cause any significant damage.

Aerodrome bombed

Boreham Aerodrome was also struck by at least four and a half ABB incendiary containers.

One fell in an apple orchard 600 yards south-west of Dukes Lodge. It failed to operate or explode and burned out on impact as did an identical device that landed 500 hundred feet to the south-east. The half container was discovered a further hundred yards to the south-east, while the third and fourth complete containers fell another 120 feet and another 600 feet to the south-east - the latter on the edge of Dukes Wood. Neither had operated correctly. An additional one-and-a-half ABB 500 containers were reported to have fallen in a field to the south-west of Mount Maskell.

Further to the north-east, a string of four SBC 50 kg firepots dropped close to Douglas Farm in Russell Green. One fell in an orchard 50 yards north-east of the farmhouse, while a second landed just 75 feet north-east of the farmhouse, spreading incendiary material up to thirty feet. The third and fourth both fell in the orchard on the west side of the road immediately opposite the farm.

THE AFTERMATH:
CASUALTIES & COMMENDATIONS

An accurate total for the number of casualties caused by the raid is difficult to ascertain with many conflicting figures given.

The following casualty reports for Chelmsford were received at the Essex Police H.Q. after the raid;

4.05 a.m. 14th May: 3 killed, 10 wounded, unknown trapped.

5.10 a.m. 14th May: 6 killed, 19 wounded.

8.30 a.m. 14th May: 9 killed, 28 wounded.

9.35 a.m. 14th May: 14 killed, 51 wounded.

5.42 a.m. 14th May: 28 killed, 52 wounded.

1.46 a.m. 16th May: 46 killed (including 5 servicemen), 49 seriously wounded (plus 2 R.A.F. & 2 Army) & 70 slightly wounded.

Most published accounts give a total of 46 killed and 226 injured, though my research would indicate that 40 civilians died during the raid, a further six died from their injuries in hospital, plus an additional five servicemen, including three balloonists and an American soldier. This gives a total of at least 51 fatalities. The true figure is likely to have been higher as some of the seriously injured may have died weeks or even months later in hospital. Chelmsford's four First Aid Casualty Stations dealt with almost two hundred cases;

Boarded Barns F.A.P.: 9 casualties plus 3 to hospital.

Chelmsford & Essex Hospital: 45 casualties plus 22 to hospital.

Coval Lane Clinic: 66 casualties plus 7 to hospital.

St. John's Hospital: 42 casualties plus 20 to hospital.

Commendations

The work of the rescue services at all the incidents of the Chelmsford Blitz was to receive praise from all quarters.

Special Constable Eric Thomas Bailey of The Cottage in Springfield Road, and a builder by trade, was later awarded the B.E.M. for his initiative and devotion to duty while rescuing patients at New Hall Emergency Hospital. He had conducted much of the highly dangerous rescue work aided by Special Constable F.L. Guttery.

The Chief Constable later commended several officers, including Special Constable F.L. Guttery, for their initiative and devotion to duty when dealing with various air raid incidents following the Blitz.

Those honoured were: Special Constables E.T. Bailey, J.C. Blooman P.A. Groves, J.F. Grinham & G.H. Ketley; Police War Reservists A.T. Watts & L.A. Fulcher; Sergeant L.R. Bridge; Constable W.E. Bake; and Special Sgt. C.J. Sweet.

Three of the officers, Messers Ketley, Watts and Fulcher, commanded by Sgt. Harry Warnes and aided by five wardens, rescued a woman, boy and girl who were trapped in a collapsing house. The woman later died. An American soldier, Cpl. Thomas Guergen, was fatally injured during the rescue attempt and died later in hospital.

Of the wardens, the highest praise went to Warden Albert W. Morton of Post C15 (Public Library). He was subsequently commended by King George VI for his instrumental part in the rescue of four people trapped in a Morrison shelter. Senior Wardens Charles A. Brett of Post B14, and Reginald C. Baker of Post B15 were praised by the Regional Commissioner, while the following Wardens were commended by the Chief Warden, W.V. Wakefield, in a letter to the Chief Constable;

Group A: Group Warden F.G. Gunn, Wardens H.V. Gard, H.M. Imrie, P.F. Lambert, H.W. Plantin & J.H. Ward; Group C: Deputy Group Warden A.E. Wiseman, Wardens W.G. Percival, A.H. Spurgeon, A.E. Young & N.F. Alexander; Group D: Group Warden C. Stubbings; Group E: Senior Warden E.A. Brown, Wardens E.A. Blandford, J. Waskett, H.G. Goodfellow, G.K. Machell & L.I. Van Roegen; Group F: Group Warden S.F. Shead; Group H: Senior Wardens E.W. Peek & B. Harvey.

Mutual assistance

Chelmsford's civil defence services were hard pressed to deal with the consequences of the raid and help was rapidly called in from neighbouring districts under the Mutual Assistance Scheme. Rescue parties, ambulances, mobile canteens and first aid squads arrived from bases at Billericay, Brentwood, Colchester Hornchurch, Maldon and Thurrock, with the last mobile canteen not returning from Chelmsford until 25th May.

The raid rendered hundreds of homes uninhabitable through bomb damage with almost 1,000 people required to be billeted out. The task was undertaken by the Council's Billeting Office, which by coincidence had been due to re-open the morning of the raid in new premises at 3 London Road, having outgrown the Vestry Hall in New Street. The new office opened its doors at 5 a.m. and such was the generous response of the public that compulsory billeting measures were not required to house the homeless. Most were housed in the town, though many found accommodation in rural areas all around Chelmsford.

The Chelmsford Blitz: Friday 14th May 1943

THE PRICE: VICTIMS OF THE BLITZ

Lilian Annie Arnold, Margaret Louisa Arnold, Lilian Ivy Taylor.

Forty-three year-old Lilian Arnold and her two daughters, 18 year-old Margaret Arnold & 24 year-old Lilian Taylor, were killed when a parachute landmine exploded close to their home, 10 Victoria Crescent. Mrs. Arnold was married to Charles Arnold, while their daughter Lilian was married to Gunner George Taylor R.A.

Elizabeth Baker and Charles Daniel Baker.

Sixty-six year-old Mrs. Baker was killed when a 500 kg H.E. exploded close to her home, 39 Lynmouth Avenue. The device demolished a wall of the air raid shelter in which she had taken cover, trapping her under the rubble. Her 59 year-old husband, Charles, was severely injured and was to subsequently die as a result of his injuries in an Epping Hospital a few weeks later. For over 20 years he had been on the G.P.O.'s engineering staff at Chelmsford. He was buried at the Borough Cemetery on 28th July 1943.

Gerald Ivor Blundell.

Aged 17, he was the son of John and Emma Blundell of 11a Widford Chase, and is believed to have been killed by a 50 kg SC H.E. that fell close to his home.

George Edward Bonner and Agnes Bonner.

Sixty-five year-old George Bonner and his 69 year-old wife, Agnes, were killed when a parachute landmine exploded behind their home, 46 Townfield Street.

Gertrude Lilian Byford and Bessie Lilian Byford.

Sixty-two year old Gertrude Byford and her 42 year-old eldest daughter, Bessie, were killed when a parachute landmine exploded close to their home, 4 Victoria Crescent. Mrs. Byford's husband, James, survived the incident. Bessie Byford worked in Chelmsford's A.R.P. Control Centre. Their funeral service was held at the London Road Congregational Church on 20th May 1943, with burial afterwards at the Borough Cemetery.

George Chapman.

Ninety-three year old George Chapman, of 44 Primrose Hill, died at the Chelmsford & Essex Hospital from injuries that he is believed to have sustained during the raid. The exact circumstances of his death are unclear but it is thought that he may have been struck by falling shrapnel or debris.

Angelo Clarke.

Aged 83, he came from 64 Stevens Road in Dagenham and was one of 7 people killed when a 250/500 kg SC H.E. scored a direct hit on New Hall Hospital.

Sarah Ann Cooper.

Aged 78, she came from 65 Kinfauns Road in Ilford and died in the Chelmsford & Essex Hospital on 14th May 1943 from injuries sustained from a 250/500 kg SC H.E. that scored a direct hit on New Hall Hospital. She was the daughter of the late Robert Cooper.

Ernest Alfred Dale.

Aged 64, he was the youngest son of Detective Inspector Dale of the Essex Police and married to Mary Dale. Mr. Dale was an employee of the County Council and had worked at Crompton's for 32 years. He was killed when a 250 kg H.E. exploded in the road opposite his house, 115 Upper Bridge Road. His daughter was also killed in the incident and they were subsequently buried together at the Borough Cemetery after a service at St. John's Moulsham.

Ellen Emily Alice Dowsett.

Aged 54, she was the daughter of George & Annie Dowsett of George Street and was killed when a 250 kg H.E. demolished 74 Duke Street.

Thomas Farrow.

Aged 92, he was one of 7 people killed when a 250/500 kg SC H.E. scored a direct hit on New Hall Hospital.

Sophia Gersen.

Aged 84, she was the widow of Henry Gersen and came from 80 Woodfield Drive in Gidea Park. She was one of 7 people killed when a 250/500 kg SC H.E. scored a direct hit on New Hall Hospital.

Elsie Ida Gledstone.

Aged 51, she was the widow of Thomas Gledstone and was killed when a 500 kg H.E. struck 46 Goldlay Road. She was killed along with Alice Snow and was subsequently buried at Holy Trinity Church on 19th May 1943.

Corporal Thomas A. Guergen.

Aged 23, he died in hospital from injuries that he sustained whilst attempting to rescue a woman and two children from a bomb damaged house in Chelmsford. He came from Charleston in Virginia and for his gallant efforts he was posthumously awarded the Purple Heart. His English girlfriend, Gladys Jones, who lived in New Street only heard of his death when she wrote to Cpl. Guergen's brother in the U.S.A. who revealed the tragic news to her.

Leading Aircraftsman Leslie Samuel Hall, R.A.F.V.R.

He was one of three balloonists killed when a 250 kg SC H.E. bomb exploded within the compound of 993 Squadron's barrage balloon site 26, north of the east end of Chelmsford City F.C.'s New Writtle Street stadium. Aged 35, he was the son of Samuel and Mary Hall, and married to Daisy Hall of Burton upon Trent. He was buried at Burton upon Trent cemetery in Staffordshire.

William Charles Hill.

Aged 73, he came from 3 Russell Road in Walthamstow and died in St. John's Hospital on 24th July 1943 from injuries sustained from a 250/500 kg SC H.E. that scored a direct hit on New Hall Hospital. He was married to Sarah Hill.

William John Holmes.

Aged 56, he came from 156 Marley Road in Barking and was one of 7 people killed when a 250/500 kg SC H.E. scored a direct hit on New Hall Hospital.

Phillipa Rowe Hook-Newman.

Aged 80, she came from 61 Oldchurch Road in Romford and was the widow of Sidney Wilkins Hook-Newman. She was one of 7 people killed when a 250/500 kg SC H.E. scored a direct hit on New Hall Hospital.

Leading Aircraftsman Thomas Harold Hunt, R.A.F. (Aux. Air Force).

He was one of three balloonists killed when a 250 kg SC H.E. bomb exploded within the compound of 993 Squadron's barrage balloon site 26, north of the east end of Chelmsford City F.C.'s New Writtle Street stadium. Aged 42, he was the son of Thomas and Gertrude Hunt of Birmingham and married to Eleanor Alice Hunt of Acocks Green in Birmingham. L.A.C. Hunt was buried at Solihull Cemetery, Warwickshire

Gwendoline Iris James.

Aged 23, she was the daughter of Mr. & Mrs. Frederick James of Violet, Beatrice Road in Laindon and was killed when a 250 kg H.E. scored a direct hit on her lodgings at 22 Lower Anchor Street. She died along with the house's occupiers, Sidney & Cissie Westrip and their baby daughter, June.

Alan Judd and Beryl Ina Judd.

Nine year-old Alan Judd was the son of George & Hazell Judd of 111 King's Road. He was killed when a 50 kg phosphorus bomb struck the property. His sister, Beryl,

Counting the cost - residents of Chelmsford checking the post raid casualty list on a noticeboard outside the library. The tall woman, second from the right is Mrs. Sharpe, a district visitor. (Battle Over Essex)

was seriously injured in the incident and died in hospital two days later. Their funeral was held at Holy Trinity Church on 26th May 1943.

William and Mary Judd.

Thirty-six year-old William Judd and his 36 year-old wife, Mary, were killed when a 250 kg H.E. fell close to their home, 19 Lower Anchor Street. Their 11 year-old daughter, Doreen, was rescued from the wrecked home, having been trapped in the rubble for some time.

Lily Harriet Lidbetter.

Aged 63, she was the wife of Arthur Lidbetter, who ran a house furnishings business from premises by their 45 Baddow Road home. Mrs. Lidbetter was killed along with George and Florrie Simms at 45 Goldlay Road.

Ida Violet May Machell.

Aged 42, she was the daughter of C.E. Dawson of Enfield, married to George Machell of 9 King Edward Avenue, and was killed when a 250 kg H.E. fell close to the property. Her husband, Mr. G.K. Machell, was the manager of The Essex Fencing Company and a warden based at the Shire Hall Post. They had a son and a daughter. Mrs. Machell was subsequently buried at the Lavender Hill Cemetery in Enfield on 22nd May 1943.

William Stacey Mason.

Aged 81, he came from 84 Cambridge Avenue in Gidea Park. He was the son of the late Mr. W. Mason of Bocastle in Cornwall, and the husband of the late Emma Mason. He was one of 7 people killed when a 250/500 kg SC H.E. scored a direct hit on New Hall Hospital.

Frederick James Middleton.

Aged 83, he came from Rothsay, Ongar Road in Brentwood and died in St. John's Hospital on 31st May 1943 from injuries sustained from a 250/500 kg SC H.E. that scored a direct hit on New Hall Hospital.

George Newman, Sarah Ann Newman, Alfred George Newman and Elsie May Newman.

Sixty-five year-old George Newman was killed along with his 64 year-old wife Sarah, their 33 year-old son, Alfred, and 28 year-old daughter-in-law, Elsie, when a parachute landmine exploded close to their home, 14 Victoria Crescent. Alfred Newman was a fireman with the N.F.S. The four victims were subsequently buried at the Borough Cemetery on 22nd May 1943.

Alfred Horace Offord.

Aged 67, he was killed at his home, 30 Dixon Avenue, possibly as a result of one of several incendiaries that fell close to the property.

Mary Ann Louisa Poulter.

Aged 81, she came from 6 Abbotsfield in Goodmayes and died in the Chelmsford & Essex Hospital on 14th May 1943 from injuries sustained from a 250/500 kg SC H.E. that scored a direct hit on New Hall Hospital. She was the widow of Benjamin Poulter.

George William & Florrie E.M. Simms.

Forty-seven year-old George Simms and his 57 year-old wife, Florrie, were killed when their home, 45 Goldlay Road, was struck by a 500 kg H.E. The couple died alongside Lily Lidbetter. Mr. Simms was the son of G.R. & R. Simms of Wood Green in London.

Henry William & Joan Miriam Smith.

Fifty-three year-old Henry Smith and his 52 year-old wife, Joan, were killed when a 250 kg H.E. demolished their home at 24 Lower Anchor Street. The couple were subsequently buried at the Borough Cemetery on 21st May 1943.

Alice Snow.

Aged 84, she was the widow of Henry Miles Snow and was killed when a 500 kg H.E. struck her home, 46 Goldlay Road. She was killed along with Elsie Gledstone and was subsequently buried at the Borough Cemetery on 19th May 1943.

Leading Aircraftsman Arthur Telford, R.A.F.V.R.

He was one of three balloonists killed when a 250 kg SC H.E. bomb exploded within the compound of 993 Squadron's barrage balloon site 26, north of the east end of Chelmsford City F.C.'s New Writtle Street stadium. Aged 36, he was the son of Jack and Lucy Telford, and married to Lily Telford of Sheffield. He was buried in Sheffield (Wisewood) Cemetery, Yorkshire.

Sidney Arthur Westrip, Cissie Kezia Westrip and June Westrip.

Thirty-seven year-old Sidney Westrip and his 31 year-old wife, Cissie, were killed when a 250 kg H.E. scored a direct hit on their home at 22 Lower Anchor Street. The explosion also killed the couple's lodger, 23 year-old Gwendoline James. Mr. & Mrs. Westrip's two year-old daughter, June, was pulled out of the wrecked property with serious injuries and died later in hospital. The Westrips were buried at the Borough Cemetery.

Vera Audrey Muriel Willis.

Aged 40, she was the daughter of Ernest and Mary Dale of 115 Upper Bridge Road and married to Mr. F. Willis. She was killed when a 250 kg H.E. exploded in the road opposite the house in an incident which also claimed the life of her father, Ernest Dale. They were subsequently buried together at the Borough Cemetery, following a service at St. John's Moulsham.

Frederick Albion Henry Wilson.

Aged 76, he came from 23 Fieldway in Dagenham and was the husband of Jessie M. Wilson. He was one of 7 people killed when a 250/500 kg SC H.E. scored a direct hit on New Hall Hospital.

THE HOME GUARD IS THREE

The day saw celebrations throughout the country to mark the third anniversary of the formation of the Home Guard.

In Chelmsford around five hundred people watched a display by members of the armed forces at the Stadium in New Writtle Street, which had followed a parade through the town's crowd-lined and bomb-damaged streets.

Dignitaries in attendance included the Mayor and Chelmsford's M.P. Unfortunately, whilst the Mayor was at the display his house, 'Ardmore' in Rainsford Road, was burgled with the stolen items including jewellery and ration cards.

Sunday 16th May 1943.

DIGNITARIES TOUR BLITZED CHELMSFORD

The Lord Lieutenant of Essex, Sir Francis Whitmore, visited Chelmsford and was accompanied by the Mayor on a tour of the blitzed parts of the town.

Tuesday 18th May 1943

HOME SECRETARY GRANTS REMISSION TO HELPFUL CHELMSFORD PRISONERS

IN PARLIAMENT the Home Secretary, Mr. Morrison, announced a fortnight's remission for fourteen prisoners who had helped prevent the prison from burning down during the raid on 15th April after incendiaries had set it ablaze.

The move came eight days after rumour had spread throughout Chelmsford that a prisoner had escaped from the gaol. No official comment was made, but it was later reported that after good conduct prisoners had finished salvage work at the gaol on premises damaged by enemy action, one of them was missing.

He was eventually found, almost suffocated under a pile of rubble. He had apparently burrowed there to hide, pending his escape, but when more debris had been heaped onto the pile, he had found himself in difficulties!

Thursday 27th May 1943.

COUNTY TOWN'S POST-WAR HOUSING NEEDS

Council discusses for first time

THE START OF THE WAR had resulted in a cessation of house-building whilst labour and materials were directed into more important projects. However, in the Spring of 1943 the Government decided that local authorities should begin preparing plans for house building in the first year after the war.

On 26th May 1943 Chelmsford Town Council discussed the matter for the first time. Members had before them a recent Ministry of Health circular which required the Council to begin formulating plans for its first post-war year's house building programme.

Programme drawn up

Upon this the Housing Committee recommended that the programme should consist of 32 flats in Upper Bridge Road, 30 houses and 28 bungalows in Rainsford Lane, and 34 houses in the unnamed road (today Fox Crescent) facing Rainsford Senior School. After much discussion on the matter it was clear that the majority of members favoured a larger and more comprehensive scheme so the Housing Committee was instructed to prepare this.

By the following month the Committee had identified sites for around a further 718 houses, comprising of approximately 548 on the Melbourne Estate (draining to the Boarded Barns Estate), 218 on the Melbourne Estate (draining to the Chignall Road), and another 12 adjoining the Widford Estate.

Tentative enquiries had also begun with local landowners with regard to purchasing additional land for council house building in Springfield and land east of Hollow Lane. It was envisaged that at least 1,000 new houses would be needed after the war, with the Housing Committee recommending that he first year's programme be limited to 250 in line with the Ministry of Health's circular, comprising of 32 flats in Upper Bridge Road, 30 houses and 28 bungalows in Rainsford Lane, and 160 houses on the Melbourne Park Estate.

Acute housing shortage

The Committee also reported that the present housing situation in Chelmsford was acute through a combination of a desperate need of accommodation for war workers and the effects of the recent Blitz. It concluded that the situation was so bad that strong representations ought to be made to the Ministry of Health for the immediate provision of 350 new houses.

The Committee's report was fully endorsed by the Council at its 30th June 1943 meeting when a four man deputation was selected to be sent to see the Minister of Health, Ernest Brown, to press for his approval for the 350 new houses. The deputation duly visited the Minister on 6th July 1943

but was told by him that the Government's policy meant that there was no possibility of the Council obtaining approval to build any new houses at present.

In fact, in the event and despite its best efforts, the Council was unable to build any new houses until after the war ended in August 1945.

The intervening period saw it attempt to develop a house-building programme in the face of endless delays during prolonged negotiations with the various Government departments it had to deal with.

High land prices

The problem was exacerbated by a severe shortage of staff necessary to conduct the work. Problems were also encountered with local landowners who sought premium prices for their land; on 29th September 1943, for example, the Council decided not to pursue offers to buy land from two local landowners; Robert Fleming of Barnes Farm, who had offered to sell land fronting Chelmer Road at a cost of £600 per acre; and Sir Alexander Livingstone, who had offered for purchase part of the 164 acre Melbourne Park Estate lying on the eastern side of Chignall Road and north of Roxwell Road at £300 per acre along with land north-east of the playing fields and College Wood at £250 per acre.

Commenting on the high price quoted for Mr. Fleming's land, Councillor Hodge complained that it was an attempt to bleed the community, while Councillor Langton opinioned that the same land had only been worth £30 to £40 per acre ten years previously. He asked 'How are we going to afford much needed houses if we can't afford the land?'.

During the war the Council and the majority of its committees comprised exclusively of men. By the end of 1943 feelings had begun to be voiced that it was time that the opinions of women in particular were heard when housing matters were discussed.

Women can help too

At the January 1944 Council meeting members considered letters sent from the Chelmsford Labour Party and the Springfield Women's Institute which protested at the Council's failure to co-opt women representatives on the Housing Committee.

After consideration the Council agreed to invite one representative each from the Women's Institute, Women's Co-operative Guild, Women's Voluntary Service, Women's Section of the British Legion, and the Rotary Club to attend meetings where plans for the erection of new houses would be considered. In the event the Women's Institute, the Rotary Inner Wheel and the Women's Co-operative Guild nominated Mrs. W.T. Unstead, Mrs. A.G. Gilling and Mrs. Ethel Cramner. The special

committee subsequently met three times during 1944 to discuss the design of post war houses and it presented its recommendations at the end of 1944.

By March 1945, with an end to the war at last in sight, the Ministry of Health wrote to the Council revealing that authorisation to begin house building would possibly be forthcoming in the summer of 1945.

Sites finally chosen

The Council discussed the matter at the end of April 1945 and instructed the Borough Engineer to prepare plans for submission to the Ministry for the erection of permanent houses on several sites in the town.

The plans were swiftly completed and comprised of the following number of houses, each of which could be subdivided into two flats; 34 on the unnamed road fronting Rainsford School (named Fox Crescent in November 1945), 10 on the Widford Estate, 3 on the vacant site between 8 and 10 Eastern Crescent, 1 on the vacant site between 47 and 49 Eastern Crescent, 4 on the vacant site between 71 and 73 Brownings Avenue, and 28 on land at the south-west end of King's Road. The programme was quickly extended to include a 23.09 acre southern extension to the Springfield Park Estate and the Melbourne Park Estate.

Building starts

Ministerial approval for the programme was received in the early summer of 1945 and finally, on 17th August 1945, 50 German p.o.w.s supervised by Council staff began the groundwork on the Springfield Park Estate extension. Building work on the other sites in the town commenced later in the year, but it was to be several more years before Chelmsford's acute housing shortage was alleviated.

CHELMSFORD BLITZ IS AVENGED

COUNTERPART IN GERMANY IS BOMBED BY R.A.F.

IN THE EVENING the R.A.F. carried out a heavy air raid on Wuppertal in the Ruhr region of Germany.

Its target was a large ball bearings factory, on which 1,500 tons of explosives were dropped at a cost of 33 aircraft lost.

In Chelmsford the raid was regarded with some satisfaction as a revenge attack for the recent blitz on the town.

Saturday 29th May 1943

WINGS FOR VICTORY WEEK

A GREAT SUCCESS

The latest National Savings campaign got under way in Chelmsford with the launch of the Chelmsford and Rural District 'Wings for Victory Week', aimed at securing £500,000 worth of investment in National Savings - enough to buy a squadron of a dozen Lancaster bombers.

The public was urged to buy at least £10 worth per head at any bank, any post office, the bus station, W.V.S. depot at 3 Tindal Square, National Savings Bureau at 19 Duke Street village selling centres. Advertising reminded them 'We have a debt to repay with interest' - a reference to the blitz on Chelmsford two weeks earlier.

The week included the usual diverse range of publicity events including a model aircraft exhibition at the library, R.A.F. exhibition at the Council chamber, dances, concerts, parades and whist drives.

By the conclusion of the campaign on 5th June a total of £757,904/19/4 had been invested by the people of Chelmsford and its Rural District, enough to pay for eighteen Lancaster bombers.

In the Borough, where the target had been £325,000, a total of £509,528/12/1 had been invested at £15/8/9 per head. In the Rural District, where the target had been £175,000, a total of £248,376/7/3 had been invested at 37/6/9 per head. The combined investment was over 50% above its target level at £11/6/9 per head.

Of the rural parishes the highest totals were Ingatestone & Fryerning (£35,499/7/11), Great Baddow (£26,986/12/1) and Broomfield (£17,984/9/0). The highest per head figure was at Mashbury with £26/16/0 for each of the parish's 120 residents. Second was Springfield with £18/18/4 per head and third, Good Easter with £15 per head.

South Woodham Ferrers was bottom of both lists with £1,665/11/5 invested at £1/11/9 per head. In the challenge between the Borough and Rural District schools the honour went to the latter with £12.951/19/7 invested as opposed to £12,766 for the former.

The three National Savings weeks, War Weapons, Warship and now Wings for Victory Week, had raised a total of £1,758, 480 for the war effort from the Chelmsford district.

Saturday 29th May 1943

In need of care and attention

In the first case of its kind at Chelmsford Juvenile Court a 15 year-old girl, said to be 'in need of care and protection', was sent to a remand home whilst suitable accommodation was found for her. She had been seen at Chelmsford railway station on 5th May 1943 with an American soldier, and had admitted spending the night with him.

Tuesday 1st June 1943.

CHELMSFORD LOOTER GETS FIFTEEN MONTHS

WARNING TO OTHERS

SIX MONTHS JAIL FOR BEING ABSENT FROM WORK

AT THE CHELMSFORD Petty Sessions a six month gaol sentence was imposed on a 20 year-old agricultural worker from Walnuts, Little Waltham, who had been summoned for absenting himself from work without reasonable cause.

Between 25th November 1942 and 23rd February 1943 he was said to have missed 255.5 of the 576 hours that he was supposed to have worked. In mitigation he explained to the court that he had trouble getting up early in the morning as he stayed out late with his pals!

Friday 4th June 1943

EYEWITNESS ACCOUNTS: WARTIME SPIRIT

"People seemed much friendlier to one another and there was a much greater feeling of neighbourliness in the war."

As told to our our Special Correspondent

"You can't describe wartime conditions - whether it was because you never knew if you were going to be killed or what, I don't know, but everyone was so friendly. You didn't meet anybody who was nasty to you or anything like that."

Mary Bateman

"People seemed much friendlier to one another and there was a much greater feeling of neighbourliness in the war than there is today.

There was a real sense of camaraderie, we were all in it together. There were always women at home so that if you didn't feel well, there was usually someone to go to, or when you went to get your rations there would be someone you could talk to on the way. People seemed to help each other more then.

If you making something your neighbour would lend you a tool, and if you were digging in the garden they'd would come round and help you. It's a pity we haven't got the same spirit nowadays."

Edna Brown

AT THE ESSEX ASSIZES Mr. Justice Oliver sentenced a 34 year-old plasterer who lodged at Hamlet Road to fifteen months imprisonment for receiving stolen property.

The man had admitted to being in possession of a stolen tweed suit valued at £4/5/0, property of Montague Burton Ltd., a pair of flanneled trousers valued at 17/10 from Messers J. Hepworth and a raincoat valued at £2/15/0 from Frank Miles Ltd.

All the items had been taken from shops damaged during the fire raid on Chelmsford on 15th April 1943. He had denied the more serious charge of looting and the police had agreed to drop that charge.

In another case a 43 year-old painter was found guilty of looting and sentenced to twelve months imprisonment. The court was told that he had been employed by the Ministry of Works for first aid repairs on bombed buildings in Chelmsford.

The offence had taken place on 19th April 1943 when the man had been working on Mr. Leslie Gannon's house at 1 Second Avenue. After Mr. Gannon had declined his offer to help move items of his property the man had asked him to give him some toys for his large family.

Mr. Gannon gave the man two or three games and a box of bricks, but not a child's scooter and wheelbarrow which he was subsequently found to be in possession of. Mr. Gannon was the organist and choirmaster at Great Waltham Church.

Thursday 10th June 1943

DRIVER NARROWLY ESCAPES DEATH BY BUTTERFLY BOMB

Around 8.45 p.m. a suspected anti-personnel SD1 'butterfly' bomb exploded at Master John's Farm, Mountnessing when it was trod on by one of two horses drawing a cutter through a hay field.

The horse which detonated the device was killed, the other wounded, though fortunately their driver, who was just 14 feet from the explosion, escaped with just shock. A subsequent investigation by the military authorities was to reveal that the bomb and several others found in a thorough search of the area were remnants of the air raid on the evening of 3rd March 1943.

The incident was to cause much concern locally, and for a time the farmer, Mr. Stevens, would refuse to allow any more hay cutting work to be undertaken in the field and a neighbouring one until fears over the presence of other bombs were allayed.

Wednesday 23rd June 1943

NEW ACK ACK DEFENCES FOR HOFFMANN'S

At Hoffmann's a dozen Home Guardsmen paraded for the first time for Light Anti-Aircraft training.

Officers within the army's 37 A.A. Brigade had been concerned about the vulnerability of factories to attack by enemy aircraft and since June 1943 had consulted various factory managers in Essex with a view to improving their defences. Consequently it had been decided to form an Essex Home Guard Light Anti-Aircraft Battery to protect industrial premises at Chelmsford, Tilbury, Shell Haven and Purfleet.

The men on parade were set to man new defences which became operational at Hoffmann's on 1st August 1943. The new battery was designated 'A troop' of the 131 (Essex Home Guard) Light A.A. Battery and was commanded by 2nd Lt.. H.H.G. Parmenter. It was armed with nine 20 mm guns. The unit was to have a short life, only remaining in operation until 1st April 1944.

Sunday 11th July 1943

SPRINGFIELD PLACE TO BECOME WOMEN WAR WORKERS' HOSTEL

THE ESSEX CHRONICLE revealed that Springfield Place. the seventeenth century home of Walter Ridley, a director of the local brewery, had been requisitioned by the Ministry of Supply for use as a hostel for transferred women war workers.

This followed the recent recruitment of large numbers of young women from the Republic of Ireland who had volunteered to work in Chelmsford's factories.

Another hostel for factory girls had recently opened in Broomfield Road and it was reported that it would be extended in the near future to accommodate twenty women , eight more than the existing total.

The Essex Weekly News revealed that blast walls were to be erected in front of 26 windows at the maternity block of St. John's Hospital at a cost of £324.

Friday 2nd July 1943

RURAL AREAS UPSET BY PRIORITY BUS SERVICE SCHEME

A meeting of the Rural District Council resolved to draw Chelmsford's M.P.'s attention to the great inconvenience caused by the experimental priority bus service which had been introduced to Chelmsford at the end of the previous month at the direction of the Ministry of War Transport.

The scheme meant that on most rush hour services weekly and season ticket holders had been the only passengers permitted to board at the Bus Station, Golden Lion, Market Road and Woolworth's. At all other town centre bus stops such passengers now had priority over ordinary ones.

The scheme had been designed to ease overcrowding and give preference to war workers and scholars who tended to have the necessary weekly and season tickets. Unfortunately it had resulted in many people in the rural areas around Chelmsford finding it practically impossible to travel by bus.

Amongst other items, the R.D.C. decided that its post-war year's housing programme would propose the erection of 227 houses.

Tuesday 22nd June 1943

PRISON ESCAPE

During the morning a 27 year-old Czech soldier escaped from Chelmsford Prison, where he had been awaiting trial for a number of charges of housebreaking in the Harwich area.

He was recaptured in a wood at Bagshot in Surrey six days later having made his way there on foot across fields to Danbury, then Latchingdon, Runwell, Aveley and thence to London where he took the train to Bagshot.

He was subsequently returned to Chelmsford and tried on 22nd July at the Quarter Sessions and given 12 months hard labour for 19 counts of theft including 7 made during his time on the run.

Wednesday 14th July 1943

TEENAGE GIRLS 'IN GRAVE MORAL DANGER'

At Chelmsford Juvenile Court two girls, aged 13 and 14, were sent to an approved home having been deemed 'in need of care and protection'. The court heard that the girls had associated with American soldiers and were considered to be in 'grave moral danger'.

Tuesday 20th July 1943

EYEWITNESS ACCOUNT:

"Military installations."

As told to our our Special Correspondent

"On the corner of King's Road and Broomfield Road the authorities installed a Blacker Bombard base. It consisted of a solid round cylinder of concrete in the ground with a spigot on the top, onto which the bombard was to be placed. As far as I know it was never put to use.

There was a Bofors gun on top of County Hall and another one, together with a searchlight station at Chignall Smealy. If you approach the village from the direction of 'The Pig & Whistle' pub there is a sharp left turn just before Dyers Hall. The searchlight station was in the field on the right-hand side immediately after that bend.

There was a barrage balloon site at the Grammar School. It was right outside 'Westfields', then used as the junior school and which has since been replaced by a private house. The concrete base at the balloon site may still be in existence.

All the local road signs and finger boards were put up across the Baddow Meads to deter enemy aircraft or parachute troops from landing there. There were acres of them."

Les Appleton

LANDLORD KILLED AS BICKNACRE PUB BOMBED

AT 12.55 A.M. a lone raider dropped an H.E. which scored a direct hit on The Brewer's Arms P.H. in Bicknacre.

The landlord of over 20 years, 54 year-old widower Charles Matthew Smith, had just returned to the premises having spent the evening with his Home Guard unit searching for the escaped Czech prisoner.

Mr. Smith was fatally injured by the bomb as he stood in the kitchen whilst another person, thought to have been Mrs. Alice Kerwin, escaped with cuts and shock from a room at the front of the premises. A second H.E. fell unexploded a hundred yards east of the pub and necessitated the evacuation of nearby residents and the temporary closure of the B1418.

Mr. Smith was subsequently buried at East Hanningford on 21st July. His funeral was attended by colleagues in the 2nd Battalion Essex Home Guard, for whom he was a Second Lieutenant. Mr. Smith was a Parish Councillor and had no local family.

Friday 16th July 1943

LORD HAW HAW

The day's Essex Chronicle revealed that Lord Haw Haw used to live at Danbury Road in Great Baddow and for a time worked in a Chelmsford factory. Before the war he had organised the British Union of Fascists in parts of Essex.

Friday 23rd July 1943.

"I had to keep an eye out for incendiaries and deal with them."

As told to our our Special Correspondent

"In August 1943 I left school and went to work for the first time at Strutt & Parker at their offices above Barclay's Bank.

As soon as I joined the firm I was put on the fire watch rota, which was something everyone who was not in military service had to do. Duty normally came round about once a fortnight when I was paid about 4/6 to spend the night at our premises.

I had a camp bed to sleep on and the idea was that if there was a raid I had to keep an eye out for incendiaries and deal with them before they could do too much damage.

If Christmas or New Year's Eve were coming up and my colleagues due to fire watch didn't want to do it they'd come up to me and ask me to do it for them instead. They'd pay me of course and I made quite a bit of money from that."

Ray Knappett

"Their equivalent to the N.A.A.F.I. was at the Saracen's Head, just a few yards down from our offices."

As told to our our Special Correspondent

"At Strutt & Parker our work comprised mainly of farm and estate management.

As an office boy at the firm's High Street offices it was part of my job to collect the various booze rations for our clients which would then be delivered to them by the firm's representatives as they visited each estate or farm.

About once a moth I'd walk up to the Taylor Walker off licence in Duke Street and pick up the booze rations which typically might be a bottle of sherry and a bottle of whisky for each client.

As I came back out of the shop, armed with the usual half dozen bottles, a crowd of chattering American servicemen would appear and follow me, offering fistfulls of dollars for the bottles. To my credit I never did business with them, or ever dropped a bottle - if I had I think that I might have got the sack.

We saw alot of the Americans in Chelmsford. Their equivalent to the N.A.A.F.I., or their P.X., was at the Saracen's Head, just a few yards down from our offices. It was a sort of social centre and frequently they'd come into town, straight of their debriefings from bombing missions, with their flying jackets still on and head for the Saracen's Head.

The Americans were most things people said they were - flamboyant, untidy, noisy and boisterous. To me they appeared to be ill-disciplined and I hardly regarded them as a fighting force compared with our own services."

Ray Knappett

TWO LARGE BOMBS ON GREAT WALTHAM

At 12.15 a.m., twenty minutes after the air raid alert had sounded in Chelmsford, a pair of 500 kg SC H.E.s were dropped on Great Waltham from an unidentified aircraft flying at about 15,000 feet.

It approached the district from the south-east and made a bomb run from the east-south-east to west-north-west, before making off to in a south-south-easterly direction.

One bomb fell in a corn field at Partridge Farm in Broads Green near Great Waltham, two hundred yards from Larks Lane. It left a crater 38 feet across by 9 feet deep, but failed to cause any significant damage. The second H.E. fell half a mile to the south-east in Sparrowhawk Wood, leaving a crater 35 feet across by 5 feet deep.

The all-clear sounded at 1.02 a.m.

Monday 26th July 1943.

TWINS 'IN GRAVE MORAL DANGER'

At the Chelmsford Juvenile Court 12 year-old twin boys, stated 'to be in need of care and protection' and said to have been 'in grave moral danger' were sent to an approved school.

The court heard that they lived with their widowed mother and others in a filthy bungalow in West Hanningfield, frequented by American soldiers.

Witnesses said that the two boys smoked, swore, stole and generally were out of hand. Their mother, who was engaged to an American Sergeant, said that the prosecution was the result of 'dirty village slander'!

Tuesday 17th August 1943

MORE LOOTERS ON TRIAL

AT THE CHELMSFORD Petty Sessions a 52 year-old man admitted stealing a rug, coat and jacket from a bombed out house in Chapel Place on 18th August.

The man was employed by a firm of wartime demolition contractors and since 26th July had been engaged in demolishing properties bombed in the Chelmsford blitz.

The man, who was described as being in a verminous condition, was fined £2. Members of the bench were reportedly surprised that a man thus described was able to earn £4/18/0 per week.

In a similar case a 35 year-old tyre examiner was given three months hard labour for stealing tyre tubes between 18th June and 18th August from Chelmsford's bus station. The premises had not been locked up since it was blitzed in May 1943.

Friday 27th August 1943

WATER TANKS

VERMINOUS WORKERS

AT THE MONTHLY COUNCIL meeting consent was given to the N.F.S. to build several more static water tanks in Chelmsford.

The tanks included one with a 10,000 gallon capacity on land to the rear of numbers 50, 51 & 52 Upper Bridge Road, one in the cul-de-sac opposite Yarwood Road, off Springfield Park Lane, one by the allotments in Writtle Road and one on the grass verge in North Avenue opposite Tennyson Road.

The Chief Billeting Officer reported that preliminary proposals had been drawn up to convert the Red House in Moulsham Street into a hostel for women war workers. The building was being used at the time to house aged evacuees. The new plans envisaged their transfer to the neighbouring property, Highfield, and to other parts of Essex.

In the wake of continuing complaints from residents over the condition of certain war workers, particularly those from Ireland, the Council instructed the Chief Billeting Officer to no longer billet 'verminous or otherwise unsatisfactory war workers'. Approval was given to transfer the Billeting Office from 3 London Road to larger premises at 19 Duke Street and for an increase in its staff. A huge increase in the office's workload, caused by the Chelmsford Blitz, had necessitated the move.

Wednesday 28th July 1943.

MINISTER IN TOWN

The Minister of Aircraft Production, Sir Stafford Cripps, visited 'a Chelmsford factory', probably Hoffmann's or Marconi's and spoke to a large gathering of workers there during their lunch break. Sir Stafford was greeted by company officials and a guard of honour from the firm's civil defence services.

Friday 10th September 1943.

JEHOVAH'S WITNESS JAILED

At the Chelmsford Petty Sessions a 49 year-old foreman mechanic of a local garage was sentenced to three months imprisonment for failing to comply with a direction given to him to undertake part time duties with a first aid party. The man, who was a Jehovah's Witness and came from 91 King's Road, had refused to do so on the grounds of his religious convictions. He had been imprisoned for two months for a similar offence in February 1942.

Friday 10th September 1943.

M.P. ABROAD

Chelmsford's M.P., Col. John Macnamara, was reported to have left the country by troopship to go on active service abroad with his regiment, the London Irish Rifles. M.P.s of Chelmsford's neighbouring constituencies were set to share his workload in his absence.

Friday 20th August 1943

MORE YOUNG GIRLS 'IN NEED OF CARE AND PROTECTION'

At Chelmsford Juvenile Court a 13 year-old girl, said to be 'in need of care and protection', was sent to an approved school after being found to have been in the habit of associating with soldiers and staying out late.

A 14-year old girl was also found to be 'in need of care and protection' having been found sleeping under a haystack at the rear of an American camp.

It was disclosed that two American soldiers had each been given 18 months hard labour for offences against the 14 year-old girl who was placed under the supervision of a probation officer for three years.

Tuesday 3rd August 1943

MAYOR EATS COVAL CUSTARD

At the invitation of a group of housewives, the Mayor, councillors and a few friends were entertained to lunch on a bomb site in Coval Lane - most likely from the air raid on 21st May 1941. A meal was cooked in blitz conditions on an emergency stove and included 'Coval custard', and a 'Combined Operations Stew', where each housewife supplied an ingredient.

Wednesday 29th September 1943

MOVES TO IMPROVE 'REC' SHELTERS

At the monthly Council meeting members considered a report from the Borough Engineer which revealed that the Recreation Ground concrete trench shelters were now in a poor state of repair following months of wanton vandalism.

The shelters, which were still used by around 100 people every night during alerts, required repairs to emergency exit covers, lavatory partitions and doors.

The Council agreed to forward a report on the matter to the Regional Commissioner and await his further instructions. Meanwhile the Borough Engineer was directed to appoint a permanent attendant to look after the shelters.

The Council also agreed to purchase 150 forty-gallon re-conditioned steel drums at a cost of between 7/6 and 10/- each from the Ministry of Supply for replenishing stirrup pumps.

An additional 50 mono static water tanks were reported to be on order and would be situated at points throughout the town.

Wednesday 29th September 1943

BISHOP'S WARNING

The Bishop of Chelmsford, speaking as president of Chelmsford Diocesan Council, expressed his concern over the lack of parental control over young girls and demanded an 8 p.m. curfew for all girls under 18.

He warned of a grave moral collapse in a society where rates of venereal disease had soared since the start of the war. His views echoed those of many leading churchmen who were deeply worried over what they saw as a collapse of morality during the war.

Tuesday 19th October 1943

FIRST REPATRIATED

At Liverpool the 17,000 ton hospital ship S.S. Atlantis berthed with over 800 sick and blind p.o.w.s, the first to be repatriated from Germany.

The first man ashore, and one of several local men on the ship, was 27 year-old Private Leslie Bloomfield R.A.O.C. He had been captured on Crete in June 1941 and was dangerously ill.

Prior to the war he had worked at Marconi's and had lived in South Primrose Hill.

Tuesday 26th October 1943.

"The Italian p.o.w.s were great fun but did bugger all work."

As told to our our Special Correspondent

"My father farmed Newland Hall at Roxwell and the Essex War Agricultural Executive Committee used to send us German or Italian prisoners of war as supplementary labour.

Hopefully as many as had been asked for would be sent, with the numbers varying according to the work that needed to be carried out. They were bussed in each day from the local p.o.w. camps, I think mainly from the one at Hylands Park, and soldiers used to stay and guard them.

The Italians were great fun but did bugger all work - all they ever wanted to do was to light fires and get around them. My father kicked them off and insisted on Germans instead.

They were absolutely superb and would work like mad. Everybody agreed that they were jolly good and jolly hard workers and admired them. I remember my father saying 'Give them a loaf of bread and they'll do anything'.

We weren't getting any particular nasty Nazi type of German, but people you could refer to, and certainly as kids we didn't have any objection to them.

Our usual farmworkers also got on well with them - in fact one of the Germans stayed on after the war and lodged with our horseman, Sid Everard, for quite a while afterwards."

Leonard Menhinick

ITALIAN P.O.W.S IN WRITTLE CRASH

At the notorious Warren Corner, on the A414 near Writtle, a coach returning some 30 Italian p.o.w.s back to their camp from work was in collision with a van. The coach was forced into the ditch by the side of the road, but all on board scrambled out unhurt.

Saturday 9th October 1943.

EYEWITNESS ACCOUNT: PRSIONERS OF WAR

"Luckily the guard stopped him from getting off - I reckon if he hadn't, the Italian would've killed us both!"

As told to our our Special Correspondent

"One day I was cycling up Duke Street with a friend of mine. When we got near to the library we had to stop behind a bus that was trying to turn into Broomfield Road.

The bus was loaded with these Italian p.o.w.s and a guard. Peering out of the window at the back of the bus was this massive great Italian with a beard. Once the bus started to move off again we both gave him the 'V' sign. He went mad!

As we passed along the side of the bus he charged up the aisle in the bus and was trying to get out the door and get hold of us. There was this poor old guard hanging on to him for dear life! I said to my friend 'Come on, we're off!', so we shot off down Coval Lane while the bus went up Broomfield Road.

Luckily the guard stopped him from getting off - I reckon if he hadn't the Italian would've killed us both!

Kenneth Smith

TAYLOR MAYOR AGAIN

AT A SPECIAL MEETING of the Council Cllr. Sidney Taylor was elected Mayor for his fourth consecutive term in office and his seventh in all.

It was the fourteenth time that a member of his family had held the post since it had been created 55 years previously. Alderman Fox was re-appointed as his deputy.

Amongst other matters, a proposal from Cllr. Thomas Howes that three women should be invited to join the Housing Committee was defeated 19 votes to 10. The move followed a request from the Women's Co-operative Guild who felt that women should have some say in housing policy as many women spent most of their time at home. At that time the Council consisted entirely of men.

Tuesday 9th November 1943.

BOMBS AT WIDFORD AND STOCK

AT 12.49 A.M. Chelmsford 's air raid sirens sounded the alert.

A few hostile enemy aircraft passed over the town, and at 1.05 a.m. one diving aircraft released a stick of H.E.s which fell in a line between Widford and Stock.

Two dropped into Hylands Park, 250 yards north-west of Hylands House, damaging thirteen military vehicles stationed in the park and windows at Hylands House.

Another fell 75 yards east of the railway line in a field two hundred yards from Private Road, Galleywood. It left a crater 13' across by 6' deep and damaged telegraph and signal lines on the railway. Nine houses were also slightly damaged; 'Lyndon', 'The Mill', 'Edwyn', 'Down', 'Amphrey', 'Arden', 'Rosedene' and 'Homelands'.

A fourth H.E. fell in a field at Stock adjoining Birch Lane and damaged some properties in the vicinity. Nobody was hurt by the bombs, though a cat which was thought to have died of shock was later discovered in Hylands Park.

The raider was met by a heavy A.A. barrage from Chelmsford's defences.

Thursday 21st October 1943

COMPLAINTS ABOUT WAR WORKERS

At the monthly Council meeting members were informed that the Regional Commissioner had recently written to the Council stating that he had received strong complaints from many people about the condition of certain war workers transferred to Chelmsford. The Chief Billeting Officer reported that the situation had improved recently and that inspections of such workers would be intensified.

Wednesday 27th October 1943

IMMORALITY DENOUNCED

At the Essex Autumn Assizes which opened at the Shire Hall Mr. Justice Atkinson denounced the recent wave of immorality in the county that had been demonstrated by a big increase in cases of bigamy and offences against young girls. He criticised many magistrates whom he felt were too lenient on offenders.

Monday 1st November 1943

WOMAN JAILED FOR HELPING DESERTER

AT THE CHELMSFORD Petty Sessions a 33 year-old French-speaking, Swiss-born woman of 27 Shrublands Close was jailed for one month for assisting a deserter from the army in concealing himself.

The court heard the extraordinary story of how, between May 1942 and November 1943, the deserter from the Free French Army had lived in a specially constructed hideout under the floor at her home.

The hideout was 11'6" long by 37" wide and just 14.5" deep. The woman's unsuspecting husband new nothing of it throughout the months that the soldier was concealed there. She had met the deserter early in the war when she had helped to entertain members of the Free French who had escaped to England.

Since then a friendship had developed between them. The deserter had been discovered when another Free Frenchman visited the house - after which the police had been called in. The deserter was to be dealt with by the French military authorities.

Friday 19th November 1943

EYEWITNESS ACCOUNT:

"Our barrage balloon."

As told to our our Special Correspondent

"One of the R.A.F.'s balloon sites was in the field we knew as Morse's meadow, opposite Springfield School. Nowadays All Saints' Close partly covers the site.

I lived just around the corner from there so my friends and I got to know the balloon crews quite well. If you behaved yourself they didn't mind you hanging around and on occasions, especially when it was windy, they would let us help them put the balloon up or bring it down.

The balloon was tethered by a wire cable that came down to a pulley wheel fixed to the ground and then on to a winch on the back of a truck.

The crew used to sleep next to the field in the Women's Institute hut. Nearby they had a tent with a radio telephone to headquarters who would send them the alarm if any German planes were approaching.

Normally the balloon was kept quite low, but when news came through that enemy planes were coming the balloonists were ordered to raise the balloon. All the various heights the balloons could be elevated to had different names. I remember one of them was 'dog height'.

One cloudy day I was at the balloon site when I heard the sound of German plane above the clouds. I told one of the balloonists there was a German plane, but he didn't believe me at first as there had been no alarm.

Eventually he did, but when he rang headquarters to tell them about the plane, they told him that there were none about.

He put the phone down and as we looked over beyond Timson's Lane towards Great Baddow, the local anti-aircraft guns began pumping up shells at the plane which then made off. After that the alarm eventually came through and the order was given to raise the balloons!

One lunchtime, I was cycling home for lunch from work at Tamkin's in Navigation Road, when a terrific thunderstorm broke out. As I passed Budd the bakers in Springfield Road there was a flash, bang and a ball of fire in the sky further up the road towards Springfield.

A barrage balloon which had been fairly low had been struck by lightning. It came down near to 'The Plough' on Bertie Culpeck's house, 1 Dukes View, Springfield Street. When I got up there it was still alight."

Eric Clark

THE FIRST 'G.I. BRIDES'

On Friday 29th October 1943 Chelmsford's local papers reported that one of the first weddings had taken place between a local woman and an American serviceman.

Miss Edna Game, a nurse at St, John's Hospital, had recently married Lt. Gietz Petersen of the U.S. Army from Wisconsin at All Saints' Springfield. Over the forthcoming months many more local girls were set to follow suit including the following;

Miss Edith M. Auger, the only daughter of Mr. & Mrs. F.J. Auger of 'Chez Nous', Broomfield to Cpl David Weir from Niagara Falls.

Miss Diana Barrett, the only daughter of Mr. & Mrs. Roland Barrett of 14 Cedar Avenue, to First Lt. Andrew Prescott U.S. Army from California.

Miss Patricia B. Black, the daughter of Mr. & Mrs. D. Black of 'Little Maynetrees' in New Street, to Walter Sullivan U.S. Army from Delaware.

Miss Linda D. Brewer, the youngest daughter of Mr. & Mrs. Brewer of Rainsford Road, to Cpl. Earl Marshall from Virginia.

Miss Sylvia Brown, the youngest daughter of Mr. & Mrs. Harold Brown of 30 Hillside Grove, to Cpl. Carl Smith U.S. Army from Indiana.

Miss Celia Chapman, the second daughter of Mr. & Mrs. Ernest Chapman of 20 Gloucester Avenue, to Ft. Lt. Bruce Watts R.C.A.F. from Toronto.

Miss Esme Cracknell, the only daughter of Mrs. & the late Mr. Cracknell of 9 Jubilee Terrace, to Cpl. Michael Dudik U.S.A.A.F. from Ohio.

Miss Stella Easter, the daughter of Mr. & Mrs. Charles Easter of 136 King's Road, to Billy Ray Baxter from Arizona.

Miss Vera Easter, the daughter of Mr. & Mrs. Charles Easter of 136 King's Road, to Military Policeman Percy Le Baron Latimer from Maine.

Miss Laura G. Eveling, the only daughter of Mr. & Mrs. Reginald Eveling of 100 Bishop Road, to Roy Wood U.S. Army.

Miss Joan Gardner, the youngest daughter of Mr. & Mrs. Oswald Gardner of Patching Hall, to Sgt. Frederick Benner U.S.A.A.F. from Pennsylvania.

Miss Joan Gregson, the only daughter of Mr. & Mrs. Thomas Gregson of 180 Rainsford Road, to Arthur Miller from Minnesota.

Miss Gweneth Harris, the eldest daughter of Mr. & Mrs. William Harris of 86 Moulsham Street, to T/Sgt. Andrew Esman U.S.A.A.F. from New Jersey.

Miss Betty Heard, the second daughter of Mr. & Mrs. Heard of 75 Swiss Avenue, to Pte. First Class Daniel Nargiso from New Jersey.

Miss Nellie A. Lodge, from Chelmsford to Cpl. Dart Mason from California.

Miss Kathleen A. Lovegrove, the daughter of Mrs. E. & the late Mr. W. Lovegrove of 29 Patching Hall Lane, to Sgt. James Ingram U.S.A.A.F. from Alabama.

Miss Mary Maher, the daughter of Mr. & Mrs. P. Maher, to Pte. First Class Harold Cromer from Chicago.

Miss Frances E. Monsey, the youngest daughter of Mr. & the late Mrs. Malcolm Monsey of 46 Broomfield Road, to Pte. Paul Hills of the U.S. Mounted Police from Idaho.

Miss Hilda Nokes, the daughter of Mr. & Mrs. Nokes of Ockelford Avenue, to Lincoln Cressey of Pennsylvania.

Miss Ruby M. Porter, the fourth daughter of Mr. & Mrs. Porter of 14 Widford Close, to Cpl. Nickolas Mancuso from New York.

Miss Peggy J. Rogers, the daughter of Mr. & Mrs. Ernest Rogers of Howe Street, to Sgt. John Bayus from Ohio.

Miss Brenda P.A. Seymour, the only daughter of Mr. & Mrs. F.G. Seymour of Wheelers Farm near Little Waltham to Sgt. Robert Wilson U.S. Army.

Miss Doreen Sorrell, of 'Ash Holt' in Springfield Road, to Clarence 'Woodie' Francis U.S. Army from Virginia.

Miss Anne Teager, the eldest daughter of Mr. & Mrs., Teager of 20 Norton Road in Ingatestone, to Cpl. Francis Zerja from New Jersey.

Miss Gladys Tutton of 107 Baddow Road to Cpl. Tillman Galt U.S. Army from California,

Miss Evelyn Watkinson, the second daughter of Mr. & Mrs. G. Watkinson of 'Landview' in Writtle, to Lt. Robert Paubert U.S.A.A.F. from Iowa.

Miss Hilda Mary Westrop of 'Ellesmere' Rettendon Common to Rev. Daniel T. Woods, an American Presbyterian minister.

Miss Phyllis S. Woodison, the only daughter of Mr. & Mrs. Frederick Woodison of 26 Brownings Avenue to T/Sgt Francis Fordyce of Montana.

Friday 29th October 1943

STRANGE MURDER TRIAL

At the Shire Hall one of Essex's most remarkable murder trials ended when a 20 year-old soldier from Rayleigh was found guilty but insane of the murder of his 47 year-old father. He was sentenced to be detained at his majesty's pleasure.

The court heard that the father, who was described as 'a man of difficult temperament' had spent the previous three years paralysed and confined to a wheelchair by illness.

Since the onset of the illness he was said to have made his wife's and son's lives very difficult and thus the son had decided to kill his father in order that his mother would be released 'from her drudgery'.

This had been achieved after the son placed a stolen Hawkins 75 Grenade Mine, (an anti-tank weapon) under the cushion of his father's wheelchair. As the father was pushed along a road in Rayleigh the mine was detonated when the father lit a cigar.

He was killed instantly with his body blown to pieces; his head and shoulders fell on to the pavement beside the wrecked wheelchair, his left leg was blown 30 feet away and landed 15 feet up in a tree, whilst his right leg was thrown 48 feet into a front garden.

Miraculously the nurse who had been pushing the wheelchair at the time escaped with shock.

Tuesday 2nd November 1943

P.O.W. CONFERENCE AT SHIRE HALL

In the afternoon nearly a thousand people crowded into the Shire Hall to try and discover the latest news on their friends and relations that were being held as p.o.w.s. The event was arranged by the Essex Red Cross & St. John's War Organisation, presided over by Lady Rayleigh, and saw one of the biggest ever gatherings in the building.

Wednesday 24th November 1943.

Council Meeting:

DOVEDALE, BARRAGE BALLOONS, SIREN, & REPAIR COSTS

At the monthly Council meeting the Chief Billeting Officer reported that Dovedale in Moulsham Street had been transferred to County's Education Committee to provide additional accommodation for the M.E.T.C., replacing that which had been lost through enemy action during the Chelmsford Blitz, and for use as a hostel for agricultural students.

The building had originally been requisitioned and earmarked by the Ministry of Supply for a hostel for war workers but had never been put to that use.

The Council resolved to write to the Air Ministry asking it to give barrage balloon crews at sites in Chelmsford authority to lower their balloons on their own initiative whenever storms appeared imminent rather than wait for the somewhat delayed instructions from the central headquarters as was the case at present.

Amongst other matters permission was given to the Police to erect an air raid warning siren on the water tower at Longstomps Reservoir, while the Borough Treasurer was authorised to obtain advances from the War Damage Commission to compensate the Council for the large payments that it was having to make to building contractors undertaking war damage repairs in Chelmsford.

Wednesday 24th November 1943.

IN GRAVE MORAL DANGER

At Chelmsford Juvenile Court a 14 year-old girl was found to be beyond the control of her parents and 'in grave moral danger'.

The court heard that she had gone missing from 30th November to 3rd December and had been discovered in the company of American soldiers. She was said to have been particularly friendly with an American corporal. The court ordered that the girl be taken into care but she was to subsequently escape from St. John's Hospital, where she was being held, saying that she didn't want to be near dead people!

By the end of January 1944, having escaped a further five times, the court was to sent her to Holloway prison for two weeks.

Tuesday 7th December 1943

THE MINOPRIO SURVEY:

POST-WAR CHELMSFORD

AT THE SHIRE HALL the Chelmsford Area Planning Group held an open conference on the future of the Chelmsford area.

The event was held in close co-operation with the local planning authorities, with many prominent guest speakers in attendance. It came at a time when the public was at last beginning to see that an end to the war was possible, and their thoughts were increasingly turning towards post-war Britain.

Nationally this had manifested itself in a growing public interest in town and country planning, while locally this was the focus of attention of the The Chelmsford Area Planning Group.

The Group was an unofficial organisation which had been established in 1935 by a number of residents of both the Borough and Rural District who were interested in planning. Its wartime chairman was Henry Cleminson, a member of the council of the Town & Country Planning Association.

Survey & report

One outcome of the conference was the news that Chelmsford's big three employers, Hoffmann's, Marconi's and Crompton's were to jointly fund a preliminary planning survey and report of the Chelmsford district with suggestions for the area's post-war development.

At the end of February 1944 Max Lock wrote to both the Council and Rural District Councils stating that he had been appointed by the Group to direct its survey and plan of Chelmsford in association with Mrs. Tyewhitt of the Association for Planning & Regional Reconstruction.

Mr. Lock requested that the Council grant him access to its records to help him complete the Survey. In the meantime the Council was invited to send representative to a meeting of the Group. Consequently Councillors Kearsley & Pigg, accompanied by the Borough Engineer, attended the the Group's meeting on 15th March 1944, and at the end of the month their colleagues on the Council invited Mr. Lock to meet them and give an outline of the proposed planning survey.

Unfortunately Mr. Lock's preoccupation with a similar survey of Middlesbrough made it impossible for him to visit Chelmsford, and so a gathering of members of the Council and Rural District Council was addressed instead by Anthony Minoprio M.A. F.R.I.B.A. A.M.T.P.I on 27th June 1944.

Council support

He revealed that the purpose of the Survey was two-fold; firstly, to collect facts and information upon which to base a plan for the future development of the Chelmsford district, and secondly, to discover what local people thought about the planning of their town and villages to. After hearing Mr. Minoprio's presentation both Council's agreed to give the survey their full support and made access available to all their relevant records.

Work on the Survey began at once under Mr. Minoprio's direction, aided by over 200 volunteers. The public's opinion on the future development of the Chelmsford area was ascertained via a questionnaire delivered to each household by members of the W.V.S. during the early spring of 1945.

Exhibition

By May of that year the Survey was practically finished, with around 30 survey maps and 10 drawings illustrating suggested improvements completed. These were displayed at a six day exhibition at the Shire Hall which was opened on 14th May 1945 by the author of the Greater London Plan, Sir Patrick Abercrombie. He was a close personal friend of Henry Cleminson. The exhibition gave the public its first chance to see in detail the Groups' recommendations and aroused considerable public interest with over 3,000 people visiting. As a result it was decided to publish an illustrated report on the proposals to include many suggestions that were made during the exhibition.

A bound copy of the report was gratefully received by the Mayor on behalf of the Borough of Chelmsford in February 1946. Though unofficial, it was to form the basis of the official Chelmsford Plan of 1950 which gave a framework around which Chelmsford's post-war development was established.

Six conclusions

The Chelmsford Planning Survey's six main conclusions were as follows; 1. Chelmsford had a bad road plan. 2. Valuable central land to the west of the High Street and around the Market was being wastefully used. 3. Sufficient attention had not been paid to architecture and amenities. 4. Chelmsford's finest natural assets, the Rivers Can and Chelmer, were being neglected. 5. There was a deficiency in houses and public buildings in the Borough. 6. Chelmsford's residential areas lacked the amenities which they should have had.

In response the Survey concluded the following;

Roads

Chelmsford lacked good roads to the west and should welcome the Orbital Parkway proposed by the Greater London Plan. In order to free the High Street and Duke Street from through traffic new roads should be built alongside the Rivers Chelmer and Can.

A new road on the west side of the town should be built to relieve the centre of north and south bound traffic; this could follow the Widford - Waterhouse Lane - Coval Lane route. London Road should be diverted westwards into Market Road in order to reduce congestion in the High Street and provide an alternative route through the centre.

An inner ring road to link Moulsham with the station and connect up radial roads should be made by extending Victoria and Market Roads southwards across the river. A new road should be built between the High Street and the River Chelmer to relieve the former and provide a service road to the main shopping centre.

The carriageway and pavements in Duke Street, New Street and the inner end of Springfield Road, which were dangerously narrow, should be widened. Public car parks with a total capacity of 850 cars should be provided at the points were that were most needed. The wholesale widening of rural roads was not necessary, but the advantages of a rural ring road as a link between the village communities could be considered.

Bus & rail stations

The Hicks bus station should be moved to the Townfield Street bomb site. If a larger goods yard became necessary, it could be built at a higher level between the River Chelmer and Arbour Lane. The railway arches at New Street and Duke Street were dangerous to traffic and should be widened. A new passenger station, forecourt and hotel were necessities to Chelmsford and should be planned in close co-operation between the Borough and L.N.E.R.

Cattle market

The cattle market should be moved to a better site in Victoria Fields in order to improve its efficiency and relieve congestion in the centre.

Town centre

Tindal Square was unworthy as the centre of the County Town and should be replanned. The Tindal Street area should be replanned in order to improve traffic circulation and provide the town with a convenient shopping centre. The Cathedral and its churchyard should be opened up by demolishing the houses which hid it from Tindal Square. A new Civic Centre with the public building which were needed should be built on and to the east of the existing Market site.

Residential areas

Residential areas in the Borough should be properly developed as self-contained units with their own facilities for worship, education, shopping, health and recreation. Vacant sites should be built on before any new development outwards was allowed from residential areas in the villages. The future development of residential areas should be kept within a green belt of one and a half miles from the Shire Hall. Rural housing should be sited in compact groups and straggling development along main roads should be avoided.

Public services

Efforts should be made to improve the water supply in the Borough and to extend the water mains and other services in the Rural District. All rural schools and new housing groups not connected to sewers should be provided with septic tanks. A refuse destructor and an abbatoir should be provided in the Borough.

Open spaces

The Can And Chelmer riversides are neglected assets which should be developed as a riverside park from Admiral's Park to Moulsham Mill. The preservation of commons as public amenities and of high-class farmland for food production is an urgent necessity.

Architecture and amenities

A fully qualified architect should be employed for the design of every building.

LAST BOMBS OF 1943

IN THE EVENING the district's last bombs of the year fell between Great Waltham and Boreham.

At 7.07 p.m. the air raid alert was sounded at Chelmsford. Twenty-three minutes later four H.E.s fell near the General's Head P.H. in Boreham, bringing down telephone lines to Park Farm and causing blast damage to several properties in the vicinity. Ten minutes later an H.E., incendiaries and a suspected firepot were dropped on Boreham Aerodrome, still under construction. No serious damage or casualties were reported. At 7.45 p.m. an H.E. fell to the south-east of Little Waltham Church, whilst four 250 kg H.E.s came down to the north of Langley's in Great Waltham between 600 and 620 feet from the house. One of the bombs failed to explode, but damage was restricted to 6 broken windows in the mansion. The all -clear sounded at Chelmsford at 8.21 p.m.

Later in the night Chelmsford had a fortunate escape when a force of around ten enemy Do 217s and Ju 88's apparently mistakenly bombed Gosfield Aerodrome near Braintree instead of Chelmsford, the intended target.

At least 65 H.E.s, weighing over 18.5 tonnes fell around the aerodrome, a load which if delivered accurately on Chelmsford, would have had devastating consequences.

Friday 10th December 1943

HOFFMANN WORKERS KILLED

Enroute to Ireland

The Essex Weekly News reported that a number of Irish women war workers from Hoffmann's were missing as a result of enemy action whilst returning to Ireland from Chelmsford for Christmas.

Friday 17th December 1943.

EYEWITNESS ACCOUNT:

"Working at Crompton's."

As told to our our Special Correspondent

"After I left King's Road School I went to the Kenmore Tutorial College in Springfield Road. After a time I decided that I'd rather work, so I got a job in the machine shop at Crompton's on a lathe, making components for switch gear for electric motors.

I used to make the same things all day long, working from 7.30 a.m. to 5.30 p.m., weekdays and also Saturday mornings. Other sections of the factory made things including hydraulic pumps that turned tanks' turrets and driving sprockets which were used to move tank tracks.

Whenever the air raid siren used to go off we all had to go to the shelters which were situated outdoors. They were rather like trenches, covered right over, with steps going down into them. On one occasion we'd been in the shelters all day long and the all-clear still hadn't sounded.

We looked at our watches and it was time to go home so we decided we'd all get out of the shelter and do that. In the grounds outside was this member of the factory's Home Guard called Mr. Hart. As we began to leave he said 'You lot can't go yet, you've got to keep in the shelters'. Everyone just carried on walking anyway and the next think I saw he was in the air, rifle and all, as the crowd pushed him out he way as we all went home!

After a time people got fed up with having to go down the shelters, so when there was anything on we used to come out and watch the aircraft battles above, although it was usually difficult to tell who was who.

Everywhere we went we used to carry our respirators with us - I kept mine in a tin. Eventually they had a system so that only when there was an immediate danger would we take cover, usually under our work benches.

There was a tall chimney at Crompton's and the spotter used to go up to the top and look round for enemy aircraft. If there were any around he'd send a warning signal down to the rest of us in the factory.

I never really enjoyed my time at Crompton's - we were watched by the foremen all the time and the wages weren't too good - by the time I left at 18 to join up I don't think that I was making £2 a week. I couldn't get out of there quick enough!

One day in early 1944 while I was at work I disappeared for about half an hour to have a little confab with my friends. When I got back the manager was stood there and demanded 'Where have you been?' 'Oh I've been having a talk' I replied, 'Don't worry I won't be here next week'. And I wasn't as I'd joined the army. I'd got fed up with factory life and I'd always fancied going into the army.

I had already been with the 5th Essex army cadets for almost two years and I couldn't see a quick end to the war so I thought of it as an adventure to join up and see the world. I didn't give a thought to getting killed - there seemed just as much chance of that happening in an air raid at home.

After initial training in Scotland I joined the Dorset's and after that I was posted to the far east with the Devonshire Regiment."

Kenneth Smith

War Damage Repairs:

ALMOST £90,000 SPENT ALREADY

At a meeting of the Council the Borough Engineer reported that up until 12th December 1943 war damage repairs in Chelmsford had cost £89,852.

At the same meeting the Council voted to earmark a site on the Melbourne Park Estate for the erection of a Junior & Infants School once the war was over. The school would help ease the severe overcrowding problems that were being experienced at the King's Road School.

Wednesday 29th December 1943

WARSHIP WEEK PLAQUE PRESENTED

At the Library in Duke Street the official exchange of plaques took place between the Council and H.M.S. Hardy in commemoration of Chelmsford's adoption of the ship after Warship Week. In attendance were the Mayor and Vice Admiral A.L. Snagge who represented the Admiralty.

Wednesday 29th December 1943

WINGS FOR VICTORY PRESENTATIONS

At separate ceremonies F.O. Hugh Ashton D.F.C. presented commemorative plaques to both the Borough and Rural District Councils in recognition of their successful Wings for Victory Week held during June 1943. F.O. Ashton, who was the son of Alderman Ashton of Highfield Road was a veteran of over seventy bombing operations over enemy territory.

Saturday 15th January 1944

LUFTWAFFE RETURNS

IN THE EVENING a small Luftwaffe force appeared over the district and the Home Guard Rocket Battery went into action for the first time since the Chelmsford Blitz eight months earlier.

No hits on enemy aircraft were recorded but several properties in the town were damaged by falling shrapnel.

Those known to have been thus affected were; 'Kiaora' in Chelmer Road, 41 Fourth Avenue, 20 Hamlet Road, 91 London Road, 'Moulsham Place' in Moulsham Street, 71 Mildmay Road, nos. 7, 8, 9, 13, 32, 50 New Street, 84 Sandford Road and 14 & 25 Yarwood Road.

In the period until 23rd January 1944 a further fifteen properties would suffer shrapnel damage in the Borough; 67 Barnes Mill Road, 'Ivydene' & 'Braemar' in Beeches Road, 73 First Avenue, 15 Longstomps Avenue, 12, 15 & 20 Roxwell Avenue, 117 Swiss Avenue, 17 Third Avenue, 5 Tudor Avenue, and 33, 34, 35 & 38 Waterhouse Street.

Saturday 15th January 1944

REGIONAL COMMISSIONER VISIT PROMPTS RESIGNATION OF CHELMSFORD FIRE GUARD CHIEF

The Regional Commissioner, Sir Wil Spens, paid a surprise visit to Chelmsford to investigate the Borough's Fire Guard in response to an unsatisfactory report from an inspector.

He had a conference lasting several hours with the Mayor, who was Chairman of the Fire Guard Committee, and other officials. The meeting led to the resignation of the Chief Fire Guard Officer, Mr. G.B. Soddy, though the exact circumstances of his departure were never made public.

When the matter was discussed at a special Council meeting no further details were revealed. Instead the public was given an up to date report on the state of Chelmsford's Fire Guard.

It consisted of 51 sectors for which 40 sector captains had been found and 19 sector points had been arranged. Of the 42 business area blocks that had been constituted 16 had block leaders appointed and 14 block points had been fixed. Of the 24 entirely residential sectors 19 had sector captains with 83 party leaders. Considerable difficulty had been experienced in dealing with business premises, primarily because a shortage of personnel - only 642 Fire Guards had been enrolled to protect the business areas when the actual requirement had been 1,183. An additional 5 independent Fire Guard schemes had been established at the various large works in Chelmsford.

With regards to training, 51 out of the 54 Fire Guards passed the short course on basic training while 34 out of 43 had passed the course in tactical training. An estimated 4,146 Fire Guards had undergone basic training, of whom 1,264 had been through the smoke hut, while 901 had undertaken tactical training.

Even so, some of the Fire Guard's officers, after three years' service, were reported to have yet to receive any training, though one or two had been to lectures. Many others had never even operated a stirrup pump and in some streets Fire Guard groups had all but ceased to function. Mr. Soddy was to remain in office until his successor, Mr. W.H. Burrell, took over on 16th March 1944.

Tuesday 11th January 1944

EYEWITNESS ACCOUNT:

"The wartime atmosphere."

As told to our our Special Correspondent

"There was a good feeling amongst the population in those days. Crime dropped off and people were more sympathetic to each other.

There was a good atmosphere from a humanitarian point of view. People were very kindly, we'd talk to anyone and everyone would help everyone else; kids and mothers with prams - you'd always help them get to a shelter.

It was a funny old life. We were all on edge, but we lived with it. We wondered 'What's going to happen next?' - yet we all went along with it.

We were a close community; we didn't go out of Chelmsford a lot and tended to make our own entertainment. Often we'd visit one another's houses for whist drives, though the air raid siren would go and that was the end of that!"

Les Manning

EYEWITNESS ACCOUNT:

"The Baby Blitz."

As told to our our Special Correspondent

One of my brother-in-laws was a regular soldier who had fought as a 'Desert Rat' in North Africa, so was no stranger to action. He was brought back to England in preparation for D Day and he stayed with us for one or two nights on his return when we had air raids.

He was quite shaken by them and told us that he hadn't realised we'd had it so bad here. He said 'At least in the army you've got something to fight back with'!"

George Brown

DORNIER DO217 SHOT DOWN AT RUNWELL

AT 5.15 A.M. a Dornier Do 217M (No. 86017) of 2/KG2, crashed in the grounds of Runwell Hospital, between the power house and farm buildings, killing all four crewmen on board. The aircraft had been shot down by A.A. fire over Pitsea.

Uffz. G. Kablitz and Uffz.. E. Kanz's bodies were identified in the wreckage but those of their companions, Uffz. G. Sauer and Lt. E. Reiner were not identified until later. Their remains were taken to St. John's Hospital and on 3rd February 1944 they were buried in a single grave at the Borough Cemetery.

Their aircraft U5 + CK was totally destroyed but fragments were subsequently excavated in 1976 and later put on display at the Imperial War Museum at Duxford.

The aircraft was likely to have been associated with an overnight raid on London which was the heaviest on England since July 1942. It marked the beginning in an upsurge in German bombing activity over Britain, a phase which was subsequently known as Operation Steinbock or 'The Baby Blitz'.

Fifteen minutes after the aircraft crash over 100 incendiaries fell into a wheat field five hundred yards west of Imphy Hall near Stock. Around 40 unignited specimens were collected by the police. No casualties were reported.

Saturday 22nd January 1944.

EYEWITNESS ACCOUNT:

"Danger, barrage balloons."

As told to our our Special Correspondent

"One very windy night I left my girlfriend's house in Bruce Grove to cycle home to Springfield. As was riding down Wood Street I heard the sound of a small explosion. Seconds later, in the darkness, I saw loads of sparks that flashed up the road towards me and stopped just short of me. I pulled up quick and stood still, not knowing what was happening and not sure what to do.

It turned out that the wind had brought down a barrage balloon, sited in the field by the Wood Street roundabout. The explosion had been the emergency charge detonating to deflate the balloon and the sparks had been caused as its cable fell down to earth.

Within a few moments a couple of R.A.F. blokes came running up to me - one said 'Don't move and don't touch anything - if that cable's in contact with a power cable then you've had it!.' They put big rubber gloves on and began cutting the balloon cable into short lengths which they took away. After half an hour or so the cable was cleared up and I was able to continue home."

Jack Palmer

BISHOP AND MORAL STANDARDS

The Essex Chronicle reported that in the latest edition of the Diocesan Chronicle the Bishop of Chelmsford had once again attacked declining moral values, 'particularly in a sexual sense', and the increase in divorce.

Friday 21st January 1944.

EYEWITNESS ACCOUNT:

"Visiting the yanks."

As told to our our Special Correspondent

"I was 15 when the American servicemen arrived in Essex during 1942. As a youngster I got on well with them - they were very friendly, popular and generous, everything that people said that they were. We used to see them in the villages, in the pubs and with the girls, as they became part of the scene.

After a time they developed Willingale Aerodrome, which was not far from where I lived in Roxwell. The aerodrome was certainly an attractive place and it was quite a thing to go and visit it. A group of us schoolboys would cycle over there and see the Yanks - they were very friendly and used to let us look all around their Marauders..

We never had any trouble getting in the base. They'd give us sweets and gum and things that we couldn't get ordinarily. We'd use the catchphrase "Got any gum chum?."

Leonard Menhinick

EYEWITNESS ACCOUNT:
AROUND TOWN

"A phalanx of cyclists would come down New Street to pour out into the town."

As told to our our Special Correspondent

"Around the early part of 1944, when I first learned to drive with my employers, you could travel out on the A12 from Chelmsford to the outskirts of Colchester and typically pass only two private vehicles en route

There would be a few trade vehicles on business too, and often you'd pass or be passed by an army convoy. There were very few cars on the roads, even in Chelmsford itself, and it was easy motoring.

At night when you came back you would have to put slotted masks over the headlights for the blackout and this made life very difficult, especially trying to get back through the country lanes.

It was very hard work, made worse in those days before the Clean Air Act by the awful smogs and fogs which we used to get during the winter months. Opposed to that Chelmsford was full of bicycles.

When the whistle blew for lunch at Marconi's and Hoffmann's a phalanx of cyclists would come down New Street to pour out into the town. If you were standing in their way you'd be bowled over!

On a Friday after market, herds of steers or bullocks would be led up from the market, across Tindal Square and up New Street to the railway goods yard. It was usually mayhem, with drovers all over the place, the occasional runaway cow from time to time, and the roads were in a pretty awful state afterwards. There was more traffic in that way in that one hour after market than there was in the whole of the rest of the week."

Ray Knappett

NIGHT RAID PROMPTS FEARS OVER INADEQUATE SHELTERS

IN THE EVENING the Luftwaffe launched a largely unsuccessful raid on London with the majority of the bombing incidents occurring instead in Essex and Kent.

The Chelmsford sirens sounded the alert at 8.15 p.m. when between 15 and 20 hostile aircraft were plotted nearing the coast. They approached the town from the north-east at about 20,000 feet, circled and began bombing the district mainly with incendiaries from soon after 9 p.m.

A combination of a heavy A.A. defence, poor visibility due to low cloud and the absence of the moon meant that only one bomb was dropped on Chelmsford, with the remainder falling in rural areas to the east and south of the town.

At 9.04 p.m. fourteen 50 kg H.E. bombs fell in the Margaretting area: one a quarter of a mile south of Whites Place; one unexploded on the east side of the L.N.E.R. embankment close to the Maldon Road bridge; two on the west side of the L.N.E.R. embankment close to the Maldon Road bridge; two unexploded in a field 100 yards east of the L.N.E.R. close to the Maldon Road bridge; one 50 feet to the west and two 60 feet to the west of the L.N.E.R./Parsonage Lane level crossing; one unexploded in a field to the east and one unexploded to the north-east of the L.N.E.R./Parsonage Lane level crossing; one 300 yards south of Durrant's Farm on the bank of the River Wid; one in a ploughed field between the River Wid and Margaretting Tye; and one in a field between Webb's and Bearman's Farms.

A minute later at 9.05 p.m. one ABB 1000-1 incendiary container fell into a field on the east side of the L.N.E.R../Parsonage Lane level crossing. The device burst on impact and all the incendiaries ignited within the crater.

A second ABB 1000-1 incendiary container fell to the west of Ingatestone railway station. It too burst on impact and ignited with about 50 of the incendiaries burned out around the crater, and the rest within it.

Nearby some 136 of the 1 kg incendiaries were spread over an area 300 yards by 150 yards close to the station. One house's roof was hit by five of them and partly burned out as a result.

Around 360 more of the 1 kg incendiaries fell in fields east of Roper's Farm, between Margaretting Road and Hylands Park in Writtle. Thirty of them came down on an A.A. gun site in the vicinity.

At 9.15 p.m. an ABB 500-1 incendiary container fell in the rear garden of 114 St. John's Road, the house on the road's southern corner at the junction with Moulsham Drive.

The container exploded on impact with most of the incendiaries burning in situ and only 38 of them spread just outside the crater. One person, believed to have been a Mr. Ryan, suffered burns to his hands whilst dealing with the device and was taken to hospital.

An airman at the barrage balloon site 28, opposite the junction, was also taken to hospital suffering from shock. They were to prove to be the only two casualties of the night. The incident resulted in the only significant damage of the raid in Chelmsford.

At Moulsham Drive numbers 44, 46, 48, 71, 73, 83 & 85 were damaged, and at St. John's Road numbers 108, 112 & 114 were similarly affected.

Two minutes later an unidentified incendiary container fell and burned out in the centre of Danbury Common. Around 200 of the 1 kg type incendiaries were spread over the Common. A further 147 of the devices, including 30 unignited specimens, were spread over an area 400 yards by 150 yards in a field adjacent to Gay Bowers, in Danbury. Some roofs were reported to have been damaged.

At 9.20 p.m. a 50 kg Phosphorus bomb fell unexploded into a field at Hylands Park to the north of Hylands House.

At the same time an ABB 1000-2 incendiary container fell and burst on impact in fields at South Gibcracks in East Hanningfield. There was no spread of incendiaries. The container was accompanied by 50 kg H.E. which fell nearby and failed to exploded. Meanwhile to the south, an ABB 1000-2 container of incendiaries fell and burst in a field 400 yards to the south of High House, between the B1012 Woodham Road and the L.N.E.R. at Battlesbridge.

Around 30 of the incendiaries spread up to 50 feet from the impact point. The container was also accompanied by a 50 kg H.E. which fell nearby and failed to explode.

Two minutes later another ABB 1000-2 container of incendiaries burst on impact with no spread when it fell 150 yards to the west of The Mill at Battlesbridge. The presence of the bombs led to the temporary closure of the A130 until around 11 a.m. the following morning.

At 9.30 p.m. around 190 of the 1 kg type incendiaries spread over an area 300 yards by 100 yards in a field south of Copt Hill and Gay Bowers Lane in Danbury. Their unidentified container is thought to have fallen at The Avenue.

At an unknown time during the raid another four bombs were dropped in the district. One ABB 500-1 container fell between Brook Farm and Baddow Park Farm in Great Baddow.

A complete ABB 500 container of incendiaries fell at the same location, burst on impact and all its incendiaries burned in situ. A 500 kg H.E. was also dropped into a field south-east of Baddow Park Farm.

Finally, one ABB 500-1 container of incendiaries fell and burst on impact in a field south-east of Linkhouse Farm in West Hanningfield. About 40 incendiaries were spread around the edge of the crater.

The all-clear was sounded at 9.47 p.m.

The Home Guard Rocket Battery opened fire on the passing raiders and pieces of shrapnel showered down onto the town, damaging at least one house, 'Newholme' in Springfield Road, where a hole was made in its roof.

At the time of the raid Chelmsford was crowded. There was a dance on at the Corn Exchange and with many people out visiting the town's pubs it soon became apparent that the local air raid shelter provision was inadequate.

The town centre's two small surface air raid shelters quickly filled up and several hundred people rushed to the cellars under the Shire Hall, leaving many others caught outside and endangered by falling shrapnel from Chelmsford's A.A. defences. The situation was exacerbated by the fact that the trench shelters at the Recreation Ground and in Bell Meadow were closed, pending their demolition as they had been found to be unsafe.

The issue was quickly taken up by the local press, and for the next few weeks the Essex Chronicle was to mount a campaign for an improvement in the town centre shelters.

It argued that should a heavy air raid occur before people could return home home to their own domestic shelters then casualties would be severe. So far Chelmsford's biggest raids had fortunately taken place in the early hours when the streets had been deserted.

Saturday 29th January 1944

TOWN SPARED AS RURAL AREAS HIT AGAIN

At 4.24 a.m. Chelmsford's air raid sirens sounded the alert as Luftwaffe aircraft approached the district as part of a two phase attack on London.

Locally numerous incendiaries and H.E.s were dropped during a half hour period beginning at 5.15 a.m. They came from some 25 to 30 enemy aircraft which made level bombing runs across the Chelmsford district at about 15,000 feet from the north-east and north to the west and south-west. Fortunately for Chelmsford the vast majority of the bombs fell in rural areas around the town and little significant damage was inflicted.

The first bombs fell at 5.15 a.m. when an ABB 1000-2 incendiary container opened in mid air and fell to the north of Seaman's Lane in West Hanningfield. Incendiaries from the device fell further north on grassland at Slough House Farm, but failed to spread significantly. A 50 kg H.E. fell nearby on wasteland by Seaman's Lane, causing a crater 10 feet across by 3 feet deep.

Fifteen minutes later an ABB 1000-2 container fell and scattered some 600 incendiaries at Edwin's Hall near Woodham Ferrers.

Meanwhile in the north-west of the district, another two ABB 1000-2 containers were dropped, one at Broad's Green near Great Waltham and the other near Bard's Hall, Pleshey. Each was accompanied by an ABB 500-1 container of incendiaries. Their contents fell at Israel's Farm, where three haystacks and a barn were damaged by fire.

Further to the north an ABB 500-1 container and an ABB 1000-2 container fell and scattered incendiaries at Old Park Farm near Ford End.

The peak of the raid was around 5.30 a.m. when bombs fell at Bicknacre, Butt's Green, Danbury, Fryerning, Rettendon, Stock, South Woodham Ferrers and Writtle.

At Bicknacre a large container with over 1800 of the 1 kg type incendiaries fell unexploded to the rear of Grange Cottage. Nearby, an ABB 1000-2 container of incendiaries fell on allotments close to the Brewer's Arms P.H. Of its contents, around 480 small incendiaries burned out harmlessly in the crater, whilst a further 120 fell on Gibcracks Camp in Danbury. Ten 50 kg H.E.s were dropped just to the west, between Butt's Green, Sandon and Great Gibcracks. Six of them, of which four were unexploded, fell in a ploughed field, whilst another four came down in a wheat field, only one of which exploded. The H.E.s were accompanied by an ABB 1000-2 which contained about 600 incendiaries. They failed to spread and burned out in the bomb's crater.

A pair of ABB 1000-2 containers, each holding 600 incendiaries fell at Fryerning; one fell complete at Fryerning Wood with the incendiaries burning out in the crater, while the other opened in mid air between Fryerning Wood and College Wood, scattering the incendiaries harmlessly over farmland.

Five devices were dropped at Rettendon; a 50 kg Phosphorus Incendiary and 50 kg H.E in a pasture at Little Hayes Farm; an unexploded flare on the north bank of the River Crouch; and a pair of ABB 1000-2 containers at Rettendon Place, of which one of which fell intact into a wheat field and the other opened in mid air and destroyed four straw ricks and three corn stacks.

At Stock ten 50 kg Phosphorus Incendiaries fell unexploded at Ramsey Tyrells. Four of the devices came down in a wheat field, two in a pasture, two in the lane leading to Stock, one in a duck pond and one in another field. The Phosphorous incendiaries were accompanied by an ABB 1000-2 container which opened in the air and spread some 600 incendiaries between Ramsey Tyrells and Stock.

At South Woodham Ferrers an ABB 1000-2 container fell intact into a pasture at Champion's Hall. Its 600 incendiaries burned out in the device's crater A pair of 50 kg H.E.s exploded at Writtle, one in a meadow at Shakestones Farm and the other on the bank of the River Wid at Lower Shakestones. The latter damaged a footbridge over the river.

At 5.40 a.m. some 450 of the 1 kg type incendiaries, including 150 unexploded, fell at Top Barn Lane near South Woodham Ferrers. The container from which they came was believed to have fallen nearby, into the River Crouch.

Five minutes later there were three bombing incidents in Chelmsford. One phosphorus incendiary caused a small crater in London Road opposite the Chelmsford & Essex Hospital. The main portion of the device was subsequently taken to the police station in New Street. A second phosphorus incendiary and a 50 kg H.E. fell in the allotments at the end of Crompton Street, injuring one person.

Meanwhile, three 500 kg H.E.s exploded in a wheat field near The Grange on the B1012 in Rettendon, each creating crates up to 50 feet across by 13 feet deep Nearby seven 50 kg Phosphorus Incendiaries fell unexploded at Grange Farm, Rettendon, three in a copse and four in a wheat field.

Finally, around 5.45 a.m. three unexploded 50 kg Phosphorus incendiaries and three 50 kg H.E.s fell into a wheat field at Peatlands Farm, South Woodham Ferrers

The all-clear was sounded by Chelmsford's sirens at 6.07 a.m.

Strong winds during the day are thought to have led to barrage balloon cables damaging six properties in Chelmsford; 16 & 18 Lower Anchor Street, 31 New Writtle Street and 5,6, & 8 The Vineyards.

Friday 4th February 1944

The Essex Chronicle reported that Brownings in Broomfield Road, the former residence of Mr. W.G. Webber, had now been taken over by the American Red Cross for use as an officers' club.

The organisation had purchased the large grey-bricked ivy-covered house and three acres of grounds for use by American officers, to be run in conjunction with the existing general club over the Saracen's Head Hotel.

Brownings was situated on the western side of Broomfield Road, nearly opposite Third Avenue, and almost hidden from the main road by trees. Among the facilities for the officers were 18 beds, meal provision and a billiard table in the basement.

Friday 11th February 1944

BABY BLITZ CONTINUES

IN THE EVENING and into the early hours of the following morning, the 'Baby Blitz' continued with another Luftwaffe raid on London.

Locally, some 34 properties had been damaged by A.A. fire in the week ended today, with the majority of the incidents likely to have occurred during the evening's raid.

In the Borough the following buildings are known to have suffered slight damaged; nos. 1, 27, 54, 55, 65, 67, 73, 79, 92, 102, 103, 122, 130, 157, 166, 167, 169, 175, 178, 185, 186, & 190 Galleywood Road, 'Briarfield' in Galleywood Road, 22, 188 & 222 Rainsford Road, 1, 3, 4, 5, 6, 7, Hylands Parade in Wood Street, the public conveniences in Viaduct Road, and 3 Laurel Cottages in Victoria Road.

Sunday 13th February 1944

B26 BOMBERS ARRIVE AT BOREHAM

The first of 64 B26 Martin Marauder aircraft arrived at their new base, the recently completed Boreham Aerodrome. It would officially open on 6th March 1944.

Thursday 24th February 1944

FACTORY GIRL 'KILLED AMERICAN'S CHILD'

At the Chelmsford Petty Sessions a young factory girl was committed for trial at the Old Bailey on the charge of infanticide.

The court was told that on 2nd January 1944 she had given birth to a baby whose father was said to be an American serviceman. The following morning the baby had been found dead at the girls' lodgings at 7 Old Court Road.

The prosecution alleged that she had asphyxiated the child by putting a cloth in its mouth.

Friday 3rd March 1944.

JU 188 BROUGHT DOWN AT GREAT LEIGHS

The remains of a Luftwaffe Ju 188 which was shot down at Great Leighs on 14th March 1944. (Courtesy Essex Chronicle)

AFTER A FORTNIGHT'S break the Luftwaffe returned to raid London with around 140 aircraft reaching the capital. Participants in the raid were probably responsible for one or two bombs that fell in the rural areas around Chelmsford.

At 10.10 p.m. Chelmsford's air raid sirens sounded the alert as around twenty enemy aircraft approached the town from the north and north-east, circled and left to the east and south-east.

Twenty minutes later an aerial torpedo (4' x 3.5") fell and exploded 350 yards west of Lilystone Hall in Stock. Soon afterwards A.A. shells were reported at West Hanningfield, but the evening's major incident occurred around 11 p.m. when a Ju 188 E-1 of KG2 (markings U5 + BM) appeared over Chelmsford.

It was engaged by anti-aircraft fire from the ground, the Home Guard Rocket Battery and by a Mosquito of Squadron Leader

Bunting D.F.C. and Ft. Lt. Reed D.F.C. of 488 Squadron from R.A.F. Bradwell Bay.

The aircraft was quickly hit and set alight, a wing was seen to fall off, and it plunged to the ground into a field at White House Farm in Great Leighs at 11.03 p.m., some 500 yards from the farm house and 200 yards from the church.

The wreckage burned so ferociously that no one was able to reach the trapped crew members. When the fire had eventually died down the bodies of all five men on board were recovered, one had been decapitated and one had no arms. They were later identified as Lt. Horst Becker, Uffz. Gerhard Bartolain, Uffz. Albert Lange, Uffz. Gunter Goecking and Oberfw. Heinrich Litschke.

At the Recreation Ground there was great jubilation shown by the members of Number 4 Relief of the Home Guard Rocket Battery, who believed that they had been responsible for the destruction of German aircraft.

Although their claims were supported by evidence from Royal Observer Corps posts, civilians and the police the kill was subsequently credited to the Mosquito of Squadron Leader Bunting D.F.C. and Ft. Lt. C.P. Reed D.F.C.

Incendiaries, believed to have been jettisoned from the doomed Ju 188 fell at Church Lane in Margaretting and at Longs Farm, Little Waltham, whilst four empty AB23 SD2 incendiary containers fell at Widford Hall Farm and a fifth empty one in the churchyard at Widford Church. The all-clear was sounded at 11.30 p.m.

Apart from two salvos fired by the Home Guard's Rocket Battery, Chelmsford's other defences fired some 1530 rounds of 3.7 inch.

At least eight properties in the Borough were damaged by shrapnel. They included; 'Sunny Corner' in Chignall Road, 166 Galleywood Road, 15 Kingston Avenue, 3 & 8 Kingston Crescent, 1 Park Avenue and 'Forestlyn' & 120 Springfield Road.

Tuesday 14th March 1944

FACTORY WORKER MURDERED

IN SOUTHEND, Kathleen Cornish, a young Hoffmann's employee, was brutally stabbed to work as she was walking to Southend Victoria Station on her way to catch her train for work.

A 27 year-old lorry driver with a previous manslaughter conviction was arrested and charged with her murder. He subsequently appeared at the Essex Assizes on 9th June 1944, was convicted and sentenced to death.

The conviction was later quashed on appeal on technicalities regarding the conduct of his trial.

Friday 17th March 1944.

HOSTEL OPENS IN BROOMFIELD RD

In the afternoon the actress Jean Forbes-Robertson opened a new Y.W.C.A. hostel and services canteen at 76 Broomfield Road,. a large house which had been specially converted for the purpose.

Saturday 18th March 1944.

JU 88 SHOT DOWN ABOVE CHELMSFORD

CRASHES IN NORTH SEA

Late the previous evening some 95 Luftwaffe aircraft had crossed the English coast, once more intent on attacking London. with many of them passing over Chelmsford.

One of the raiders, a Junkers Ju 88 A-4 of KG54. was engaged above Chelmsford by Ft. Lt. J.C. Surman and Ft. Sgt. C.E. Weston in a Mosquito from 604 Squadron R.A.F. and came down in the sea off the Isle of Sheppey. Three of the aircraft's crew perished, but a fourth baled out and was captured at Southend.

The Chelmsford A.A. defences had another busy night, with 787 rounds of 3.7 inch fired, and the Home Guard Rocket Battery once more in action, narrowly missing one enemy raider.

Bomb damage was minimal. At 12.55 a.m. a container of incendiaries landed in the garden of 3 Avenue Road in Great Baddow, just five yards from the house,

causing a crater six feet across in the front garden. The house was superficially damaged, but no one was hurt. Ten minutes later other incendiaries fell and damaged a house at Mill Lane in Stock.

Wednesday 22nd March 1944

ROCKET BATTERY FIRES LAST SALVOES

In the early hours around 120 enemy aircraft attempted to raid London. Locally, the enemy aircraft were attacked by the Home Guard Rocket Battery which was in action for what transpired to be the last time.

Saturday 25th March 1944.

"Fifth Columnists."

As told to our our Special Correspondent

"During the war everyone was suspicious of strangers and if saw someone doing something a bit unusual you'd say 'You wanna watch, him he could be a spy'.

There was one man, a middle aged tramp I suppose, who used to wander around Springfield at night wearing this old mac. Whenever you went out you always seemed to meet him and each time his hair would have changed colour from the last time.

People used to say he was a spy or a fifth columnist so if we saw him we'd shout out 'This is the FIFTH time we've seen you!'. Then all of a sudden he disappeared and we never saw him again."

Gerald Carter

COUNCIL MEETING:

ROAD SIGNS ARE BACK

At the monthly Council meeting members were informed that following instructions from the Ministry of War Transport direction signs had been re-erected on the A12.

They had been removed during the invasion scare of 1940. Amongst other matters the Council urged consumers to exercise economy in their consumption of water and gas, both of which were in short supply.

Wednesday 29th March 1944

CAT SURVIVES 21 HOURS IN BARRAGE BALLOON!

The Essex Chronicle reported that a cat recently adopted by one of Chelmsford's barrage balloon sites had been discovered asleep in a barrage balloon's air pocket when it had been brought down for inspection after 21 hours airborne!

Friday 31st March 1944.

PARISH COUNCIL NEWS

POST WAR HOUSES FOR GREAT BADDOW

The Essex Chronicle reported that Great Baddow parish Council had recently held its annual meeting where it had been revealed that a dozen houses had been allocated to the village in the R.D.C.'s first post-war year's house building programme. Some 14 acres of land had been purchased for the erection of 125 houses whilst another 4.5 acres and 'The Vineyards' were also earmarked for purchase.

Friday 31st March 1944.

THE SHELTERS THAT NEVER WERE

FOLLOWING THE RECENT upsurge in enemy aerial activity there had been considerable public concern that Chelmsford's air raid shelter provision was inadequate.

These concerns had been expressed vehemently in recent articles in the Essex Chronicle, letters to the Council from the local branches of the Amalgamated Engineering Union and the Communist Party, and by a petition signed by residents of Goldlay and Rochford Roads.

When the Council held its monthly meeting on Wednesday 29th March 1944.the matter was consequently top of the agenda.

The Borough Engineer had prepared a report on the current position relating to air raid shelters in Chelmsford. At the outbreak of the war the initial provision had been limited by the Government to shelters for 10% of Chelmsford's population using town's shopping facilities - this had been provided by basement shelters accommodating 1,550 people and trench shelters accommodating 2,100 people.

During 1941 a dozen 50 person shelters had been built around the town but despite changes made by the Luftwaffe's bombing tactics the Government had adopted and maintained a policy whereby the dispersal of the population in their own domestic shelters had been seen as a better safeguard than the construction of large public shelters.

As a result of this basement shelter for 1,180 people and trenches for 2,380 people had been abandoned on Government instructions. These had comprised of:

Basement Shelters:
Congregational Church 400 people
Shire Hall 380 people
F. Spalding Ltd. 150 people
Chelmsford Club 150 people
Freeman, Hardy & Willis Ltd. 80 people
F. Luckin Smith Ltd. 60 people
Wenley Ltd. 60 people

Trench Shelters:
Recreation Ground 600 people
Bell Hotel site 600 people

With those reductions taken into account plus the Council's domestic air raid shelter schemes the existing provision thus stood at:

Basement shelters 240 people
Trench shelters 600 people
Surface shelters 600 people
(12 x 50 people)
School shelters out of school hours 2,210 people plus a further 500 places under construction
Domestic - brick surface
6 person 527 - 3,162 people
Domestic - brick surface
9 person 74 - 666 people
Domestic - Anderson
6 person 61 - 366 people
Domestic - Morrison single tier
4,933 - 12,333 people
Domestic - Morrison double tier
46 - 230 people
Domestic - blast walled refuge
rooms12 - 45 people

In addition there was a considerable shelter provision at the town's factories and from privately provided domestic and business shelters.

After the enemy begun to undertake heavy concentrated raids of a short duration the Borough Engineer had approached the Regional Commissioner with regards increasing the shelter provision for the town.

He had then been informed that only in very exceptional circumstances would there be any possibility of further shelters being sanctioned. Following the heavy raids of April and May 1943 a shortage of building labour and materials prevented any further moves in that direction.

However, consultations had continued with the Regional Technical Advisor of the Ministry of Home Security in October 1943, January 1944 and had culminated with a meeting on 6th March 1944 when the Regional Technical Advisor had revealed that although the domestic shelter provision was well above the country's average and could not be improved, a case could now be put forward for the erection of several additional public shelters within the town centre.

After carefully reviewing the whole position and considering the Borough Engineer's report the Council voted to seek Government approval to build brick surface shelters at four sites; the corner of Duke Street and Victoria Road, Tindal Square, top of the High Street near the Shire Hall, and in Barrack Square opposite Baddow Road.

The Council deferred consideration of the provision of a further shelters until its next meeting at the end of April 1944, when it opted for one to be erected outside Woolworth's store.

However, any hopes the Council had for the scheme were quickly dampened when, at the Council's meeting in May 1944. the Borough Engineer reported that the Ministry of Home Security had written stating that owing to difficulties with labour and materials and also speed of erection, consideration should be given to building the shelters using an alternative method of construction, namely surface concreted Anderson shelters.

The Ministry advised that such shelters would would occupy less room and that it would be possible to arrange a better dispersal by building eight sets of shelters each comprising of two 12 person Anderson shelters built facing each other and covered with concrete.

After considering the Borough Engineer's report on the shelters the Council voted to build one group of four of the Anderson shelters at a site at the junction of Victoria Road with Duke Street and another group in Tindal Square - both sites thus having accommodation for 48 people. In addition it would seek to build one pair of Anderson shelters placed end to end in the High Street outside Woolworth's store, another pair at the far end of Barrack Square, opposite Baddow Road, and a third pair in front of the Saracen's Head Hotel at the top of the High Street.

The Council concluded that the scheme, combined with existing shelters, would provide sufficient cover for all those members of the public likely to be caught in the open during alerts.

Throughout the summer, whilst the V-1 campaign was at its height, no start was possible on the new shelters due to a delay in the delivery of the shelter sections. Finally, on 28th September 1944, the Ministry of Home Security wrote to the Council and suggested that in view of 'the changing war conditions, the continuing difficulties in obtaining the necessary parts and the likely shortage of labour to erect them', the Council should consider cancelling the shelters.

A special Council meeting on 9th October 1944 discussed the matter, the outcome of which was a vote 17 to 1 in favour of the scheme's cancellation.

Wednesday 29th March 1944

VISITORS BANNED FROM CHELMSFORD

With an Allied invasion of north-west Europe expected during the summer the Government designated the English coast a protected area from the Wash to Land's End as a security measure.

Visitors were banned from entering the zone which went many miles inland and included the Chelmsford district. Increased police checks were expected to be implemented to enforce the ban.

Saturday 1st April 1944

B.B.C. AT SHIRE HALL

IN THE EVENING the B.B.C. recorded an edition of the popular radio programme 'The Brains Trust' at the Shire Hall.

The question master was Donald McCulloch, whilst the guest speakers were the President of the Board of Education, R.A. Butler M.P., an agricultural expert, M.L. Easterbrook, Secretary of the T.W.U., T.H. Hodgson and the President of the N.F.U., J.C. Knowles. The recording was expected to be broadcast to the U.S.A.

Friday 21st April 1944

PERMISSION FOR BLITZED HOUSES TO BE REBUILT AFTER 3 YEAR WAIT

At the monthly meeting of the Council members granted outline consent was given to Messers Stamp Worthy & Company's request for rebuilding numbers 70, 72, 74 and 76 Marconi Road. The houses had been destroyed as a result of the raid on Marconi's on 9th May 1941.

Wednesday 26th April 1944.

AMERICAN BOMBER CRASHES AT MARGARETTING

During the afternoon a B26 Martin Marauder crashed at Margaretting between The Wantz and Ivy Barn Lane, killing all five crewmen on board the aircraft. It was believed to have been a member of the U.S.A.A.F. 387th Bomb Group based at Chipping Ongar (Willingale) Aerodrome.

Thursday 27th April 1944.

D DAY PREPARATIONS CONTINUE

As part of the preparations for Operation Overlord, the forthcoming Allied invasion of France, orders were given that members of the Home Guard were to man guard posts at several locations in the Chelmsford area until July 4th 1944.

They included; The Eagle P.H. crossroads in Galleywood, Church Street in Great Baddow, the River Chelmer railway bridge in Springfield, The Oasis junction in Springfield, and the Broomfield Road/Rectory Lane junction. Additionally, two mobile platoons, with one on immediate notice, were to be based at the Territorial Offices in Market Road.

Thursday 27th April 1944.

DANBURY WOMAN LEAVES £1/4 MILLION

The death occurred of Mrs. Eva Perry of St. Clere's Hall in Danbury. She left an estate worth a massive £227,424/10/0, including £10,000 and St. Clere's Hall Farm to its manager.

Saturday 29th April 1944.

KING'S HEAD MEADOW FOR THE YANKS

KING'S HEAD MEADOW, the former home of Chelmsford's amateur football club, was officially made available free of charge to the U.S. Red Cross for use as a sports ground for American servicemen.

The field had previously been rented from the Council at £3 per annum by Messers W. & H. Marriage who had used it for grazing purposes. Other facilities made available to the Americans included the Essex Home School (boxing), Chelmsford Golf Course at Widford and the 'big three' firms' sports grounds.

Monday 1st May 1944.

FIRST ESSEX WOMEN POLICE

The Essex Joint Standing committee agreed to select women police constables to serve within the Essex Constabulary.

Of the 25 set to be appointed, five were to be based at Chelmsford's New Street police station from early August 1944. The first woman officer was a former sergeant in the Metropolitan Police and she was subsequently joined by two w.p.c.s transferred from the Lancashire force.

Wednesday 3rd May 1944

BIKE THEFT EPIDEMIC

AT THE CHELMSFORD Petty Sessions two soldiers were fined £5 each for stealing bicycles from outside the Ritz Cinema.

The case highlighted the continuing epidemic of the offence, usually committed by servicemen taking them to return to their bases, Since the start of 1944 209 bicycles had been stolen in Chelmsford.

The Petty Sessions also saw the first prosecutions against people who had entered the town in contravention of the Government's recently introduced visitor ban. Throughout the summer dozens of people, mainly from London, were to be convicted of the offence and given fines typically of between five shillings and £5.

Friday 19th May 1944

SALUTE THE SOLDIER WEEK:

A GREAT SUCCESS NEARLY £1 MILLION INVESTED

THE DAY SAW THE START of the Chelmsford and district 'Salute the Soldier Week', the latest in a series of campaigns which had been designed to encourage investment in National Savings to help pay for the war.

The Borough had been set a target of £500,000 and the Rural District one of £250,000, representing an investment of around £10 per head of population.

The week was opened at 11 a.m. when a mounted knight in armour challenged Chelmsford to meet the target. The knight was in fact Major Alan Mills of the Home Guard, from Danbury, who rode a horse belonging to Ernest Seabrook.

Following the challenge a two mile long military parade proceeded through the town with salute taken by Major general J.A. Aizlewood M.C. Further events publicising the campaign, such as parades, speeches, concerts, and

dances, were set to take place throughout the following week.

The campaign, like the previous three similar events, had proven to be a great success. A total of £939,800/8/9 was invested in National Savings, including £629,407/18/8 in the Borough at £19/3/10 per head, and £310,392/11/6 in the Rural District at £8/13/5 per head.

Over £114,000 of the Borough's total had come from the employees of Marconi's. The top parish was Ingatestone & Fryerning with £34,453/7/9 at £13/9/2 per head, whilst in terms of investment per person it was Springfield with £11,615/9/16 at £23/14/10.

The wooden spoon went to Runwell where only £22/15/6 had been invested at a pitiful 3s/7d per head. The weeks' events had also made a surplus of over £900 of which £445 was subsequently given to the Essex Regiment Association and £164 to the Essex Yeomanry Benevolent Fund.

Saturday 20th May 1944

AIRCRAFT CRASHES NEAR BOREHAM AERODROME

Around 11 a.m. an American aircraft crashed 100 yards from the Waltham Road junction at Russell Green, just to the north of the U.S.A.A.F.'s base at Boreham Aerodrome.

One crewman was injured and on the instruction of the U.S. police the road was closed between Russell Green and Little Waltham whilst residents from the vicinity of the crash were evacuated for a few hours.

Wednesday 31st May 1944

EYEWITNESS ACCOUNT: D DAY

"It seemed to me that the sky was full."

As told to our our Special Correspondent

"One episode which stands outs in my mind was D Day afternoon when all around Chelmsford the invasion gliders were mustered for a massive airlift. It seemed to me that the sky was full, mostly of Dakotas towing grey gliders with white invasion stripes. They were going round and round in circles until they assembled in formation, before flying off. They were all at different altitudes, different distances as they gradually mustered from a series of airfields. It was incredible and almost nightmarish - great echelons of planes, each towing a glider, completely filling the sky. We knew from that what was going on. It was an incredible sight which I shall never forget."

Ray Knappett

D DAY

In the early hours the Allies launched their long awaited invasion of Europe with the D Day landings in Normandy.

In the Chelmsford area great fleets of aircraft could be seen forming up ready for their departure for France.

Tuesday 6th June 1944

HOFFMANN'S 'BOMBED' BY THE AMERICANS

DURING THE MORNING spotters on the roof of Hoffmann's saw several objects falling from an aircraft flying high above the factory.

Suspecting that they were bombs, they issued an immediate take cover warning to employees who rushed to the shelters.

Seconds later the objects came crashing through Hoffmann's roof and into the garden of a nearby cottage - however, they were in fact a steel helmet, pullover, pair of airman's shoes and a large box containing a dingy.

It was subsequently discovered that the items had been accidentally dropped by a passing American aircraft!

Americans were also thought to have been responsible for another incident which occurred during the morning when an Eastern National bus which had been parked behind the cattle market was discovered to have gone missing.

Later, after a search, the bus was found the next day near Rivenhall Aerodrome and a group of American soldiers were detained in connection with its disappearance.

Monday 12th June 1944

FIRST V-1 HITS LONDON

CHELMSFORD TRAIN SERVICES DISRUPTED

In the early hours Hitler's much vaunted secret weapon, the Vergeltungswaffe 1 (reprisal weapon 1), or V-1, was launched on London from sites in north-eastern France.

In the first morning of the offensive four of the devices reached England, with the worst incident at Bethnal Green where one struck the L.N.E.R. bridge over Grove Road.

Six people were killed and railway services between Liverpool Street Station and Chelmsford and beyond were subsequently diverted to Fenchurch Street Station. Initially the Government kept the V-1s secret, with the incidents put down to aircraft crashes.

However, on the morning of 16th June the Home Secretary announced their existence during a speech in the House of Commons. Very soon the V-1 was nick-named 'the doodlebug'.

Tuesday 13th June 1944

CHELMSFORD'S FIRST V-1s

Since late the previous afternoon until lunch time today more than 200 V-1s were launched on London as their use began in earnest. Locally the Chelmsford district suffered its first V-1 attacks.

At 3.50 a.m. a large explosion occurred near Boreham Aerodrome. Almost immediately it was identified as a V-1 incident. The device came down 100 yards north-east of Russell Green Fruit Farm, just off the Little Waltham Road. In doing so it was the dis-

trict's first enemy bombing for almost two months. No casualties were caused though some nearby piggeries and fruit trees were damaged by the blast.

Later in the morning, at 10.20 a.m., an unidentified aircraft was reported to have crashed some 400 yards west of Weilt Cottages, Creephedge Lane, between East Hanningfield and Rettendon. By 12.30 p.m. the suspected aircraft was confirmed to have been a second local V-1. Again no casualties were reported though several cottages were badly damaged and required evacuation.

Friday 16th June 1944

DOODLEBUG ON SWIMMING BATHS

Waterloo Cottages which were severly damaged by the Swimming Baths V-1. (Author)

AT 6.06 A.M., on what was a warm summer's morning, a V-1 fell on soft open land immediately to the south of the Public Baths at the bottom of Waterloo Lane.

The doodlebug had approached Chelmsford from a point midway between Danbury and Galleywood, at an altitude of only a few hundred feet. Although the explosion damaged a considerable number of properties there were only nine casualties, mainly caused by flying glass. Two people required hospital treatment, including a woman who was seriously injured. One employee at the Gas Works' Hydrogen Plant was blown over by the blast and suffered from

severe shock, while parts of the V-1 fell on the Gas Works and damaged several buildings there. Chelmsford was fortunate. Had the V-1 fallen a few hundred yards away in most directions it would undoubtedly have caused far more casualties. The Home Guard Rocket Battery was not ordered to engage this or any of the subsequent V-1s.

A total of over 560 properties were affected by the blast. The worst affected were the Public Baths which were partly demolished, and the four Wellington Cottages which were seriously damaged. The wartime nursery in Waterloo Lane was to remain closed until 3rd July 1944 pending its repair.

EYEWITNESS ACCOUNTS: SWIMMING BATHS V-1

"We heard this doodlebug getting louder and louder making an incredible noise."

As told to our our Special Correspondent

"One Sunday morning in 1944 a V-1 buzz bomb dropped on the swimming baths in Chelmsford. The baths were notorious for their poor state and I remember a pensioner who lived in Sandon was quoted as saying 'It must have been a very dirty bomb if it needed a bath in Chelmsford!'.

I worked in an office above Barclays Bank at 2 High Street, and the back of our premises faced the direction of the swimming baths. Although we had no windows on that side of the building the blast from the V-1 blew out the whole of the contents from our stationery cupboard. I had to go in to work that morning and put all the items back again ready for work the next day."

Ray Knappett

I was in the Cathedral Vestry in New Street on fire watching duty early in the morning. We had had a reasonably quiet night when we heard this doodlebug approaching, getting louder and louder making an incredible noise. It was common knowledge that once the noise stopped it would fall out of the sky and explode. Well suddenly the noise stopped. I was with one of the Cathedral's clergy, Mr. Mitchell, and we stood there looking at each other for about ten seconds before there was an almighty crump as it came down and exploded. The doodlebug landed by the open air baths only a few hundred yards short of, and in line with, the Cathedral. "

Dennis Hance

Sunday 18th June 1944

NO MORE IRISH WORKERS FOR CHELMSFORD

At the monthly Council meeting the Mayor revealed that in the wake of mounting public protests, and after consultations on the matter with the Regional Commissioner, no more Irishmen would be compulsorily billeted on householders in Chelmsford.

Over recent months dozens of men had been recruited from Ireland to work in the town's factories in an attempt to solve the acute labour shortage. However, in recent weeks there had been growing resentment towards the Irish from some Chelmsford people who felt that the Irish were being given preferential treatment over them. Criticism had also been levelled at the unhygienic condition of many of the Irishmen.

In a similar vein, the Council discussed the increasing problems caused through the misbehaviour of members of the armed forces in Chelmsford. Consequently the Town Clerk was asked to write to the Military Police asking for greater supervision of the military in the town.

Wednesday 28th June 1944.

DOODLEBUG AT MARGARETTING CAUSES FIRST LOCAL FATALITY

AT 12.20 A.M. a V-1 fell at Bearman's Farm in Margaretting and in the process caused the first V-1 fatality in the Chelmsford district.

The device demolished one house and seriously damaged farm buildings and two other properties.

At 'Tuhfaut', a newly built house fronting the Writtle Road, four women were trapped in the debris, Miss M. Clarke, Mrs. Radford, Miss Radford and Miss Marjorie Carter. Rescuers, who included American soldiers, were quickly on the scene and managed to extricate the women who were rushed to hospital.

However, 60 year-old Miss Carter subsequently died at the Chelmsford & Essex Hospital.

She was the younger daughter of the late Dr. Edward Carter and a member of the W.V.S. During the First World War she had been an ambulance driver on Lady Gooch's staff at Hylands Park and in her younger days had been a fine golfer, tennis player and horsewoman.

She was a former captain of the Chelmsford Ladies golf team and noted as a keen gardener. Miss Carter's funeral was held at Margaretting Church on 27th July 1944.

Sunday 16th July 1944

EYEWITNESS ACCOUNT:

"When they began it was as a complete surprise to us."

As told to our our Special Correspondent

"When the doodlebugs began coming over it was as a complete surprise to us; we hadn't been warned about them and so we didn't know a thing about them.

With the first one the siren came on about 7 a.m. one morning. No all-clear was sounded until the evening so we had to stay on alert all day, even though nothing else came over.

Afterwards they gradually became more frequent until they started coming every ten minutes or so."

Les Manning

V-1 BETWEEN RETTENDON & WOODHAM FERRERS

The Chelmsford district's fourth V-1 fell between Rettendon and Woodham Ferrers around 6.30 p.m., in a field three-quarters of a mile west of Ilgars Manor Farm and 300 yards from the old barn at Hyde Hall. No casualties were caused and damage was restricted to a few broken windows at nearby cottages.

Saturday 1st July 1944

AMERICAN BOMBER CRASHES NEAR FORD END

A Liberator aircraft crashed in flames and exploded with its bombs on board some 400 yards north of the A130 east of Appletree Corner near Ford End (junction with B1417) at 12.55 p.m. All the aircraft's crew had managed to bale our safely before impact and no casualties were caused. Some 22 properties in the vicinity of the crash site suffered superficial blast damage.

Sunday 2nd July 1944

NEW V-1 WARNING

A new air raid warning system was introduced in the Rural District Council area at 10 p.m. in an effort to combat the V-1 menace.

Previously wardens had given an immediate warning by sounding their whistles, and the all-clear by ringing hand bells. However, in recent attacks such warnings had been known not to have occurred until after a V-1 had hit the ground.

The new system involved each wardens' post in the Borough area 'adopting' a counterpart in the Rural District for the purpose of passing on warnings. In theory the warning could now be given almost simultaneously in Chelmsford and the rural areas around the town.

Thursday 27th July 1944

V-1 AT BATTLESBRIDGE RAILWAY STATION

At 11.10 p.m. a V-1 fell on the L.N.E.R.'s goods yard adjacent to Battlesbridge Station. Five people were seriously hurt, two houses extensively damaged and 30 others superficially so.

Monday 3rd July 1944

DOODLEBUG AT WEST HANNINGFIELD

At 10.13 a.m. a V-1 fell 500 yards to the east of Linkhouse Farm in West Hanningfield. No casualties were reported and damage was restricted to Linkhouse Farm, Patten's Farm and a number of cottages in the vicinity.

Wednesday 19th July 1944.

V-1 AT INGATESTONE

The district's ninth V-1 fell at 12.08 a.m. at The Hyde, a listed county house just to the north of Ingatestone. No one was hurt in the incident, though the blast damaged the house, its outbuildings and around two dozen other properties in the vicinity.

Thursday 20th July 1944

RETTENDON DOODLEBUG

At 11.42 a V-1 fell at Great Elms Farm in Rettendon, 200 yards south of Roman's Farm. No one was hurt, though 29 properties and Bevin Brothers munitions factory were damaged by the blast. Production at the factory was not affected.

Tuesday 25th July 1944

TWO MORE V-1s FRYERNING AND CHIGNALL ST. JAMES

At 3.57 a.m. a V-1, the district's twelfth, fell at Fryerning in fields just to the south of Grange Farm and Maisonette.

No casualties were reported, though between 25 and 30 houses were damaged by the blast and several small fires were started.

In the early evening residents in Chelmsford looked anxiously into the sky as a V-1 appeared in the east and tracked its way right across the town. Fortunately it continued past Chelmsford and at 6.30 p.m. it came down in a barley field 500 yards north-west of Grays Farm on land belonging to Chignall Hall Farm at Chignall St. James. No one was injured by the explosion. Some fifteen nearby properties, including the Pig & Whistle P.H. were damaged by the blast.

Saturday 29th July 1944

V-1 IN ARBOUR LANE GRAVEL PIT

The districts' sixth V-1 fell at 11.35 a.m. in Bolingbroke's gravel pits (Springfield Quarries), a site west of the junction of Arbour Lane and Church Lane, Springfield.

Fortunately just one slight casualty was caused, though several tame rabbits were killed. Although no precise records survive, it is known that the roof of Hoffmann's, only a few hundred yards away across the Chelmer valley (its likely intended target), and 125 properties in Arbour Lane, Church Lane, First Avenue, Green Close, Second Avenue, Springfield Green, and Springfield Road, suffered blast damage. Windows were smashed by the explosion at the Cathedral and All Saints' Church in Springfield.

Sunday 9th July 1944

GALLEYWOOD DOODLEBUG

At 3 a.m. a V-1 fell in a field close to a large barn at Parklands Farm (also known as Howard's Farm) on the outskirts of Galleywood.

No casualties were reported, though extensive blast damage was inflicted on the farmhouse and outbuildings, whilst around ten cottages in Lower Green suffered superficial blast damage.

Late in the evening at 10.20 p.m. a railway truck containing a 100 lb phosphorus and magnesium bomb was reported to be on fire at Boreham.

Saturday 22nd July 1944.

COUNCIL ANGER AT MILITARY TRAFFIC

At the monthly meeting of the Council the Borough Engineer was once again directed to contact the army's Eastern Command in an effort to divert the large numbers of military vehicles that were currently passing through Chelmsford's narrow town centre streets. The Council hoped that greater use could be made by military vehicles could make greater use of the A12 by-pass and Victoria Road.

Wednesday 26th July 1944

WOMAN FINED FOR ENTERING CHELMSFORD ILLEGALLY

A Walthamstow woman was fined £1 for entering Chelmsford contrary to the existing Government travel restrictions at the Chelmsford Petty Session.

In mitigation she told the court that she had come to Chelmsford 'for a change from the flying bombs which came over night and day and we got no rest'.

Friday 11th August 1944

EYEWITNESS ACCOUNT:

"The doodlebug babies."

As told to our our Special Correspondent

"I had just given birth to my second daughter, Sally, at St. John's Hospital. The maternity block so full up so that those of us who had had their babies and were getting on had to sleep in the day room there. It was a half-circular room with glass windows all around. All our babies were kept in the corridor next door.

On this particular night we were laying there when suddenly a doodlebug went past the window, making a horrible noise and spitting flame out the back. It was rather uncanny. We were all terrified that it was about to explode and we'd all get showered with glass from the windows. It was a bit dangerous really."

Maud Manning

EYEWITNESS ACCOUNT:

"The cost of living."

As told to our our Special Correspondent

"In wartime if you were earning £5 a week you were thought to be doing quite well. For example, the officer in charge of the book-keeping section at County Hall, a Mr. Pates, had a salary of £500 a year. On that he was able, not only to run a car, but he actually lived at the County Hotel.

For a penny you could buy a box of matches, or a newspaper. A packet of Players was sixpence, as was admission to the cinema and cider cost about four pence a pint.

A cheap day return rail ticket to London was 4/9d and if you caught a train before 7.30 a.m. you could buy a workman's ticket for even less. I used to get one to Romford and that was only one and three pence halfpenny return per day."

Les Appleton

SANDON DOODLEBUG

A V-1 fell on farmland near Little Baddow Hall, Little Baddow, to the west of Sandon Brook and north of Hurrell's Lane at 3.20 a.m. No casualties were caused, though some blast damage was reported at a neighbouring farm.

Sunday 30th July 1944

THE DISTRICT'S LAST V-1 FOR SIX WEEKS

At 6 a.m. a V-1 fell 150 yards north-west of Humphrey's Farm, around three-quarters of a mile to the west of Great Waltham.

No casualties were caused though around two dozen properties and farm buildings were damaged by the blast. Cows in nearby fields were cut by fragments of the V-1 and their milk supply was adversely affected for a few days afterwards. The V-1 incident was to prove to be the district's last for over six weeks.

Thursday 3rd August 1944

EYEWITNESS ACCOUNT:

"My first doodlebug."

As told to our our Special Correspondent

"I remember my first doodle-bug quite well. I was in lodgings at 11 Old Court Road and we had a table-top shelter there. An alert was on and I had been in the shelter quite a while.

Everything was still quiet so I got out and stood by the front door and there was this terrific noise. The man of the house, Mr. Saul who worked in the drawing office at Hoffmann's, was with me and said 'What the hell is that?'. I replied I don't know, whatever could it be, perhaps its the drone of planes or something like that coming over.'

Then all of a sudden there was silence and it came down with a thud some distance away. We soon became used to them but the noise was more frightening than anything because you were waiting for the thing to stop. When it did you knew it would come down any minute."

Mary Bateman

NEW SHELTER TRENCHES AT BADDOW REC

The Essex Chronicle reported that slit trenches at the Great Baddow Recreation Ground were now available for use by the public during air raids. They had been dug by soldiers for the Parish Council after a delay caused by a lack of labour.

Friday 18th August 1944

BISHOP SUGGESTS WELCOME HOME SCHEME

The Essex Chronicle reported that the Bishop of Chelmsford had written in the Diocesan Chronicle suggesting that a 'welcome home to the boys' week should be held at the end of the war for returning servicemen.

In several of the villages around Chelmsford thoughts had already turned towards such an idea with 'Welcome Home' fundraising already beginning.

Friday 25th August 1944

VISITOR BAN ENDS

THE VISITOR BAN which had been imposed on Chelmsford and many other coastal districts during April 1944 as part of the preparations for D Day was lifted.

Even so the public were warned that they were still required to carry their identity cards, the military could still impose restrictions and that certain areas would still remain closed due to the presence of mines. Nevertheless at the Chelmsford Petty Sessions three women were fined ten shillings each for illegally entering the Chelmsford area during the previous few weeks.

Friday 25th August 1944

WOMAN GETS ONE MONTH IN JAIL FOR BREAKING VISITOR BAN

A WOMAN WAS sentenced to one month's imprisonment for entering Chelmsford contrary to the Government's travel restrictions at the Chelmsford Petty Sessions.

The severity of the sentence caused some controversy, especially as the woman had arrived by train at Chelmsford Station, had then been made aware of the offence and had returned to London on the next available train. In the following weeks the Home Secretary, Herbert Morrison, when asked about the case in the House of Commons was to reply, somewhat surprisingly, that he saw no grounds for recommending any interference with the sentence!

Friday 18th August 1944

MARGARETTING MAN IS FIRST INTO PARIS

The Allies entered Paris, and the first Englishman to do so was said to have been Ft. Lt. Jeffrey 'Chippy' Barclay', the elder son of Mr. & Mrs. E.L. Barclay of Ivy Hill in Margaretting.

As an air information pilot his job was to fly his Hurricane to and from France to London, twice a day, to bring war reporters' dispatches back from the front. On this particular day he had landed at an aerodrome on the edge of French capital.

Friday 25th August 1944

COUNCIL SEEKS 'CRASH' AIR RAID WARNINGS

AT THE MONTHLY COUNCIl meeting members agreed to approach the Ministry of Home Security to obtain a system of immediate danger or 'crash' air raid warnings for Chelmsford and to suggest a shortening of the current alert periods.

The matter had arisen out of a recent letter to the Council from the local branch of the A.E.U., whose members had expressed concern that their families outside of the town's factories were receiving inferior air raid warnings to those that they were receiving inside.

In the letter the union had suggested that the immediate air raid warning systems used in the factories ought to be spread to residential areas with the use of klaxons.

Wednesday 30th August 1944

V-1 ON DISPLAY

At Broomfield over 2,000 people attended a horse show and gymkhana which raised some £450 for the Red Cross. A captured V-1 was one of the main attractions on display.

Saturday 9th September 1944

CHELMSFORD STREET LIGHTS TO BE RE-LIT AFTER 5 YEAR BLACKOUT

The day saw the publication of a Ministry of Home Security circular which revealed that the Government would now permit the relaxation of the blackout and the introduction of reduced street lighting not yet up to the pre-war standard.

In Chelmsford the matter was discussed by the Council at its meeting at the end of September 1944 when members were informed that the cost of adapting street lights would be 13/6 for each main road lamp and 2/6 for their counterparts on the town's minor roads.

Delay

The work would be undertaken in co-operation with C.L.E.S.Co., the local electricity company. In view of the high costs involved and the likelihood of further reductions in lighting restrictions the Council resolved to postpone any action on the matter until a later date.

The decision to delay was immediately met with a largely unfavourable reaction from the people of Chelmsford. Somewhat chastened the Council reconsidered the matter at its October 1944 meeting and voted to adopt a limited programme of reduced street lighting and seek the necessary approval from the Ministry of Home Security.

The programme involved 33 lamps at certain junctions in Baddow Road, Broomfield Road, Duke Street, High Street, London Road, Moulsham Street, New Street, Roxwell Road, Springfield Road, Writtle Road and the A12 By-pass. The initial cost of adaptation was put at £22 for the 33 lamps. The Council was informed that the figure would rise to approximately £753 if spread to every street lamp in the Borough. Despite the decision the Essex Chronicle was to complain that Witham, with a population of a third of Chelmsford's, had already decided to relight 79 lamps.

Lights on

In any event the first 33 modified street lamps in Chelmsford were illuminated during the evening of 4th November 1944. However, the initial general consensus of the public was that the lamps had very little effect except for illuminating a small area directly underneath them!

At its November 1944 meeting the Council agreed to a major expansion of the reduced street lighting scheme. Members voted to illuminate a further 63 lamps on the town's main roads, 36 on main tributary roads such as Mildmay Road and North Avenue, and 146 on residential roads. By mid January 1945 all the main road lights and 107 of those in side roads had been relit and finally on 3rd March 1945 all the lights were illuminated to the restricted standard.

Shortages

The German surrender on 7th May 1945 ended the chance of any further air raids and thus, in theory, permitted the introduction of street lighting to the pre-war standard.

However, with a national fuel shortage the Government was keen to economise on electricity consumption and so it requested that the Council temporarily extinguish all Chelmsford's street lights immediately and prepare for the introduction of full lighting at the end of double summer time on 15th July 1945.

At the end of May 1945 the Council voted to accede to the request and so Chelmsford was temporarily plunged back in the Blackout conditions it had suffered for more than five years from the outbreak of the war.

On 15th July 1945 Chelmsford's street lights were illuminated at full power for the first time since the outbreak of the war. However, within months of the end of the war the continuing national fuel shortage was to lead to the introduction of further lighting restrictions as Chelmsford experienced its first taste of post-war austerity.

Saturday 9th September 1944

THE V-2 ROCKET ARRIVES

In the evening, at 6.43 p.m., almost simultaneous explosions at Parndon Wood near Epping and Chiswick in London marked the arrival of the first two V-2 rockets to fall on England.

Immediately the Government imposed a news blackout on any V-2 incidents, which was to stay in force until 10th November 1944, when the Prime Minister would announce their existence.

Friday 8th September 1944

ROCKET BATTERY TAKES IT EASY

With the threat of invasion from Germany now gone, compulsory Home Guard duty and drills ceased. The 211 (101 Essex Home Guard) Rocket Battery in the Recreation Ground also ceased operational duties, having not fired in anger since 25th March 1944.

The day was also the last before a relaxation in Fire Guard duties was allowed in many parts of the country, though the Chelmsford area was not yet included in the relaxation.

The Home Guard's Rocket Battery at the Recreation Ground 'stood easy' on Monday 25th September 1944.

Monday 11th September 1944

GLIDER DOWN AT MASHBURY

During the day a glider crashed-landed into a field at Mashbury. None of its crew were hurt. The aircraft is believed to have been part of the 'Market Garden' invasion force, briefed to attack and capture three bridges over the River Rhine including that at Arnhem.

Tuesday 19th September 1944

EYEWITNESS ACCOUNT:

ARNHEM GLIDERS

"We looked and saw these great big planes towing gliders."

As told to our our Special Correspondent

"I was at home in Chignall St. James when I heard this terrific roar and I said to my brother 'What ever's happening now?',

We looked into the sky and saw these great big planes towing gliders, with the parachute troops on board. There must have been at least a hundred of them.

Later when the planes returned, many of them were missing and those that were left had their doors swinging open from when the troops had gone."

Winifred Wales

EYEWITNESS ACCOUNT:

"An American glider had come down."

As told to our our Special Correspondent

"All day at school in Great Waltham we watched droves of gliders flying across the sky towards Europe.

In the afternoon when I came home to Bailey's Farm, Mashbury, my grandmother said to me 'Hey boy, there's one of them gliders in that field across the road'.

Excitedly I rushed outside and went to have a look. An American glider had come down 300 yards to the south of the farm in a field on the opposite side of the road known as Dowsett's or Mill Field.

Several Americans were there on guard duty. They made me quite welcome and treated me like royalty - we chatted and they gave me chewing gum out of their packed rations. They told me that they were hoping to get a rope and hook the glider up again - For a few days I refused to go to school as I didn't want to miss that happening. I used to eat my tea and dinner there with the Americans.

In the end it was decided to dismantle the glider on site rather than try and fly it away. It was taken apart and driven away by lorry and I had to go back to school. Some of the ladies in the village had been pleased by the arrival of the Americans. One woman down the road was especially keen on them, and later on I heard that her husband used to say 'I don't care, as long as it's there when I want it'!"

Bernard Wrenn

V-1 ATTACKS RESUME

ONE DOWN AT RETTENDON

The lull in enemy activity over the Chelmsford district which had begun on 3rd August 1944 was rudely broken at 4.50 a.m. when a V-1 fell 100 yards east of the Rettendon Turnpike at The Piggeries in Woodham Road (B1012).

The V-1 may well have been launched from a German aircraft over the North Sea, a tactic recently introduced by the Luftwaffe. The explosion seriously damaged buildings at High House Farm and six houses in the vicinity, of which four were rendered uninhabitable. A further 40 suffered superficial damage. Four people, cut by flying glass, were taken to hospital in Chelmsford, whilst another, suffering from serious shock, was admitted to Runwell Hospital. A number of pigs, heifers and chickens were also hurt.

Tuesday 19th September 1944

BATTLE OF BRITAIN LEADER IN CHELMSFORD

Lord Dowding, of Battle of Britain fame, spoke at a meeting of the Chelmsford Spiritualists Society at the Shire Hall on the subject of spiritualism. His visit also raised £28 fro the R.A.F. Benevolent Fund.

Wednesday 20th September 1944

M.P. NOW IN GREECE

The Government announced that British troops had landed in Greece, some three and a half years after they had been driven from the country by the Germans. Chelmsford's M.P., Col. John Macnamara was reported to be in command of the R.A.F. Regiment in the invasion.

Thursday 5th October 1944

"Meeting the Americans."

As told to our our Special Correspondent

"In the latter part of the war I worked at Weathersfield where we were building a school near the Aerodrome. One evening, after work, we were coming back to Chelmsford by bus and there were some American airmen on the bus with us.

One of them was a coloured chap, and one or two of the others who were white were sat behind him and kept taking the mickey out of him because he was dark. I was angry and I had to hold myself back from interfering. I couldn't understand it.

He was just the same as them, doing the same job on an equal footing, yet they kept putting this fella down. That did annoy me."

Norman Hume

WOMAN KILLED BY LITTLE BADDOW V-1

AT 1.35 A.M. CHELMSFORD'S air raid sirens were sounded. Eight minutes later a very low flying V-1, travelling in a westerly direction and on course for Chelmsford, was interrupted in mid flight when it reached the high ground of the Little Baddow - Danbury ridge.

With its propulsion unit still running the V-1 collided with trees approximately 20 feet above the ground, just 30 feet to the rear of 'Dukes Orchard' in Spring Elms Lane, Little Baddow. The device dived into the earth and exploded with devastating results, killing one person.

Dukes Orchard, a well-built large brick detached property, was almost completely demolished. The property's owner, 82 year-old Ann Jane Nicholson who was in a bedroom directly facing the back garden, was buried under tons of debris and it was not until 8.20 a.m. that rescuers were able to recover her body.

Her sister, Mrs. Young, who was in a bedroom on the opposite side of the house escaped serious injury but was severely shocked. A maid in a third bedroom also suffered shock and cuts. Severe blast damage was inflicted within a radius of 40 yards, mainly to trees and the garden, whilst the house across Spring Elms Lane, opposite 'Dukes Orchard' was seriously damaged.

A total of 34 properties suffered superficial blast damage. The nearest undamaged building was 1,460 feet away and the furthest damaged one was 2,280 feet away.

Among other people injured by the explosion were Mr. & Mrs. Cooper and Mr. & Mrs. Ennals who were saved serious injury by their Morrison shelter.

Chelmsford's sirens sounded the all-clear at 2.45 a.m.

Mrs. Nicholson was the daughter of the late John and Ann Gregory, and the widow of Henry Nicholson who had died in March 1944. She was described as gracious, talented, and greatly interested in amateur dramatics and was secretary of the Essex Drama League. She had been a student of the actress Leah Bateman and had written and produced plays, often performing in the leading roles. She was also a gifted musician and with her husband had played in an orchestra for more than a quarter of a century.

Subsequently Mrs. Nicholson was buried at Little Baddow on 23rd September.

Wednesday 20th September 1944

DOODLEBUG ON DISPLAY AT FIRE STATION

A captured V-1 which was put on display at the Market Road Fire Station helped to raised £176 from admission fees and donations for the N.F.S. Benevolent Fund. After its stay in Chelmsford the V-1 was to be taken to Epping for exhibition there.

Friday 6th October 1944

CHELMSFORD'S FIRST ROCKET

FALLS AT THE RETTENDON BELL CROSSROADS

At 5.05 a.m. the Chelmsford district suffered its first V-2 attack. The device came down on farmland 40 yards north-west of the Rettendon Bell P.H. crossroads beside the A130 at Rettendon.

The V-2, which was the only one to fall on England during the day, was the 83rd V-2 to reach the country since the offensive had begun on 8th September 1944. The explosion left a huge crater, 61 feet across by 25 feet deep in the clay soil, surrounded by a large ring of spoil which had been thrown up.

Fortunately there were only two slight casualties, a man and a child, neither of whom required hospital treatment. A fox was, however, killed by the blast. Four properties, including the post office, were severely damaged and another forty, including houses and farm buildings were superficially damaged.

Sunday 15th October 1944

V-1 FALLS AT BICKNACRE

At 7.50 p.m. the district's 18th V-1 fell to the rear of Woodham Hall in Bicknacre, and extensively damaged the farm buildings and some 26 houses up to a distance of three-quarters of a mile.

There were just two slight casualties. Eight people who were made homeless were accommodated by neighbours.

Friday 6th October 1944

HOUSE DESTROYED IN LT BADDOW ROCKET ATTACK

The country's 84th V-2 came down at Little Baddow, in a small plantation behind Lubman's House on the north side of Fir Tree Lane at 3.50 p.m.

The explosion left a crater 33 feet across by 10 feet deep in the clay soil. The house, which was a two storey detached dwelling of wood and asbestos construction, was only 106 feet from the impact point and was practically destroyed by the blast.

King House, a two storey, timber framed thatched property, some 500 feet to the south-west in Chestnut Walk, was struck by hot fragments. They set the thatch ablaze and burned the house down to the first floor. Six houses were seriously damaged and 16 others slightly.

Overhead electricity and telephone cables were also severed. Despite all of this there were only two slight casualties, one man and one woman.

Tuesday 17th October 1944.

"Coping with the Shortages."

As told to our our Special Correspondent

"During the war it was difficult for people to travel around the country, and this caused certain problems.

A girl I knew in Broomfield planned to marry a chap in the R.A.F. who came from another part of the country, and their wedding was arranged to take place at Great Bardfield. Unfortunately none of his relatives or friends could obtain the consent to travel down so the girl asked me to be the best man. I was only about nineteen at the time and I'd not even met the groom but I agreed to do it.

After the wedding ceremony we went over to Great Saling to the Saling Oak pub for a celebratory drink. There were always shortages of beer, and pubs were often not open for the full licencing hours as they had nothing to sell. When we arrived at the hostelry in the absolute darkness there was a notice on the door of the pub saying 'no beer, sold out'.

The rural publicans used to do this to exclude the Americans from the nearby bases since they would go and drink a pub dry and the locals would then have no beer. To get in the pub the bride's father gave a special knock on the door. There was a response from inside and the door opened to let us in. I think we stayed in there till around two o' clock the following morning!

In a similar way if you knew the right people you were able to obtain other scarce goods. There was a tobacconists along Broomfield Road from which I used to buy my cigarettes. When anyone went in, there were never any cigarettes visibly on sale, but I got to know the girl behind the counter. She'd tell me when they were going to be delivered and would save a pack of twenty for me.

It was the same with sweets. There used to be a little sweet shop right on the corner of Tindal Street and London Road called Peachey's. One of my former masters at the Grammar School had an interest in the business and occasionally he would be in there behind the counter after school hours. I would go into the shop, he'd recognise me and consequently I was usually able to purchase a bar of chocolate or something equally rare."

Les Appleton

V-1 DESTROYED OVER HYLANDS

AT 7.30 P.M. the district's 19th V-1 became the first one to be shot down by a pursuing aircraft.

The doodlebug was exploded in mid air between the south-western corner of Hylands Park and the northern side of Chapel Wood in Margaretting.

No one was hurt, though the blast and machine gun fire damaged several properties, including Messers G.S. Last's premises at 144 Moulsham Street, Southwood Farm in Writtle, the White Horse P.H. in Widford and Widford Garage.

Wednesday 25th October 1944

BOARDED BARNS PROPERTIES HIT BY CANNON SHELLS

At 3.45 a.m. cannon shells, thought to have come from an Allied aircraft pursuing a V-1, damaged several houses near and on the Boarded Barns Estate.

At 82 Swiss Avenue one passed through a bedroom window and fell onto the floor, whilst at 36 Dixon Avenue the front door and staircase were damaged by another.

Roof windows were broken at King's Road School and windows and doors were broken at 1, 2 and 3 Jubilee Terrace. Other damaged properties included numbers 25, 26, 29 & 33 Corporation Road and 25 Woodland Road.

Wednesday 27th September 1944

BABY LEFT IN DITCH FOR TWO DAYS

At the Essex Quarter Sessions a 22 year-old land worker who admitted exposing her two week-old child at Little Baddow was bound over and put on probation for two years.

The court heard that she had left the illegitimate baby girl in a ditch for two days, before it had been discovered unharmed by Mrs. Currie of Hammond's Farm. The land worker admitted to have associated with American soldiers. It was revealed that the baby was her second illegitimate child.

Friday 29th September 1944

FIRST INTO GERMANY

Around 11 a.m. Major R. Guy Matthews, of the Dorsetshire Regiment and from Bedell's Hall in Chignall Smealy, crossed the frontier and entered Germany. He was thought to be the first local man to do so.

Saturday 7th October 1944

"I could feel the heat from the explosion."

As told to our our Special Correspondent

"During the early evening I was coming into Chelmsford by train from Shenfield on my way to work at Hoffmann's. It was dark and the train was creeping over the viaduct by the Recreation Ground when suddenly a doodlebug appeared, flying parallel to the train in the opposite direction to the west.

It was not much higher that the train and on its tail there was a nightfighter chasing it and firing into to it. It flashed before my eyes and suddenly there was a terrific explosion with myriads of white sparks as the doodlebug was hit an blew up.

The fighter flew clean through the debris and as I sat by the closed window I could feel the heat from the explosion. The whole carriage shook and had it been much closer I think that it train could have been blasted over."

Bill Wilson

EYEWITNESS ACCOUNT:

"Farmers didn't go hungry!"

As told to our our Special Correspondent

"I used to spend my holidays on my uncle's farm the other side of Colchester. When I arrived there one day he said, 'You're just the man I wanted. Come out to the cow shed'. I went out there and in an old bath was a twenty score (or four hundred) pound pig he'd just killed.

I spent half the morning scraping it to get the bristles out and then after this had been done he cut it up into joints. All the local farmers took turns at killing the odd animal. It was illegal to do so without official permission but most farmers, including my uncle, did it anyway. One would occasionally kill an animal and they'd all share it to help one another out. Farmers didn't go hungry!

I was sitting in the farmhouse having breakfast the next morning, when I heard the gate open. I looked out and there was the village policeman who had just got off his bike. I said to my uncle 'Look out, the police have arrived!'

My uncle went out to the back door to meet him and I heard a murmuring going on. After about five minutes the policeman left with a brown paper parcel under his arm. I'd been worried about him learning that we'd killed a pig, when he'd known about it all along and had only come to take his share!"

Les Appleton

FOUR MONTHS JAIL FOR THRICE MARRIED WOMAN

The problem of an increase in the number of bigamy cases was demonstrated with three cases being heard at the Essex Assizes, which opened at the Shire Hall,

A 38 year-old Llanelly woman was imprisoned for four months for the offence, having been concurrently 'married' three times; once at Wethersfield, for a second time at Richmond in Yorkshire and for a third time in Chelmsford during August 1943.

In the other cases, a 32 year-old lorry driver from Romford was given six months and another Romford man was given three days imprisonment.

Monday 6th November 1944

V-1 ON SANDON/EAST HANNINGFIELD BORDER

At 10.55 a.m. the districts' fourth, and Britain's 276th, V-2 fell on Little Claydon's Farm on the Sandon/East Hanningfield border. The explosion demolished the farmhouse, severely damaged farm buildings and slightly damaged four cottages. Two women were badly injured by flying debris, another suffered shock and a man was slightly hurt. They are believed to have been Mr. F. Law, Rose Tiley, Cecilia Tiley and Miss V. Day.

Wednesday 29th November 1944

994 BOTTLES OF CHAMPAGNE FOUND IN MANOR ROAD HOUSE

AMERICAN AIRMEN SUSPECTED OF SMUGGLING

THE ESSEX CHRONICLE reported that His Majesty's Customs & Excise had discovered 994 bottles of champagne in cases at a house in Manor Road.

The bottles had apparently been 'liberated' from France by American airmen and flown to 'a base near Chelmsford', most likely Boreham Aerodrome. From there the cases had been driven to the house by lorry.

A number of Americans were said to have been questioned by the police and customs authorities, who were naturally concerned about the duty liable to be paid on the champagne.

In the West End of London bottles could frequently cost £10 each. The whole episode brought national attention, with The Times describing the Manor Road house as a 'champagne orgy'.

As a footnote, in reference to the incident, on 14th November the Chancellor of the Exchequer was asked in the House of Commons whether he was aware of the wholesale smuggling that was going on?

Friday 27th October 1944

MAYOR AGAIN

Cllr. Sidney Taylor was unanimously elected to be Chelmsford's Mayor for the fifth successive year and a record equalling seventh time in all. Alderman Fox was re-appointed as his deputy.

Thursday 9th November 1944

HOME GUARD STAND DOWN COMMEMORATED

During the morning some 900 representatives of detachments of the Home Guard from all over Essex packed the Cathedral for a special service to commemorate the stand down of the Home Guard which had been ordered on 1st November 1944.

The sermon was taken by the Bishop of Chelmsford. The service attracted a great array of the county's dignitaries and was followed by a half mile long procession of detachments of the Essex Home Guard through the town centre.

The salute was taken by the Lord Lieutenant of Essex, Sir Francis Whitmore, and a number of his deputies at the Shire Hall.

Sunday. 19th November 1944

POLICE TARGET ILLEGAL BOOZE

Following the find of illegally imported champagne at a house in Manor Road, the local papers reported that detectives were now investigating the illegal sale of the spirit Hooch.

In recent weeks bottles of the drink had been discovered on sale in Chelmsford shops at prices as high as £5 a bottle. It was often made using methylated spirits or wood alcohol and despite its obvious health dangers it was very popular amongst American servicemen in the town.

Friday 24th November 1944

DOODLEBUG AT NEWNEY GREEN

At 7.40 p.m. the district's 21st V-1 fell near Little Moor Hall, Newney Green. No casualties were caused, though numerous cottages and nurseries in the vicinity were damaged by the blast.

During the day 115 Baddow Road suffered war damage.

Friday 10th November 1944

V-1 EXPLODES OVER LAWN LANE

AT 6.06 A.M. AN ALLIED fighter shot and destroyed a V-1 in mid air above Lawn Lane in Springfield.

The explosion damaged several properties, but the only casualty was Mrs. Peacock of 72 West Avenue who sustained shock and a slight wound in her right leg from a stray cannon shell fired by the fighter. Among properties known to have been damaged were: Holders Farm & cottages, Bowers Farm; nos. 8, 9, 10, Springfield Hall Lodge, & Brambles in Arbour Lane; Kent House & La Lorna in Broomfield Road; Pantiles & Greengates in Church Lane; no. 38 Fifth Avenue; nos. 33, 65 & 71 First Avenue; Beverley & The Lodge in Lawn Lane; no. 3 Lionfield Terrace; Mrs. Clarke's, Mrs. Carlick's, nos. 1, 2, 3, 4, P.J. Tyler's, Grayfields, Willow Cott, The Little Gem. Greenview, Mrs. Harvey's, The Almshouses, & Springfield Place Cottages in Springfield Green; and nos. 83, 96, 108, 109, 110, 125, 126, & The Plough Inn in Springfield Road.

Friday 24th November 1944

HOME GUARD FAREWELLS

Throughout the country detachments of the Home Guard took part in their final parades. The main event took place at Hyde Park in London where the King took the salute from representatives of every Home Guard battalion. Locally most villages held farewell suppers and other celebratory event.

Sunday 3rd December 1944

V-1 DESTROYED OVER DANBURY

At 5.24 a.m. a V-1 was destroyed in mid air between Brock's Farm and Old London Road, Runsell Green near Danbury. No one was hurt, though some 30 houses suffered superficial blast damage.

Sunday 29th October 1944

FIRE GUARD TO BE HALVED

The Home Secretary announced that the Fire Guard in Chelmsford and other areas was to be halved in size. The decision caused some concern to the County Council, which was to decide at a meeting later in the month to press the Government to postpone any cut back in civil defence.

Thursday 2nd November 1944

MARGARETTING V-1

A V-1 fell in Margaretting; to the west of the River Wid and in a ploughed field north-east of Rook Wood and east-south-east of Margaretting Church at 5.30 p.m. The device left a crater 30 feet across by about 9 feet deep. No casualties were reported and damage was restricted to around ten nearby houses and a farmhouse.

Friday 17th November 1944

NEW Y.M.C.A.

Some 18 months after it had been devastated by a German bomb the Y.M.C.A. was reopened in Victoria Road by the County's Chief Education Officer, Dr. B.E. Laurence, in a ceremony attended by the Mayor and Bishop of Chelmsford.

The new building was a temporary wooden structure which had formerly been used as a hall by the Childerditch Women's Institute. It had been placed adjacent to the lounge of the old Y.M.C.A. building which had survived the bombing and was also available. A second, smaller wooden building was set to be erected almost directly opposite the Y.M.C.A. in the near future for use as a Y.W.C.A.

Saturday 2nd December 1944

V-1 & V-2 FALL

At 8.30 p.m. the Chelmsford district's 24th V-1 fell 200 yards south of Chignall Hall Farm in Chignall St. James.

No casualties were caused, though one house was seriously damaged and 16 others, plus a number of farm buildings, suffered superficial damage. Among them were Chignall St. James School and the village church where windows were broken by the blast.

Later on, at 10.34 p.m., a V-2, Britain's 314th, fell around a quarter of a mile east of Potters Farm in Rettendon, between Hyde Hall and Grays Farm. It left a crater 35 feet across by 12 feet deep. No casualties were reported though slight damage was caused by the blast at Salesfrith Farm and cottages in East Hanningfield.

Tuesday 5th December 1944

HYLANDS HOUSE NEAR-MISS

A V-1 was reported to have blown out windows at Hylands House at 7.43 p.m. A daylight search was to find no evidence of any impact and it was subsequently assumed that the damage had been caused by a V-1 that had passed the area and gone on to crash outside the district at Bushwood Farm near Hutton.

Saturday 4th November 1944

LITTLE WALTHAM ROCKET

THE DISTRICT'S THIRD V-2, and Britain's 228th, fell at 12.03 p.m. in a sugar beet field to the south-west of the junction of Chatham Hall Lane and the A131 Roman Road near Little Waltham.

No serious injuries were caused, though two people were treated for shock at the Little Waltham first aid post. Around 95 properties were damaged by the blast including greenhouses along Roman Road, the Congregational Chapel and the village's school only 150 yards away.

At the latter windows facing the explosion were blown in and a several of the twenty or so children awaiting their school dinners were thrown to the ground, though none was hurt. Two others, on their way home for lunch were blown off their feet and flung into a heap of straw in the corner of a field.

A few minutes later they would have been passing the spot where the V-2 exploded. The school was shut for one or two days afterwards pending repairs, and subsequently, on the following Sunday, a thanksgiving service was held at the village's Congregational Church in gratitude that no one had been seriously hurt.

Tuesday 21st November 1944

ANOTHER V-2 FOR WOODHAM FERRERS

THE DISTRICT'S SIXTH, and the country's 317th. V-2 fell at Holland's Farm near Woodham Ferrers at 4.46 a.m.

Typically no one was injured, though many properties within a two mile radius were damaged by the blast, including Salesfrith Farm and cottages, Charity Farm, Edwin's Hall Farm and Holland's Farm.

The rocket left a crater 25 feet across by 12 feet deep on Holland's Farm road. Its propulsion unit was subsequently found in the stackyard of Charity Farm and parts of its casing on the former aerodrome at Stow Maries.

The close proximity of this and the previous evening's V-2 caused some initial confusion until wardens were able to confirm that there had been two incidents and give their locations.

Wednesday 6th December 1944.

V-2 ROCKET SCORES A DIRECT HIT ON HOFFMANN'S

30 FACTORY WORKERS KILLED

EYEWITNESS ACCOUNT:

"Springfield doodlebug."

As told to our our Special Correspondent

"About 7 p.m. one evening we were at home in Springfield with my father's dinner on the stove, waiting for him to come in from work.

Suddenly, without warning, there was a loud bang, the back door flew open, a load of soot came down the chimney, and there was the sound of glass shattering. We soon realised that a doodlebug had landed not far from our house.

The next morning I went to see what if I could find any bits of it for souvenirs. It had come down in the field between the Ridley family's house 'Gernons' and 'Pendennis', on the boundary with 'Gernons'.

There was very little to be seen, just a shallow crater and little bits and pieces of wreckage scattered about. I managed to find the doodlebug's gyro and I took that into work at Hoffmann's. They inspected it, measured it up and took it away, and I never saw it again after that.

The strange thing was that the field where the doodlebug came down already had a crater in it, twenty or thirty yards from Springfield Road.

My father had told me that during the First World War a Zeppelin had dropped a bomb there and afterwards it had filled up with water to make a small pond. After the Second World War a house was built in the field, but the old crater was left there and it has now been made into a sunken garden."

Eric Clark

EYEWITNESS ACCOUNT:

"Watching the doodlebugs."

As told to our our Special Correspondent

"In the latter part of the war I helped build ships such as landing craft and motor patrol boats in Burnham-on-Crouch.

During the week I used to lodge in Latchingdon, but on Fridays I'd catch the bus home to Chelmsford for the weekend. Often I travelled home on the bus and on both sides of it there were doodlebugs flying parallel to it.

Later on when we'd developed jets I can recall watching them chase the doodlebugs and blow ing them up. At the time we couldn't understand how the planes could fly with no propellers."

Norman Hume

HARMLESS V-1 IN THE HANNING-FIELDS

The district's 26th V-1 fell 200 yards from Patten's Farm on the boundary between East and West Hanningfield at 11.12 p.m.

No casualties were caused, though superficial damage was reported to have occurred at Patten's Farmhouse and buildings, Glebe Cottages, Hills Farm and Rough Hills Farm.

Monday 11th December 1944

BISHOP INJURED BY SPRINGFIELD V-1

THE RECENT UPSURGE IN V-1 and V-2 activity continued when, at 7 p.m., a V-1 fell between Springfield Road and the L.N.E.R., on ground to the rear of Gernons (today's number 331 Springfield Road).

Dozens of properties were damaged and at least six people were slightly hurt by flying glass and debris. Amongst them was Percy Gray of Gernons, and the Bishop of Chelmsford.

The latter received 16 cuts to his face from glass fragments as he was pulling down the blackout at a window at his Bishopscourt home. Fortunately none were serious and his eyes were unharmed.

At least a dozen aged and blind residents were made homeless from the County Council's hostel at Springfield Rectory in Springfield Road. The property stood between Gernons and Bishopscourt. The residents were taken in by friends or transferred to St. John's Hospital.

Further up Springfield Road N.F.S. staff at Pendennis were reported to have felt the whole building shudder with the blast, whilst at the Endeavour P.H. glasses were shaken off the bar to smash on the floor.

At Springfield All Saints' Church every window on the southern side of the building was damaged as were parts of the chancel roof.

Nearby the three Almshouses in Springfield Green also suffered badly from the blast, with the one nearest the L.N.E.R. losing nearly all of its roof tiles. Its elderly occupier, Mrs. Banks, was reported to have declined shelter elsewhere and said that her only grievance was not the damage to the roof, but the fact that the back door would no longer shut!

Thursday 7th December 1944

CHELMSFORD HOME GUARD'S FAREWELL TO THE TOWN

AT 9.15 A.M. SOME 500 members of the 101 (Essex Home Guard) Rocket Battery assembled in Market Road for the unit's farewell parade.

Many present had taken part in the Home Guard stand down parade a week earlier. The salute was taken by the G.O.C. Major General E.A.E. Tremlett with numerous other officers and dignitaries in attendance.

The Mayor thanked the battery on behalf of the people of Chelmsford. In the evening a farewell concert was held for the battery's members at the Regent Theatre.

It had been organised by the regulars at the battery and was paid for by Messers Christy Brothers, Messers Christy & Norris, Hoffmann's, Crompton's and Marconi's.

Sunday 10th December 1944

GREATER LONDON PLAN PROPOSES NEW TOWN AT MARGARETTING

Professor Abercrombie's Greater London Plan was published, outlining proposals for the post-war development of the capital and surrounding areas.

Its main thrust was to propose the removal of large numbers of Londoners to new and expanded towns around London. In Essex expansion was proposed at Braintree, Bocking, Halstead, Witham and Chelmsford, with new towns at Harlow, Margaretting and Chipping Ongar.

The plan described Chelmsford as 'having a hopelessly congested town centre', despite the A12 bypass, and an acute shortage of housing. Drastic replanning of the town centre was deemed to be necessary. Meanwhile the proposed new town at Margaretting would have a population of about 30,000 people and would be a twin of Chelmsford with many amenities and services shared.

The railway line from London to Ongar (today's Central Line) would be extended to Chelmsford via a new stretch of line to a junction near Widford.

Professor Abercrombie also proposed that the new arterial route 7 from the capital to Ipswich should be built to the west of the existing A12 from London, skirt around the north of Chelmsford and rejoin the A12 at Boreham.

Thursday 14th December 1944

NINE OTHERS DEAD IN HENRY ROAD

GOOD FORTUNE CAME TO an abrupt and tragic end at 1.28 a.m. when the country's 367th V-2 , and the district's 8th, fell close to Hoffmann's works, causing the Chelmsford's greatest loss of life from a single wartime incident.

Official figures put the total fatalities of the V-2 incident at 39 dead and 138 injured, including 47 seriously so.

To date the majority of the twenty-seven V-1s and seven V-2s which had exploded in the Chelmsford district had done so in rural areas with relatively few casualties and little significant damage.

Back garden

The V-2 came down in the vicinity of Hoffmann's and the back gardens of houses on the eastern side of Henry Road.

It is believed to have struck the extreme western edge of the roof of Hoffmann's C Factory's Cage & Assembly Department approximately level with the garden of 11 Henry Road.

It exploded before reaching the earth bank which ran alongside the outer west wall of the factory, leaving a small crater, 12 feet across by 6 feet deep. The blast devastated a large area of Hoffmann's, demolished several properties in Henry Road and damaged hundreds of others in the town.

Night shift

At Hoffmann's the night shift had just returned to their benches and machines to continue their work after singing Christmas carols to the accompaniment of the visiting Salvation Army band.

Tuesday 19th December 1944

EYEWITNESS ACCOUNTS:

"He would never talk about what he had seen."

As told to our our Special Correspondent

"My father, John McPherson, was a turner at Hoffmann's and was working the night that when the V-2 struck. The experience affected him quite badly and afterwards he couldn't face going back to work there. He got another job at the County Council's Supplies Department but he would never talk about what he had seen that night at Hoffmann's."

Sheila Wrenn

"I used to lodge along with a workmate of mine, Janet Bacon, at Mr. Mace's house at 2 Yarwood Road. As we were walking along Victoria Road on our way to work at Hoffmann's we suddenly heard a sound in the sky behind us. We turned our heads and saw a V-2. As we watched it I said to her 'It's coming down on Hoffmann's!'. We went on to work and carried on as usual. Fortunately no one from our department was killed or injured."

Joan Taylor.

Spirits had been high with the end to the war at last in sight and the festive season already begun. Many of the workers were young women who were still singing when without any warning the V-2 exploded yards away from them. In an instant the blast swept across the factory and neighbouring streets with devastating consequences.

V-2 AT LOVES GREEN

A V-2, the county's 354th and the district's seventh, fell in a field at Loves Green, a quarter of a mile west of the hamlet's wardens post and a few hundred yards north of Highwood Road at 11.39 p.m.

It left a crater about 20 feet across and 6 feet deep in the gravel soil. No casualties were reported, though the blast damaged around thirty houses, the school and church. Meanwhile number 124 Vicarage Road suffered war damage during the day.

Thursday 14th December 1944

V-1 ON BOREHAM AERODROME

At 6.40 a.m. a V-1 fell midway between Drakes Farm and Cranham Farm in Little Waltham, landing in the orchard of a house called Boscombe, just south of the Russell Green to Little Waltham road.

The land was part of the Air Ministry's Boreham Aerodrome Estate. No casualties were caused and damage was restricted to Drakes Farmhouse & buildings, two houses at Cranham's Farm, Lawns Farm in Great Leighs and to around 200 fruit trees and seven chicken houses.

Monday 18th December 1944.

Rocket on Hoffmann's: Tuesday 19th December 1944

'THE CAGE' IS DEVASTATED

The worst affected part of the factory was the Cage & Assembly Department. It was housed in a single-story, north light roofed building, 514 feet long by 81 feet wide, running parallel to and behind houses on the eastern side of Henry Road.

Demolished

A considerable length of the Department's external western wall and a smaller internal wall which divided it from the Turret Department were immediately demolished by the blast, along with a paraffin washing plant and various shelters and internal steel and timber partitions.

The entire north light-type roof of C Factory was stripped of its poilite sheeting, slate and asbestos covering and the roof structure displaced. Stanchions and girders near the crater were wrenched apart and badly twisted and several air raid shelters built against the outside wall were demolished.

The neighbouring Turret Department suffered no serious damage except that to its roof which was moved some eight inches eastwards through its gable ends, whilst the roofs of A and B Factories were also considerably damaged by the blast.

Fire

A split second after the blast damage, a ferocious fire was started in bays 1 to 10 of the Cage & Assembly Department when a 200 gallon tank of paraffin was ignited by the explosion - either through an electrical short circuit when cables were damaged or sparks from falling steelwork.

The paraffin tank was part of a bearing washing plant, partly housed in a brick and concrete building and partly enclosed by steel partitions and was situated some sixty feet from the impact point of the V-2. Burning paraffin was distributed over wooden benches, boxes, timber partitions and debris that had had already been wrecked by the blast.

Within a minute of the explosion fire watchers at Hoffmann's had informed the works fire brigade of the fire and two pumps were immediately ordered to deal with it - one from the River Chelmer at Mill House and the other to C Factory Engine Room to boost the fire mains.

On their arrival at the fire the works brigade found that there was only low pressure on their hoses from the factory mains and then discovered that the overhead mains had been fractured by blast and debris. The pump at the C Factory Engine Room was then ordered to 'knock off' and get to work from the River Chelmer near the factory's gas plant.

Outside assistance

By 1.29 a.m. it was clear that outside help would be necessary and a call for assistance was telephoned through to the National Fire Service. It sent four pumps to the incident, with the first arriving at 1.32 a.m. They were got to work from the hydrant in Rectory Lane and a static water tank in Henry Road which was supplied by a stationary pump from Mill House.

Within minutes other civil defence staff were on the scene, aided by considerable numbers of American servicemen from Boreham Aerodrome and members of the returning Salvation Army Band.

At 1.50 a.m. a pump and crew arrived from Marconi's and got to work from the River Chelmer at the side of the works fire station. In addition to these seven pumps hoses were also put into action from three fire hydrants in the factory, enabling the blaze to be tackled from all directions.

At 2.12 a.m. the Essex Police

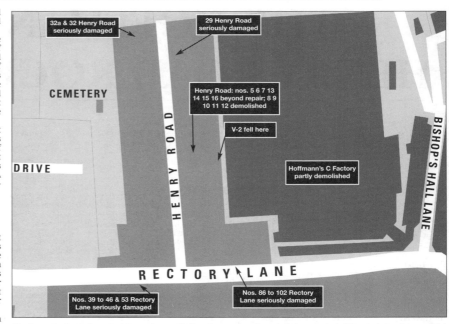

Sketch map showing the Henry Road, Rectory Lane and Hoffmann's area, where 39 people died as a result of a V-2 rocket in the arly hours of 19th December 1944. (Author)

(Map labels: 32a & 32 Henry Road seriously damaged; 29 Henry Road seriously damaged; Henry Road: nos. 5 6 7 13 14 15 16 beyond repair; 8 9 10 11 12 demolished; V-2 fell here; Hoffmann's C Factory partly demolished; CEMETERY; DRIVE; HENRY ROAD; BISHOP'S HALL LANE; RECTORY LANE; Nos. 39 to 46 & 53 Rectory Lane seriously damaged; Nos. 86 to 102 Rectory Lane seriously damaged)

H.Q. received its first casualty report from Hoffmann's. It spoke of being inundated with victims. Five minutes later the A.R.P. authorities, aware that the incident was of a very serious nature, called for mutual assistance from neighbouring districts. Their response was magnificent and the next few hours would see the arrival of additional ambulances, rescue squads, first aid parties, heavy lifting equipment and canteen facilities from other parts of Essex. Rest centres were quickly opened in Chelmsford for the bombed out and some of the homeless were driven to Boreham Aerodrome by the Americans.

Casualties

As rescue work continued against the back drop of the large fire so the number of reported casualties began to rise. At 2.50 a.m. one person was said to have been killed, four were missing and 52 were slightly injured.

Twenty-eight minutes later, almost two hours after the explosion, Column Officer Bowden of the N.F.S. rang his superiors at the Market Road Fire Station and reported that no further pumps were needed as the fire was now under control.

At 4.32 a.m. the Marconi's pump was sent back to its base and eight minutes later the updated casualty list read 'ten dead, over 100 injured with more believed hurt'. Ten minutes after that the fire was finally extinguished.

One pump was kept standing by until 11.30 a.m. and raking over continued until mid day. By that time casualties spoke of 'approximately 20 dead and over 100 injured at Hoffmann's'.

As recovery of the victims continued during daylight the number of confirmed fatalities continued to rise to eventually number thirty. The majority them were thought to have been caused either by being struck by falling debris or by being thrown by the

Recent view of the the rear of the houses on the eastern side of Henry Road. When the V-2 came down in the early hours of 19th December 1944 it detonated just behind number 11. (Author)

Recent view of the Rectory Lane site of Hoffmann's C Factory from Globe House. Shortly after this photograph was taken work began here on the construction of Anglia Polytechic University. (Author)

blast against some object. However, many of the victims had subsequently been burned in the fire. Chief Fire Officer D. Ricketts later reported that he had personally retrieved two charred bodies and placed them in to blankets prior to their removal, and that he was convinced that their deaths had been not through the fire but by being blasted against shelter 28c.

In the morning following the incident the scene was inspected by Regional Commissioner, accompanied by the Mayor and County A.R.P. Controller.

They gave the highest praise to all those who took part in the difficult, hazardous and harrowing task of rescuing the casualties and removing the remains of the victims of the V-2.

EYEWITNESS ACCOUNT:

"I was working as usual in the grinding floor when without warning I heard a sudden terrific crack in the sky."

As told to our our Special Correspondent

"The night that the V- 2 fell on Hoffmann's I was working as usual in the grinding floor when without warning I heard a sudden terrific crack in the sky.

I dived under my steel topped bench as quick as I could - you instinctively crouched down whenever you heard bangs and other noises. Then the V- 2 hit the factory.

The blast brought t down all the asbestos tiles which had been put over the reinforced Georgian glass in the roof for the blackout. They came crashing down all around me and there were cuts galore as they struck the chaps that were still in the open.

Fortunately I was alright. There was a bit of chaos for a while afterwards, but the factory doors were opened and we were all allowed out into the streets.

People were wandering about and I walked up Rectory Lane to opposite Henry Road. I couldn't see a great deal apart from something had happened.

It was only afterwards that we heard that the V-2 had come down between Henry Road and Hoffmann's, the explosion had drawn out the factory wall and its flash had set fire to oils and god knows what and killed a lot of people

It was obvious that no more work could be done that night so we were sent home. The trouble was there were no buses until the schedules began later in the morning, so for a time it looked like we were going to be stuck there.

Luckily around 3 or 4 a.m. the Americans brought their army trucks round and they drove us to our homes all over Essex. I got on board one that was going to Southend and it dropped me off home in Rayleigh.

Even as I sat on that truck I could hear other V-2's going off with a thump in the distance."

Bill Wilson

Rocket on Hoffmann's: Tuesday 19th December 1944

COUNTING THE COST: THE HOFFMANN'S AND HENRY ROAD ROCKET VICTIMS

THE HOFFMANN'S V-2 INCIDENT claimed the lives of 30 workers on the night shift at the factory, including ten men, nineteen women and one unidentified body.

The youngest was aged 19 and the eldest 64, with many of the victims coming from outside the Chelmsford area. The average age of the women who died was just under 25 years old.

A memorial service, conducted by the Rector, was held at the Cathedral four days later. It attracted a large congregation including representatives and survivors from Hoffmann's, the Home Guard, Police, Civil Defence Services and local dignitaries. On 29th December 1944 nineteen of those killed at the factory were buried in a communal grave in the Borough Cemetery. Their funeral service was conducted by the Bishop of Chelmsford, who said 'They died for their country. They died at their post of duty. We honour their memory.'

On the second anniversary of the incident a memorial garden at the mass grave in the Borough Cemetery, designed by a member of Hoffmanns' staff, was dedicated by the Provost. Memorial services were also held at the Cathedral and London Road Congregational Church and a memorial plaque to the victims was unveiled in the factory's canteen.

The thirty victims at Hoffmann's were as follows:

Leonard Charles Bailey
Aged 36, he was the eldest son of Mr. & Mrs. G. Bailey of 1 Dukes Farm Cottages in Springfield, and married to Phyllis Bailey of 127 Baddow Hall Crescent in Great Baddow. He had two young sons and had worked at Hoffmann's for some 16 years. He was buried at the Borough Cemetery on 30th December after a funeral service at Springfield All Saints' Church. Mr. Bailey is commemorated on the Great Baddow war memorial.

Vera Joan Baker
She was the 19 year-old daughter of Mr. & Mrs. E.J. Baker of 6 Council Houses in Bradwell-on-Sea, and was resident at 22 Marconi Road. She was buried at the mass grave in the Borough Cemetery on 29th December.

Winifred Edith Boyce
Aged 26, she was the daughter of Mr. & Mrs. Andrews of 32 Easterford Road in Kelvedon and married to Ft. Sgt. Frederick Boyce R.A.F. She was buried at the mass grave in the Borough Cemetery on 29th December.

Henry John Brown
He was the 42 year-old son of Henry Brown and married to Ella Brown of 30 Station Road in Braintree. He was buried at the mass grave in the Borough Cemetery on 29th December.

Cissie Alice Devenish
Aged 28, she was the daughter George Devenish of 'Rose Cottage', The Street in Little Waltham and was buried at the mass grave in the Borough Cemetery on 29th December. She is commemorated on the Little Waltham war memorial.

Edward David Driscoll
He was the 38 year-old son of Mr. & Mrs. James Driscoll of 9 Sandgate Road in Brighton and lived at 7 East Street in Coggeshall. He was a member of the Home Guard.

Phyllis Maude Evans
Aged 27, she was the daughter of Harry and Nellie Evans of 14 Pentland Avenue in Shoeburyness and was buried at the mass grave in the Borough Cemetery on 29th December.

Edith Annie Everitt
She was the 51 year-old daughter of the late Mr. & Mrs. Smith of Robins Bridge Road in Coggeshall and the widow of James Smith. They had one son. She lived at 5 Oak Road in Rivenhall, having formerly resided in Kelvedon. She was buried at the mass grave in the Borough Cemetery on 29th December.

Harold Leonard Foley
Aged 30, he was the son of John and Elizabeth Foley of Little Baddow Post Office. His wife, Grace, and two children lived at the same address. He was subsequently buried at St. Mary's Church in Little Baddow.

Constance Ester Franklin
She was the 33 year-old daughter of Mark and Bertha Franklin of 8 Redcliffe Road and was buried at the mass grave in the Borough Cemetery on 29th December.

Dorothy Maud Hancock
Aged 22, she was the daughter of Mr. & Mrs. Frederick Hancock of 29 Stonard Road in Dagenham. She was buried at the mass grave in the Borough Cemetery on 29th December.

Emily Kate Harvey
She was the 23 year-old daughter of Mr. & Mrs. Harvey of 10 Dickenson Villas in Maldon Road, Tiptree. She was buried at the mass grave in the Borough Cemetery on 29th December.

Charles Frederick Hollis
Aged 51, he lived at 101 Broomfield Road.

Lilian Grace Horne
She was the 21 year-old daughter of Mr. F.B. and Florence Horne of Bridge Cottage in Jackson's Lane, Billericay. She was buried at the mass grave in the Borough Cemetery on 29th December.

Arthur Edmund Jackson
Aged 56, he was married to Florence Jackson of The Stores in Well Lane, Galleywood and was buried at the mass grave in the Borough Cemetery on 29th December. He is commemorated on the Galleywood war memorial.

Winifred Joan Johnson
She was the 21 year old daughter of Mr. A.E. Johnson of 12 Sunnyside in Stansted and was buried at the mass grave in the Borough Cemetery on 29th December.

Muriel May Mullender
Aged 30, she was the daughter of Mrs. A.M. and the late Mr. C. Mullender of 118 Kimberley Road in Lowestoft. She was rescued alive from Hoffmann's but died later in the day at the Chelmsford & Essex Hospital.

Joan Munson
She was the 21 year-old daughter of Charles and Annie Munson of 2 Oaklands in Great Bentley near Colchester.

Catherine Murphy
Aged 28, she was the daughter of Mr. & Mrs. Murphy of Portmagee, Killarney in the Irish Republic. She lived at 10 Cramphorn Road.

Leonard George Outten
He was the 48 year-old third son of Mrs. P. and the late John Outten of 1 Prospect Cottages in Oxney Green, where he lived with his mother. He had worked at Hoffmann's for nearly 20 years and was a member of the Home Guard, having only handed his equipment in the previous night. He was also well qualified in First Aid and attached to the St. John's Ambulance Brigade. He was buried at Writtle All Saints' Church on 23rd December and is commemorated on the village's war memorial.

Muriel Jean Outten
Aged 20, she was the younger daughter of Joseph and Florence Outten of 4 Victoria Road in Oxney Green, and a niece to Leonard Outten who was also killed at Hoffmann's. She had been employed at the factory for three years, having previously worked as a maid at the Widford Lodge Preparatory School. She was engaged to marry Driver Vincent Wakeling R.A. on his next visit home on leave from service in Italy. Miss Outten was buried at the mass grave in the Borough Cemetery on 29th December. She is commemorated on the Writtle war memorial.

Joyce Dorothy Phillibrown
She was the 24 year-old daughter of Alice and the late Albert Phillibrown of Stanford Rivers near Ongar. She was buried at the mass grave in the Borough Cemetery on 29th December.

Edith Maud Piper
Aged 24, she was the daughter of Mr. & Mrs. William Piper of 138 South Street in Bishop's Stortford and lived at 39 Rectory Lane. She was buried at the mass grave in the Borough Cemetery on 29th December.

Marjorie Lilly Scott
She was the 34 year-old daughter of Mr. & Mrs. F.C. Scott of Sunnyside, Powers Farm in Little Waltham. She was buried at the mass grave in the Borough Cemetery on 29th December and is commemorated on the Little Waltham war memorial.

Arthur Seager
Aged 45, he was the son of Mrs. Seager of 39 Oakhurst Road in Southend-on-Sea and married to Mrs. D. Seager of 16 Gayton Road also in Southend-on-Sea. He was buried at the mass grave in the Borough Cemetery on 29th December.

Annie May Sterry
She was the 38 year old wife of James Sterry and lived at 29 New Street. She was buried at the mass grave in the Borough Cemetery on 29th December.

Alfred William Stuart-Smith
Aged 49, he was a native of East Ham and had lived in Chelmsford for around eight years. He was married to Gladys Stuart-Smith of 17 Second Avenue. They had one son who was then serving in the R.A.F. He was buried at the Borough Cemetery on 28th December after a requiem mass at the Church of Our Lady Immaculate.

Barbara Olive Thorogood
She was the 31 year-old daughter of Mr.

& Mrs. E.J. Thorogood of Bridge Cottage in Southend Road, Great Baddow. She is commemorated on the village's war memorial.

William Alfred Thorpe
Aged 64, he was a native of Bury St. Edmund's and had lived in Chelmsford for some 34 years. He had worked at Crompton's for the first twenty of them, and for the remainder of that time at Hoffmann's. He was married to Lilian Thorpe of 79 First Avenue and they had four sons and a daughter. He was buried at the Borough Cemetery on 23rd December.

Unidentified
One unidentified person was buried at the mass grave in the Borough Cemetery on 29th December 1944.

Clara Joiner
She is thought to have died as a result of shock from the Hoffmann's incident on 24th December 1944.

As well as the thirty victims at Hoffmann's a further nine people were killed in houses in neighbouring Henry Road:

Pamela Christine Howse
She was the 2 year-old daughter of William and Doreen Howse and was killed at the family's home, number 6 Henry Road.

Phyllis Joan Webb
She was the 25 year-old daughter of Mr. & Mrs. Charles Marshall of 7 Patching Hall Lane. She was married to Reginald Webb with an eight-month old daughter, and was killed at the family home, number 7 Henry Road. Her father was a horseman at Patching Hall Farm.

Emily Maud Everitt
Aged 60, she was the widow of Reuben Everitt of Sparrow Hall in Ford End, died at 9 Henry Road. She had lived with her daughter, Mrs. P. Lucking at the house since his death. She was buried at Ford End on 23rd December.

Stanley Richard Harrhy
Aged 39, he was a lodger at 9 Henry Road and was buried on 23rd December.

Eva Joan Turp
Aged 21, she was the daughter of Mr. & Mrs. F. Pennock of 'Avondale' in Rickstones Road, Witham. She was married to Kenneth Turp and was killed at 10 Henry Road, where she was thought to have been lodging.

Edith Hull
Aged 59, who was the wife of Henry Hull, and was killed at their home, number 11 Henry Road.

Frank Benjamin Baxter
Aged 50, he was killed at his home, 12 Henry Road. His wife Mabel M. Baxter, aged 52 and their ten year-old daughter, Dulcie Baxter, also died.

Mabel M Baxter
Aged 52, she was killed at her home, 12 Henry Road. Her husband Frank and their ten year-old daughter, Dulcie Baxter, also died.

Dulcie Baxter
Aged 10, she was killed along with her parents at 12 Henry Road.

Rocket on Hoffmann's: Tuesday 19th December 1944

LUCKY ESCAPES IN HENRY ROAD

OUTSIDE OF HOFFMANN'S considerable destruction was inflicted to Henry Road where a further nine people lost their lives in houses backing on to the factory's Cage & Assembly Department.

Five house were demolished, numbers 8, 9, 10, 11 and 12, whilst either side of them numbers 5, 6, 7, 13, 14, 15 and 16 were damaged beyond repair.

A dozen small fires were started in residential properties, but all were quickly dealt with by Fire Guards. Contents and debris from the houses were strewn all over the road and included a doll, parts of a Christmas Tree, Christmas decorations and a teddy bear.

At one house a child sleeping in a cot escaped injury when a wardrobe became wedged above it and sheltered the child from tons of debris. At another an electric light remained switched on after the explosion whilst a motorcycle could be seen where it had been blasted into a blazing upstairs room.

Subsequently it was discovered that four gas meters from damaged houses had been opened and approximately £2/6/0 stolen from them.

As with all bombing incidents many people had narrow escapes. One young woman's father had died the previous morning so she had stayed at home with her mother. Had she gone to work as usual at Hoffmann's she would have surely been killed too.

Another worker at home at the tine was in bed when the side of her house was demolished by the blast and caved in on her. She was unhurt, as was a year-old baby daughter in the same house, who escaped despite half a ton of masonry crashing on the end of her bed.

Another young child was to spend some 16 months in Orsett Hospital in plaster recovering from her injuries caused by the collapse of her house onto her as she slept in her cot.

A domestic argument saved another couple. The husband had a premonition and refused to sleep upstairs. His wife said that he was talking nonsense and the V-2 fell as they were arguing. It demolished practically every room in the house save for the front room in which they were standing.

At 9 Henry Road one elderly woman was killed but her daughter, Mrs. P. Lucking, was trapped in her Morrison shelter before being rescued by two postmen who heard her screams for help. She was four months pregnant at the time but her baby was subsequently born safely, named Roger and known locally as the 'miracle' or 'rocket baby'.

HOFFMANN'S PROFITS SLASHED AS PRODUCTION HIT

Most of the damaged roofs at Hoffmann's, except for those in the immediate vicinity of the explosion, were covered with poilite sheets and tarpaulins within 36 hours to prevent weather damage - an impressive task given the size of the job.

Morale of those involved in the repairs and cleaning up operations was said to have remained good and determined.

The first and last stages of production were most disrupted in the incident, though all but 17 machines escaped serious damage and were subsequently moved to other parts of Hoffmann's to be working within a few days.

Work in more distant parts of the factory was able to continue practically unaffected. After clearance of the site rebuilding work would subsequently start on 17th January 1945. The incident was to have serious financial implications on Hoffmann's. Its annual profits would shrink from £217,930 in 1943-4 to just £77,608 for the following financial year.

Tuesday 19th December 1944

This garden is dedicated to the memory of 29 employees of the Hoffmann Manufacturing Company Limited, 18 of whom lie in this grave, who were killed by enemy action on 19th December 1944; and to the memory of 7 employees who were killed by enemy action on19th July 1942 and 19th October 1942.

They shall remind faith the Lord of hosts in that day when I make up my jewels.

Inscription at Hoffmann memorial garden, Chelmsford Borough Cemetery.

Recent view of the memorial garden to all those Hoffmann workers killed during the war. The garden is situated at Chelmsford Borough Cemetery in Writtle Road. (Author)

CHELMSFORD'S M.P. KILLED IN ITALY

WHAT HAD ALREADY BEEN a black couple of weeks for Chelmsford were made worse with the death on active service in Italy of the town's M.P., 39 year-old Colonel John Robert Jarmain 'Jack' Macnamara.

He was killed by a mortar bomb while going up to visit former colleagues in a forward company of the 1st Battalion London Irish Rifles on Friday 22nd December 1944, though news of his death was not to reach home until the first week of 1945.

He had been due home on leave on New Year's Day after which he had been expected to have returned to his Parliamentary duties.

Col. Macnamara was born in India on 11th October 1905, the son of the late Dr. J.R. Macnamara of Nazina Assam and Mrs. Stewart Orpen of Windmills in Little Waltham. His father, who died in 1923, had been a doctor on a tea planting estate. After early life in India, where he learned to speak English, Hindustani and Assamese, Col. Macnamara came to England and was educated at Cheam and Haileybury.

In 1926 he enlisted as a special constable in London during the General Strike. In the same year he was also arrested as a suspected spy in Tunisia and imprisoned for a month. A year later he returned to India to serve with the Royal Fusiliers in which he had held a Territorial commission, but came back six years later. In 1934 he was commissioned in the London Irish Rifles, a territorial regiment he commanded from 1938.

Col. Macnamara's first attempt to enter parliament was in 1934 when he unsuccessfully contested the Upton By-Election in West Ham. A year later, however, he was chosen from 17 candidates to stand for the Conservatives in Chelmsford in the General Election. He beat his Labour opponent, Fred Hughes, in a straight fight by 23, 314 votes to 11,690. In 1938 he was one of a group of M.P.s who visited Madrid to report on the Spanish Civil War.

At the outbreak of the Second World War he was still with the London Irish Rifles and later went to Northern Ireland to help organise the R.A.F. Regiment. Subsequently he joined Combined Operations and was Chief of Staff, Adriatic Command, seeing action in Greece, Yugoslavia and Italy.

He was a bachelor, quiet, extremely modest and popular. He was said to possess a deep seriousness and intensity of purpose.

Col. Macnamara's memorial service was held at the Cathedral on 6th January 1945, conducted by the Provost W.E.R. Morrow. An address was given by the Bishop of Chelmsford who said "A very sad event has brought us here today. We have lost one of those men who possessed in a generous measure those qualities of leadership and strong conviction which will be desperately needed in the rebuilding of the ruined world in the years in which we shall shortly be entering. We cannot afford to lose people like him who we mourn today. The country needs them, and the world needs them."

On 11th July 1945 the Bishop of Chelmsford dedicated a silver communion chalice and paten at Little Waltham Church in memory of Col. John Macnamara, who had been both a parishioner and worshipper there. The objects had been presented by his mother, Mrs. Orpen.

Col. Macnamara is also commemorated on the Little Waltham war memorial.

Friday 22nd December 1944

CHELMSFORD SUFFERS NEW V-2 ONSLAUGHT

ROCKET AT RAMSDEN HEATH

At 12.35 a.m. the district's ninth V-2, and Britain's 411th, exploded in countryside at Ramsden Heath, some 500 yards north-east of Cox Green. It left a crater 44 feet across by 15 feet deep.

No casualties were reported, though a number of properties in the vicinity were damaged by the blast.

Sunday 31st December 1944

ANOTHER V-2 FOR RAMSDEN HEATH

At 6.51 p.m. Britain's 431st V-2 exploded, apparently in mid air, near Ramsden Heath, the second such device in three days in the locality.

Fragments of the rocket were subsequently discovered as far afield as Ramsden Heath and Wickford. No one was hurt. The blast damaged houses in the Runwell Road area. Telephone and electricity cables were also damaged around Brock Hill.

Tuesday 2nd January 1945

MYSTERY OF SANDON V-2

At 6.22 a.m. a V-2, the country's 422nd, fell at Sandon. Details of the incident remain scarce.

The day also saw the closure of the wartime first aid posts at St. John's Hospital and at the Coval Lane Clinic.

Monday 1st January 1945

GT. BADDOW ROCKET NEAR BEEHIVE LANE

FOR THE FOURTH consecutive day the Chelmsford district was hit by a V-2 when, at 3.32 a.m., one fell on farmland west of Beehive Lane, some 400 yards north-west of Lathcotes Farm.

It was Britain's 433rd V-2. The location of the explosion has since been obscured by post-war housing development, its position roughly coinciding with the junction of the modern day Lime Walk and Laburnum Drive.

The V-2 left a crater some 30 feet across and 9 feet deep in the clay soil. No one was injured though around 90 properties in Great Baddow were damaged by the blast.

Wednesday 3rd January 1945

V-2 AT RUNWELL

At 3.43 p.m. the district's 13th V-2, and the county's 444th, fell in a ploughed field to the south-west of Browns Avenue in Runwell. The road was a cul-de-sac which ran off the southern side of the B1002 (today's A132) Runwell Road, about half a mile east of Runwell Church. Around a hundred properties were damaged as a result and ten people were slightly injured.

Thursday 4th January 1945

GREAT BADDOW ROCKET

At 6.12 a.m a V-2 fell approximately 600 yards west of Baddow Park Farm in Great Baddow and left a crater 20 feet across by 25 feet deep.

It was country's 474th V-2. No one was hurt in the incident though superficial damage was inflicted on Parklands Farm, Rignal's Farm and Baddow Park Farm.

In the Chelmsford Borough some 26 properties suffered blast damage; nos. 166, 168, 170, 176, 206 & White House in Baddow Road; 49 Gainsborough Crescent; 21 Galleywood Road; 23 Hill Road; 42, 44 & 46 Hillside Grove; 95, 101, 117 & 119 Lady Lane; 116, 117, 122 & 124 Longstomps Avenue; 5 Moulsham Chase; 21 Moulsham Drive; 95 Moulsham Street; 264 Rainsford Road; and 138 & 140 Vicarage Road.

Sunday 7th January 1945

18TH V-2 FALLS AT BICKNACRE

The district's 18th V-2, and the country's 546th, fell into a ploughed field some 200 yards west of the B1418 Main Road in Bicknacre, near Horseshoe farm and opposite the Council Houses at 8.32 p.m..

The explosion created a crater 40 feet across by 14 feet deep in the heavy clay soil. No casualties were caused, though local 31 houses were damaged by the blast along with overhead electric cables. A further 14 houses in the neighbouring parish of Danbury were similarly affected.

Tuesday 16th January 1945

FINED FOR COLLECTING A MEMENTO

A Woodham Ferrers man was fined £1 at the Chelmsford Petty Sessions for failing to deliver to the police 'a certain enemy article' that he had found.

The object was a V-2 valve which he had taken from a field, perhaps from the V-2 which had fallen at Woodham Ferrers on 6th December 1944. The man had been liable for a fine of up to £100 for the offence and the case was seen as a warning to deter other souvenir hunters.

Friday 19th January 1945

BROOMFIELD SUFFERS ITS FIRST V-2

THE DISTRICT'S 15TH V-2 fell into Church Lands Field (number 139) at Priors Farm in Broomfield, between Priors and Daffy Wood and about 50 yards from Pingley Pond at 2.31 p.m.

The explosion created a crater 38 feet across by 14 feet deep. Fortunately no one was seriously hurt in the incident, though three students suffered from shock.

Many properties in the vicinity were damaged by the blast, including some 83 in the Borough area: Cuckfield, Radlett, Fir Cottage, Mon Abri, Elmcroft & 7 The Parade in Broomfield Road; 4, 63 & 76 Brownings Avenue; 6 & 7 Burgess Well Road; 60 & 61 Corporation Road; 2 Dixon Avenue; 7 & 30 The Drive; 2 & 9 Eves Crescent; 8, 11, 27, 34, 36, 39, 77 & 135 Eastern Crescent; 23 First Avenue; 16 Fifth Avenue; 22, 35 & 41 The Green; 2a, 22, 27 & 30 Highfield Road; 20, 22, 28, 34 & 45 King's Road; 37 Nalla Gardens; 57, 78, 85 & 93 North Avenue; 10 Norton Road; 37, 43, 3 Claypits Cottages, Patching Hut, Manora, Barlhoys, Maisondingle & Destiny in Patching Hall Lane; 94 Ockelford Avenue; 9 Roxwell Road; 3 Seventh Avenue; 28, 45 & 61 South Primrose Hill; 7, 9, 11, 16, 18, 20, 22 & 24 Sunrise Avenue; 9, 58, 65, 66, 75, 79, 80, 84, 99 & 122 Swiss Avenue; 27 & 74 Tennyson Road; 18 Third Avenue; and 148 & 151 West Avenue.

Wednesday 10th January 1945

ROCKET NEAR MOUNTNESSING

At 9.45 a.m. Britain's 623rd V-2 fell close to Fitzwalter's Farm, south-west of Mountnessing, leaving a crater 50 feet across by 20 feet deep. One person was slightly hurt. Although the impact point was just inside the Brentwood district a number of properties were damaged in the Chelmsford district.

Saturday 27th January 1945

ROCKET AT RAMSDEN HEATH

Britain's 685th V-2, and Chelmsford's 21st, fell some 300 yards south of White House in Ramsden Heath at 9.51 a.m. Three slight casualties were caused and around thirty properties were damaged by the effects of blast.

Tuesday 6th February 1945

RETTENDON V-2

At 3.43 p.m. Britain's 701st V-2 fell at Pound Farm, Rettendon, 200 yards south of The Bell P.H., leaving a crater 40 feet across by 25 feet deep in the clay soil.

The V-2, which was the district's 22nd, landed less than a mile south of where one had fallen four days earlier. No casualties were caused and damage was limited to around 25 properties.

Thursday 8th February 1945

"It looked big enough to take a couple of double-decker buses! "

As told to our our Special Correspondent

"I was at home in Patching Hall Lane when I heard a big bang, to the west, apparently not that far away. Whenever there was an explosion or a plane crash or something of that sort, it was the usual thing to go and find out exactly what it was and where it had happened. This occasion was no exception.

A V-2 rocket had come down in the field immediately to the west of the wood on what is now known as Newland Spring around half a mile from home. The field was part of Priors Farm, which at that time was farmed by Dora Christy.

When I arrived on the scene there were little groups of people, mainly youngsters, looking down into a huge crater which had been formed by the explosion in the middle of the field. It looked big enough to take a couple of double-decker buses!

I was told that two farmworkers, including a Mr. Franklin who lived in the lane, had been working in a ditch at the edge of the field and had heard nothing when the the V-2 had come down. The first they'd known about it was when huge boulders of clay suddenly flew over their heads. Fortunately they were unhurt and no harm had been done except for the unwanted large hole.

The village bobby P.C. Jordan from Broomfield turned up on his bike to inspect the scene. Once I'd had a good look and a chat with my pals, there was not a great deal more to do, so I, like most people, drifted back home."

Les Appleton

COUNTRY'S FIRST & LAST ROCKETS FALL AT BICKNACRE AND RETTENDON

At 2.48 p.m. Britain's 664th, and Chelmsford's 19th, V-2 fell into a field south-east of The Swan P.H. in Bicknacre, only a few hundred yards east of where an identical device had fallen on 16th January 1945.

No one was hurt in the incident though some 19 properties in Bicknacre and Sandon Rectory were superficially damaged by the blast.

The V-2 was the first to fall in the country during the day, and the day's last, number 674, also fell in the Chelmsford district. At 11.57 p.m. it exploded 200 yards north of Rolph's Farm, Rettendon. No casualties were caused, but around a dozen houses suffered slight blast damage.

During the day 85 Sandford Road sustained damage through wartime activities.

Sunday 4th February 1945.

TWO MORE ROCKETS: WRITTLE AND BOREHAM HIT

In the evening the district was hit by two more V-2s, the county's 508th and 509th.

The first, Chelmsford's 16th, fell at 5.55 p.m. in a field belonging to Skegg's Farm in Writtle, some 200 yards south of the River Wid bridge. The V-2 left a crater 30 feet across by 20 feet deep and extensively damaged 19 properties and superficially so a further 218. Among the latter was Writtle All Saints' Church where the roof and windows were damaged and White Thorns in Highwood. At one factory, code-named XX115, the blast damaged the sprinkler system and the glass substitute in its vertical windows and roof lights. Production was, however, unaffected.

Fortunately no casualties were reported though two families in Bridge Street, Writtle were made homeless. Ten properties in the Borough area were damaged: 2 Lodge Farm Cottages in Goat Hall Lane; 3 Hart Street; 74 London Road; 92 Moulsham Street; Dukes in Stump Lane; 190 Upper Bridge Road; Dalston in Waterhouse Lane; Lorretta in Writtle Road; 26 Victoria Road; and Willow Cottage in Springfield Green.

At 7.35 p.m. the day's second V-2 came down at Paynes Lane in Boreham to the north of the railway and west of the road to Little Waltham. The explosion left a crater 40 feet across by 16 feet deep in the clay soil. One nearby house was demolished and 20 others superficially damaged. Five people were hurt including including a man and a woman who were cut by flying glass and taken to hospital. Other adults suffered shock and a child was slightly hurt.

Friday 12th January 1945

THANKS FROM EISENHOWER

The Essex Chronicle reported that the Mayor had received a letter from Lt. Gen. John C.H. Lee, thanking the people of Chelmsford for their hospitality towards American servicemen in recent months. It had been sent on behalf of General Eisenhower.

Friday 12th January 1945

50 YEARS A COUNCILLOR

At the monthly meeting of the Rural District Council Cllr. Frederic Marriage J.P., who represented Little Waltham, was congratulated for achieving fifty years' service as a member of the Rural District Council. He was the only survivor of the original 1895 Council.

Tuesday. 23rd January 1945.

"We heard this terrific whizzing sound in the sky. It was a V-2"

As told to our our Special Correspondent

"One evening I was cycling home along Chignall Road with my husband towards Chignall St. James when we heard this terrific whizzing sound in the sky. It was a V-2 which fell on Writtle. My husband said 'Quick, get in the ditch!, so we jumped off our bikes and went into the ditch for cover. What we never knew was that the ditch was full of water!. We were soaking wet and a mess."

Winifred Wales

"We were provided with an armlet, whistle and steel helmet."

As told to our our Special Correspondent

"Like many others I did not believe that the war would happen and consequently I did not enroll in Air Raid Precautions. But when on the night that war was declared we had an air raid warning I decided that sheltering indoors (with young evacuees), with knowledge of what might be going on, was not for me. So on the following morning I went to the Police Station and enrolled as a warden.

My wife joined the following May as the authorities wanted someone to be available during the day when the men were at work. We were all voluntary but later on paid wardens were recruited to man posts during the day.

We were provided with an armlet, whistle and steel helmet (black with a white 'W' on the front). In time we were issued with a uniform, heavy black boots and a service gas mask which would provide better protection than the small civilian issue.

The whole of the area (under the control of a Chief Warden) was divided into groups which were subdivided into sectors. Our sector was Navigation Road, Brockley Road, Wharf Road and that part of Springfield Road from Navigation Road to the bridge, which of course contained Brown's timber yard and the Gas Works. The personnel to cover this sector was six wardens.

During the first winter there was little aerial activity but there were 'purple' alerts when enemy aircraft were detected approaching the area and wardens were called out by telephone to patrol the streets and see that car headlights were sufficiently dimmed. The sirens only sounded for 'red' alerts, while the all-clear was given by a 'white' alert.

After the Battle of Britain had started there were frequent red alerts which often lasted for many hours, without any aircraft in the immediate vicinity. All the wardens turned out during the evening but after 10 p.m. if nothing was happening the watch was kept by two wardens in two hour periods until the all clear was sounded."

Gerald Hockley

"Lights in sky."

As told to our our Special Correspondent

"On several nights during the war the whole sky was lit up from what appeared to be lights scattered about the countryside around Chelmsford. No one knew what was causing the light but we knew it wasn't from normal searchlights because there was never any beam, just brightness. Local rumour had it that the idea behind them was that our night fighters would fly high above the light so that when the German planes were caught in it below them they could be easily spotted and shot down."

Norman Hume

MOUNTNESSING ROCKET

Chelmsford's 25th V-2, and the country's 739th, fell at Burnthouse Farm in Mountnessing at 1.46 p.m. It landed south of the railway line and left a crater 50 feet across by 20 feet deep. Slight damage was inflicted on properties in Burnthouse Lane, Padham's Green and houses on the Heybridge Estate near Ingatestone.

Monday 12th February 1945

V-2 FALLS BESIDE A12

THE DISTRICT'S 26th V-2, Britain's 769th, fell at 5.12 p.m. in a field at Mountnessing just ten yards from the A12.

Half the houses in the village were damaged by the blast with the Congregational Chapel, opposite the explosion, demolished. Fortunately casualties were restricted to just one person detained in hospital and two dozen others with slight injuries.

Within a radius of about 200 yards the blast damaged every ceiling including those of the day school, 80 yards away, which had most of its windows blown in and was subsequently closed for five weeks for repairs.

A Chelmsford bound bus narrowly missed disaster by passing the impact point just three minutes before the explosion occurred.

Wednesday 14th February 1945

"Mountnessing Rocket."

As told to our our Special Correspondent

"I was at home, 'Bethany' which was next door to the Congregational Chapel. When the rocket exploded everything seemed to turn upside down. We were covered with plaster from the ceiling, wallpaper was ripped off in large streamers, the walls appeared to bellow out then back again, our piano in the front room slithered all round the floor, and in the process lost all the works inside! Dishes in the sideboard kept their shape, but on being touched fell to pieces. I got a superficial cut on the head. My wife and I were taken in the ambulance to hospital but we soon recovered."

John Sawyer, from 'Battle Over Essex' 1946.

'WELCOME HOME' COMMITTEE MEETS

The Essex Chronicle reported that a newly formed committee had met under the Mayor's chairmanship to prepare Chelmsford's 'Welcome Home' for the town's returning servicemen.

Friday 9th February 1945

3 MONTHS JAIL FOR BIGAMY

At the Essex Assizesin Chelmsford a 32 year-old woman factory worker was jailed for three months for bigamy. It was her second conviction for the offence. Previously she had been bound over.

Friday 9th February 1945

TWO MORE ROCKETS IN THE SOUTH

At 9.24 p.m. and ten minutes later the county's 781st and 782nd V-2s fell to the south of Chelmsford. Neither caused any casualties.

The first V-2, which was the district's 27th, fell between South Hanningfield and Rettendon near the tile works and in the vicinity of Bromley Lodge. Four houses and Lacey's Farm were superficially damaged. The second incident occurred at Tinsley's Farm in West Hanningfield where a number of properties sustained slight blast damage.

Friday 16th February 1945

MAN KILLED AS ROCKET FALLS AT WOODHAM FERRERS FARM

A MAN DIED from the injuries he received when a V-2 fell at Brazil's Farm near Woodham Ferrers at 7.32 a.m. It was Chelmsford's 29th, and the country's 801st, V-2.

The explosion left a crater 40 feet across and a dozen feet deep, demolished farm buildings and rendered the farmhouse uninhabitable. Ten cows and three pigs died though more importantly four people were hurt, one of them seriously.

The latter was Douglas Henry Evemy, aged 35, who was taken to Chelmsford & Essex Hospital where he later died from his injuries. He lived with his wife, Marie, and young child at Mon Abri in Woodham Road, Woodham Ferrers, and was to turn out to be the district's last civilian fatality of the war.

He was subsequently buried at St Mary's Church in Woodham Ferrers on 24th February 1945.

Sunday 18th February 1945

THREE ROCKETS IN ONE DAY

RADLEY GREEN, MARGARETTING, & HYLANDS PARK

OF THE 13 V-2S that fell on Britain during the day three did so in the Chelmsford district.

At 6.34 a.m. one came down on Norton Church Farm, Radley Green and left a crater 20 to 25 feet across by 15 to 20 feet deep in the clay soil. The farm buildings were completely demolished and livestock injured.

Radley Green School and some fifteen nearby houses suffered from the blast whilst telephone wire were brought down. The only casualty was a woman who was taken to hospital, suffering from shock. The V-2 was the 715th to fall on the country.

In the afternoon, at 3.29 p.m., Britain's 722nd V-2, and the district's 24th, fell in a filed between Pound Wood and the River Wid in Margaretting. No one was hurt and no damage was reported though the explosion left a crater 45 feet across and 15 feet deep.

The day's third local V-2, and the country's 725th in all, fell at 8.01 p.m. in the middle of South Wood in Hylands Park, about half a mile west of Hylands House.

The device left a crater 45 feet across by 14 feet deep and seriously damaged nine army huts.

A dozen others were superficially damaged by the blast, as was Hylands House and several other properties including; 3 Belle Vue; 99 Coval Lane; Goat Hall & Lodge Farm in Goat Hall Lane; 32 Grove Road; 43 Nursery Road; Lyndon, The Pines, Minfreida, Edwyne, Braemar, Ivydene, Hill View, Rosedean, Arden & Homelands in Private Road; 14, 15 & 17 Prykes Drive; 69 Rainsford Lane; 6, 52 & 62 South Primrose Hill; 15 Stewart Road; Widford Garage, Widford Hall, The White Horse P.H., School Cottage, A.R.P. Stores at Widford School, Widford Church, Widford Rectory, Hillside & 3 Hall Cottages in Widford; and Hall View, Lyston & 49 Writtle Road

Saturday 10th February 1945.

LUCKY ESCAPE: ROCKET FALLS NEAR ROXWELL ROAD

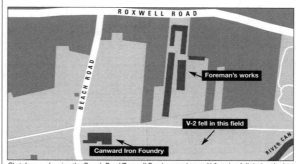

Sketch map showing the Beach Road/Roxwell Road area where a V-2 rocket fell during the late afternoon of 24th February 1945. (Author)

CHELMSFORD'S 31ST V-2, and Britain's 863rd, fell in a field to the east of Beach Road and south of Roxwell Road, behind L.P. Foreman & Son's works.

The explosion, at 4.59 p.m., left one person very seriously injured and 16 others, including workers at Foreman's, slightly hurt.

Had the rocket landed a few hundred yards nearer the town centre the casualties would have been far greater, perhaps into the hundreds, as Chelmsford enjoyed its traditional market day crowds.

Over 360 properties were damaged by the blast in the Borough including the Canward Iron Foundry and Foreman's, both of which were undertaking Government work. The audience at the Pavilion Cinema was showered with pieces of the ceiling that were dislodged by the blast. A further eight properties were also damaged in Lawford Lane, Writtle.

The most serious casualty was a joiner, Edward Kemp of Molerams Lane in Great Baddow. When first found by rescuers his injuries looked so serious that he was thought to have been killed, so his body was removed to the mortuary. However, in a bizarre turn of events, some hours later workers at the mortuary realised that he was in fact still alive and immediately took him to the Chelmsford & Essex Hospital where he was treated for a collapsed lung.

Thanks to the skills of the staff there his life was saved and he was able to return home during April 1945. Mr. Kemp was to enjoy a further 50 years of life and eventually died in the summer of 1995 aged 82.

Friday 23rd February 1945

GREAT LEIGHS ROCKET

At 2.34 a.m. a V-2, the district's 33rd and Britain's 888th, fell to the rear of The Croft in Great Leighs, leaving a crater 20 feet across by 20 feet deep.

No casualties were caused. Damage was restricted to Little Leigh's Hall and Rectory, eight houses in Little Leighs, around 200 fruit trees and some two dozen houses in Great Leighs.

Thursday 1st March 1945

SALUTE THE SOLDIER PLAQUES

Plaques and certificates of honour giving a permanent record of Chelmsford's achievements during Salute the Soldier Week were presented to the town by the Vice Chairman and past President of the National Savings Movement, Lord Mottistone, at ceremonies at the Shire Hall and R.D.C. Offices.

At the Shire Hall the Mayor, as President of the Borough Savings Committee, accepted the award, accompanied by local dignitaries. Since the start of the war £6,637,000 of National Savings had been purchased by the people of Chelmsford.

Saturday 10th February 1945.

FRYERNING V-2

Chelmsford's 30th V-2, the country's 833rd, fell at 3.38 p.m. within the north-east corner of Fryerning Wood near Fryerning. No casualties were caused and damage was restricted to Woodcock Lodge and a number of properties in Bicknacre.

Tuesday 20th February 1945

32ND V-2: FALLS AT INGATESTONE

At 10.51 a.m. the country's 882nd V-2, Chelmsford's 32nd, fell near Shoulder Hall in Ingatestone. No casualties were reported and the only damage was cracks in the wall at Elmbrook Farm, Buttsbury.

Tuesday 27th February 1945

£200,000 WAR DAMAGE REPAIR COST

The Borough Engineer reported at the monthly Council meeting that war damage repair work totalling some £214,000 had now been carried out in the Borough, excluding work undertaken by the Ministry of Works special repair squads.

Wednesday 28th February 1945

"Night V-2"

As told to our our Special Correspondent

"One night during a break I had managed to lose my watch in Hoffmann's so in the early hours

I was given permission to go down to the police station in New Street to report it missing and give a description. Just as I was walking past The Wheatsheaf, suddenly the whole place was lit up by a brilliant light that lasted no longer than a second or two.

I looked up into the sky and there was a V-2 going towards London with a terrific long bright belch of flame out of its tail that must have lit up the whole town. It didn't make a sound at all and though I listened out for it exploding I never heard anything. I don't suppose many people in Chelmsford saw it at that time of night."

Bill Wilson

COUNTY TOWN'S FINAL V-1 SHOT DOWN

Chelmsford's 27th V-1 was shot down by an R.A.F. aircraft some 150 yards to the south of Sandon Garage, and to the west of the A130, between Sandon Brook and Little Sir Hughes at 2.25 p.m.

One woman and two men were slightly hurt, while six houses were badly damaged and another two slightly so. It was the first V-1 to fall on the district since 18th December 1944, and was to turn out to be the last of the war.

Tuesday 6th March 1945

STOCK V-2 40 FOOT DEEP CRATER AT

Chelmsford's 35th V-2, Britain's 1028th, fell in Seven Ponds Field, Imphy Hall near Stock at 6.51 a.m.

The explosion left a crater 50 feet across by 40 feet deep. No one was hurt despite the damage inflicted to a number of properties in the vicinity.

Friday 16th March 1945

HOFFMANN HEROS TO RECEIVE DECORATIONS

THE DAY'S LONDON Gazette announced that several members of Chelmsford's civil defence staff were to receive decorations following the V-2 attack on Hoffmann's shortly before Christmas 1944.

Dr. Charles Bateman, a medical officer with the civil defence first aid service was to get the M.B.E., and David James, a staff officer with the civil defence rescue service was to receive the B.E.M.

Both men had tunnelled 12 feet through rubble at immense risk to rescue a woman trapped in wreckage.

For his actions at another incident the M.B.E. was to go to Dr. William Boul, officer in charge with the civil defence casualty service. Alfred Dandy was awarded the B.E.M. as were two other men, Benjamin A. Garwood and Frederick Marshall, who were party leaders with the civil defence rescue service.

Commendations went to Harry K. Brown, a staff officer with the civil defence rescue service, and P.c. (War Reserve) Alfred P. Drake.

Tuesday 6th March 1945

BATTLESBRIDGE ROCKET

At 1.41 a.m. the district's 36th V-2, and Britain's 1043rd, fell in the vicinity of Don's Farm and Gosses Farm, near Battlesbridge` and close to the River Crouch. The device left a crater 24 feet across by 5 feet deep. No one was hurt, but both farms and five other properties sustained slight blast damage.

Sunday 18th March 1945

FINAL DAY OF ENEMY ACTION:

LAST THREE ROCKETS FALL

ON WHAT WOULD turn out to be the last day of enemy activity over the Chelmsford district three V-2s fell.

The first, which was Britain's 1078th, came down at 5.22 a.m. near Ramsey Tyrells in Stock, only a few hundred yards from where one had fallen six days earlier. Imphy Hall, Whites Tyrells and Ramsey Tyrells all suffered superficial blast damage to roof tiles, windows, plaster work and telephone cables. Fortunately no one was hurt.

At 5.47 a.m. Britain's next V-2, and Chelmsford's 40th, fell in a field at Culverts Farm in Boreham. Again no casualties were reported, though the farm

and two cottages were superficially damaged by the blast and a timber cart shed was set ablaze and destroyed..

Finally, at 9.52 p.m., the country's 1084th V-2, the Chelmsford district's 41st and last, fell at Woodham Ferrers. It exploded in a field opposite the police house and some 400 yards north of Grange Cottage, South Woodham Ferrers, leaving a crater 15 feet across by just 2.5 feet deep.

An empty school bus that was passing by was blown into a ditch and its driver seriously injured.. Four other people were slightly hurt and around twenty houses were damaged by the blast. This was to be the last bombing incident of the war.

Thursday 22nd March 1945

ILLEGAL DRINKS: STILL A PROBLEM

An elderly and grey-haired woman from 11a Park Avenue was fined £21 plus £2/2 analyst's fee at the Chelmsford Petty Sessions for 'selling watered-down whisky, whisky not on a licensed premises, whisky without a licence and obstructing a detective constable'.

The court heard her admit to having bought the whisky from a man in a dark pin-striped suit at the Lion & Lamb P.H. and then to have sold bottles on to American

servicemen at £4 a bottle. The £1 a bottle profit she made was, she claimed, "My only way of getting a living."

The court was told that when arrested she had become very abusive to the detective constable and had to be restrained after attempting to hit him with one of the bottles of whisky!

In another case, a butcher from Springfield Park Road was given fines totalling £15 after admitting to four charges relating to the sale of the illegal cocktails 'Red Lady' and 'Parasue'.

Friday 23rd March 1945

37TH ROCKET

Britain's 1060th V-2, and Chelmsford's 37th, fell in a field at Little Preston's Farm on the border between South Hanningfield and West Hanningfield at 4.10 a.m.

It created a crater 42 feet across by 30 feet deep in the clay soil. No casualties were caused though seven houses and some telephone wires were damaged by the blast.

Tuesday 20th March 1945

EYEWITNESS ACCOUNT:

"Wartime atmosphere."

As told to our our Special Correspondent

"It was an exciting time for people of my age - those in their late teens and early twenties. We knew that people were being killed and that was very sad.

It was hard with the rationing and being bombed out, but we felt that we were really living. The pressure we were under was so high that we felt that we lived every minute of every day."

Eileen Hance

GLIDER DOWN AT RUNWELL

At 8.15 a.m. an Allied glider (markings RN O 493) became detached from its parent aircraft and came down in a field of parsley 150 yards east of Hillside, Brock Hill in Runwell, and some 600 yards south of Fleming's Farm, South Hanningfield. The aircraft was only slightly damaged and none of the five crew on board was injured.

Saturday 24th March 1945

TRIBUTES TO AMERICAN PRESIDENT

Abroad, American President Roosevelt died of a cerebral haemorrhage at the age of 63. In Chelmsford most local churches flew their flags at half-mast during the subsequent Sunday services in his honour, whilst the Cathedral was to host an all day memorial service to him on 17th April 1945.

Thursday 12th April 1945

ELDERLY COUPLE IN REMARKABLE ESCAPE FROM ROCKET

At 3.24 a.m. Britain's 959th V-2, the district's 34th, fell in the garden of Stoke Cottage, a picturesque thatched cottage close to the A414 between Writtle and Roxwell.

The device fell little more than a dozen yards from the property which was demolished by the explosion. Remarkably its elderly occupants, Mr. & Mrs. Stephen Nelson, who had been asleep upstairs, escaped without any serious injury.

A huge crater was left in the garden with its lip right up to the entrance of an air raid shelter that Mr. Nelson had constructed. Had an alert sounded before the V-2 fell the couple would have made their way to the shelter and would have certainly been killed.

Thursday 8th March 1945

ROCKET AT WOODHAM FERRERS

Britain's 1071st V-2, the district's 38th, fell some 200 yards south-east of Woodham Ferrers railway station at 10.40 p.m., close to Hullbridge Road. One woman sustained a slight head injury in the incident while around fifty houses and the station were superficially damaged by the blast.

Wednesday. 21st March 1945

FIRE GUARD FINISHED

The Ministry of Home Security finally authorised the complete relaxation of Chelmsford's Fire Guard.

Just four weeks earlier the Council had unsuccessfully requested the Ministry of Home Security to make the move following reports that Colchester had already been granted a similar request.

The Council had argued that although the Fire Guard had originally been formed to deal with the threat posed by incendiary bombs, none had been dropped on Chelmsford for many months and there was now little likelihood of a resumption in such attacks.

Subsequently all the Fire Guard's full-time staff would lose their jobs by 20th July 1945.

Thursday 22nd March 1945

BIKE FOR SOLDIERS

The Galleywood British Legion was reported to have purchased a bicycle to be lodged at Chelmsford Police Station for the use of men from Galleywood arriving home on leave in Chelmsford after the last bus from the town to Galleywood had gone.

Friday 13th April 1945

EYEWITNESS ACCOUNT: V-2

"We hadn't the faintest idea where the front or the back of the cottage was."

As told to our our Special Correspondent

"When I came to my senses my first fleeting impression was that there had been an earthquake. I cannot quite describe the sensation. Everything around us and both of us seemed to be suspended in mid air. There was a terrific crack, as though all the thunder I had heard in my life had been rolled into one awful roar. Then everything around us collapsed.

But as the roof of the cottage was thatched and not slated, the whole heap of thatch, a couple of feet thick, fell upon my wife and I, and instead of killing us, protected us from the bricks and timber.

When my wife and I realised that we were still alive and apparently uninjured, we found we were on the ground floor, having fallen through the bedroom floor, with part of the thatched roof still forming a sort of triangle over us.

We started crawling through bits of smashed furniture. We hadn't the faintest idea where the front or the back of the cottage was.

Then groping, half-stunned, through a hole, we found ourselves out in the open at the back of where the cottage had been. The earth seemed to be still quivering from the effects of the explosion.

It was dark but we could dimly see some of the fine old trees in the garden snapped and torn as though they had been matchsticks. Then the ambulance came and took us away. We both suffered from shock. The A.R.P. workers quite expected to find us badly hurt, but that was not so. We had no more than a few scratches between us.

What would have happened had we been in our outdoor shelter I tremble to think; the lip of the crater came right up to it. And we should have gone there if the alert had sounded!"

Stephen Nelson

HARD LABOUR FOR POSSESSION OF MILITARY EQUIPMENT

At the Chelmsford Petty Sessions three local men were given three, six and twelve months hard labour after being found in possession of U.S. Army clothing and other goods.

The three had formerly been employed at Boreham Aerodrome.

Their conviction came a week after a South Woodham Ferrers man was jailed for a year, fined £50 and given ten guineas costs on similar charges relating to his possession of a large quantity of stolen 'Government articles', mainly army blankets, clothes and boots.

Friday 13th April 1945

SURPRISE VICTOR IN CHELMSFORD BY ELECTION

TOP A.R.P. MAN GIVEN EIGHT MONTHS HARD LABOUR

At the Essex Quarter Sessions Chelmsford's Air Raid Precautions (A.R.P.) Officer, 44 year-old William Fellas, was given eight months hard labour for stealing a large quantity of A.R.P. equipment. He had pleaded not guilty.

Mr. Fellas, who was in charge of the A.R.P. stores in the Essex Central A.R.P. Area, was said to have sold a considerable amount of the equipment to a local taxi proprietor.

Thursday 19th April 1945

THE BY ELECTION caused by the death on 22nd December 1944 Chelmsford's M.P., Col. John Macnamara, on active service in Italy was held on 26th April 1945.

Nationally the major political parties had maintained a truce since the outbreak of war which meant that they would not normally nominate a candidate in a by-election against the party of the former M.P. for the duration of the war. As it transpired, in Chelmsford's case, no such truce was observed.

No truce

On 5th January 1945 the Essex Chronicle reported that the Chelmsford branch of the Communist Party had suggested in an open letter that Col. Macnamara be replaced, not by a party's candidate, but one chosen by all parties - via a selection conference attended by representatives of the Conservative, Labour, Liberal, Co-operative, Common Wealth and Communist Parties.

A week later the paper reported that the local Conservative party had responded to the suggestion, welcoming the idea but urging that any jointly selected candidate should pledge to support the current National Government. However, the newly formed Common Wealth Party was not satisfied, and announced that it would select its own candidate to contest seat, a policy it had undertaken elsewhere with some success. Meanwhile the Communist, Labour and Liberal Parties all decided to observe the truce.

A few days later on 14th January 1945 over 200 people attended a Common Wealth meeting at the County Hotel. The party's chairman Sir Richard Acland revealed to the packed audience that its candidate would be an as yet unnamed R.A.F.

bomber pilot. Incidentally a similar meeting held the week before Col. Macnamara's death had only attracted around 45 people and the increase was some measure of the popular surge in left-wing popularity which the Common Wealth had tapped since its formation in July 1942.

Candidates

Over the next fortnight the Common Wealth and Conservatives selected their candidates for the by-election. Somewhat surprisingly the Conservatives chose an outsider, 34 year-old Ft. Lt. Brian C. Cook R.A.F., of Gerrards Cross Bucks. He was a director of Batsfords, the well known publishers & had reputation as a fluent public speaker. He had served with the R.A.F. since 1940, and although trained as a member of aircrew, had spent much of the war in an administrative post within the Air Ministry.

The Common Wealth candidate was Wing Commander Ernest Millington R.A.F., the 28 year-old commander of a Lancaster squadron. He was an experienced airman and was close to achieving the 30 operation flights which would complete a tour of duty. He had joined territorials in 1938, spent time as a sapper with the Royal Engineers, as a non-commissioned officer, had gone to O.C.T.U. and had gained a commission into the Royal Artillery in 1940.

After serving in the defence of London during the blitz he had volunteered pilot duties with R.A.F. and had been transferred in 1941. After gaining his wings he then spent nearly two years as a flying instructor before his transfer to R.A.F. Bomber Command. Unlike Ft. Lt. Cook he had good local connections - he had been educated at Chigwell, while his mother lived Ilford. He was married with three daughters and

was a former Labour Party member.

On 2nd February 1945 the Essex Chronicle reported that a third candidate had announced his intention to stand in the by-election. He was 40 year-old Pte. Ronald Cornwell, a London businessman coincidentally living at Gerrards Cross. Pte. Cornwell was to stand for the Independent Progressive Party.

The candidates embarked on their vigorous election campaigns with a series of public meetings, debates and newspaper articles. Pte. Cornwell was an early casualty in this and on 16th March 1945 the Essex Chronicle announced that he had withdrawn his candidature. The by-election was left as a straight fight between the Conservatives and Common Wealth, a choice between the status quo or a socialist programme of 'public ownership and a fairer society'.

Churchill letter

On 25th April 1945, on what was the eve of the Chelmsford By-Election, a letter, signed by Mr. Churchill (Conservative), Mr. Brown (National Liberal), Mr. Atlee (Labour) and Mr. Sinclair (Liberal), the leaders of their respective parties, was issued, urging Chelmsford's voters to support the Government's candidate, the Conservative Ft. Lt. Brian Cook.

The electors were asked to 'make it plain to the world that the Chelmsford Division of Essex stands behind the National Government that is bearing so heavy a burden'.

The release of the letter did, however, reveal a certain incompetence in the Conservative's campaign, for although primarily intended for the local press to publish, the letter was released too late to be included in the local papers before the election. The next issues of the Essex Chronicle

and Essex Weekly News were not due until two days later, a day after voters went to the polls!

The vote

Voting took place on Thursday 26th April 1945, with a relatively low turnout of around 54% It was the first election under the new register which comprised of 44,371 voters in Chelmsford, 16,488 in Brentwood, 1,882 in Billericay, 974 in Runwell, 2,873 in Ingatestone, 1,070 in the Romford postal area, 3,097 in Ongar, 3,051 in other districts and around 5,000 service voters.

The following morning the High Sheriff of Essex, Sir Adam Ritchie, declared the result to a crowd of around three thousand people outside the Shire Hall. He announced:

Ernest Millington
(Common Wealth) 24,548 votes
Brian Cook
(Conservative) 18,117 votes

The result was seen as a disaster for the Conservatives and Winston Churchill was said to have been extremely annoyed at the result. Outside of Chelmsford the result had been unexpected with a Conservative victory regarded as a formality. However, locally the hardships of the war had encouraged a growth in socialist sympathies and here the result was not a great surprise.

Just over a week later, on 2nd May 1945, Wing Commander Ernest Millington M.P. took his seat at the House of Commons for the first time, joining the two other Common Wealth M.P.s. He was loudly cheered from the Labour benches.

Exactly two weeks after that he made his maiden speech, appropriately enough during a parliamentary debate on the release and resettlement of members of the armed forces.

Thursday 26th April 1945

CHELMSFORD CELEBRATES V.E. DAY

At 3 p.m. Winston Churchill spoke in the House of Commons and announced that Germany had signed the final act of capitulation and that the war in Europe had been concluded. The news brought scenes of jubilation throughout Britain.

M.P. in controversy

Controversy, however, surrounded Chelmsford's new M.P., Wing Cdr. Ernest Millington, days after taking his seat in Parliament.

He was one of a handful of M.P.s who failed to rise to cheer Churchill's entrance into the House of Commons.

Later Wing Cmdr. Millington was to explain that his behaviour had not been a gesture of ingratitude to the Prime Minister, but one of disgust at the 'dishonest use of Churchill's justified popularity by the Conservative Party which knew that there was soon to be a General Election'.

Tindal Square

In Chelmsford the V E Day celebrations were centred around Tindal Square, where a large dancing and singing crowd developed outside the Corn Exchange, and spread into Tindal Street and the High Street.

Arthur Beeton and members of the Chelmsford Dance Club made arrangements for the dance band to play music from the Corn Exchange until into the early hours. As dusk fell a huge 'V for Victory' sign was illuminated over the building, whilst spot and floodlights where shone onto those in the square below. It was a scene of unrestrained joy. The King's speech was relayed to the huge crowd via loud speakers and three cheers were given for the King, the Allies, and the Prime Minister.

Floodlit

In a floodlit Baddow Road and Mildmay Road revellers danced in

the street outside The Ritz (Odeon) cinema to the accompaniment of the resident dance band.

In other parts of the town bonfires were lit, children danced around them, and parties were held in dozens of homes. Searchlights were aimed high in the sky, an illuminated 'G R' sign was erected outside the Chelmsford Club in London Road, whilst K.E.G.S. was floodlit by enterprising scholars. Chelmsford's pubs had their licences extended till 11 p.m., but most were forced to shut around half an hour before that as beer supplies became exhausted. Further afield, at Writtle, a ten feet high bonfire, surmounted with an effigy of Hitler, was constructed on The Green with much assistance from the local N.F.S.

Cathedral

The Cathedral paid host to thanksgiving services, at hourly intervals throughout the day, whilst, perhaps most poignantly, the war memorial in Duke Street

was floodlit in recognition of those who had not survived to see the day.

As the V.E. Day celebrations continued onto Wednesday 9th May 1945, throughout the country the first of dozens of street parties were held in Chelmsford. They were to continue to take place throughout the summer months.

Statistics

Since the outbreak of the war the Chelmsford area had suffered around 1225 air raid warnings and had been hit by an estimated 1326 H.E.s, 60 parachute landmines, 136 phosphorous and oil bombs, 25,056 small incendiaries, 27 V-1s and 41 V-2s.

In the Rural District enemy action had resulted in the demolition of 27 properties, a further 19 damaged beyond repair, 108 seriously damaged and another 6,475 slightly damaged. Of the Rural District's 1,000 council houses 550 had been damaged or demolished as a result of enemy action.

Tuesday 8th May 1945

"We were thankful that it was over and the fear of air raids at night had all gone. At long last, after night after night when the sirens had gone off, we would be able to have a full night's sleep without worrying."

As told to our our Special Correspondent

"At the end of the war I was almost 18 years-old, but my father wouldn't allow me to go out with boys and I had to be home by ten o' clock at night. Things were far more strict in those days!

On V.E. Day afternoon I walked into Chelmsford with our lodger, Rita, who was a few years older than me. In town everybody was merry - people were drinking and dancing in the street all around the Shire Hall. It was a lovely atmosphere.

We met a couple of soldiers and we were walking through one of the alleyways from the top of the High Street to Back (Tindal) Street when to my horror I saw my father coming towards us. 'Rita', I said, 'My dad's coming!' So we turned and ran like mad to get away from him. The soldiers couldn't understand it!

We dropped them and carried on having a good time with other girls and fellas until it was quite late. When we eventually got home my father gave me a good hiding for being with the soldiers and forbade me from going out again for weeks afterwards."

Betty Pryke

"It was a wonderful day. Chelmsford was 'on fete' with celebrations all over the town. It was lovely, there was such a sense of relief and happiness, I shall never forget that. I don't think that I've ever experienced anything lie it , apart perhaps from when my children were born.

I was a senior boarder at K.E.G.S. and Company Sgt. Major. of the school's Cadet Corps. in the morning we celebrated by setting up the floodlighting for the school.

In the evening we went down the town for a real celebration, and it was quite some long time before I got back. We visited the pubs, which were all packed, and every one in the town must have been drunk dry that night. It was the first time I'd ever been drunk and how I got back to school I don't know!

Apparently I was hidden in one of the classrooms so that the headmaster couldn't find me until I'd sobered up. When I eventually left the school in July 1945 the headmaster, dear old 'Nobby' Squire, a wonderful man, said to me "Tell me, where did they hide you that night?'. The old beggar had known about it all the time."

Leonard Menhinick

"We had the day off work. I spent the morning looking out at the view from the top of the Cathedral tower with my friends. In the evening we wandered about the town and stuck our heads in various pubs.

The was great elation - everyone was singing things like 'Roll me over in the clover'. After that we went up to Tindal Square and danced with the crowds till around midnight before we went home. There were loads of British soldiers let out, but the Americans were shut up in their camps."

Peggy Brown

"The end of the war in Europe came as a great relief for us. We were thankful that it was over and the fear of air raids at night had all gone. At long last, after night after night when the sirens had gone off, we would be able to have a full night's sleep without worrying. At work we were relieved too because, we knew that we'd be able to ease up and not have to do all the overtime.

To celebrate V.E. Day we held a street party in Dorset Avenue organised by the local wardens. There was a line of tables down the street and the houses were decorated with flags and buntings. At the junction with Chelmerton Avenue neither corner plot had been built on in those days, so a tent was put up on one of them. The kids had over party there and there was also a baby show. It was a time of great relief."

George Brown

CHELMSFORD'S CIVIL DEFENCE STAFF IN STAND DOWN CELEBRATIONS

IN BRIGHT AFTERNOON sunshine around 500 men and women of the local civil defence staff took part in Chelmsford's stand down celebrations.

They assembled, along with a large number of members of the public, in the car park behind the market for a brief thanksgiving for victory service conducted by the Rev. H. Pike of Widford, himself a warden.

Afterwards a parade was formed which then marched through the town centre, past the Shire Hall, where the salute was taken by the Chief Constable, and finally to the Ritz Cinema car park. There each Chief Warden addressed his personnel and gave the final stand down order.

Among those taking part in the ceremonies were Wardens R. Crozier and A.W. Morton, both of whom had been commended for their bravery by the King, Senior Wardens C.A. Brett and R.C. Baker who had been commended by the Regional Commissioner, and 22 other wardens who had been commended by the Chief Constable.

Many of those who attended the events were set to join a civil defence association which was to be formed in Essex.

Sunday 24th June 1945

PUB BOMBED BY THE AMERICANS

During the afternoon a practice bomb from a passing American aircraft was accidentally dropped onto the lawn at The White Hart P.H. in Springfield, shattering windows in nearby buildings. No one was injured in the incident.

Thursday 31st May 1945.

FREEDOM OF THE BOROUGH TO BE GIVEN TO U.S. GENERAL

Members of the Council unanimously approved a motion to grant the Freedom of the Borough of Chelmsford to General G. Anderson U.S.A.A.F.

For the previous three years he had commanded the air force's Essex based units, in acknowledgement of the efforts by the Americans during the war.

The suggestion to offer the honour had been made by the Lord Lieutenant of Essex, Sir Francis Whitmore, in a recent letter to the Mayor. The official offer to General Anderson had to wait until January 1946.

Tuesday 5th June 1945

ANGER AT ITALIAN PRISONERS

The Essex Weekly News reported that the Great Leighs Branch of the British Legion had passed a resolution protesting to the Government at the manufacture and sale locally of baskets and other items by Italian p.o.w.s.

The branch objected 'on the grounds that no purchase tax was being paid, no hawkers licences were in operation and it was unfair on members who were disabled ex-servicemen'. The issue was certainly a thorny one, as many of the village's housewives regularly traded with the p.o.w.s who were mainly engaged in agricultural work.

Friday 15th June 1945

AT LAST: CHELMSFORD'S STREET LIGHTS ON FULL BEAM

With the ending of double summer time Chelmsford's street lights were able to light up again at full power for the first time in nearly six years.

In the town centre and at the main road junctions all 187 Merca 400W and 250W lamps were put into full operation whilst most of side streets were illuminated by 150W lights.

By the following Wednesday all forty miles of the town's street lighting were back to the prewar standard. Similar scenes were to be seen in towns and cities throughout the country as the blackout finally came to an end.

Sunday 15th July 1945

AMERICANS PULL OUT

The Essex Chronicle revealed that the American forces had relinquished their sports facilities on King's Head Meadow, whilst the officers' club at Brownings in Broomfield Road had now closed down.

Friday 8th June 1945

CIVIL DEFENCE WORKERS' FAREWELL

At Hyde Park in London the King addressed a farewell parade of some 2,500 members of the civil defence forces. Chelmsford was represented by three civil defence staff from Marconi's.

Sunday 10th June 1945

CHELMSFORD SOLDIER BRINGS 'LORD HAW HAW' BACK

In the late afternoon Lord Haw Haw, alias William Joyce, was flown back to Britain from Brussels to stand trial for treason. The soldier in command of the escort that guarded him on his return was Cpl. Harry George Hudson C.M.P. of 14 Regina Road. He handed Joyce over to Scotland Yard detectives on their arrival at 'a south-eastern aerodrome'. Joyce was subsequently tried, convicted and hanged for treason on 3rd January 1946.

Saturday 16th June 1945

"Lord Haw Haw."

As told to our our Special Correspondent

"I remember listening to Lord Haw Haw from Hamburg - his voice was unmistakable, He would make nasty, taunting remarks, trying to prove to us that he knew exactly what was going on.

I can't remember the exact details, but I do recall him, on one occasion, talking about the Shire Hall clock in Chelmsford. People had one of two views about him - there were those who thought it was treason just to listen to him, but most people liked to listen to him just to get a good laugh. You wondered what ridiculous comment he was going to come up with next."

Ray Knappet

CITY TO RESUME WITHOUT THEIR KIT!

With Chelmsford City set to resume Southern League football in a few weeks time, with their new manager Arthur Rowe, souvenir hunters were reported to have been responsible for the theft of all of the club's playing kit and most its towels which had disappeared during the war. Meanwhile, Southend United were said to have had their goal posts stolen!

Friday 3rd August 1945.

S.A.S. KILL FARMWORKER

At a Chelmsford inquest a verdict of accidental death was returned on 78 year-old farmworker James Carter.

He had been knocked down by an army jeep near his home at Gable Cottages in Margaretting Road, Writtle. The jeep, driven by a soldier of the S.A.S Regiment which was based at Hylands Park, had met an oncoming lorry loaded with Austrian p.o.w.s on a narrow bend where the road was just 13 feet wide.

In trying to avoid a collision the jeep's driver struck Mr. Carter as he walked along the edge of the verge.

Saturday 9th June 1945

LUFTWAFFE MODEL OF CHELMSFORD FOUND IN GERMANY

Officers of C Squadron, 6501 Wing R.A.F. discovered a scale model of the Hoffmann and Marconi works, prepared from aerial photography, in the firegutted photographic building at Quedlingburg Aerodrome in Germany.

The officers were to subsequently present the model to Marconi's and for many years after the war it was to be seen on display at the Chelmsford & Essex Museum in Oaklands Park.

Tuesday 12th June 1945

YOUTHS CAUGHT STEALING WEAPONS FROM AERODROME

At Chelmsford Juvenile Court one 16 year old and two 15 year-old boys admitted stealing three R.A.F. service revolvers, 48 rounds of ammunition and other items from Boreham Aerodrome. All three were sent to an approved school.

Tuesday 19th June 1945

COUNCIL REBUILDING FOR PEACETIME

At the monthly meeting of the Council members were informed that around 500 houses in Chelmsford still required war damage repairs.

More than 400 others which had been evacuated pending repair had now been repaired sufficiently for the return of residents.

The Council agreed to urgently prepare and submit final plans for the extension of the town's sewage works for Government approval. The scheme was necessary in order that the works have sufficient capacity to cope with Chelmsford's rapidly rising population.

Weds. 25th July 1945

1945 General Election

COMMON WEALTH HOLDS CHELMSFORD SEAT - BUT ONLY JUST

THE DAY SAW BRITAIN'S first General Election since November 1935. The Chelmsford seat was contested by the Liberal, Conservative and Common Wealth Parties, with a close contest expected between then the latter two.

Throughout the district's polling stations brisk business was reported even though over a thousand electors were said to have been left of the electoral register and were thus unable to vote.

Their omission was blamed on a shortage of labour and a lack of time in which to have prepared for the election. Results were not expected to be announced until 25th July as up to 6,500 service votes had to be collected from around the globe.

The General Election had come only a matter of weeks after the Chelmsford by-election, caused by the death of Col. John Macnamara in Italy. Since then the local political scene had seen a great deal of activity as the various parties geared themselves up for the fight.

Candidates

After their disastrous defeat in the by-election, the Conservatives had met a month later to select their candidate for the General Election.

As expected the local party president, Brig. Gen. J.T. Wigan and the chairman, Major R.K. Magor announced their retirements to allow younger men to succeed them.

Brian Cook, the defeated Conservative candidate in the by-election, withdrew his candidature so that the replacement executive committee could have complete freedom in choosing any candidate, though he he still wished to be considered.

Somewhat unexpectedly Brian Cook was not chosen, and in his place the Conservatives selected Hubert Ashton M.C., the 47 year-old former High Sheriff of Essex, triple blue and England cricketer who lived at South Weald near Brentwood.

After serving with the Royal Field Artillery during the First World War he had spent much of his career with the Burmah Oil Company. The Conservatives considered that his main strength over Brian Cook was his strong local connections.

The Liberal Party's candidate was Miss Hilda Buckmaster, a chief officer with the W.R.E.N.S. She was aged in the middle forties and had unsuccessfully fought the Maldon seat in the 1935 General Election. She was only the second woman to contest the Chelmsford seat. Chelmsford's only Liberal M.P. had been Sir Sydney Robinson from 1923 to 1924.

Campaigning

Campaigning began in ernest during the last week of May though it was not until 5th June 1945 that a conference of representatives from the local branches of the left-wing parties met in Chelmsford to discuss their selection of a single candidate to stand in the General Election.

The Labour, Common Wealth, Communist and Co-operative Parties agreed that the current M.P., Ernest Millington of the Common Wealth, should stand in that capacity. Cllr. Baker Smith who had previously been selected as the official Labour Co-operative candidate for the seat withdrew in favour of Millington.

The Liberals who also attended that conference decided that they would not support him and would maintain their own candidate, Hilda Buckmaster.

Three days later, in separate

meetings, the left wing parties and the Conservatives attempted to persuade Miss Buckmaster to withdraw from the contest. Neither approach could persuade her to stand down.

The General Election results were finally declared on 26th July 1945, three weeks after the voting had taken place. Nationally the Labour Party swept to a dramatic landslide victory.

In Chelmsford the result was announced by the High Sheriff shortly after 11.30 a.m. to a small crowd that gathered outside the Shire Hall.

Onslaught

Despite a strong local Tory onslaught, which was contrary to the national pattern, Wing Cmdr. Millington had managed to retain the seat for the Common Wealth Party, albeit with a much reduced majority. The Liberal candidate lost her deposit, having failed to obtain the necessary one eighth of the poll. The full result was:

Ernest Millington Common Wealth	27,309
Hubert Ashton Conservative	25,229
Miss Hilda Buckmaster Liberal	5,909
Turnout 73.4%.	

After the result was declared it was announced that Millington had purchased a house, 'Chestnuts'. in Boreham. Previously he had resided near his aerodrome in Grantham, but his release from the R.A.F. was expected shortly.

In the new Parliament he was set to be in the unique position of being the only Common Wealth M.P., and thus the leader of the smallest party in the House of Commons. In the event he was to rejoin the Labour Party in April 1946.

Thursday 5th July 1945

The day saw the closure of the U.S. Red Cross American Club at the Saracen's Head Hotel.

Tuesday 31st July 1945.

CHELMSFORD AND ESSEX HOSPITAL ANNUAL MEETING: WAR SERVICE & AN UNCERTAIN FUTURE

THE 126TH ANNUAl meeting of the Chelmsford & Essex Hospital took place, where Figures were given illustrating the number of patients treated at the hospital since the outbreak of the war.

In 1939 there had been 2,279 patients, peaking at 3,042 in 1942, with 2,640 in 1944. Out patients had risen from 24,429 in 1939 to 48,658 in 1944.

During the war the hospital had treated 15,903 service patients, plus 595 victims of air raids. They had included 90 men wounded at Dunkirk and 20 wounded at D Day.

Concern was expressed at the future of voluntary hospitals such as it under the Government's new N.H.S. proposals. The hospital now faced the problem of replacing the income from Government fees for service patients which had totalled almost £10,000 p.a.

Tuesday 31st July 1945.

ONE THIRD OF TOWN HAS AN AWAY DAY

In parts of Britain the day was celebrated as the third V.E. Day holiday and for many people it was their first chance in several years to have a break from home.

An estimated 10,000 of Chelmsford's 35,000 inhabitants left for the seaside, London and the countryside, leaving the town deserted.

The most popular destinations for them were Maldon, Southend, Clacton and Walton. However, freak storms in the afternoon brought many rushing back and the cinemas reported good attendances for the afternoon and evening showings.

Unfortunately, the holiday once again showed the shortcomings of the local bus services. Despite the end of the war in Europe services were still severely restricted through an acute labour shortage.

Many villages were reported to have been virtually cut off with potential passengers having to resort to lifts to get home.

Tuesday 7th August 1945.

MEMORABLE BANK HOLIDAY

It was a typical August Bank Holiday with violent thunderstorms sweeping across Essex during the afternoon.

At Great Totham two people were killed by lightning as they sheltered under a tree, whilst more locally, a chimney stack was struck at 26 Cedar Avenue.

Abroad, the Allies dropped an atomic bomb on the Japanese city of Hiroshima.

Monday 6th August 1945

BISHOP REACTS TO ATOM BOMB

Abroad, the Allies dropped their second atomic bomb, this time on the Japanese city of Nagasaki. Two days later The Times was to publish a letter from the Bishop of Chelmsford in which he spoke of his regret over the Allies' use of the devices.

Thursday 9th August 1945.

JAPAN SURRENDERS

Japan surrendered unconditionally to the Allies and for Britain the war was over after almost six long years. The official announcement was made by the Prime Minister in a wireless broadcast at midnight.

Tuesday 14th August 1945.

EYEWITNESS ACCOUNT:

"Atom bombs."

As told to our our Special Correspondent

"After V.E. Day there was a sense of relief and euphoria that the war in Europe was over, but in the back of many people's minds there was the thought that Japan still had to be beaten. At the time that appeared to be a very daunting task and few of us could see it happening in the foreseeable future.

However, when the first atom bomb was dropped, it seemed that at last we had the means to end the war, and end it far more quickly than anyone had ever thought possible."

Les Appleton.

END OF WAR THANKSGIVING

A LARGE CROWD gathered in Tindal Square to attend a simple, yet impressive, open air thanksgiving service to mark the end of the war.

It was conducted from the steps of the Corn Exchange by six local clergymen of differing denominations and attended by dozens of local dignitaries, members of the services and pre-service organisations. Music was provided by the Salvation Army Band.

Missing was the Chairman of Chelmsford's Joint A.R.P. Committee and twice former Mayor in 1936-7 and 1938-9, Cllr. Bellamy, who died the same day at the age of 62.

Sunday 19th August 1945.

THE WAR IS OVER
Chelmsford Celebrates

THE GOVERNMENT declared the day V.J. Day, and it was to be the first day of a two day holiday.

With most people asleep when news of the end of the fighting was announced initial celebrations were muted, but as news spread the streets became crowded.

In Chelmsford town centre bunting and flags were hastily put up during the morning. The Cathedral paid host to well attended special services throughout the day and its bells were rung to celebrate the end of the war. Similar scenes were witnessed at churches all around the Chelmsford district.

As the streets became crowded rain began to fall and the crowds quickly dispersed for

shelter in the pubs, leaving them almost empty by 7 p.m.

An hour later, with an improvement in the weather, several thousand people mysteriously appeared and crowded into Tindal Square where the celebrations repeated those of V.E. Day.

At the Corn Exchange entertainment was provided by the Salvation Army Band and then Dave Cleminson's Band. Loudspeakers conveyed the King's evening wireless broadcast, with the arrangements once again in the hands of the Chelmsford Dance Club with Arthur Beeton as m.c.

Most of Chelmsford's pubs had one hour extensions until 11 p.m. Once they had closed dancing and celebrating got into full swing, lasting until around 3 a.m.

In one incident a sailor found

himself minus his bellbottoms and whilst running along the street came right into the path of a naval officer. He gave the customary salute, which was acknowledged, and to the amusement of the crowd carried on as if nothing had happened.

In Moulsham Street a soldiers' cafe was opened by Miss Mead where all men in uniform were given free refreshments and cigarettes.

Around twenty people had to be treated by the Red Cross First Aid Post at the Corn Exchange for minor injuries sustained during the festivities.

In other parts of the town fireworks were set off and the first of dozens of V.J. parties that were to be held over the coming weeks took place.

Wednesday 15th August 1945

ADAMS F	Killed, of Rettendon
ADAMS Gnr Ernest	Killed, of Writtle
ADAMS Lt Richard	Killed, of Margaretting
ADAMS Trooper Vincent W	Killed, of Nelson Rd
ADEY J C	Killed, of Ramsden Heath
AGER Sgt Leonard	Killed, of Leigh-on-Sea
AHRENS Obergefr F	Luftwaffe, shot down, killed
AINSLEE-WILLIAMS Ft Lt Edward J	Killed, late of Broomfield
ALEXANDER A	Killed, of Runwell
ALLARD Sgt Geoffrey	DFC, DFM, bar award, killed
ALLEN Pte William H	Pow, killed of E hanningfield
AMOS J	Killed, of Ramsden Heath
ANDERSON L/sgt Robert	Killed, of Runwell
ANDREWS A A	Killed, of Downham
ARNOLD Lilian A	Killed air raid Victoria Cres
ARNOLD Major John G	Killed, of Baddow Rd
ARNOLD Margaret L	Killed air raid Victoria Cres
ASHBY LAC Gordon G A	Killed, of Nalla Gdns
ASHFIELD AFC Sqn Ldr Glyn	DFC award, killed, born Writtle
ASHTON Sqn Ldr Claude T	Killed, of Ingatestone
ASTELL N F	Killed, of Ramsden Heath
AUSTIN J R	Killed, late of KEGS
BABBAGE Bernard	Killed, of Woodham Ferrers
BAILEY Leonard C	Killed air raid Hoffmann's
BAINBRIDGE Gnr Robert J	Killed, of Howe Green
BAINBRIDGE Tpr George W	Killed, of Gt Waltham
BAINES J	Killed, of Runwell
BAKER Charles D	Killed air raid Lynmouth Ave
BAKER Elizabeth	Killed air raid Lynmouth Ave
BAKER Ft Lt Thomas D	Killed, of Danbury
BAKER P C	Killed, late of KEGS
BAKER Sgt Frank H	Killed, of Manor Road
BAKER Vera J	Killed air raid Hoffmann's
BANKS John A T	Killed, of Woodham Ferrers
BANNISTER Sgt D P	Killed, of West Ave
BARKER Sgt Jeffrey W	Killed, of Baddow Rd
BARNARD Stf/Sgt John R	Killed
BARRACLOUGH Lt Ernest	Killed, of Stock
BARRETT Edwin G	Killed, of Broomfield
BARRETT Walter B	Killed, of Broomfield
BARRITT Ellen	Killed air raid Coval La
BARTOLAIN Uffz G	Luftwaffe, shot down, killed
BARTRUPT L G	Killed, late of KEGS
BATTERSHILL Peter	Killed, of Ingatestone
BAXTER Dulcie	Killed air raid Henry Rd
BAXTER Frank B	Killed air raid Henry Rd
BAXTER Mabel M	Killed air raid Henry Rd
BEARMAN Ft Lt Cecil E	Killed, former policeman
BECKER Lt H	Luftwaffe, shot down, killed
BECKWITH CSM Walter	Killed, of Lt Baddow
BEFALL Derrick C	Killed air raid Bristol
BENFORD Cptn QMS E	Pow, killed, of South Woodham
BENNETT Dvr Leslie H	Killed
BEVERS Harold W	Killed air raid Marconi's
BEVINGTON 2nd Lt Guy C	Killed, of Bicknacre
BEWERS Alfred	Killed, of Rettendon
BIRT Frederick W	Killed air raid Hoffmann's
BLAKE Sub Lt Arthur	Killed, of Langley
BLOOMFIELD LAC Albert F	Killed, of Woodham Mortimer
BLOOMFIELD Pte Leslie	Pow, killed
BLUNDELL Gerald I	Killed air raid Widford Chase
BLUNDEN Pte Lloyd G	Killed, of Maltese Rd
BODY FO G	Killed
BOLINGBROKE DFC Flt Lt Hale W	Killed, of Springfield
BOND Cpl Frederick A	Killed, of Sandford Rd
BONE Major William J	Killed, of Lt Waltham
BONNELL H E	Killed, of Runwell
BONNER Agnes	Killed air raid Townfield St
BONNER George E	Killed air raid Townfield St
BONSEIGNEUR PO Camille R	Killed, of Canada
BOREHAM A	Killed, of Rettendon
BOREHAM E H	Killed, late of KEGS
BORLEY Pte Reuben	Pow, killed, Sprngfield Pk Ave
BOURNE Harold	Killed, of Stock
BOWLES Pte Alexander A	Pow, killed, of Haycocks Row
BOWRING George F J	Killed, of Park Ave
BOWTLE Leonard G	Pow, killed, of Christy Ave
BOYCE Winifred M E	Killed air raid Hoffmann's
BRABURY Lt John	Killed, of Baddow Rd
BRAY Lt Herbert E	Killed, of Rectory La
BRENNAN James A	Killed air raid Hoffmann's
BRETT Charles R	Killed air raid Hoffmann's
BRETT Sgt George A	Killed, of Lwr Anchor St
BREWSTER Gnr George T	Killed, of Mountnessing
BREWSTER Pte Albert J	Killed, of Gt Waltham
BREWSTER Pte James W	Pow, killed, of Boreham
BREWSTER Sgt Norman J	Killed, of Roxwell
BRICKELL Frederick J	Killed air raid Runwell
BRIGGS Eric S	Killed, of Gt Leighs
BRIGGS FO P J	Killed
BROWN A D	Killed, late of KEGS
BROWN Henry J	Killed air raid Hoffmann's
BRUCE Cpl David	Killed, of Scotland
BRUNNING LAC George	Killed, of Galleywood
BUCHANAN K	Killed, of Danbury
BUNN Sgt John	Killed, of Wood St
BURDETT Pte Harry	Killed, of Primrose Hill
BURGESS Pte Ronald	Pow, killed, of Danbury
BURMAN Pte Frank	Killed, of Writtle
BURRELL Ord/Sea C J	Killed, of Boreham
BURT Cpl Walter	Pow, killed, of Broomfield Rd
BURTON Spr Arthur K	Killed, of Brook End
BYAM George V	Killed, of E Hanningfield
BYFORD Bessie L	Killed air raid Victoria Cres
BYFORD Gertrude L	Killed air raid Victoria Cres
CAMPBELL Colin H	Killed, of Woodham Ferrers
CAMPBELL Joseph	Killed, of Chandlersford
CANDLER LAC Reginald A	Killed, of Gt Baddow
CARTER Marjorie	Killed V-I Margaretting
CARTER Pte Cecil J	Killed, of Glebe Rd
CHADWICK S F	Killed, of Good Easter
CHANCELLOR Sgt Charles W	Killed, of Maltese Rd
CHAPMAN George	Killed air raid Primrose Hill
CHAPMAN Pte Edward A	Killed, of Broomfield
CHARLTON Ord/sea Ronald H	Killed, of Eastern Cres
CHARNLEY Sub Lt John B	Killed, of Sandon & Gt Baddow
CHILDS AC T H	Killed, of Glebe Rd
CHINNERY L/cpl Reginald A	Killed, of Ford End
CHLOPIK Ft Lt Tadeusz	Killed, of Poland
CLARK E	Killed, late of KEGS
CLARK PO John Allen	Killed, of Lt Baddow
CLARK Pte George E A E	Killed, of Boreham
CLARK WO Eric G	Killed, of Widford
CLARKE Angelo	Killed air raid New Hall
CLARKE Pte George W	Killed, of Baddow Rd
CLAYTON 2nd Lt Leonard W C	Killed, of Bicknacre
CLEGG Cptn Ernest G	Killed, of Stanhope Terr
CLEMENTS W	Killed, of W Hanningfield
COARD PO David	Killed, of Gt Leighs
COLE Alfred E	Killed air raid Boreham
COLE Cpl Leonard W	Pow, killed, of Widford
COLEMAN Pte Kenneth	Killed, West Ave
COLVIN FO J	Killed
COLYER Douglas W C	Killed, of Highwood
COOKE Lt Arthur R	Killed, of Gt Baddow
COOMBES 2nd Lt Stanley C	Killed, Home Guard
COOPER Sarah A	Killed air raid New Hall
CORNELL L/sgt Arthur E	Killed, of Railway St
CORNWELL Cpl Frederick C B	Killed, of Writtle
CORP Ord/sea Douglas R	Killed, of Gt Baddow
CORPUS Oblt H-G	Luftwaffe, shot down, killed
COTTIS Arthur	Killed, of Woodham Ferrers
COTTON Sgt Walter	Killed, of London
COULCHER Lucy Emma	Killed air raid Coval La
COUSINS George	Killed air raid Marconi's
COUSINS Lt David G	Killed, of Gt Leighs
COX Pte George	Killed, of Eastern Crescent
COX Pte George	Killed, of Gt Baddow
COX Pte Lenoard	Pow, killed, of Ingatestone
CROOKS Ronald	Killed, of Mountnessing
CROSIER Pte Jack L	Killed, of Upper Br Rd
CROSIER Pte Leslie G	Killed, of Upper Br Rd
CROUCH Able/sea Victor J	Killed, of Tudor Ave
CROZIER Sgt Douglas	Killed, of West Ave
CRUTTENDON Eric C	Killed, late of Chelmsford
DAWSON O N	Killed air raid London
CUTTS Cecil V R	Killed air raid Marconi's
CUTTS FO Kenneth L	Killed, of New London Rd
DAINES Sgt Gwyn B	Killed, of Boreham
DALE Ernest A	Killed air raid Upper Br Rd
DALZIEL Sgt William E	Killed, of Stock
DANCE L/cpl R G	Pow, killed of Ash Tree Cres
DANCE R	Killed, of Widford
DAVIDSON David E	Killed air raid Marconi's
DAVIES Bdr Robert R	Killed, of Springfield Pk Ave
DAWSON P.O. Norman F	Killed, of Victoria Rd
DAY J	Killed, of Good Easter
DAY L/cpl Stanley J	Pow, killed, of Kings Rd
DE VILLE Sgt Sidney J	MM award, killed, of Boreham
DEBARR Albert J	Killed, of Writtle
DEBARR Ft Sgt Frederick H	Killed, of Burns Crescent
DENT Cpl Thomas E	Killed, of Springfield Pk Rd
DERRY S	Killed, of Rettendon
DEVITT Lt John B	Killed air raid west country
DEVENISH Cissie A	Killed air raid Hoffmann's
DEWAR FO Charles E	Killed, of Chelmsford
DIAMOND Sgt Thomas D	Killed, of Writtle
DOBLE L	Killed, of Ramsden Heath
DOBSON Harry A	Killed, of Woodham Ferrers
DOCHERTY Spr Bil	Killed
DOWNS Gdsmn Douglas	Killed, of Van Dieman's Rd
DOWSETT Ellen E A	Killed air raid Duke St
DOWSETT Sgt Alfred W M	DFM, killed of Gt Baddow
DRISCOLL Edward D	Killed air raid Hoffmann's
EATON Frederick C L	Killed, of Danbury
EKE Cadet Desmond J	Killed, late of Manor Rd
ELKINS V N	Killed, of Sandon
ELLIOT Walter	Killed, of Stock
EMERY Alice M	Killed air raid New London Rd
ETHERTON Sgt Randle R	Killed, late of Third Ave
EVANS AC2 Harold L	Killed, of Eastern Crescent
EVANS H R	Killed, of Runwell
EVANS Phyllis M	Killed air raid Hoffmann's
EVANS Sgt Clifford J	Killed, of Mildmay Rd
EVANS William	Killed, of North Ave
EVEMY Dougal H	Killed air raid Woodham Ferrers
EVERETT Cpl Leslie R	Killed, of Roxwell
EVERETT Eric J	Killed, of Roxwell
EVERITT Edith A	Killed air raid Hoffmann's
EVERITT Emily M	Killed air raid Henry Rd
EVERITT Frederick J	Killed, of Roxwell
EWERS Sub Lt Bertrum T A	Killed, of Swiss Ave
FARISH Cptn William W	Killed, of Fryerning
FARROW Ft Sgt J R	Killed, of Kings Rd
FARROW PO Reginald E	Killed, of Cramphorn Rd
FARROW Thomas	Killed air raid New Hall
FAULKS C	Killed, of Rettendon
FENNER L/cpl James E	Pow, killed
FIELD Spr Thomas V	Killed, of Galleywood
FISHER Leslie	Killed, of S Woodham Ferrers
FITCH Ft Lt Headley W	Killed
FLETCHER Norman	Killed, of Mountnessing
FOLEY Harold L	Killed air raid Hoffmann's
FORD Ernest J	Killed, of Boreham
FOREMAN Ft Lt Douglas M	DFC award, killed
FORSYTH A	Killed, of Danbury
FRANCIS Charles H	Killed air raid Galleywood
FRANCIS Pte Bertie	Killed, of Howe Green
FRANCIS Sgt Douglas J	Killed, of Gt Baddow
FRANCIS Sgt Jack T	Killed, of Gt Baddow
FRANK Gnr Christopher	Killed, of Railway St
FRANK Richard	Killed, of Gt Leighs
FRANKLIN Charles T	Killed air raid Marconi's
FRANKLIN Constance E	Killed air raid Hoffmann's
FRANKLIN PO R N	Killed, late of KEGS
FRENCH Able/Sea Charles	Killed, of Battlesbridge
FRENCH Pte Sidney L	Killed, of Lt Baddow
GALE Ft sgt Thomas	Killed, of Prykes Dr
GALLEY Pte Edward H	Killed, of Manor Rd
GALLEY Tpr Maurice C	Killed, of Writtle
GANNON Daniel	Killed air raid Hoffmann's
GARNETT H O	Killed, of Danbury
GARWOOD Louis J	Killed, of Broomfield
GERSEN Sophia	Killed air raid New Hall
GIBBS Cptn David M	Killed, of Danbury
GIBSON L/cpl Henry W	Killed, of Widford Chase
GIBSON W	Killed, of Widford
GILBERT Bmdr Thomas R	Killed
GILBERT D T	Killed, of Ramsden Heath
GLEDSTONE Elsie I	Killed air raid Goldlay Rd
GODDEN Jack	Killed, of Writtle
GOECKING Uffz G	Luftwaffe, shot down, killed
GOSLIN Sgt R A J	Killed, of Danbury
GOWEN Barry John	Killed air raid Coval La
GOWEN Winifred	Killed air raid Coval La
GOWER PO Jack G	Killed, of Arbour La
GOWERS PO Arthur V	Shot down, DFC award, killed
GOWERS Pte Maurice	Killed, of Ford End
GOZZETT Pte Arthur J	Killed, of St John's Rd
GREAVES Stf Sgt Robert J	Killed, of Gt Baddow
GRIGGS Alfred H	Killed air raid Marconi's
GRILL Sgt Gordon A	Killed, of Woodland Rd
GRIMWADE Ab/sea Frederick W	Killed, of Rainsford Lane
GRIMWADE Pte Herbert	Pow, killed, of Hart St
GRIMWOOD Frederick P S	Killed, of Woodham Ferrers
GRINHAM Sub Lt Dennis F	Killed, of Boreham
GROGAN Pte George I	Killed, of Tindal St
GROSS Oberfw W	Luftwaffe, shot down, killed
GUERGEN Cpl Thomas A	Killed air raid Chelmsford
GUNN Gnr F	Killed, of Ford End
HAMMOND FO Francis C	Killed, of Gt Waltham
HANBURY PO John C M	Killed, of Hylands
HANCOCK Dorothy M	Killed air raid Hoffmann's
HARCOURT L/cpl Alfred J	Killed
HARNACK 2nd Lt Waldo	Killed, of Springfield
HARNACK Mr & Mrs Frederick W	Killed, of Springfield
HARRHY Stanley R	Killed air raid Henry Rd
HARRINGTON Gnr Walter A	Pow, killed, Woodham Ferrers
HARRIS Gnr Henry W	Killed, of Stock
HARVEY Emily K	Killed air raid Hoffmann's
HARVEY Harold J	Killed air raid Marconi's
HARVEY Pte Edward G	Killed, of Oxney Green
HARVEY Sgt Frank C	Killed, of Brownings Ave
HAYES John	Killed, of Roxwell
HAYES Pte Charles W	DCM award, pow, killed
HAYWARD Sgt David	Killed, of Lynmouth Ave
HAYWARD Stoker Herbert	Killed, of Baddow Rd
HAZEL LAC Walter	Pow, killed of Galleywood Rd
HAZELL Pte Derek	Killed, of Danbury
HEAD Hector F	Killed air raid Marconi's
HEARD Cpl Ernest	Killed, of Haycocks Row
HEAVON Gnr Thomas W	Killed, of Bootle
HEDGES Henry	Killed, of Boreham
HENNESEY-NOLAN PO Maurice	Killed, of Great Baddow
HERBERT Pte Elsie M	Killed, of Upminster
HERD Pte Gladstone F	Killed of Park Ave
HIBBLE Able/sea Joseph F	Killed, of Gt Baddow
HIBBLE Joseph F	Killed, of Gt Baddow
HIGDON P W	Killed, of Sandon
HILL William C	Killed, of Woodham Ferrers
HILL William C	Killed air raid New Hall
HOBART AC2 Ronald W G	Killed, of Writtle
HOLLIS Charles F	Killed air raid Hoffmann's
HOLLIS E K	Killed, of Ramsden Heath
HOLMES CEA Leonard J	Killed, of E Hanningfield
HOLMES Dudley W	Killed, of Margaretting
HOLMES Sgt Arthur A	Killed, of Margaretting
HOLMES William J	Killed air raid New Hall
HOOK-NEWMAN Phillipa R	Killed air raid New Hall
HORNE Lilian G	Killed air raid Hoffmann's
HOTSON Gnr Geoffrey	Killed, of Radley Green
HOUCHINS Ft Lt Victor G	Killed, of Ingatestone
HOWARD William	Killed air raid Coval La
HOWSE Pamela C	Killed air raid Henry Rd
HUDSON Harry	Killed, late of Tindal St
HUDSON Pte Ernest E	Killed, of Tindal St
HUDSWELL Pte Richard W	Killed, of Prykes Dr
HUGHES Cpl Fred	Killed, of Ingatestone
HUGHES Sgt W F G	Killed, of Runwell
HULL Edith	Killed air raid Henry Rd
HULL LAC Alan	Killed, of Gt Leighs
HUME George S	Killed, of Writtle
HUMPHREY Ft Sgt Alfred G	Killed, of Waterhouse Lane
HUMPHREYS 2nd Lt Stanley	Killed, of Danbury
HUMPHRIES A S	Killed, late of KEGS
HYAM Sgt Stanley E	Killed, of Moulsham Chase
JACKSON Arthur	Killed air raid Hoffmann's
JAKES Pte Thomas F	Killed
JAMES Gwendoline I	Killed air raid Lwr Anchor St
JARMAN Pte John W	Killed, of East Hanningfield
JARVIS CQMS Herbert G	Killed, of Roxwell
JOHNSON Winifred Joan	Killed air raid Hoffmann's
JOINER Clara	Killed air raid Hoffmann's?
JONES R H	Killed, of Runwell
JONES S	Killed, of Rettendon
JONES Sgt Claude	Killed, of Hayes Close
JONES Sgt Edwin	Killed, of Hayes Close
JOSLIN Cpl Leslie J	Killed, of Boreham
JOSLIN Pte Christopher	Killed, of Corporation Rd
JOSLIN Victor A	Killed air raid Marconi's
JUDD Alan	Killed air raid King's Rd
JUDD Beryl I	Killed air raid King's Rd
JUDD Ernest	Killed, of Woodham Ferrers
JUDD Mary	Killed air raid Lwr Anchor St
JUDD William	Killed air raid Lwr Anchor St
JUPP Leslie	Killed, of Ingatestone
KABLITZ Uffz Gunter	Luftwaffe, shot down, killed
KANE Cadet Bryan D U	Killed, of Hayes Clo
KANZ Uffz Erich	Luftwaffe, shot down, killed
KARSTEN Dvr Phillip W	Killed, of Rainsford Rd
KAYE Lt Norman	Killed, of Baddow Rd
KEDDIE DSO Lt Richard G D	Killed, of Downham
KEDDIE Ft Lt Wallace A R	Killed, of Downham
KEDDIE Sgt John M	Killed, of Downham
KEEBLE Pte Walter	Pow, killed, Woodham Ferrers

KEMP Pte Cyril	Pow, Killed, of Gt Baddow
KENNEDY 3rd Officer Keith	Killed, of Gt Baddow
KENT Fireman James W	Killed, of Baddow Rd
KETLEY R C	Killed, of Runwell
KETLEY Sister Annie	Killed, of Sandon
KIMMENCE William A	Killed, of Vicarage Rd
KING Leslie	Killed, of Galleywood
KING Pte Douglas J	Killed, of Widford Chase
KING Sea/Steward Raymond W	Killed, of Old Court Rd
KIPLING Bernard	Killed, of Broomfield Rd
KIPLING Cpl Peter N	Killed, of Broomfield Rd
KIPLING Sgt Guy	Killed, of Eastern Cres
KIRKBY Leading Stoker Robert	Killed, of Ingatestone
KNOCK AC1 Frederick	Pow, killed, of Ingatestone
LADKIN Sister Ellen A	Killed, of Gt Baddow
LANGE Uffz A	Luftwaffe, shot down, killed
LANGFORD George & Florence	Killed, of Dixon Ave
LANZIER Pte Reggie	Killed, of Galleywood
LATIMER Frank	Killed, of Rainsford La
LAUGHTON Ernest A G	Killed, of Hornchurch
LEE Det Cons Maurice G	Killed, of Springfield Pk La
LEET Bert L	Killed, of Broomfield
LEET Edward J	Killed, of Broomfield
LEET L/Cpl Edward J	Killed, of Broomfield
LETCH Sgt Keith	Killed, of First Ave
LIDBETTER Lily H	Killed air raid Goldlay Rd
LINEGAR Sgt Leonard	Killed, of Sandford Rd
LITSHKE Ober H	Luftwaffe, shot down, killed
LITTLE Dvr Sidney G	Killed, of Stock
LITTLE Robert W	Killed, of Writtle
LLOYD LAC William H	Killed, of Gt Baddow
LOCKE Dennis W	Killed air raid Henry Rd
LOCKE Elizabeth	Killed air raid Henry Rd
LODGE Nellie	Killed air raid Galleywood
LODGE Sgt E A	Killed, of Galleywood
LOVETT DFC Ft Lt Reginald	Killed, of Golders Green
MacFADDEN Cpl Cecil L	Killed
MACHELL Ida V M	Killed air raid King Edward Av
MACHIN Sgt William H	Killed, of Handsworth
MACMORLAND Sgt William G	Killed, of Stock
MacNAMARA Lt Col John R Jj	Killed
MAGGS Cyril E	Killed air raid Marconi's
MANN 2nd Lt Kieth W M	MC award, killed, Rainsford Rd
MARJORUM Cpl Arthur W	Killed, of Roxwell
MARKHAM Vivian M	Killed, of Woodham Ferrers
MARSH Edward H	Killed, of Gt Waltham
MARSH Pte E	Killed, of Chelmsford
MASON William S	Killed air raid New Hall
MAYHEW Ernest	Killed, of Rettendon, E Hannfld
MAYHEW S	Killed, late of KEGS
MAYLON Pte Edward C	Killed, of Ingatestone
McBIRNEY Harold A R	Killed, of Margaretting
McGOWAN Robert	Killed, of Margaretting
MEGGY Ester	Killed air raid Coval La
MENZIES Andrew F	Killed air raid Henry Rd
METSON Pte Thomas J	Killed, of Broomfield Rd
MICKLEFIELD Ft Sgt George R E	Killed, of Boreham
MIDDLETON Frederick J	Killed air raid New Hall
MILES Tpr Denis	Killed, of Danbury
MILLER Edward C	Killed air raid Hoffmann's
MILLINGTON L/cpl Brian R	Killed, of Fifth Ave
MILLS Herman J	Killed, of Galleywood
MILLS LAC Robert G	Killed, of Springfield
MILLS Leslie A	Killed, of Sandon
MINDEN Max	Killed, of Boreham
MITCHELL Bernard	Killed, of Hall St
MOFFATT Walter P	Killed air raid Hoffmann's
MOLYNEAUX-BERRY C T B	Killed, of Danbury
MOORE Gnr Alexander	Killed, of Woodham Ferrers
MOORE Robert G	Killed, Rec explosion
MOORE Sgt Jack	Killed, of Ingatestone
MOORE Sgt John M	Killed, of Upper Br Rd
MORRIS Pte George D	Killed, of Gt Baddow
MORSE Sgt Olive M	Killed, of Springfield
MOSS Cpl Brian	Killed, of Hatfield Peverel
MOUSER John E	Killed, of Boreham
MULLENDER Muriel M	Killed air raid Hoffmann's
MULLINER A R	Killed, of Ramsden Heath
MUNSON Joan	Killed air raid Hoffmann's
MURPHY Catherine	Killed air raid Hoffmann's
NASH James	Killed, of Woodham Ferrers
NEWMAN Alfred G	Killed air raid Victoria Cres
NEWMAN Elsie M	Killed air raid Victoria Cres
NEWMAN George	Killed air raid Victoria Cres
NEWMAN Sarah A	Killed air raid Victoria Cres
NEWMAN Sgt Victor C	Killed, late of Good Easter
NICHOLSON Ann J	Killed V-1 Lt Baddow
NORRIS Cadet John W G	Killed, of Warrington
NUTTALL Sgt Kenneth E	Killed, of Blackpool
O'SHEA Stf/sgt Joseph C	Killed, of West Ave
OAKLEY Alice L	Killed air raid Gainsborough Cres
OAKLEY Gwendoline M	Killed air raid Gainsborough Cres
OAKLEY Ivy B	Killed air raid Gainsborough Cres
OASTLER Gnr Leslie	Killed, of Edney Common
ODDY Marine Leslie	Killed, of Roxwell
OFFORD Alfred H	Killed air raidDixon Ave
OGIER PO Michael O	Killed, of Sandon
ORRIS Sgt Robert H	Killed, Rec explosion
OUTTEN Leonard G	Killed air raid Hoffmann's
OUTTEN Muriel J	Killed air raid Hoffmann's
OWEN Craftsman Harry	Killed, of Bootle
OWEN LAC Terrance W	Killed, of Gt Waltham
OWERS Nellie E	Killed air raid Galleywood
PAGE L	Killed, of Rettendon
PAGE LAC Leonard A	Killed, of Galleywood
PARKER Edwin M	Killed, of Margaretting
PARKER Pte John H	Killed
PARNALL Ft Lt Denis G	Killed, of Cornwall
PARNELL Sgt Anthony W	Killed, of Nelson Rd
PARNELL Sgt Anthony W	Killed, of Nelson Rd
PARRISH Kenneth	Killed, of Railway Sq
PASSFIELD L/cpl Alexander	Killed, of Gt Waltham
PASSFIELD Pte Alfred	Killed, of Highwood
PATTERSON Ft Sgt James R	Killed, of Mashbury
PATTERSON J A B	Killed, late of KEGS
PATTERSON Major S	Killed, of Mashbury
PAWSEY L/cpl Joseph R	Killed, of Sandon
PEARCE Herbert J	Killed air raid Marconi's
PEDDAR Able/sea Ernest A J	Killed, of Runwell
PEMBER MC Cptn R C G	Killed, of Ingatestone
PERRY Sgt D	Killed, late of KEGS
PHILLIBROWN Joyce D	Killed air raid Hoffmann's
PICKERING Cpl John W	Killed, of Nottingham
PICKERING FO G H J	Killed, of Coval La
PIGERHAM LAC Harry C	Killed, former policeman
PIPER Edith M	Killed air raid Hoffmann's
PORTER Rflmn Ernest J W	Killed, of Baddow Rd
POTHAM Sarah A	Killed air raid Brockley Rd
POULTER Mary A	Killed air raid New Hall
PRATT Ft Sgt H G	Killed
PRATT Ian F	Killed, of Margaretting
Pte MAPES Leslie	Killed, of Stock
PURNELL-EDWARDS W E P L	Killed, of Danbury
RADLEY Albert	Killed air raid Hoffmann's
RANSON PO Jeffrey B	Killed, of E Hanningfield
RAYCharles E	Killed air raid Marconi Rd
RAYNER Pte Harry W C	Pow, killed, of W Hanningfield
REA 2nd Lt John C	Killed, of Newport
REDDALL Boy Sig Peter E A	Killed, of Ingatestone
REED Benjamin G	Killed air raid Marconi's
REED Ord/sea William	Killed, of Chignall St James
REED Spr Alfred B	Pow, killed, of Gt Leighs
REINER E	Luftwaffe, shot down, killed
REYNOLDS Ivy R L	Killed air raid S Woodham Ferrers
REYNOLDS Pte Ray L	Pow, killed, of Roxwell
RICHER Sgt Cecil J B	Killed, of Second Ave
RIDGEWELL Pte Leonard C	Killed, of Wallace Crescent
RIDLEY Ft Lt Raymond N	Killed, of Broomfield
RIGLIN John	Killed, of Highwood
ROBINSON AC1 Frank C	Killed, of Corporation Rd
ROBINSON Sgt Eric A	Killed, of Runwell
RODD PO G	Killed, late of KEGS
ROGERS LAC Albert	Killed, of Runwell
ROLFE Louisa	Killed Home Guard explosion
ROPER Edmund	Killed air raid Upper Br Rd
ROPER Emily S	Killed air raid Upper Br Rd
ROSE Cpl Leslie W	Killed, of Lwr Anchor St
ROSE Cpl Valentine H	Killed, of Maltese Rd
ROSS AC James M	Killed, body in river
ROYCE Pte Ernest E	Pow, killed, of Springfield Rd
RUDDY Pte Alan	Killed, of Leeds
RUDLING Ray E	Killed, of Broomfield
RUSH Dvr Harold	Pow, killed, of Tindal St
RUSH Sgt Alfred E	Killed, of Chatham Green
SADLER John	Killed, of Writtle
SAFE Cadet Peter	Killed, of Mildmay Rd
SALTMARSH Gnr Christopher E	Killed, of Manor Rd
SANDFIELD Albert	Killed
SANKEY W F	Killed, of Good Easter
SANKEY W G	Killed, late of KEGS
SANSOM Arthur H	Killed, of Anchor St
SANSOM Frank	Killed, of Anchor St
SAUER Uffz G	Luftwaffe, shot down, killed
SAVEALL Arthur	Killed, of Writtle
SAVEALL Elijah G	Killed air raid Galleywood
SCHICK Uffz K	Luftwaffe, shot down, killed
SCOTCHMAN William H	Killed air raid Marconi's
SCOTT Marjorie L	Killed air raid Hoffmann's
SCOTT Police Cons Alexander S	Killed, of Springfield Pk Rd
SEABROOK Sgt John A	Killed, of Broomfield
SEAGER Arthur	Killed air raid Hoffmann's
SELBY Major M B	Presumed Killed, of Lt Baddow
SELLICK FO Eric Tom	DFC, Killed, of Rainsford Rd
SELLICK FO George	Killed, of Rainsford Rd
SHARPLES Ft Sgt Emrys F	Killed, of Rainsford Rd
SHAW LAC Bernard V	Killed, of Billericay
SHAW PO Richard E	Killed, of Lt Baddow
SHAW Sqn Ldr John L	Killed, of Lt Baddow
SHEAD Ft Lt Derrish A	Killed, of Battlesbridge
SHEAD Pte Jack L	Killed, of Ramsden Heath
SHEARING L/cpl John E	Pow, killed, of Broomfield
SHERRINGTON Ft Sgt Roy C	DFM, killed, of Lady Lane
SHERRINGTON LAC Stanley V	Killed, of Marconi Rd
SHERWIN Sgt Obs Robert W	Killed, of Sandon & Gt Baddow
SHIPMAN L/cpl Cecil E	Killed, of Corporation Rd
SHIPMAN Tpr Robert E	Killed of Greenways
SHIPP Sgt James K	Killed, of Gt Baddow
SHORTT PO Harry A	Killed, of Lt Baddow
SIDGWICK Mrs Mary	Killed by runaway cow
SIMMONDS Bdr Reginald J	Killed, of Bradford St
SIMS Florrie E M	Killed air raid Goldlay Rd
SIMS George W	Killed air raid Goldlay Rd
SLIMAN Sgt Allan M	Killed, of Scotland
SMITH Alice L	Killed air raid Galleywood
SMITH Charles M	Killed air raid Bicknacre
SMITH E F	Killed, of Runwell
SMITH George W	Killed air raid Galleywood
SMITH Henry W	Killed air raid Lwr Anchor St
SMITH Joan M	Killed air raid Lwr Anchor St
SMITH John K	Killed air raid Marconi's
SMITH Leslie A	Killed, of Lt Waltham
SMITH Major John V P	Killed, of Lt Waltham
SMITH N P S	Killed, of Danbury
SMITH Pte Bertie W	Killed, of Springfield Rd
SMITH Pte Denis	Killed, of Danbury
SMITH Robert	Killed, of Bruce Grove
SMITH Sgt Hector N	MM award, killed, of Boreham
SMITH William	Killed, of Woodham Ferrers
SNOW Alice	Killed air raid Goldlay Rd
SNOWBALL Musician William	Killed, of Moulsham Dr
SOLE horace	Killed, of Ingatestone
SPEARMAN Spr Ernest J	Killed, of Oxney Green
SPRINGETT LAC Reginald	Killed, of Goldlay Ave
STAINES Sgt Arthur H	Killed, of Oxney Green
STANDIDGE Thelma D	Killed, of Scarborough
STANNARD L/cpl Arthur E	Killed, of Downham
STEBBINGS Eva	Killed air raid London
STERRY Annie M	Killed air raid Hoffmann's
STEWARD Sgt Bryan R	Killed, of Eastern Crescent
STIFF Jack	Killed, of Ingatestone
STOKES Winifred K	Killed air raid Coval La
STONEHAM LAC John W	Killed, of Vicarage Rd
STUART-SMITH Alfred W	Killed air raid Hoffmann's
SWALLOW Fred	Killed, of Galleywood
SWEETING Pte Alfred J	Pow, killed, of Patching Hall La
SYMMONS H	Killed, of Rettendon
TATUM Gerald H	Killed, of Galleywood
TAYLOR Lilian I	Killed air raid Victoria Cres
THOMPSON Audrey M	Killed air raid New London Rd
THOMPSON CBE DL JP John Od	Killed air raid New London Rd
THOMPSON Deana L	Killed air raid New London Rd
THOMPSON Emma	Killed air raid New London Rd
THOMPSON MC Lt Col Thomas C	Killed air raid New London Rd
THOROGOOD Barbara O	Killed air raid Hoffmann's
THORPE William A	Killed air raid Hoffmann's
THREDDER Pte Robert	Killed, of Gt Dunmow
THURMER J T	Killed, late of KEGS
THUROGOOD Alfred B	Killed, of Woodham Ferrers
TINGLE Cptn Harold C	Killed, of Galleywood
TONNISON Frederick	Killed, of Woodham Ferrers
TOON Fl Lt Frederick K	DFC award, killed, of Brmfld Rd
TORRIE Sgt Robert W	Killed, of Pentland Ave
TOTTERDELL Able/sea Gerald N	Killed, of Springfield
TOTTERDELL Ldg/tel Ronald G	Killed, of Springfield
TOWNEND Alfred B R	Killed, of Gt Leighs
TOWNSEND G	Killed, of Downham
TREMAR FO James H	Killed, of Gt Baddow
TULL J E	Killed, late of KEGS
TURP Eva J	Killed air raid Henry Rd
TURRALL Cptn John E	Killed, of Swiss Ave
TUTT PO W H	Killed, of Fourth Ave
UNIDENTIFIED	Killed air raid Hoffmann's
UPSON ft Sgt Jim	Killed, of Stock
VAN SOMERSEN A B	Killed, of Downham
VAUGHAN Cpl John	Killed, of Merton Park
VEEVERS Cpl Thomas	Killed, of Burnley
VERNON Laura	Killed air raid Rectory La
VERNON Leonard W	Killed
VERNON Walter R	Killed air raid Rectory La
VIALL Cpl John A	Killed
VICK FW W	Luftwaffe, shot down, killed
VOWLES George F	Killed air raid Marconi's
VOYCE Pte Joseph H C	Killed, of Ramsden Heath
WADE John	Killed, of Woodham Ferrers
WAKELING Pte Horace J	Killed, of Gt Waltham
WALKER Pte Andrew	Pow, killed, of Writtle
WALLIS Pte Cyril W	Pow, killed, of Gt Waltham
WAREHAM Sgt William H	Killed, of Springfield Pk Rd
WARNE Tpr Geoffrey	Killed, of Gt Baddow
WARNER PO Gordon G	Killed, former local policeman
WARREN AC1 John B W	Killed, of Writtle Rd
WARREN DSC Lt Arthur L W	Killed, of Moulsham St
WARREN Ernest G	Killed air raid Newney Green
WASKETT AC1 Reginald A	Killed, of Baddow Rd
WATKINSON Derek	Killed, of Woodham Ferrers
WATLING FO Victor G	DFC, killed, of Mountnessing
WATLING Sub Lt Brian V	Killed, of Sth Primrose Hill
WATSON J A	Killed, of Danbury
WATT Spr Richard	Killed, of Edinburgh
WAYLETT Pte Douglas	Killed, of Widford
WEBB Douglas	Killed, of Stock
WEBB Phyllis J	Killed air raid Henry Rd
WELSH Pte Brian N	Killed, of Galleywood
WEST FO Denis L	Killed, of Trinity Rd
WESTON Lt John B	Killed, of Broomfield
WESTRIP Cissie K	Killed air raid Lwr Anchor St
WESTRIP David A	Killed air raid Henry Rd
WESTRIP June	Killed air raid Lwr Anchor St
WESTRIP Sidney A	Killed air raid Lwr Anchor St
WHITE AC2 Edwin T W	Killed, of Rainsford Rd
WHITE Pte William V	Pow, killed, of Baddow Rd
WHITE Sidney V	Killed air raid Marconi's
WHYBROW Hannah	Killed air raid Marconi Rd
WHYTE WO Robert A	Killed, of Shrublands Clo
WICKS Sub Lt Deryck E T	Killed, of Galleywood Rd
WIGG Ac1 Vernon	Killed, of Gt Baddow
WIGGINS Sgt Ronald R	Killed, of Danbury
WILKINSON Dvr Walter J	Killed, of Ealing
WILKINSON Pte Leonard G	Killed
WILKS Cptn John	Killed, of Widford
WILKS Evelyn M P	Killed, of Widford
WILLETT Gnr Herbert G	Killed, of Highwood
WILLIAMS 1st Radio Op Billie	Killed, when torpedoed
WILLIAMS Wyndham L	Killed, of Aberdare
WILLIS Vera A M	Killed air raid Upper Br Rd
WILSON Arthur & Chrissie	Killed air raid Ilford
WILSON Frederick A H	Killed air raid New Hall
WILSON Gerald	Killed, of Townfield St
WILSON Gnr Robert	Killed of Writtle
WILSON Henry	Killed, of Ingatestone
WILSON LAC Kenneth D G	Killed, of Townfield St
WILSON Pte John	Killed, of Eves Cres
WISEMAN Charles	Killed, of Woodham Ferrers
WOOD AC1 Harold	Killed, of Sth Primrose Hill
WOOD Cpl Arthur E	Killed, of Nalla Gardens
WOOD Ft Lt H F G	Killed
WOOD Gnr Francis H	Pow, killed, of Ockelford Ave
WOOD Terrance J	Killed of Galleywood
WOODBRIDGE Henry	Killed, of Stock
WOODS Harry J	Killed air raid Marconi's
WOOLLARD Ft Sgt Peter	Killed, of Burgess Well Rd
WOOLTON Sgt James H	DFM award, killed
WORNLEIGHTON Stf Sgt Clifford G	Killed, of Coventry
WRENN May Ellen	Killed air raid Henry Rd
WRENN Pte Charles	Killed, of Tottenham
WRIGHT Able/sea William	Killed, of Roxwell
WRIGHT Ernest	Killed, of Mountnessing
WRIGHT Pte Walter E	Killed, of Lt Waltham
WYATT Denis	Killed air raid Hoffmann's
YEO Pte William C	Killed, of Rettendon
YOUNG ERA IV Royston H	Killed, of Upper Br Rd
YOUNG FO Peter N	Killed, of New London Rd
YOUNG Tpr John H	Pow, killed, of Roxwell Ave

INDEX
compiled by
Ian & Pamela Wilkes

1 Squadron 8
17 Squadron 8
19 Squadron 8,11
41 Squadron 8
46 Squadron 8
56 Squadron 8
73 Squadron 8
151 Squadron 6
249 Squadron 8
257 Squadron 8
264 Squadron 7
302 (Polish) Squadron 8
603 Squadron 8
604 Squadron 51
993 Squadron 33
A T S 21
A12 9,41,50,52,63
A12 by-pass 4,12,18,54,55,58
A130 50
A414, Writtle 47
Abbess Close 3
Abercrombie, Patrick 48
Acland, Richard 65
Admiral's Park 2,18,24
Ainsworth, George 29
Air Training Corps 13,21,25
Air Raid Precautions see ARP
Aizlewood, J C 53
Albert Road, SWF 9
Alexander, N F 42
All Saints' Church, W 3,13-4,22,26,47,54,58,60,
62
All Saints Close 47
Allen, Mrs E E 12
Alston, E 24
Amalgamated Engineering Union 5,52,55
American Red Cross 21,25,51-2,67
Anchor House 24
Anderson, G 66
Anderson, John 18
Anderson shelters 23,52
Anthony, Christopher 18
Anti-Aircraft Batteries 18,21,24-7,29,31-2,45,47,
50-1
Appleton, Les 3,5,7,31,33,45,54,56-7,62,67
Appletree Corner 54
Arbour Lane 3,11,20,24,27-8,33,41,48,54,57
Archer, E P 21
Archer's Suet Factory 28-30
Area Planning Group 48
Army & Navy Roundabout 4,33
Army Cadets 49
Arnold, Arthur J 2,21,38
Arnold, Lilian A 35,43
Arnold, Margaret L 35
ARP 3,5,7,12-6,26,28,37,39,41-2,59,62-5,67
Ash Tree Corner 25
Ash Tree Crescent 1,24,39
Ashford, Mr & Mrs 35
Ashton, Hubert 67
Ashton, Hugh 49
Ashworth, F 39
ASLEF 5
Assheton, William 8
Assizes 45,47,57,63
Atkinson, Justice 47
Auger, Edith M 47
Austen, C 13
Auxiliary Fire Service 12-14,16
Avenue Road, GB 6,41,51
Back Lane 41
Back Street 65
Bacon, Janet 31,58

Baddow Hall Crescent 60
Baddow Meads 4,9-10,45
Baddow Park Farm 50,62
Baddow Road 11,13,16,21,24-5,31,40-1,43,47,
52,55, 57,62,65
Bailey, Eric T 42
Bailey, Leonard C 60
Bailey's Farm 23,26,55
Bainbridge, Beatrice 20
Bake, W E 42
Baker, Charles D & Elizabeth 40,43
Baker, Reginald C 37,42,66
Baker, Vera J 60
Baker Street 30
Banks, Mrs 58
Bannister, Mrs 12
Barber, H R 3
Barclay, Jeffrey 55
Barclay's Bank 46,53,65
Barnes Farm 44
Barnes Mill 9
Barnes Mill Road 49
Barrack Square 52
Barrage Balloons 24-7,29,32-3,37,39,43,47-9,52
Barrett, Diana 47
Barritt, Albert & Ellen 16
Bartolain, Gerhard 51
Batchelor, Alfred 25
Bateman, Charles 64
Bateman, Mary 23,45,55
Bates, Alfred 14
Bates, Edmund 14
Battlesbridge 6,8,26,31,50,54,64
Baverstock, Reginald 28
Baxter, Billy R 47
Baxter, Dulcie 60
Baxter, Frank B & Mable M 60
Bayus, John 47
Beach Road 63
Bearman's Farm 8,54
Beavers, Harold W 15
Becker, Horst 51
Beeches Road 49
Beehive Lane 13,15,22,26,41,61
Beeleigh Lock 2
Beeton, Arthur 65,67
Bell Hotel 3,52
Bell Meadow 4,39,50
Bell Yard, GB 18
Bellamy, Cllr 5,67
Belle Vue 15,63
Belstead Hall 41
Belstead Hall Farm 26
Belsteads Farm 41
Belsteads Farm Lane 41
Benner, Frederick 47
Bevin Brothers 54
Bevington, Captain 9
Bicknacre 45,50,56,62-3
Bicknell, John 18
Billericay 65
Billeting Officer 16,42
Birch Lane, S 47
Birt, Anne 22
Birt, Frederick W 22
Bishop of Chelmsford 3-4,7,10-1,25,46,49,55,
57-8,60-1,67
Bishop Road 14,19,47
Bishop's Hall 33
Bishop's Hall Lane 20,25
Bishop's Hall Mill 24
Bishopscourt 4-5,7,41,58
Black, Patricia B 47
Blake, Arthur 11
Blake's Wood 8,31
Blande, A 24
Blandford, E A 42

Blooman, J C 42
Bloomfield, Leslie 46
Blue Lion Inn 31
Blundell, Gerald I 41,43
Board of Education 17
Boarded Barns Estate 20,32,34,42,44,56
Bocking, Cecil 38
Bodmin Road 28
Bomb Disposal Squad 6,9,13-4,18,28,41
Bond, Bertie 28
Bond, J G 16
Bond's 29
Bonner, George E & Agnes 36,43
Bonnet, L P 24
Bonseigneur, Camille 8
Boreham 5,7,9,17,27,31,33,41,48,62,64,67
Boreham Airfield 31,42,48,51,53,57-9,64,66
Boreham Hall 7,12
Borough Treasurer 48
Borough Engineer 4,5,17-8,24,44,46,48-9,52,54
63
Boswells Schol 28
Boul, William 64
Bouverie Road 18,40
Bowden, CO 59
Bowling Club 10
Boy Scouts 14,41
Boyce, Winifred E 60
Boys' Club 25
Boyton Cross 9,26
Bradford Street 12
Braemar Avenue 1,10
Brazil's Farm 11,63
Brennan, James A 20
Brentwood 65
Brett, Charles A 42,66
Brett, Charles R 20
Brett, Mr 39
Brewer, Linda D 47
Brewer's Arms P H 45,50
Brick House Farm 31
Bridge, L R 42
Bridge Street 62
Bridges, Sgt 2
British Legion 64,66
British Legion: Women's Section 44
British Restaurant 17,18
Broads Green 46,50
Brock Hill 61,64
Brock's Farm 57
Brockley Road 7,18,24,62
Bromley Lodge 63
Brook Farm 7,8,26,50
Brook End Farm 11
Broomfield 9,33,44,47,55,62
Broomfield Church 41
Broomfield Court Sanitorium 2
Broomfield Hall 41
Broomfield Mill 41
Broomfield Road 2-4,21,24,27,29,34-6,47,51-2,
55-7,60,62,66
Broomfield School 41
Brown, E A 42
Brown, Edna 13,45
Brown, George 1,3,5,7,13,25,31,49,51,66
Brown, George & Hannah 7
Brown, Harry K 64
Brown, Henry J 60
Brown, Peggy 36,66
Brown, Sylvia 47
Brown's Yard 2,4,19,62
Brownings Avenue 15,22-3,44,47,62
Browns Avenue 62
Bruce Grove 49
Brumwell, Mr 16
Buckley, Robert 5
Buckmaster, Hilda 67

Buckton, P 11
Budd the bakers 47
Bullard, Mrs 20
Bunny Walk 3,36
Bunting, S/L 51
Burgess Well 4
Burgess Well Road 62
Burnham Road 28
Burns Crescent 25
Burnthouse Farm 63
Burnthouse Lane 63
Burrell, W H 49
Burton, Montague 45
Burton, Mrs R W 26
Bus Station 1,36-7,45-6,48
Butler, R A 52
Butt's Green 50
Buttsbury 63
Buttsbury Church 26
Buttsbury Hall Farm 26
Byford, Bessie L 35,43
Byford, Gertrude L 35,43
Byford, James 43
C.L.E.S Co. 55
Cadet Corps 3
Can River 24,30,33,38-9,48
Canfield 21
Cannon's Restaurant 30,38
Canward Iron Foundry 63
Carlick, Mrs 57
Carr, Mr. 31
Carter, Annie 37
Carter, Gerald 5,20,23,25,52
Carter, James 66
Carter, Marjorie 54
Carter, William 5
Cass, Ernest 40
Cass, P G 40
Cathedral 10,15-6,18,23,30,38,48,53-4,57,60-1,
  64-7
Catholic Church Hall 27
Catholic School, C 24
Catholic School, Stock 8
Cattle Market 24,30-1,33,38,48,50,53
Cedar Avenue 2,47,67
Cemetery 4,10,14-6,18-20,22-4,43,49,60-1
Chalk End Farm 26
Channels Farm 41
Chapel Place 20,36,46
Chapel Wood 56
Chaplin, Harry E A 23
Chaplin, T 26
Chaplin's Farm 8
Chapman, Celia 47
Chapman, George 43
Charity Farm 57
Chatham Hall Lane 57
Chelmer & Blackwater Canal 29
Chelmer Place 11,28
Chelmer River 2-4,7,11,25,28-9,41,48,52,59
Chelmer Road 4,12,27,29,31,44,49,51
Chelmerton Avenue, GB 8,13,66
Chelmerton Road 41
Chelmsford & Essex Hospital 4-6,8,11-3,15
  -6,18-9,22-3,39,42,50,54,60,63,67
Chelmsford & Essex Museum 66
Chelmsford Brewery Co 7
Chelmsford Citizens' Air Raid Shelter Committee 5
Chelmsford City F C 30,33,39,43,66
Chelmsford Club 52,65
Chelmsford Dance Club 65,67
Chelmsford Dry Cleaners 37
Chelmsford Spiritualists Society 56
Cherry Garden Lane 40
Cherry Tree 12
Chestnut Walk 56
Chief Billeting Officer 26,46-8

Chief Education Officer 24,57
Chignall Hall Farm 54,57
Chignall Road 44,51,62
Chignall St. James 37,54,55,57,62
Chignall Smealy 45,56
Childerditch Women's Institute 57
Chlopik, Tadeusz 8
Christy, Dora 62
Christy & Norris 58
Christy Brothers 58
Christy's 3
Church Lane 13,51,54,57
Church Street 23,52
Citizens' Air Raid Shelter Committee 5
Civil Defence 15,22-3,27,42,60,64,66
Clark, Dudley 8
Clark, Eric 3,5,9,58
Clark, Leslie 40
Clark, Reggie 3
Clark, R 31
Clark, Sam 9
Clarke, Angelo 42,43
Clarke, Miss M 54
Clarke, Mrs 57
Clements Green Creek 26
Cleminson, Dave 67
Cleminson, Henry 48
Cloake, Kate 42
Co-op Bakery 37
Co-operative Party 65,67
Coe, Frank 14
Coggeshall 15
Colam Lane, LB 8
Colchester Street Construction 3
Cole, Alfred E 31
Colleybridge Farm 11,26
Common Wealth Party 65,67
Communist Party 5,52,65,67
Congregational Chapel, L W 57
Congregational Chapel, M 63
Congregational Church 3,52,60
Conservative Party 65,67
Cook, Brian C 65,67
Cooper, Sarah A 42,43
Cooper, Mr & Mrs 56
Cooper's Row 34
Copsey, Ada 36
Copsey, John 30
Copsey, Sidney 36
Copt Hill 50
Coptfold Hall 11
Corn Exchange 1,21,50,65,67
Cornish, Kathleen 51
Cornwell, Ronald 65
Corporation Car Park 33,39
Corporation Road 21,24,29,34,56,62
Corpus, H-G 4
Cottage Place 30,38
Coulcher, Lucy E 16
County Council 2,4,5,18,25
County Cricket Ground 39
County Gardens 8
County Hall 2-3,30,38,45,51,54
County Hotel 54,65
County Motor Works 38
County Surveyor 5,25,28
Cousins, George 15
Cousins, William 23
Coval Lane 4,15-6,21,30,36-7,42,46-8,61, 63
Cox Green 61
Cracknell, Esme 47
Cramner, Ethel 44
Cramphorn Road 30,60
Cramphorn's 24
Cranham's Farm 58
Creephedge Lane 53
Cressey, Lincoln 47

Crisp, John 19
Crittall's 14
Cromer, Harold 47
Crompton Street 30,50
Crompton's 5,12-4,18,21,24,26-7,30,33, 40,43,48-
9,58,60
Crondon Hall 15
Crondon Park 8,26
Crouch River 26,31,50,64
Crows Lane, WF 7
Crozier, Robert 11,66
Crozier family 18
Culpeck, Bertie 47
Culverts Farm 31,64
Currie, Mrs 56
Curries' Field 3
Customs & Excise 57
Cutts, Cecil V R 15
Daffy Wood 62
Dale, Ernest A 40,43
Danbury 9,13,17,31,50,52-3,57,62
Danbury Church 15,26
Danbury Common 8,50
Danbury Park 1-2,25,36
Danbury Road, G B 45
Dandy, Alfred 64
Dartmouth Road 28
Davidson, David E 15
Dawes Farm 8
Dawson, Leslie 36
Day, Miss V 57
Deadman's Lane, GB 8
Deal, G A 13
Denham & Archer 29
Deputy Mayor 21
Devenish, Cissie A 60
Digby, Mrs G 28
Dixon Avenue 24,34,43,56,62
Don's Farm 64
Dorset Avenue, GB 2-3,7-8,13,31,41,51, 66
Douglas Farm 42
Dowding, Hugh C T 56
Dowsett, Ellen E A 38,43
Dowsett's Field 55
Dr Barnardo's 4
Drake, Alfred P 64
Drakes Farm 58
Drews, Uffz 8
Drill Hall 1,3
Driscoll, Edward D 60
Driver & Ling 29
Driver's Ironyard 24
Dudik, Michael 47
Duke Street 3,7,17,24,30,32-3,37-8,43-4,46
  -9,52,55,65
Dukes Farm 12,28,60
Dukes View 47
Durrant's Farm 50
Eagle PH 52
East, Herbert & Audrey 6
East Hanningfield 45,50,53,57-8
East Street 37
Easter, Stella 47
Easter, Vera 47
Easterbrook, M L 52
Eastern Crescent 20,44,62
Eastern National 15,24,26,37,39,53,63
Edgar-White, Claude 23
Education Committee 48
Edwin's Hall, WF 8,57
Elm Road 18
Elmbrook Farm 26,63
Emery, Alice M 10
Emery, William 10
Endeavour, P H 3,5,58
Ennals, Mr & Mrs 56
Esman, Andrew 47

Essex Home School 52
Essex Home for Boys 34
Essex Regiment 21,53
Essex Volunteer Regiment 10
Essex Yeomanry 53
Evacuees 1-2
Evans, Phyllis M 60
Eve, Jack 9
Eve, Joseph 18
Eve, W G 38
Eveling, Laura G 47
Everny, Douglas H 63
Everard, Sid 46
Everitt, Edith A 60
Everitt, Emily M 60
Eves Crescent 33,62
Ewan's Farm 11
Fairfield Road 36
Farnsworth, George 23
Farrant, Robert & Sarah 16
Farrow, Thomas 42,43
Fellas, William 65
Felton, Valerie 36
Fifth Avenue 57,62
Finch, Stanley 9
Fir Tree Lane 56
Fire Guard 49,55,57,61,64
Fire Station 56
First Avenue 11,29,33,49,54,57,60,62
Fish, Reginald 34
Fisher, Kathleen 18
Fitzwalter's Farm 62
Fleming, Robert 44
Fleming's Farm 64
Flexman's 38
Flight of Fighters Fund 7,10
Foley, Harold L 60
Forbes-Robertson, Jean 51
Ford, Ray 8
Ford End 26,50,54,60
Fordson Estate 42
Foreman, L P, & Sons 63
Forest Road 30
Fourth Avenue 15,49
Fox, Frank 2,11,21,47,57
Fox Crescent 44
Francis, Charles H 11
Francis, Clarence 47
Franke, Rudolf 8
Franklin, Albert 41
Franklin, Charles T 15
Franklin, Constance E 60
Franklin, Mr 62
Freeman, Kathleen 41
Freeman, Hardy, Willis 3,52
French, F J 20,21
Friars School 24
Fristling Hall 8,21
Fritz Farm 8
Frost, Mrs A 15
Fryerning 17,44,50,53-4,63
Fulcher, L A 42
Furness Farm 8
Furze Hill 8
Gainsborough Crescent 5-7,9,12,62
Galleyend 15
Galleywood 7-8,11,18,47,52-4,60,64
Galleywood Racecourse 3,15
Galleywood Road 8,11,24,51,62
Game, Edna 47
Gannon, Daniel 20
Gannon, Leslie 45
Gard, H V 42
Gardner, Joan 47
Garwood, Benjamin A 64
Gas Works 5,7,17,21,24,29,40,53,62
Gasiorowski, Edith 24

Gaskell, Richard 7
Gauernack, O 15
Gault, Tillman 47
Gay Bowers 50
General's Head P H 48
Gersen, Sophia 42-3
GI Brides 47
Gibbs Farm 12
Gibcracks Camp 50
Gilling, Mrs A G 44
Glebe Road 35-6
Gledstone, Elsie I 40,43
Gloucester Avenue 18,47
Gloves, L/Bdr 13
Goat Hall Lane 62-3
Goddard, Frank 28
Goecking, Gunter 51
Golden Lion 45
Goldlay Road 21,40,43,52
Golf Course 8,52
Good Easter 17,26,44
Gooday, Peggy 15
Goodenough, George 12
Goodfellow, H G 42
Goods Yard 3,24,29,50
Gordon, John 6
Gosses Farm 64
Gowen, Arnold 16
Gowen. Barry J 16
Gowen, Winifred 16
Gowers, Jesse 21
Graces Walk 27,32
Grammar School 1-3,10,20,23-4,33,45, 56,65-6
Grange Farm 50,54
Grant, H W 17
Gray, Percy 58
Grays Farm 41,54,57
Great Baddow 8,11,15-6,23,31,33,41,44, 50-2,55,60-3
Great Baddow High Street 18
Great Elms Farm 54
Great Gibcracks 50
Great Leighs 51,58,63,66
Great Mascall's 11
Great Sir Hughes 11,31
Great Tey 15
Great Totham 67
Great Waltham 31,46,48,50,54-5
Green Close 54
Greenacre Farm 8,26
Greenways 2
Gregson, Joan 47
Griffths, Eunice 20
Griggs, Alfred H 15
Grimwade, James E 14
Grinham, J F 42
Gross, W 4
Grove Road 40,63
Groves, P A 42
Guergen, Thomas A 42-3
Gunn, F G 42
Guttery, F L 42
Hadler's Garage 14
Hagger, Frederick 3
Hagger, Percy 35
Haines, Leonard 8
Haldane air raid shelters 5
Hall, Leslie 39
Hall, L S 33,43
Hamlet Road 45,49
Hammond's Farm 9,56
Hamshire, Caroline 42
Hance, Dennis 9,30,53
Hance, Eileen 15,29,36,64
Hancock, Dorothy M 60
Harrhy, Stanley R 60
Harrhy, Winifred 18

Harris, Gweneth 47
Hart, Mr 49
Hart Street 62
Harvey, B 42
Harvey, Emily K 60
Harvey, Harold J 15
Harvey, Mrs 57
Hatfield Peverel 15,25,35
Hawkes' 38
Hawkin's Wood 11
Hay, Mrs 17
Hayes Close 39
Hayes Farm B 26,31
Head, Hector F 15
Heard, Betty 47
Henry Road 1,3,22-3,27-8,58-61
Hepworth, J 45
Herbert, Albert 23
Heybridge Estate 63
High Street 2-3,17.21,23,31,38,46,48,52-3,55,65-6
High House Farm 56
Highfield Road 36,49,62
Highwood 62
Highwood Road 58
Hill, William C 42,43
Hill, Mrs 20
Hill Crescent 18
Hill Farm, Broomfield 26,41
Hill Road 28
Hilliard & Ward 38
Hills, Paul 47
Hills Farm 58
Hillside Grove 47,62
Hilton, James 20
Hobson, H F L 39
Hockley, Gerald 5,7,62
Hodge, Albert 2,5
Hodge, Councillor 44
Hodges Farm 42
Hodgins, Charles 1
Hodgson, T H 52
Hodgson, W J 14
Hoffman's 3-5,7,11,13-29,31,33,36,41,45-6,48,50-1,53-6,58-61,63-4,66
Holder, Frank 13
Hollands Farm 57
Hollis, Charles F 60
Hollow Lane 44
Holmes, William J 42-3
Holy Trinity Church, S 1,7,14-5,19,28,43
Home Guard 3,14-6,18,21,25-7,30,38,44-5,49-53,55,57-8,60
Hook-Newman, Phillipa R 42-3
Hornchurch 5
Horne, Lilian G 60
Horseshoe Farm 62
Housing Committee 44,47
Howard, William 16
Howard's Farm 54
Howe Street 47
Howes, Thomas 47
Howse, Pamela C 60
Hubner, Willi 8
Hudson, Harry G 66
Hughes, Thomas 25
Hull, Edith 60
Hullbridge Road 64
Hume, Norman 2,12-3,56,58,63
Humphrey's Farm 54
Hunt, David 8
Hunt, H 33,43
Hunt, Thomas 39
Hurrell's Lane 54
Hyde Hall 54,57
Hylands House 57
Hylands Parade 11,51
Hylands Park 11,26,46-7,50,54,56,63,65-6

Hylands School 39
Ilgars Manor Farm 54
Imphy Hall 49,64
Imrie, H M 42
Independent Progressive Party 65
Ingatestone 1,8,17,44,47,50,53-4,63,65
Ingatestone Road 13
Ingram, James 47
Israel's Farm 50
Ivy Barn Lane 52
Ivy Hill 55
Jackson, Arthur E 60
Jackson's Farm 8
James, David 64
James, Gwendoline I 39,43
Jehovah's Witnesses 18,46
Johnson, Alice 29
Johnson, Winifred J 60
Joiner, Clara 60
Jones, Bill 6
Jones, Frederick 38
Jones, Gladys 43
Jordan, PC 62
Joslin, Cyril 23
Joslin, Frank 18
Joslin, Victor A 15
Jubilee Farm 13
Jubilee Terrace 47,56
Judd, Alan & Beryl I 34,43
Judd, Doreen 39,43
Judd, William & Mary 39,43
Juvenile Court 44-6,48,66
Kablitz G 49
Kanz E 49
Kearsley, Frederick 11,48
Keen, Frederick 13
Keene, Mrs J H 7
KEGS see Grammar School
Kemp, Edward 63
Kenmore Tutorial College 49
Kent, Duke of 18
Kerwin, Alice 45
Kettley, G H 42
Ketley, Laurence 18
Killegrews 8
King Edward Avenue 32,38,43
King's dentist 35
King's Head Farm 26
King's Head Meadow 51,66
King's Road 4,22,34,43-4,46-7,62
King's Road Boys' School 2,24,34,49,56
Kingston Avenue 51
Kingston Crescent 6,51
Kloss, Lt 14
Knappett, Ray 1-2,5,7,23,46,50,53,65-6
Knowles, J C 52
Kruger, O 15
Labour Party 44,65,67
Lacey's Farm 63
Lady Lane 40,62
Lambert P F 42
Lange, Albert 51
Langley, Charlie 3
Langton, Councillor 44
Larks Lane 46
Last, G S 56
Latchingdon 8,58
Lathcotts Farm 61
Latimer, Percy LeB 47
Laurence, B E 57
Law, F 57
Lawford Lane 63
Lawn Lane 11,28,41,57
Lawns Farm 58
Layer Breton 31
Leadbetter, LAC 30
Lee, Maurice G 12

Legg Street 38
Lewis, Sgt 38
Lexden Lodge 18
Leylands 8
Liberal Party 65,67
Lidbetter, Lily H 40,43
Lilystone Hall 13,51
Lindenmayer, Gefr 15
Linkhouse Farm 8,50,54
Links Drive 18,41
Lion & Lamb 30,64
Lionfield Terrace 57
Lionmead Recreation Ground 28
Litschke, Heinrich 51
Little Baddow 2,9,12,27,31-2,56,60
Little Baddow Church 12
Little Baddow Hall 54
Little Claydon's Farm 57
Little Dunmow 18
Little Hayes Farm 50
Little Leighs 63
Little Leighs Rectory 8
Little Moor Hall 57
Little Preston's Farm 64
Little Sir Hughes 64
Little Waltham 16,25-6,45,47,51,53,57-8, 60,62
Little Waltham Church 48,61
Little Waltham Road 41,53
Littley Park Farm 26
Livingstone, Alexander 44
Lloyd, A 28
Local Defence Volunteers 3
Lock, Max 48
Locke, Dennis W 23
Locke, Elizabeth 23
Locke, Florence 23
Locke, Will 7
Lockwood, Mr 37
Lodge, Ernest 23
Lodge, Nellie A 11,47
Lodge Farm 8
Loftin Way 41
London Road 3,9-11,17-8,20-1,30,39,42-3,46,48,50,
55-6, 62,65
London Road, Widford 4
Lonebarn Farm 31
Longfield Road 16,18,23
Longmeads 8
Longs Farm 51
Longstomps Avenue 4,49,62
Longstomps Reservoir 48
Lord Lieutenant 44
Lord's End House 8
Love Lane 8
Loveday & Wilson 38
Lovegrove, Kathlen A 47
Loves Green 26,58
Lovett, Reginald 8
Low, James 18
Lower Anchor Street 24,33,39,43,50
Lower Green 54
Lower Stock Road 26
Luckin & Sheldrake 7
Luckin Smith 3,21
Lucking, Mrs P 61
Lucking, Roger 61
Lynmouth Avenue 40,43
Lyster, Dr. 31
MacArthur, S H 1
McClellan, A W 4
McCulloch, Donald 52
Mace, Mr 58
Machell, G K 42
Machell, Ida V M 38,43
Machin, William H 7
Macnamara, John R J 2,11,25,44,46,56, 61,65
McPherson, John 58

McShane, Mr 37
Maggs, Cyril E 15
Magor, R K 67
Maguire, Fraser 9
Malan, Adolph 4
Maldon Road 50
Maltings Cottages 19
Mancuso, Nickolas 47
Manhard, Ltn 8
Manning, Les 6,9,12,49,54
Manning, Maude 54
Manning, Sally 54
Manor Farm 31
Manor Road 57
Marconi College 20
Marconi Road 14,15,19,24,35,52,60
Marconi's 5,11,14-6,23-4,26-30,33,35-6,
38,46,48,50,52-3,58-9,66
Margaretting 8,11,26,50,51,52,54-6,58,63
Margaretting Church 54,57
Margaretting Mental Hoispital 2
Margaretting Road 4,66
Margaretting Tye 15,50
Market Road 1,3,18,31-2,38,45,48,52,56, 58-9
Marks Farm 8
Marlborough Road 15
Marriage, Frederic 62
Marriage, W & H 52
Marriage's Farm 41
Marsh Farm SWF 26
Marshall, Alfred 8
Marshall, Earl 47
Marshall, Frederick 64
Martin, C E 13
Mashbury 9,23,44,55
Mason, Dart 47
Mason, William S 42,43
Master John's Farm 45
Matthews, R Guy 56
Mayes, Mr & Mrs 13
Mayher, Mary 47
Mayor 5,7,10-1,17-8,20-1,23,44,46-9,54,57-9,63
Mead, E 25
Mead, Rodney 10
Mead, Miss 67
Meggy, Esther 16
Meggy & Stunt 16
Melbourne Park Estate 44,49
Menhinick, John 1
Menhinick, Leonard 1,9,46,49,66
Menzies, Andrew F 23
Meon Close 28
Mersea marshes 3
Metson, Leslie 20
Mid-Essex Technical College 21,24,38,48
Middleton, Frederick J 42-3
Mildmay Ironworks 8
Mildmay Road 9,18,21,40,49,55,65
Miles, Frank 45
Mill Hill Farm 8
Mill Lane 3,36,41,51
Mill Road 36-7
Miller, Arthur 47
Miller, Edward C 22,23
Millington, Ernest R 65,67
Mills, Alan 53
Minoprio, Anthony 48
Mitchell, William 21
Mitchell, Mr 53
Moffatt, Walter P 20
Molerams Lane 63
Monsey, Frances E 47
Moor Hall 13
Moore, H G 18,21
Moore, Maurice 25
Moore, Robert G 25
Morrison shelters 16,19,23,31,33-5,42,52, 55-6,61

Morrow, William E R 10,15,30
Morton, Albert W 42,66
Morton, Gordon 14
Mottistone, Lord 63
Moulsham 6,30,32,48
Moulsham Chase 62
Moulsham Drive 24,50,62
Moulsham Grange 2
Moulsham Lodge 3,4,6
Moulsham Mill 48
Moulsham Schools 2,4,6,11,24
Moulsham Street 2,4,10-1,17,24,30,46-9,55-6,62,67
Mount Maskell 42
Mountey's Farm 1
Mountnessing 11,45,62-3
Moy, Thomas 37
Mullinder, Muriel M 60
Munson, Joan 60
Murphy, Catherine 60
Murray, H A D 18
Nabbott's Farm 26
Nalla Gardens 62
Nargiso, Daniel 47
Nathans Lane 4
National Savings 17
National Fire Service 18-20,22,27-8,31-2,37-8,43,
  46,56,58-9,65
Navigation Road 1,6-7,18,28,47,62
Nelson, Stephen 64
New Hall, Boreham 5,26,31
New Hall Hospital 42-3
New Street 2-3,14-5,19,25-6,28-30,33,36, 42-
3,47,49-50,53,55,60,63
New Writtle Street 24,30,33,39,43-4,50
Newcombe's Cycles 37
Newland Hall, Roxwell 1,9,21,46
Newland Spring 62
Newman, Alfred G & Elsie M 35,43
Newman, George & Sarah A 35,43
Newney Green 13,31,57
Newney Hall 8
Nicholson, Ann J 56
Nield, William 18
Noakes, Hilda 47
Norman, Alfred 13
North Avenue 20,23,46,55,62
Norton, Mrs 21,24
Norton Church Farm 63
Norton Road, I 47,62
Nurseries 21
Nursery Road 10,63
Oaklands Park 2,4,10,21,24,33,66
Oakley, Albert 6
Oakley, Alice L 6
Oakley, Gordon 6,7
Oakley, Gwendoline M 6
Oakley, Ivy B 6
Oasis 9
Oasis Junction 52
Observer Corps see Royal Observer
  Corps
Ockleford Avenue 15,47,62
Offord, Alfred Horace 34,43
Old Court Road 51,55
Old Lodge Farm 31,42
Old London Road 57
Old Park Farm 50
Oliver, Mr 37
Ongar 65
Orange Tree P H 39
Orrin, Harold & Winifred 1
Orris, Robert H 25
Osbourne Place 9
Our Lady Immaculate Church 20,60
Outten, Leonard G 60
Outten, Muriel J 60
Owers, Nellie E 11

Oxney Green 8,60
Padham's Green 63
Palmer, E 39
Palmer, Jack 5,12,15,27-8,33,49,51
Palmer & Harvey 9
Park Avenue 6,34,51,64
Park Farm, Boreham 26 ,48
Park Road 24,34,38
Parkes, Philip 38
Parklands Farm 54,62
Parmenter, H H G 45
Parnall, Denis 8
Parsonage Farm 8,41
Parsonage Lane 50
Partridge Farm 46
Patching Hall 47
Patching Hall Lane 5,33,47,60,62
Paterek, Edward 8
Pates, Mr 54
Patten's Farm 54,58
Paubert, Robert 47
Paverley, George 13
Pavilion Cinema 63
Paynes Lane 62
Peachey's 56
Peacock, Mrs 57
Peagram family 6
Pearce, Albert 30
Pearce, Herbert J 15
Peatlands Farm SWF 26,50
Peek, E W 42
Percival, W G 42
Perry, Eva 52
Perry, Lord 13
Petersen, Gietz 47
Petty Sessions 2,25,45-7,51,53-5,62,64
Phelps, Gnr 13
Phillibrown, Joyce D 60
Phoenix House 9
Pig & Whistle PH 54
Pigg, Cllr 48
Pike, H 66
Pingley Pond 62
Piper, Edith M 60
Pipers Farm 26
Pitts, Robert 31
Pitts, Lt 3
Plantation Road 31
Plantin, H W 42
Pleshey 50
Plough Hotel 37,47
Plough Inn 57
Plumtree, Cecil 1
Plumtree, John 1,10,65
Police 15,42,53,57,60
Police Headquarters 6,12,16,28,42,59
Police Station 2,3,8,15-6,50,63-4
Pollard's Garage 2
Porter, Ruby M 47
Porter, Mr 7
Post Office 7
Potham, Sarah A 7
Potham, Thomas 7
Potkins, H 39
Potter, Henry (William Sharpe) 17,36
Potters Farm 57
Pottery Lane 33
Poulter, Mary A L 42,43
Pound Farm 62
Pound Wood 63
Powers Farm 9,60
Pratt's Farm Lane 26,41
Prescott, Andrew 47
Price, Robert 25
Primrose Hill 17,43
Prince's Road 4,11,18
Priors Farm 41,62

Prison 28,44,45
Private Road, G 47,63
Pryce, B Vaughan 34
Pryke, Betty 1-2,20,35,66
Prykes Drive 63
Public Library 3-4,21,42-4,47,49
Pump Lane 9
Pyne, Arthur 31
Quarter Sessions 56,65
Queen Street 10,26,37
Queen's Head PH 24,39
Radford, Mrs 54
Radford, Miss 54
Radley, Albert 22
Radley, Ivy 22
Radley Green 11,26,63
RAF Biggin Hill 8
RAF Bradwell Bay 51
RAF Felixstowe 24
RAF Hornchurch 4,7-8
RAF North Weald 6-9,24
Railway 3,18,24,26-8,30-2,36,38,40-2,50,52
  -4,56,62-3,67
Railway Station 36-8,44,48
Railway Street 23,36-7
Rainsford House 21
Rainsford Lane 5,17,24,44,63
Rainsford Road 3,8,11,15,18,44,47,51,62
Rainsford School 17,24,34,44
Ramsden Heath 61,62
Ramsey Tyrells 12,50,64
Rawreth 8
Ray, Charles E & Martha 14
Ray Farm 8
Rayleigh, Lady 48
Reader's Corner 51
Recreation Ground 1-3,18,21,24-7,30,33,
  36,38-9,46,50-2,55-6
Rector of Springfield 5
Rectory Lane 1,3,15,19,20,22-4,52,59-60
Red Cross 1,5,48,55,67
Redcliffe Road 60
Redgwell, Jean 35
Reed, Benjamin G 15
Reed, C P 51
Reed, Frederick K 24
Regent Theatre 58
Regina Road 14,29,66
Registry Office 16
Reiner E 49
Rettendon 6,8,31,50,53-4,57,62-3
Rettendon Bell PH 56,62
Rettendon Common 47
Rettendon Place 8
Rettendon Turnpike 56
Reynolds, Frank & Ivy 9
Richardson, Bill 23
Ricketts, D 59
Ridley, Walter 45
Ridley, Viscount 17
Ridley family 2,58
Ridley's Flour Mill 14,36
Rignal's Farm 62
Rippon, Mr 13
Ritcher, Emma 42
Ritchie, Adam 65
Ritz Cinema 21,24,29,33,53,65-6
Rivenhall 60
Rivenhall Aerodrome 53
Riverside car park 17
Roberts, Mrs 21,24
Roberts Adlards 3,19
Robinson, Sydney 67
Robinson King's 12
Rochford Road 15,40,52
Rogers, Peggy J 47
Rolfe, Frederick 18

Rolfe, Louisa 18
Rollestones Farm 8
Rolph's Farm 62
Roman Road 31,40,42,57
Roman's Farm 54
Romford 33,54,57,65
Rook Wood 57
Roper, Edmund & Emily 12
Roper's Farm 50
Rose Brothers 30,36-7
Rosebery Hotel 27,28
Rotary Club 44
Rothmans Aveenue 31
Rough Hills Farm 58
Rout, L J & Phyllis 19
Rout, Norma 19
Rowe, Arthur 66
Roxwell 8-9,26,31,49,64
Roxwell Avenue 49
Roxwell Road 28,44,55,62-3
Royal Army Service Corps 1
Royal Artillery 13,21
Royal Engineers 11,14,29
Royal Horse Artillery 3
Royal Navy 41
Royal Observer Corps 9,33,51
Royal Steamer P H 36
Ruggles-Brise, Edward 3
Runcom, Frederick 3
Runsell Green 57
Runwell 17,53,64,65
Runwell Church 62
Runwell Hospital 49,56
Runwell Road 61,62
Rural District 17-8,27,44-5,48-9,52,54,62, 65
Russell Green 42,53,58
Rutter, Robert 8
Ryan, Mr 50
St Anne's Place 28
St Clere's Hall 52
St John's Ambulance Brigade 22,48
St John's Church, M 12,15,17,18,43
St John's Green, W 26
St John's Hospital 4,6,11,26,42-3,45,47-9,
    54,58,61
St John's Road 9,24,30,50
St John's Vicarage 9
St Mary's Church, GB 16,25,60
St Mary's Church, WF 9,63
St Michael's G 11,15,22
St Peter's Hospital, Maldon 8
St Peter's School 24
Salesfrith Farm 57
Salmon, A 12
Saltcoats Farm 9
Salute the Soldier Week 53,63
Salvation Army 35-7,58-9,67
Sam's Coffee Bar 38
Sandford Road 6,9,12,28,49,62
Sandon 50,53,57,61-2
Sandon Brook 54,64
Sandon Garage 64
Sandon Hall 8
Sandon Lodge Farm 8
Saracen's Head 7,21,25,46,51-2,67
SAS 65-6
Sauer G 49
Saul, Mr 55
Saunders, Ken 5
Saveall, Elijah G 11
Saville, Derek 18
Sawyer, John 63
Scheidweiler, Frederick 18
School View Road 8,13
Scotchman, William H 15
Scotchman, Mr 3

Scott, Alexander S 12
Scott, Marjorie L 60
Scott, Myrtle 12
Scott, Mr 15
Scravels 9
Seabrook, Ernest 53
Seabrook, William 28,41
Seabrook, Miss 37
Seager, Arthur 60
Seaman's Lane, WH 8,50
Second Avenue 24,29,45,54,60
Sedgwick, Mary 31
Selby, Mr 15
Select Cinema 39
Selwood, V G 20
Seven Ash Green 11
Seven Ponds Field 64
Seventh Avenue 62
Seyfang, Horace 19
Seymour, Alfred 16
Seymour, Brenda P A 47
Seymour Street 21,30,39
Shakestones Farm 50
Shanks, John 13
Sharman, Mrs 9
Sharp, LAC 30
Sharpe, Mrs 36,43
Shaughnessy, F B 14
Shead, S F 42
Shellow Bowells 15
Shepheard, PC 6
Sheppard, Mrs G C 17
Ship Inn 15
Shire Hall 3,5,16,18,47-8,50,52,56-7,63, 65-7
Shrublands Crescent 47
Silver End 15
Simms, George & Florrie E M 40,43
Simon, E 4
Sixth Avenue 18
Skegg's Farm 30,62
Skinners Lane 11
Skreens Road 8
Slade, Mrs 21,24
Slennett, Christopher 25
Slough House Farm 50
Slythe, J B 15
Smallholders Hall 8
Smith, Baker 67
Smith, Carl 47
Smith, Charles M 45
Smith, Fred 37
Smith, F Luckin 52
Smith, Henry W & Joan M 39,43
Smith, George W & Alice L 11
Smith, John K 15
Smith, Kenneth 20,37,47,49
Smith, P N 15
Smith, William 36-7
Snagge, A L 49
Snow, Alice 40,43
Soddy G B 49
Sorrell, Doreen 47
Sorrell, Ernest 3
South Gibcracks 50
South Hanningfield 63-4
South Primrose Hill 36,46,62-3
South Weald 3
South Woodham Ferrers 8-9,26,31,44,50, 64
Southborough Road 10
Southend Road 16,60
Southwood Farm 26,56
Spalding's 3,23,52,65
Spalding's (Whitehouse) Farm 31
Sparrow's Farm 9
Special Constabulary 38
Spens, Will 4,11,49
Spring Elms Lane 56

Springfield 3,9,11-2,17,20,28,31,33,44,52
    -3, 66
Springfield Green 3,24,54,57-8,62
Springfield Hall 28,33,41
Springfield Park 44
Springfield Park Avenue 2,7,28,35
Springfield Park Lane 46
Springfield Park Parade 28
Springfield Park Road 12,15,64
Springfield Place 45
Springfield Road 2-5,21,26-8,31,33,47-51,54-5,57-
    8,62
Springfield School 2,3,47
Springfield Street 9,47
Springfield Tyrells 4
Spurgeon, A H 42
Squire, 'Nobby' 66
Stampworthy & Co. 52
Steamer, The 2
Steamer Terrace 22,36
Steel's Farm 8
Sterry, Annie M 60
Steven's Farm 37
Stevens, Mr 45
Stewart Road 63
Stewart-Smith, Alfred W 60
Stock 8,12,18,21,26,47,49-51,64
Stock Church 13,26
Stock Common 8
Stock Lane 26
Stock Rectory 13
Stock Road 15,26
Stock Wash 13
Stokes, Winifred K 16
Stomps Garage 11
Stow Maries 8,57
Strutt & Parker 46,65
Stubbing's Farm 41
Stubbings, C 42
Stump Lane 41,62
Stump Road 3
Stunt & Sons 38
Sturgeon's Farm 8-9
Sullivan, Walter 47
Sunningdale Road 34
Sunrise Avenue 33,62
Surman, J C 51
Sutterby, J 28
Suttons Institution, Hornchurch 5,42
Swallows Cross Farm 11
Swan P H 62
Swan Lane, Stock 11
Sweet, C J 42
Swimming Baths 24,53
Swiss Avenue 29,34,47,49,56,62
Sylvester, Gorky 23
Tabors Avenue 16
Tabors Hill 31
Tabriums Farm 6
Taffs, Elizabeth 25
Taffs, Arthur & Violet 25
Tamar Rise 41
Tamkin's 47
Tanfield Tye 8
Tanner, Emma 10
Taylor, George 11
Taylor, Joan 30-1,58
Taylor, John 11
Taylor, J W 13
Taylor, Lilian I 35,43
Taylor, Sidney 11,17,21,47,57
Taylor, Rex 19
Taylor Walker 46
Teager, Anne 47
Telephone Exchange 32,38
Telford, Arthur 39
Telford, H 33,43

Tennyson Road 46,62
Tentest Fibreboard Co 22
Territorial Offices 3,52
Thacker, Percy 28
The Avenue 50
The Drive 33,62
The Green, Wr 24,62
The Vineyards 50
The Street, L W 60
Third Avenue 49,51,62
Thompson, Audrey M 10
Thompson, Deana L 10
Thompson, John O 10-1
Thompson, Muriel 10
Thompson, Thomas 10
Thorogood, Barbara O 60
Thorpe, William A 60
Threadneedle Street 36,38-9
Three Cups 5
Thrift Farm 8
Tilekiln Farm 8,11
Tiley, Cecilia 57
Tiley, Rose 57
Timson's Lane 47
Tindal Square 1,3,18,44,48,50,52,65-7
Tindal Street 31,48,56,65-6
Tinsley's Farm 8,63
Top Barn Lane, SWF 50
Torquay Road 28
Torry, Gilbert 1,16
Totterdell, Gert 6
Tower Gardens 2
Tower House 24,28,33
Town Clerk 7,54
Townfield Street 2,14,35-7,43,48
Traffic lights 2
Tremlett, E A E 58
Trigg & Moore 21,25
Trinity Road 1
Trinity Road Schools 2,17,23-4,27-8
Trinity Church 28
Tudor Avenue 49
Tulip, The 13
Tunman Close 17
Turp, Eva J 60
Tutton, Gladys 47
Tyewhitt, Mrs 48
Tyler, P J 57
Tyrell's Close 4,5
Unstead, Mrs W T 44
Upper Arbour Lane 24
Upper Bridge Road 12,15,30-1,40,44,46, 62
Van Roegen, L I 42
Vernon, Walter R & Laura 19-20
Viaduct Road 51
Vicarage Lane 31
Vicarage Road 4,9,11,19,58,62
Vick, W 4
Victoria Crescent 1-2,20,35,43
Victoria Fields 48
Victoria Road 3,8,16-7,19,21,24,28-9,36,
    38,48,51-2,54,58,62
Victoria School 16,23-4,29
Vowles, Geirge F 15
Wade, W J 17
Wakefield, W V 42
Wales, Jack 37
Wales, Winifred 1,5,37,55,62
Walls Ice Cream Co 17
Walter Hall 42
Waltham Road 31,53
War Damage Commission 48-9
War Memorial Fund 10
War Weapons Week 11
Warburton-Lee, B A W 18
Ward, Frank 28
Ward, J H 42

Ward, W 28
Warnes, Harry 13,18,28,42
Warren, Ernest G 13,31
Warren, Joseph 13
Warren Farm Field 6
Warship Week 17-8,49
Waskett, J 42
Watchouse Lane 8
Watchouse Road 11
Water Hall 9
Waterhouse Lane 30,33,39,48,62
Waterhouse Street 4,10,24,49
Waterloo Lane 7,21,53
Watkinson, Evelyn 47
Watts, A T 42
Watts, Bruce 47
Waveney Drive 28,41
Weathersfield 56
Webb, Phyllis J 60
Webber, W G 51
Weight Road 5,7
Weir, David 47
Well Lane 8,60
Wenley's 18,28,52
Wesley's 3
West Avenue 4,18,20,22,30,57,62
West Hanningfield 8,26,46,50-1,54,58,63-4
Westmacott, Innes 8
Weston, C E 51
Westrip, David A 23
Westrip, David & Florence 23
Westrip, June 39,43
Westrip, Sidney A & Cissie K 39,43
Westrop, Hilda M 47
Wharf Road 17,18,62
Wheatsheaf, The 35,63
Wheelers Farm 16,47
Whipps, Irene 24
White, Sidney V 15
White Hart P H 66
White Hart Lane 9
White Horse P H 36,56,63
Whitehead, Mr & Mrs 21,24
Whitehouse Farm 51
Whites Tyrells 64
Whitley, J T 18
Whitley, Stella 23
Whitmore, Francis 44,57,66
Whittles Hall Farm 24
Whybrow, Hannah 14
Wickford 61
Wid River 26,39,50,57,62,63
Widford 7,32,52
Widford Chase 41,43
Widford Church 51,63
Widford Close 47
Widford Estate 44
Widford Garage 56
Widford Hall Farm 51
Widford Lodge 18
Widford Rectory 8,63
Widford Road 18,41
Widford School 63
Wigan, J T 67
Wigan, Mrs J T 1
Wilkinson, Walter J 25
Wilks, Bertie 6-7
Wilks, Marjorie 5-7
Wilks, Vic 1
Willingale 21,49,52
Willis, Vera A M 40,43
Willis, Vincent 5
Wilson, Arthur & Chrissie 26
Wilson, Bill 15,20,56,59,63
Wilson, Frederick A H 42,43
Wilson, Robert 39,47
Windey, C G 13

Windus, Ernest 6
Wings for Victory 44,49
Wiseman, A E 42
Witham 24,55,58
Women's Co-operative Guild 44,47
Women's Institute 3,35,44,47
Women's Voluntary Service 38,44,48
Wood, Helen 16
Wood, Roy 47
Wood, Mrs 19
Wood Street 10,11,51
Woodham Ferrers 9,11,31,50,54,57,62-4
Woodham Hall 56
Woodham Road 50,56,63
Woodison, Phyllis S 47
Woodland Road 21,56
Woods, Daniel T 47
Woods, Harry J 15
Woolford, A H 51
Woolford, Iris 51
Woolpack P H 40
Woolworth, F W 52
Worrell, Michael & Diana 24
Worrell, Stanley & Doris 24
Wrenn, Bernard 23,55
Wrenn, Mary E 23
Wrenn, Sheila 10,58
Writtle 4-5,8-9,18,21,24,26,32,37,47,50,56,60,62,
    64
Writtle Green 65
Writtle Mill 39
Writtle Park Hospital 2
Writtle Road 4,12-3,21,26,30,39,46,54-5, 62-3
Wyatt, Dennis 22
Yarwood Road 5,27,46,49,58
YMCA 21,29,36,38,57
Youell, H W 13
Young, A 39
Young, A E 42
Young, Mrs 56
YWCA 51,57
Zerja, Francis 47

Permission has been given to reproduce material from

Essex Chronicle
Marconi's
Essex Police Museum
Gordon Oakley
Changing Chelmsford
The blitz then and now

which is gratefully acknowledged.